KITCHI-GAMI

JOHANN GEORG KOHL, 1854

KITCHI-GAMI

Life Among The Lake Superior Ojibway

JOHANN GEORG KOHL
Translated by
LASCELLES WRAXALL

With a new introduction by
ROBERT E. BIEDER
and additional translations by
RALF NEUFANG and ULRIKE BÖCKER

 MINNESOTA HISTORICAL SOCIETY PRESS
St. Paul • 1985

Frontispiece: From Herman Albert Schumacher, *J. G. Kohl's Amerikanische Studien* (Bremen, Germany, 1885)

MINNESOTA HISTORICAL SOCIETY PRESS, St. Paul 55101
Originally published in 1860 by Chapman and Hall, London
New material copyright © 1985 by the Minnesota Historical Society

International Standard Book Number 0-87351-172-7

Manufactured in the United States of America

10 9 8 7 6 5 4 3 2

Library of Congress Cataloging in Publication Data
Kohl, J. G. (Johann Georg), 1808–1878.
  Kitchi-Gami: life among the Lake Superior Ojibway.

  Translation of Kitschi-Gami.
  Originally published: London : Chapman and Hall, 1860.
  Includes index.
  1. Chippewa Indians – Social life and customs.
2. Indians of North America – Wisconsin – Social life and
customs. I. Title.
E99.C6K713   1985   977.5'00497   85-11499

CONTENTS.

CHAPTER III.

CHAPTER IV.

CHAPTER V.

CHAPTER VI.

CHAPTER VII.

CHAPTER XIII.

CHAPTER XIV.

CHAPTER XV.

CHAPTER XVI.

CONTENTS.   xi

APPENDIX I.

TALES FROM THE OJIBWAY.

APPENDIX II.

OBSERVATIONS ON THE OJIBWAY LANGUAGE.

INDEX.

INTRODUCTION

THE windy shores of Lake Superior probably seemed like
another world to Johann Georg Kohl when, in the summer of
1855, he visited the Ojibway Indians in northern Wisconsin.
Kohl, a German geographer, ethnologist, and travel writer,
extended his trip in order to spend four months with the Indians, who were themselves adjusting to a new way of life. Only
the year before they had been placed on four reservations: Lac
Courte Oreilles, Lac du Flambeau, and, farther north, Red

Author's note: The writing of this introduction was greatly facilitated
by a generous grant from the American Philosophical Society that
allowed me to purchase microfilms of the J. G. Kohl papers from the
Universitätsbibliothek Bremen. I am grateful also to others who con-
tributed to the completion of this project. They are Signe Seiler, who
"tracked down" the Kohl papers in Germany; Ulrike Böcker, who
aided in establishing contact and communicating with the library in
Bremen; Emanuel J. Drechsel, who helped with some early translations; and Gerhard Knoll, archivist at the Universitätsbibliothek
Bremen, who graciously expedited our request for the Kohl microfilm. My greatest thanks, however, go to Ralf Neufang, who worked
long hours reading and translating old German from microfilm. His
help and suggestions were invaluable.

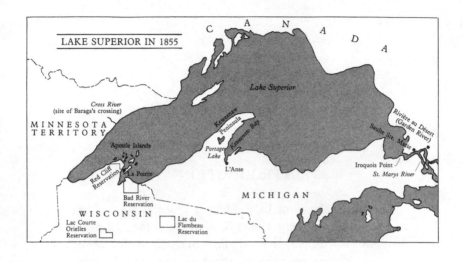

LAKE SUPERIOR IN 1855

C A N A D A

Lake Superior

Cross River
(site of Baraga's crossing)

MINNESOTA
TERRITORY

Apostle Islands

Keweenaw Peninsula

Keweenaw Bay

Portage Lake

L'Anse

Rivière au Désert
(Garden River)

Sault Ste. Marie

Iroquois Point
St. Marys River

Red Cliff
Reservation

La Pointe

MICHIGAN

Bad River
Reservation

WISCONSIN

Lac Courte
Orielles
Reservation

Lac du
Flambeau
Reservation

Cliff and Bad River, on the south shore of Lake Superior near their old villages at La Pointe.[1]

The change was one of many the tribe had experienced. The Ojibway first encountered the Europeans early in the seventeenth century when the French pushed westward into the upper Great Lakes searching for furs. At that time the Ojibway lived in small family bands for most of the year, which enabled them to survive the region's harsh weather. They hunted during the fall and winter months. In early spring each family would go to its "sugar bush" to make maple sugar, an important staple used to flavor many foods. In the summer, bands congregated for ceremonies, trading, social exchange, and fishing. Many Ojibway favored Sault Ste. Marie, the falls on the St. Marys River at the eastern end of Lake Superior, for a summer encampment, as it was an excellent spot for catching whitefish.[2]

Although traditional Ojibway culture changed continually in response to different environmental conditions, the arrival of the French and the advent of the fur trade accelerated the process. Upon entering the fur trade, the Ojibway unknowingly linked themselves and their future to an international market economy; they began hunting furs for the trade, not just for their own use. Change was more apparent to the Ojib-

1. Nancy Oestreich Lurie, *Wisconsin Indians* (Madison: State Historical Society of Wisconsin, 1980), 20; Edmund Jefferson Danziger, Jr., *The Chippewas of Lake Superior* (Norman: University of Oklahoma Press, 1978), 89; Robert E. Ritzenthaler, in "Southwestern Chippewa," *Handbook of North American Indians* (Washington: Smithsonian Institution, 1978), 15:745.

2. Here and below, see E. S. Rogers, "Southeastern Ojibwa," in *Handbook of North American Indians* 15:760–64; Harold Hickerson, "The Southwestern Chippewa: An Ethnohistorical Study," *Memoirs of the American Anthropological Association* 92 (June 1962): 2; Harold Hickerson, *The Chippewa and Their Neighbors: A Study in Ethnohistory* (New York: Holt, Rinehart and Winston, 1970), 13, 39–40; Harold Hickerson, "Ethnohistory of Chippewa of Lake Superior," in *Chippewa Indians* (New York: Garland Publishing, Inc., 1974), 3:33.

way when the French decided to make Sault Ste. Marie a fur trade center and encouraged other tribes to congregate there. What had once been an Ojibway summer village, shared at times with their linguistic neighbors the Ottawa and Potawatomi, now drew other tribes like the Huron, the Dakota, the Sac and Fox, the Menominee, and the Winnebago. This promoted marriages between Ojibways and Indians from other tribes. While such contact tended to alter the system of clans and affect the social structure in the bands, it also enriched the ceremonial life of the Ojibway. The tribes exchanged not only songs and dances but also legends and creation stories.

When the British defeated the French in 1763, the Ojibway, enmeshed in the fur trade, merely switched trading partners. After the American Revolution, some Ojibway began trading with the Americans. Throughout the 1820s and 1830s, the British Hudson's Bay Company vied with the American Fur Company under John Jacob Astor for the Ojibway fur trade. The Ojibway benefited from this competition and wisely played the companies off against each other. The trading advantage did not last, however. The heavy hunting of fur-bearing animals depleted their population and the Ojibway along the south shore of Lake Superior were forced constantly to remove westward in search of new hunting areas. By the 1830s and 1840s the fur trade economy in this area was in a state of near collapse. Some Ojibway moved farther west beyond the Mississippi and even beyond what is now Minnesota in an attempt to continue the old hunting life, while others remained in Michigan and Wisconsin and tried to hold on to old ways in a world of rapid change. A series of treaties reduced the Ojibway to virtually landless people in their old homeland.[3] Although many still trapped, few could survive by trapping alone. White farmers, lumbermen, and miners increasingly cut down the forest and further depleted the game. Some Ojibway found jobs as guides for mineral prospecters or as laborers in the nascent Lake Superior fishing industry, in lumbering, and in berry picking, but all such positions were seasonal and economic survival was difficult. Others attempted farming but had little luck. The Wisconsin Ojibway lived with the constant threat of removal until 1854, when they were provided with reservations.[4]

Some traditional ways were given up, their usefulness no longer apparent or their meaning clear in the new world of the mid-nineteenth century. Still other traditions were altered, blending cultural elements derived from Euro-Americans and from other tribes.

Into this Ojibway world of 1855 stepped the German traveler Johann Georg Kohl. Who was Kohl? Why was he in America and why would he want to spend several months among the Ojibway of northern Wisconsin and Michigan? Why would he want to write a book about his wilderness experience?

Born on April 28, 1808, Kohl spent his youth in the city of Bremen in northern Germany. The eldest of twelve children, he attended schools in Bremen but seemed to gain much of his education from his uncle, also named Johann, whose life as a seafarer fascinated the youth. His uncle had traveled over much of the world, especially in the Far East, and he possessed an extensive collection of maritime maps and atlases. Kohl studied these avidly and spent long hours talking with

3. Ritzenthaler, "Southwestern Chippewa," 744–45; Hickerson, "Southwestern Chippewa," 89. On the depletion of game near Lake Superior, see R[amsey] Crooks to George Wilder & Comp., December 16, 1835, Crooks to Warren, June 26, 1837, Crooks to John Holiday, June 26, 1837, Crooks to Stephen A. Halsey, September 5, 1838, and Crooks to Daniel Kurtz, March 21, 1840 – all in the American Fur Company Papers, New-York Historical Society. The patterns in this region differed from those described in Rhoda Gilman, "Last Days of the Upper Mississippi Fur Trade," *Minnesota History* 42 (Winter 1970): 123–24.

4. Lurie, *Wisconsin Indians,* 20; Danziger, *Chippewas,* 89.

sea captains in Bremen, acquiring early a wanderlust that would determine much of his later career.[5]

In 1827 Kohl entered the University of Göttingen to study law. After a year he transferred to the University of Heidelberg and then, in 1829, to the University of Munich. In the spring of 1830, Kohl's father died, precipitating a family financial crisis that forced Kohl to abandon his university studies.

Kohl left Munich in the fall of 1830 and for the next five years served as a tutor in Courland (Latvia) and Russia. In Russia, he began a study of the effect of topography on the movements of people and trade. After giving up his position as tutor, Kohl remained in Russia, living on his savings, traveling, and writing on the geography and rivers of Russia. Unable to persuade the Academy of Sciences in St. Petersburg to publish the results of his study, Kohl returned to Germany in 1839 and took up residence in Dresden.

Although Dresden was to be his official residence for the next ten years, he more often could be found traveling around Europe. His books on Russia, published shortly after he arrived in Dresden, were quite popular and were translated into English, Russian, and Italian. In addition, they established him as an important travel writer and led to the publication of his books on other countries. Kohl also continued to work on his study of topography and its influence on migration, placement of cities, and trade.

By 1850, however, he abandoned this study. Just why is not entirely clear; one biographer claims that Kohl believed the

5. Here and three paragraphs below, see W. Wolkenhauer, "J. G. Kohl," *Aus allen Weltteilen* 10 (1879):138–41; Johann G. Kohl, "Lebensbeschreibung, 1859," MS, AUT XX, p. 1, 2, 5, 6, Kohl Collection (Kohl, Literarischer Nachlass), Staats- und Universitätsbibliothek, Bremen. Much of the following material on Kohl's life is taken from the latter, an autobiography written shortly after his return from America. Quotations from this source and from other German works cited below have been translated by Ralf Neufang.

work to be useless. This may be true, but Kohl, who seemingly had little difficulty finding publishers for his more popular travel accounts, may also have encountered resistance when seeking to publish this more scholarly work. At any rate, the early 1850s represented a turning point in his career.[6]

In 1848 and especially in 1849, Kohl had begun to think about a trip to America. His father had often mentioned America as a land of opportunity, a land of new beginnings. One of his younger brothers was an emigrant to Canada.[7] Furthermore, his fellow Germans had evinced a certain fascination with America since the time of the Revolution. Germans who had emigrated sent news of the great American political experiment to friends in the old country. Books describing the American land and people were eagerly sought after. Some volumes, like those by Gottfried Duden and Francis Joseph Grund, were written to encourage immigration and the formation of societies to colonize the Mississippi Valley. While some Germans were repelled by stories decrying the lack of culture or ideals in the new nation, many others, attracted by reports of freedom and opportunity, crossed the Atlantic and embarked on a new life in a new land. German immigrants to the United States numbered in the thousands each year from the 1830s to the mid-1850s, when immigration peaked.[8]

6. Hermann A. Schumacher, "Kohls Amerikanische Studien," *Deutsche Geographische Blätter* 11 (April 1888): 116; Kohl, "Lebensbeschreibung," 7–8. Kohl's large scientific work on the rivers of Germany and their influence on the history of the Fatherland was published in three volumes as *Der Rhein* (2 vols.) and *Die Donau von ihrem Ursprunge bis Pesth*, because the publisher sought more popular travel titles.

7. J. G. Kohl to Adolph Kohl, September 27, 1854, AUT XVIII/ 17 Briefe aus Amerika, Kohl Collection. Since Kohl met his brother in 1855 in New York City – his brother having recently moved there from Halifax, Canada – it seems safe to assume that this brother preceded Kohl to America.

8. Paul C. Weber, *America in Imaginative German Literature in the First Half of the Nineteenth Century*, Columbia University Germanic Studies 26 (New York: Columbia University Press, 1926), 2–10, 13, 14, 107, 117–19,

Another factor prompting greater interest in America was the social uneasiness in Germany produced by the 1848 revolution. Liberals eager to combine the many separate German political units into one unified Germany convened a parliament in Frankfurt in 1848, but disagreements and bickering among the members resulted in failure. It was a bloodless revolution of patriotic fervor and its failure produced increased frustration among the general population. Whether or not this frustration led to an increase in German emigration to the United States after 1850 is difficult to say, but after the revolution emigration increased dramatically.[9]

In 1849 Kohl wrote, "In the chilling context of the political at-

198–99, 235–66; Duden, *Report on a Journey to the Western States of North America and a Stay of Several Years along the Missouri "During the Years 1824, '25, '26, and 1827,"* ed. James W. Goodrich, trans. George H. Kellner et al. (Columbia: State Historical Society of Missouri and University of Missouri Press, 1980), especially Goodrich's introduction, p. vii-xxiv; Grund, *The Americans in Their Moral, Social, and Political Relations* (Boston: Marsh, Capen and Lyon, 1837); Peter Boerner, "From the Promised Land to the Land of Promises, or European Dreams and Their Lot in the New World," in *Germans in America: Aspects of German-American Relations in the Nineteenth-Century*, ed. E. Allen McCormick (New York: Brooklyn College Press, 1983), 181–92. On German immigration, see Leo Schelbert, "Emigration from Imperial Germany Overseas, 1871–1914: Contours, Contexts, Experiences," in *Imperial Germany*, eds. Volker Durr et al. (Madison: University of Wisconsin Press, 1985), 112–33.

9. Ray Allen Billington, *Land of Savagery, Land of Promise: The European Image of the American Frontier in the Nineteenth Century* (New York: W. W. Norton, 1981), 34; Georg G. Iggers, *The German Conception of History: The National Tradition of Historical Thought from Herder to the Present*, rev. ed. (Middletown: Wesleyan University Press, 1983), 22, 92–94; Mark Wyman, *Immigrants in the Valley: Irish, Germans, and Americans in the Upper Mississippi Country, 1830-1860* (Chicago: Nelson-Hall, 1984), 56–57. On immigration after the revolution, see Marcus Lee Hansen, *The Immigrant in American History* (Cambridge: Harvard University Press, 1940; New York: Harper and Row, 1964), 79–80; Wolfgang Köllmann and Peter Marschalck, "German Emigration to the United States," *Perspectives in American History* 7 (1973): 523.

mosphere one hears of a new world, of a distant place, of a country of the future, and always one thinks here of America. 'The train of world history goes west' is being proclaimed. . . . Everywhere I find a new element, hitherto unknown to me, which I can only name the American element."[10] Several of Kohl's friends reflected this national interest, and two were especially influential in urging his visit to America. Karl Andree, a friend who had studied under ethnologist-geographer Carl Ritter at the University of Berlin, strongly supported Kohl's proposed venture. Andree seemed to embody this "American element" in his praise for the land beyond the sea, often speaking of the "flight of history westward." Another friend, Arnold Duckwitz, a senator of the state of Bremen, also urged Kohl to make the trip. His interests in America were more economic than academic, however, for he contemplated opening a shipping line between Bremen and New York.[11]

During the winter of 1850-51, Kohl secluded himself to work on a new project that would focus on the Americas. In Dresden that winter, he read extensively in American literature and in accounts of travel to the Americas. It is not known whether Kohl read the highly popular German ethnographic novels of Charles Sealfield (Karl Postl) and Friedrich Gerstäcker on American Indian life or the travel accounts of Prince Maximilian of Wied-Neuwied and Duke Paul Wilhelm of Württemberg describing the Indians on the upper Missouri. But it is probable that he studied an account of travels among the Indians of South America by Alexander von Humboldt, linguist, ethnologist, and natural historian. Kohl also

10. Schumacher, "Kohls Amerikanische Studien," 110.

11. Anneli Alexander, "J. G. Kohl und seine Bedeutung für die deutsche Landes- und Volksforschung," *Deutsche Geographische Blätter* (1940): 21; Schumacher, "Kohls Amerikanische Studien," 112.

read the works of such Americans as Washington Irving, William Prescott, and George Bancroft.[12]

Drawing on his interest in cartography, geography, culture, and history, Kohl envisioned a work that would record the European conquest and settlement of the Americas. This "History of the Discovery of the New World," would occupy him, off and on, for the rest of his life. He had collected numerous maps and completed twenty-two chapters by 1852, when he was nearly diverted from his American project. Carl Ritter strongly pushed for Kohl's appointment to a position in geography at the University of Graz in Austria. Kohl declared himself ready to assume the post but then discovered that there were no funds to support it.[13] Disappointed, he returned to his American project.

Mindful of the need for more maps and documents, Kohl decided he would have to go to America. His route, however, proved rather circuitous and time consuming. His first stop was in Berlin, where in 1853 he addressed the Berlin Geographical Society on the discovery of America. Through this talk he hoped to gain the support of Ritter and von Humboldt. His speech did not produce the desired effect. Neither came forward with enthusiastic support for his project. In 1854 he again addressed the Berlin Geographical Society, speaking on American geographical names derived from European names. Whether Ritter and von Humboldt were more impressed with this talk is not known. Von Humboldt, however, provided Kohl with letters of introduction to the distinguished geographer Edmé François Jomard and to the Geographical Society of Paris where Kohl hoped to find numerous maps on the

12. Schumacher, "Kohls Amerikanische Studien," 117.
13. Alexander, "J. G. Kohl," 21; Kohl, "Lebensbeschreibung," 9. Schumacher gives a different interpretation of this episode, pointing out that Kohl did not think himself ready for such a position (p. 115). Schumacher is not always accurate, however, especially in his quotes.

Americas. Although Kohl enjoyed the opportunity to address the Geographical Society of Paris, he saw disappointingly few maps there.[14]

From Paris Kohl traveled to London, where his luck improved. Friendships made on an earlier trip to England resulted in greater opportunities for research. Both he and his projected study on America were mentioned in the opening speech before a meeting of the London Geographical Society. In London he saw the maps at the Admiralty and worked at the British Museum and the Hudson's Bay Company Archives. In Oxford he saw the map collection of Thomas Bodley.

Finally, on September 7, 1854, Kohl sailed for the United States. He arrived in Philadelphia on September 26, but after a short stay he hurried on to New York City. Before settling down to pursue his quest for maps and documents, Kohl journeyed to Canada. It was on this trip that he first encountered Indians. He gathered enough notes to write a two-volume work entitled *Travels in Canada, and Through the States of New York and Pennsylvania,* which would be published in Germany in 1856 and in London in 1861.[15]

Once again in New York, Kohl began his research in earnest. He thoroughly enjoyed the opportunities the city provided: meetings with important scholars, talks before the New-York Historical Society and the New-York Geographical Society, and a renewal of family ties with his brother, who had moved to New York from Halifax. Through Charles P. Daley of the New-York Geographical Society, he met Washington

14. Kohl, "Lebensbeschreibung," 7–8, 10; Alexander, "J. G. Kohl," 21–22; Schumacher, "Kohls Amerikanische Studien," 121–22.

15. Alexander, "J. G. Kohl," 22; Kohl, "Lebensbeschreibung," 11; J. G. Kohl, *Reisen in Canada, und durch die Staaten von New-York und Pennsylvanien* (Stuttgart: J. W. Cotta, 1856) and *Travels in Canada, and through the States of New York and Pennsylvania,* 2 vols., trans. Mrs. Percy Sinnett (London: George Manwaring, 1861).

Irving; he also discussed ethnology with Henry Wadsworth
Longfellow. In January of 1855, while Kohl was in New York,
he signed a contract with D. Appleton and Company to write
a book on the states of the Upper Mississippi.[16]

A trip to Washington, D.C., early in 1855 widened Kohl's
circle of friends. Although Kohl did not find the city very
interesting, he there met Alexander Dallas Bache of the
United States Coast Survey. So impressed was Bache with
Kohl's knowledge of cartography and his collection of maps
and documents on America that he hired Kohl to write a survey of America's coasts. Kohl accepted the assignment and
shortly thereafter submitted a survey of the west coast of the
United States.[17]

With this part of his project completed, Kohl turned to writing his book for Appleton. Lacking empirical knowledge of
the country he was to describe, he planned a three-month trip
to the Upper Mississippi Valley. This expedition stretched to
six months and took Kohl among the Dakota Indians of Minnesota and the Ojibway Indians of northern Wisconsin and
Michigan. The events of this journey among the Indians of
Lake Superior greatly impressed Kohl. According to a biographer, the trip was the high point of his travels and yielded
the most results. Appleton would publish *Reisen im Nord-
westen der Vereinigten Staaten* (*Travels in the Northwestern
United States*) in 1857; Kohl had also taken notes for a separate
book on the Ojibway.[18]

When Kohl returned to Washington in the fall of 1855, he
resumed work on the coast survey, submitting the gulf coast
section in April 1856 and the east coast section the following
August. In an 1856 address before the Smithsonian Institu-

16. Alexander, "J. G. Kohl," 22; Schumacher, "Kohls Amerikanische Studien," 135–37.

17. Kohl, "Lebensbeschreibung," 12.

18. Schumacher, "Kohls Amerikanische Studien," 143–44.

tion, Kohl suggested a compilation of maps for an atlas of the American coastline. This plan, submitted to Congress, won approval, and Kohl was allowed $6,000 to carry it out.[19]

Kohl worked on this project in Boston from 1857 to 1858, but a depression in 1857 dissolved any plans for its publication. The rejection of a year's labor was a great disappointment. He resented not only the loss of time but also the delay that it meant in returning to Germany. Yet the year did not prove a total loss. Kohl enjoyed Boston and his close association with the Brahmins of Harvard. In May 1858 Kohl bade farewell to America and returned to Europe, spending the summer of 1858 in Freiburg. There he worked over the notes covering his weeks among the Ojibway of Lake Superior and prepared for press *Kitchi-Gami*, which was published in Germany in 1859. The English edition, translated with Kohl's approval by Lascelles Wraxall, was published the following year.[20]

Kohl never traveled to America again. Eventually he returned to Bremen, where he took up the position of city librarian. His grand project on the conquest of the Americas was never published, but at the request of the Maine Historical Society he wrote a work on the discovery of the east coast of

19. J. G. Kohl, "Substance of a Lecture Delivered at the Smithsonian Institution on a Collection of the Charts and Maps of America," *Annual Report of the Board of Regents of the Smithsonian Institution* (Washington, D.C., 1857), 145–46; Kohl, "Lebensbeschreibung," 14–15; Schumacher, "Kohls Amerikanische Studien," 159; Justin Winsor, *The Kohl Collection of Early Maps Belonging to the Department of State, Washington, U.S.A.*, Library of Harvard University Bibliographical Contributions, no. 19 (Cambridge: The Library, 1886), 3.

20. Kohl, "Lebensbeschreibung," 12, 18; Schumacher, "Kohls Amerikanische Studien," 173–74; Winsor, *Kohl Collection*, 3–4; Kohl, *Kitschi-Gami, oder, Erzählungen vom Obern See: Ein Beitrag zur Charakteristik der Amerikanischen Indianer* (Bremen: C. Schünemann, 1859) and *Kitchi-Gami: Wanderings Round Lake Superior*, trans. Lascelles Wraxall (London: Chapman and Hall, 1860; Minneapolis: Ross and Haines, 1956).

North America and particularly the coast of Maine.[21] Friends
like the ethnologist Adolph Bastian urged Kohl to do more
work in ethnology. Since *Kitchi-Gami* did not include all of
Kohl's data on the Ojibway, perhaps he intended to write
another book on the subject. Although he published some
articles on Indians in the Bremen newspaper and presented
talks on aspects of Ojibway culture before groups in Bremen,
no subsequent book on Indians appeared before his death in
1878.[22]

But the question remains: why would this educated, urbane
German want to spend weeks among Ojibway Indians in the
wilderness of northern Wisconsin? One could say that as a

21. Winsor, *Kohl Collection*, 3; R. Hoche, "Kohl," *Allgemeine Deutsche Bib-
liographie* (Leipzig, 1882), 427; "Kohl," *Deutsches Literatur Lexikon* (Bern,
1953), 1347; J. G. Kohl, *A History of the Discovery of Maine*, Collections of
the Maine Historical Society, 2d series, Documentary History of the State of
Maine, vol. 1 (Portland: Bailey and Noyes, 1869). See also Leonard Wood to
J. G. Kohl, February 22, September 21, 1868, and other letters from Wood
and Edward Ballard during the spring and summer of 1868, AUT XI, Kohl
Collection. The grand project was evidently never published, but in October
1859 Kohl began a series of twelve lectures that were published as *Geschichte
der Entdeckung Amerika's von Kolumbus bis Franklin* (Bremen: Strack, 1861),
published in English as *A Popular History of the Discovery of America, from
Columbus to Franklin*, 2 vols., trans. R. R. Noel (London: Chapman and Hall,
1862).

22. Schumacher, "Kohls Amerikanische Studien," 180–81. Some of the
material Kohl possessed but did not include in *Kitchi-Gami* were further collections of Ojibway legends and biographies, notes on Ojibway linguistics,
sketches of missionary work among the Ojibway, and an account of a visit to
a Dakota village on the Minnesota River. For examples of Kohl's writing, see
"Besuch in einem Dorfe der Sioux-Indianer am Minnesota-Flusse," *Ausland*
49 (1858): 1153–59; "Bemerkungen über die Bekehrung canadischer Indianer
zum Christenthum und einige Bekehrungsgeschichten," *Ausland* 2 (1859): 2;
"Eine kleine Sammlung von Ausdrücken aus dem canadisch-französischen
Dialekt," *Ausland* 33 (1859): 783–87; "Schingebis oder der Muschel-Prinz,
eine Chippeway-Sage," *Ausland* 34 (1859): 793–96; "Aufzeichnungen über
einige Eigenthümlichkeiten der Sprache der Chippeway-Indianer," *Ausland*
47 (1859): 1108; "Die Sagen der Indianer Nordamerikas," *Bremer Sonntags-
blatt* (1859), 9:65, 10:76, 11:81.

writer of travel books, Kohl saw an opportunity for yet another travel account, apart from the volume he had contracted
to do with Appleton; he knew of the German market for books
about American Indian cultures. His planned work on the
conquest of the Americas may have helped motivate him. But
these are only partial answers. Kohl was a student of the inter-
relationship of culture and geography. Intrigued by the ethnological questions that Indians and mixed-bloods posed, he
probably saw his trip to Wisconsin as an opportunity to test
assumptions and verify what he had read and heard about
these peoples. Added to this was Kohl's firm belief in the need
to observe people directly before writing about them. On his
trip to Wisconsin he set out to gather his own data, guided by
his dictum, "from life itself everything is taken."[23]

But if Kohl wanted to see the "real Indian," why did he not
go among the plains tribes, as his Canadian friends suggested?
Certain bits of information suggest reasons for his actions.
Kohl traveled to the Upper Mississippi Valley because he had
signed a contract with Appleton. Undoubtedly he also was
familiar with the published works of Henry Rowe Schoolcraft,
ethnologist and Indian agent, and so already had a passive
introduction to Ojibway culture. Furthermore, Longfellow's
use of Ojibway legends in his soon-to-be published poem, *The
Song of Hiawatha* (1855), impressed Kohl. Longfellow may
have urged Kohl to visit the Ojibway and gather their legends
firsthand. Perhaps while in Washington, but certainly while
in Chicago, Kohl learned of the annuity payment that would
take place at La Pointe, Wisconsin, during the summer of
1855. "For an observer," Kohl explained, "this was naturally
the best opportunity he could desire to regard more closely

23. Alexander, "J. G. Kohl," 59. On the German market for books on
Indians, see Weber, *America in Imaginative German Literature*, especially
chapters 3 and 4; Billington, *Land of Savagery*, chapter 3.

these curious American aborigines, and collect information as to their traditions and customs."[24]

Kohl's attitudes and contributions are more fully appreciated when compared with those of other ethnologists who had previously published works on the Ojibway.[25] Some of the first studies on the tribe were written by Lewis Cass, territorial governor of Michigan. Cass stressed the utilitarian function of ethnology: ethnographic data were to be used to advance the government's program of "civilizing" Indians. Such ethnology – what might be called frontier ethnology – emphasized field research and eschewed what Cass considered the theoretical pirouettes of library-bound ethnologists in eastern cities: "Our Indian relations generally are a concern, not of speculation, but of action; and a just and intimate knowledge of the Indians, of their mode of life, of their peculiar opinions, and of all that they feel, and suffer, and want, can only be acquired in their villages, camps, and hunting grounds."[26] In an earlier essay, Cass was even more emphatic. "No rational estimate can be formed of the character of any people, without

24. Kohl, *Travels in Canada* 1:227; Schumacher, "Kohls Amerikanische Studien," 148; Kohl, *Kitchi-Gami*, 2.

25. There were, of course, others besides Cass and Schoolcraft, discussed below, who wrote on the Ojibway, but they did not consciously strive to present a "scientific" account of these people. For example, Edwin James, ed., *A Narrative of the Captivity and Adventures of John Tanner during Thirty Years Residence among the Indians* (New York: G. & C. & H. Carvill, 1830) contained much ethnographic data. Less informative on the subject of Ojibway customs was Thomas L. McKenney's *Sketches of a Tour to the Lakes* (Baltimore: Fielding Lucas, 1827). Several works by the Ojibway Indian George Copway also attracted some attention. See, for example, *The Life, History, and Travels of Kah-ge-ga-gah-Bowh (George Copway), a Young Indian Chief of the Ojebwa Nation,* . . . (Albany: n.p., 1847), and *The Traditional History and Characteristic Sketches of the Ojibway Nation* (London: n.p., 1850). Other than the works of Schoolcraft, there is little evidence that Kohl was aware of these works (or those of Alexander Henry and G. C. Beltrami), or that he drew upon them for writing *Kitchi-Gami*.

26. [Lewis Cass], "Removal of the Indians," *North American Review* 30 (January 1830): 70.

viewing them at home, in their own country, engaged in their ordinary duties and occupations. This is particularly the case with the Indians."[27]

Cass believed that Indians acted "from impulse more than from reason." Collectively, he wrote, "there seems to be some insurmountable obstacle in the habits or temperaments of the Indians, which has heretofore prevented, and yet prevents, the success of these [missionary] labors." This obstacle, Cass was sure, lay imbedded deep within Indian society. "There is a principle of repulsion in ceaseless activity, operating through all their institutions, which prevents them from appreciating or adopting any other modes of life, or any other habits of thought or action, but those which have descended to them from their ancestors."[28]

Cass's frontier ethnology did not exist to collect sterile facts for spinning theories and filling books. Instead, its purpose was to ferret out what in Indian culture made Indians so resistant to new ways, or what Cass called civilization. If ethnologists in league with government agents could isolate this factor and destroy it, if ethnologists could render Indians amenable to civilization, then ethnology would merit the thanks of a grateful government.

An intellectual and political protégé of Cass was the ethnologist Henry Rowe Schoolcraft, noted not only for his writing on the Ojibway and other Indians but also for his years as Indian agent among the Ojibway of Michigan. A hard-working, ambitious, and religious man, Schoolcraft put forth this utilitarian orientation with even more zeal than did Cass.

Schoolcraft, however, believed that spiritual change must precede secular change. The dual forces that propelled his ethnological studies were the assertion of his belief in mono-

27. [Lewis Cass], "Indians of North America," *North American Review* 22 (January 1826): 58, 59.
28. [Cass], "Removal of the Indians," 93, 69, 67.

genism, or the single creation of all of mankind, and the bringing of Christianity to Indian tribes. (Schoolcraft never questioned that the Indians were descended from Adam, as some
of his contemporaries did, for to do so would have countered
the religious teachings in which he so fervently believed.)
Thus one goal of his ethnology was to trace Indian history
back to Asia using language, legends, and customs. The other
was to reveal how morally degenerate Indians had become in
their wanderings and what a difficult yet rewarding task it
would be to save them and lead them back to the light of
"true" religion.[29]

To stress the baseness of Ojibway culture, Schoolcraft often
portrayed the Ojibway and their institutions in negative
terms. He proclaimed that what he called "the society of
Wabeno" was "little more than a midnight revel; and the Evil
Spirit is solicited to give efficacy to the incantations with
which it is celebrated. It is a mere worship of Baal." A year
later he pointed out that "the Indian seldom thinks, but [ex-
cept] when he is compelled to think, and then he is not slow
to suggest plausible arguments to fortify himself in heathenish
practices."[30]

Schoolcraft collected a mass of ethnographic data, but in his
presentation the information became less a contribution to
ethnology than an indictment of what he saw as Indian savag-
ism and degeneration. Always there were subtle qualifications:

29. Schoolcraft expressed these views in various works. See, for example,
[Henry R. Schoolcraft], "Civilization and Conversion of the Indians," *North
American Review* 28 (April 1829): 354–68; Henry R. Schoolcraft, "Mythology,
Superstition and Languages of the North American Indians," *Literary and
Theological Review* 2 (March 1835): 96–121; [Henry R. Schoolcraft], "Catlin's
North American Indians," *North American Review* 54 (April 1842): 283–99;
Henry R. Schoolcraft, *Plan for the Investigation of American Ethnology* (New
York: Edward O. Jenkins, 1846).

30. [Henry R. Schoolcraft], "Travellers among the Aborigines," *North
American Review* 27 (July 1828): 101; [Schoolcraft], "Civilization and Conversion of the Indians," 367.

"they had skill enough" to make canoes, "knew sufficient of the elementary art of weaving" to make bags and mats, "knew enough of pottery to form a mixture" that could be used for food utensils. Although Schoolcraft granted that Indians were formal and stately in their councils and "expert in the arrangement and discussion of minor matters," they "failed in comprehensive views, deep-reaching foresight, and powers of generalization."[31]

The ethnology of Kohl was a sharp contrast to that of Schoolcraft. Kohl seemed to have an empathy for Indian cultures that the American lacked. As Kohl noted in *Travels in Canada*, "When I was in Europe, and knew them [Indians] only from books, I must own I considered them rude, coldblooded, rather uninteresting people, but when I had once shaken hands with them, I felt that they were 'men and brothers,' and had a good portion of warm blood and sound understanding, and I could feel as much sympathy for them as for any other human creatures."[32]

The differences between Kohl and Schoolcraft are quickly evident in a comparison of how each described Ojibway religion. Schoolcraft saw Ojibway religious practices as the "darkest and gloomiest picture of Indian life"; he asserted that Indians live "in an atmosphere of moral darkness" with "their mental faculties bound down . . . for generations, with the subtle cords of sorcery, magic, and daemonology." Kohl, in contrast, was willing to see much of value in Ojibway practices that compared favorably with the teachings of Christianity. He pointed out that the act of charity, which Christians claimed as a feature distinguishing their religion from "all other religious dogmas," was not exclusively Christian: "Char-

31. Henry R. Schoolcraft, *Algic Researches, Comprising Inquiries Respecting the Mental Characteristics of the North American Indians* (New York: Harper and Brothers, 1839), 1:19.

32. Kohl, *Travels in Canada* 2:81.

ity and liberality, as regards the goods given by God, and noble hospitality, are praised as the principal virtues among non-Christian nations equally as with us. Among the Indians this reaches such a pitch, that it is one of the chief obstacles to their conversion." Kohl found it "most remarkable" that Ojibway youths would fast and suffer physical torment in quest "of an idea, a dream, or the fulfilment of a religious duty." When, Kohl asked, "was it ever known, among us Europeans, that boys or girls were able, at the tenderest age, to fast for days on behalf of a higher motive . . . and fix their minds so exclusively on celestial matters?"[33]

Where Schoolcraft found "a body of subtile [sic] superstitions, and widely-spread popular error . . . in the masses of the Indian tribes," and a society of Wabeno "most impure, and . . . most diabolical in its rites and ceremonies," Kohl found merely another way of approaching the unknown. Indeed, he did not find that such rituals really differed from those practiced in Europe. "The Indians have for a lengthened period been great spiritualists, ghost-seers, table-rappers, and perhaps, too, magnetisers, which we 'educated' Europeans have only recently become, or returned to."[34]

Kohl's description of Ojibway culture differs sharply from those of the Americans, not because Kohl was more sensitive or perceptive than Schoolcraft and all the others, but because his concerns were different. He was not hampered by American preoccupation with the removal of Indian tribes or the acculturation of Indian peoples. Kohl's objective was to produce an ethnological account of a rich and unique culture. In his preface to the German edition of *Kitchi-Gami*, Kohl explained, "I only take the credit for having endeavored to

33. Henry R. Schoolcraft, *Information Respecting the History, Condition, and Prospects of the Indian Tribes of the United States* (Philadelphia: J. B. Lippincott, 1856), 5:415 (hereafter cited as *History*); Kohl, *Kitchi-Gami*, 65, 228.
34. Schoolcraft, *History* 5:441, 71; Kohl, *Kitchi-Gami*, 278.

understand them [Ojibway stories and ways of life] correctly and to present them clearly. Everything is taken from life itself, and as much as possible I have carefully avoided repeating what has been said in other works. Some of the legends, traditions, and stories may well have already been told elsewhere. But since I took them from the mouths of the people themselves, these too seemed to me very new and characteristic."[35]

But there were other reasons Kohl's work differed from that of Schoolcraft and others. For one, he drew upon different ethnological traditions. Kohl inherited a German tradition of travel ethnography, the practice of keeping a travel journal that described people, places, and traditions, which made an important contribution to German ethnology. Around 1800, travel writers had shifted from recording only noteworthy places to recording events and objects common to a particular culture. The focus thus changed from merely external observation to a conscious effort to interpret what was seen.[36] Kohl's travel accounts were in this tradition; he recorded, but he also interpreted and compared.

Kohl also inherited the German folk-culture tradition, which reaches back to Herder's "Ossian and the Songs of Ancient Peoples" (1773). This essay, according to one scholar, "led the way toward an interest in folk culture in Germany; and in the following decades there was much collecting of folk material: folksongs, legends, folktales, and fairy tales."[37] Kohl's efforts to gather Ojibway legends must be viewed in

35. Kohl, *Kitschi-Gami*, 1:vi.

36. Justin Stagl, "Der wohl unterwiesene Passagier: Reisekunst und Gesellschaftsbeschreibung vom 16. bis zum 18. Jahrhundert," in *Reisen und Reisebeschreibungen im 18. und 19. Jahrhundert als Quellen der Kulturbeziehungsforschung*, eds. B. I. Krasnobaev et al. (Berlin: Ulrich Camen, 1980): 353–84.

37. John M. Ellis, *One Fairy Story Too Many: The Brothers Grimm and Their Tales* (Chicago: University of Chicago Press, 1983), 6–7.

the context of the same folklore tradition that raised the works of Jakob and Wilhelm Grimm to such prominence.

Finally there was the anthropogeographical tradition of Carl Ritter, Kohl's friend and sometime sponsor. Anthropogeography, the study of the interaction of man with his environment, was both embracive and interdisciplinary. Its students held that culture, language, religion, economy, and geography must be studied together in order to fully comprehend a people; that it is necessary to observe how a people live and act within their environment; and that both geography and race are important in determining the capabilities of a people. In short, people behaved in different ways not only because of racial variations but also because they lived in different environments. While several of these assumptions today seem rather commonplace, in the mid-nineteenth century, when many believed race determined a people's culture and capability, such thinking proved controversial.[38]

In *Kitchi-Gami* Kohl combined his practiced hand as a journal keeper and his appreciation for folklore with Ritter's approach to ethnology. The ethnographic data he collected is astonishing. He was a dedicated and accomplished fieldworker who knew how to ask questions and solicit answers. He also believed that one must see and experience before one sets about building theories.

This inductive emphasis is clear in *Kitchi-Gami*. Kohl carefully noted Ojibway relationships to the environment: how and where they lived. He stayed as much as possible among the Indians, even hiring women to build him a wigwam in one

38. For a discussion of Ritter, see W. E. Mühlmann, *Geschichte der Anthropologie* (Wiesbaden: AULA, 1984), 67, 70, 125, 162; James N. Ryding, "Alternatives in Nineteenth-Century German Ethnology: A Case Study in the Sociology of Science," *Sociologus* 25 (1975–76): 6–8; George W. Stocking, Jr., *Race, Culture, and Evolution: Essays in the History of Anthropology* (New York: The Free Press, 1968), 141; Ernst Plewe, "Ritter, Carl," in *International Encyclopedia of Social Science* (New York: Macmillan, 1968), 13:517–20.

of the Ojibway villages. He was fascinated by aspects of their religion and wrote perceptively about their Midewiwin ceremony, as he did about their hieroglyphics or bark writing, their songs, and especially their folktales. Given the number of tales he collected, it is obvious that he believed (as did Ritter, the Grimm brothers, and Kohl's friend the ethnologist Adolph Bastian) that such tales provided insight into a people's beliefs and cultural identity. He wrote elegantly on how the Ojibway lived; the foods they ate; the clothes they wore; how they painted their faces; their methods and implements of travel, hunting, and fishing. He noted differences between plains and woodland tribes, in particular between the Dakota and the Ojibway. He also caught differences in life-styles between the Ojibway who lived near Lake Superior and those who lived further inland.

Kohl was intrigued by the differences among the Ojibway, the people of mixed blood, and the Euro-Americans. When a friend chided him about his interests in mixed-bloods, Kohl assured him that they possessed an ethnological importance: "In ethnography, as in all nature, mixed and mongrel races are often specially important to the observer. Many questions can only be solved among Indians who have come more or less into contact with civilisation. Of what degree of culture are they capable? To what diseases, physical and moral, are they most liable? From which do they remain free, &c.? The comparisons and contrasts with Europeans are also more easily made, and more striking, and thus the results of psychological observation are often much more surprising."[39]

Kitchi-Gami is not without its faults, but they are minor and can be attributed more to the ideas of the age than to errors in judgment by Kohl. There are some overtones of racism in Kohl's perception of relative uniformity among Indian cultures because all Indians lived in what Kohl considered a

39. Kohl, *Travels in Canada* 1:278.

wilderness environment: while he saw differences among them, he found all Indians similar in their uncivilized state when compared with Euro-Americans. This was carrying anthropogeography too far. Kohl also sometimes saw cultural traits in racial terms. This is not surprising, however, when one considers ethnological assumptions at mid-century, when some German ethnologists like Bastian believed in polygenism and others like Ritter could talk about "passive-indolent" races and "active-energetic" ones. Yet with this said about *Kitchi-Gami*, one is struck by Kohl's rather modern notion of the acculturation process. It is also significant to note that Kohl stoutly refuted charges that Indians were dirty or indolent. In general, Kohl portrayed Ojibway culture with great sensitivity and found among the Ojibway people beauty, honor, and integrity.

These sentiments betray a certain tinge of romanticism for which Kohl may be excused. He deeply respected what he saw of Ojibway culture and the sentiments he expressed regarding this culture, aspects of which he sometimes criticized, were sincere. His romanticism is best displayed in the two-volume German edition of *Kitchi-Gami*. It is divided into three sections or books, each appropriately titled to evoke within the reader a sense of nature's grandeur: "The Island," dated August 1855 at La Pointe (Chapters 1 through 11 of the English edition); "The Bay," dated September 1855 at L'Anse (Chapters 12 through 18); and "The Cataract," dated October 1855 at Rivière au Désert or Garden River near Sault Ste. Marie (Chapters 19 through 25). Like other works by Kohl, the German edition of *Kitchi-Gami* followed another popular structure of the day: letters to an anonymous friend replaced chapters. Thus the chapters (letters) are at once more intense and more forceful. To increase the personal tone, Kohl began each letter with a poem fragment – often about nature, sometimes by a romantic poet – that set the mood for what follows.

For example, before the letter on "A Religious Festival" (Book I, Letter 5), Kohl quotes from a poem by Gottfried Keller:

> I search the spray,
> Don't know for what,
> Long lost dreams
> Awaken in me.

And from Friedrich Schiller, before the chapter on the death of a boy (Book I, Letter 11), Kohl quotes:

> Bring hither the last gifts
> Bewail the dead!
> With him all be buried
> That may bring him joy!

These passages were deleted from the English edition, which thereby lost some of the charm of the original German edition, but *Kitchi-Gami* still absorbs the reader and remains a delightful account of earlier days among the Ojibway of Lake Superior. Wraxall also omitted several Ojibway legends and abridged some of the German text. The legends, now translated, are published in Appendix I of this edition. The abridgements are characterized in Ralf Neufang's "Note on the Translation," which follows this introduction; a longer sample of the elisions it describes is printed in Appendix II.

How does one measure the importance of Kohl's *Kitchi-Gami*? If the criterion is the number of times the work has been cited, then *Kitchi-Gami* is a significant work indeed. Kohl's book won plaudits among his contemporaries. One reviewer noted that it was a careful work free of sentimentality and exaggeration. "He did not carry a ready-made theory . . . with him; but applied himself to collect carefully the facts about the race, and classified and reasoned from them as he went along . . . details are handled well, and made more intelligible in their relation to the climate, circumstances, and traditions of the people." This reviewer ended proclaiming, "Mr. Kohl's book is a concise and superior contribution to the ethnography of the west." The bibliophile Thomas W. Field was effusive: "Mr. Kohl has given one of the most exhaustive and valuable treatises on Indian life ever written."[40]

In 1859 Kohl wrote, "In the course of the winter of 1858–59, I also prepared for printing a 'small work' on the Objibbewas on Kitchigami (Lake Superior) which I gave the title: Kitchigami or Narratives from Lake Superior: A Contribution to the Ethnography of the American Indians. . . . [I] hope that one will acknowledge it as a small ethnographic contribution."[41] Ethnologists have not only acknowledged Kohl's work but have utilized many of his observations on Ojibway culture.[42]

For historians, *Kitchi-Gami* supplements knowledge of midwestern frontier life and provides corroborating data regarding the payment of annuities, the hardships and rewards of missionary life on the frontier, and an array of regional racial and ethnic attitudes. Like other European travelers, Kohl saw and recorded his observations with a European bias. Historians who have examined the writings of other European trav-

40. "[Review of] *Kitchi-Gami, Wanderings Round Lake Superior,*" *Littell's Living Age*, 3d series, 9 (June 9, 1860): 612–13; Field, *An Essay Towards an Indian Bibliography* (New York: Scribner, Armstrong and Co., 1873; Detroit: Gale Research Company, 1967), 205–6.

41. Kohl, "Lebensbeschreibung," 18.

42. For examples, see Ritzenthaler, "Southwestern Chippewa," 743–59; Eva Lips, *Die Reisernte der Ojibwa-Indianer. Wirtschaft und Recht eines Erntevolkes* (Berlin, G.D.R.: Akademie-Verlag, 1956); A. Irving Hallowell, *The Role of Conjuring in Saulteaux Society*, Publications of the Philadelphia Anthropological Society, no. 2 (Philadelphia: University of Pennsylvania Press, 1942; New York: Octagon Books, 1971); Victor Barnouw, *Wisconsin Chippewa Myths and Tales and Their Relation to Chippewa Life* (Madison: University of Wisconsin Press, 1977); Christopher Vecsey, *Traditional Ojibwa Religion and Its Historical Changes* (Philadelphia: American Philosophical Society, 1983); Meinhard Schuster, "Wolkenhaupt auf der Rottanne. Ethnologische Aspekte des Traumes," in *Traum und Träumen. Traumanalysen in Wissenschaft, Religion und Kunst*, eds. Therese Wagner-Simon and Gaetano Benedetti (Göttingen: Vandenhoeck & Ruprecht, 1984), 133–49.

elers and studied their perspectives on American life will appreciate Kohl's account.

Kohl's *Kitch-Gami* also contributes to the history of anthropology. As a European or German perspective on Ojibway culture, the work is refreshing, but what it reflects of German ethnology at mid-century is also noteworthy. When compared with American works of ethnology of the time, *Kitchi-Gami* gives greater emphasis to the environmental and geographical aspects of cultural change and development. Although one might attribute this orientation to Kohl's interest in cultural geography, it is important to remember that German ethnology, especially as practiced by Ritter, had just such a direction.

The English edition of *Kitchi-Gami* was published on the eve of the American Civil War, a conflict that would turn brother against brother over such issues as how one race treats another. Kohl's work had a message for Americans, which is best expressed in his treatment of Ojibway legends. Kohl gathered his stories shortly after Schoolcraft's collection of Ojibway legends was published. Schoolcraft used the stories to demonstrate how totally alien the "Indian world" was from that of the Euro-American. To Schoolcraft, the tales revealed the fantastic, rigid world of the Oriental mind and as such were something to be deplored. In contrast, Kohl sought to show how similar Ojibway legends were to those of Europe and thus, with grace and elegance, he underscored how little the races of mankind really differed.

ROBERT E. BIEDER

A NOTE ON THE TRANSLATION

THIS edition of *Kitchi-Gami* is a reprint of the 1860 English translation by Lascelles Wraxall. Although Kohl approved Wraxall's work, many of Kohl's words are left out of the translation. The first appendix to this edition offers five legends that were published in Kohl's original text but were omitted by Wraxall, who explained, "my readers will be familiar with them in the pages of Hiawatha, to which I recommend Mr. Kohl's book as a famous supplement" (p. 299). The second appendix contains the only other major piece of text not translated.

The shorter abridgements that Wraxall made, interspersed throughout the text, cannot be corrected in this fashion, but some examples will characterize the elisions. Kohl often related his experiences with the Indians of Lake Superior to European culture, customs, and traditions. As Robert E. Bieder explains in his introduction to this edition, this indicates Kohl's more comparative approach to ethnographic research and more understanding attitude toward the Indians. Sometimes Wraxall translated these passages, as in his description of the preparation of birch bark for canoe-building: "The inner side of the fresh bark is cleansed and scraped with knives (just as our tanners treat leather) . . . " (p. 29; German edition, vol. 1, p. 43).

Usually, however, Wraxall did not include these passages. For example, Wraxall's translation reads, "Although my women were busy enough after their fashion, I had no occasion to warn them against injuring their health by excessive toil" (p. 5 – 6). A complete translation of Kohl's original would say, "Although my women were busy enough after their fashion, I had no need to shout to them what farmers in Austria shout to each other when they meet: 'Take your time! Take your time!' " (vol. 1, p. 11). Similarly, where Wraxall wrote, "He swung the tomahawk and pointed to the scars and wounds on his naked body, in confirmation of his story, giving the post a heavy blow now and then. Many had painted their scars . . . " (p. 19), a full translation would read, "He swung the tomahawk and pointed to the scars and wounds on his naked body, in confirmation of his story, giving the flagpole a heavy blow now and then, just as in our country a speaker may pound with his hand on the lectern. Some had painted their scars . . ." (vol. 1, p. 31).

Wraxall occasionally omitted details of various length about Ojibway life and customs. In translating Kohl's description of how birch bark is obtained (p. 29), Wraxall left out the remark that "Usually they peel the trees in June and July" (vol. 1, p. 43). After his general discussion of Ojibway face-painting (p. 17), Kohl provided descriptions of four specific designs; Wraxall omitted all of these, including the striking "second example: The basic color of the face is crimson. The chin: rubbed in jet black. From the lips as the center, black lines run in all directions, left and right past the nose and across the cheeks to the ears, like the quills of a porcupine. Horizontal lines run parallel across the forehead and look like deep wrinkles, which make the young warrior look thirty years older than he actually is" (vol. 1, p. 27–28).

The few examples of untranslated material given here underline again Kohl's keen sense of observation and the sometimes humorous touch of his writing.

RALF NEUFANG

KITCHI-GAMI

KITCHI-GAMI.*

TALES FROM LAKE SUPERIOR.

CHAPTER I.

THE small island on which I am taking my first
notes about the tribe of the Ojibbeways, their traditions, manners, and customs, lies on the western side
of the Canadian Lake Superior, which is as large as
the kingdoms of Bavaria and Würtemberg together.

In the language of the Indians, my island is called

* These two mysterious words are the Indian equivalent for the "big
water," known as Lake Superior. Longfellow, in "Hiawatha," spells
them "Geetchee-Gumee," but I decidedly prefer M. Kohl's spelling, for
it looks more natural. I doubt whether Indians would double the vowel
in the way Longfellow proposes. At any rate, all the other authors I have
consulted agree with M. Kohl's spelling. Geetchee-Gumee may, however,
be the true spelling in some dialect of the Ojibbeway.—L. W.

Shaguamikon, which means, literally, "something gnawed on all sides," or a promontory. The old French missionaries, who discovered and visited this strip of land two hundred years ago, translated this, consistently enough, into La Pointe. A sandy promontory, jutting out from the island, and covering its principal port or landing, was the originator of the name, which has been transferred to the village and the whole island.

La Pointe belongs to a larger group of islands, which the French missionaries named Les Isles des Apôtres. They play a great part in the Indian traditions, and seem to have been from the earliest period the residence of hunting and fishing tribes, probably through their geographical position and the good fishing in the vicinity. The fables of the Indian Creator, Menaboju, often allude to these islands, and the chiefs who resided here have always laid claim, even to the present day, to the rank of princes of the Ojibbeways.

The French missionaries had here one of their chief missions, whence many of their celebrated "lettres édifiantes " were dated.

The great fur companies, too, which, after them, ruled on Lake Superior, had one of their most important stations at La Pointe; more especially the once so powerful North-West Company, which carried on a lively trade from this spot as far as the Polar Seas.

Even now it is one of the most important places on Lake Superior; and when I was staying on the lake, in the summer of 1855, the American authorities summoned to this island the principal tribes of the Ojibbeways residing round the lake, for the purpose of holding a consultation with them, and paying them their yearly tribute. For an observer, this was naturally the best opportunity he could desire to regard more closely these curious American aborigines, and collect information as to their traditions and customs.

Besides the Indians, several hundred half-breeds had come in, many Indian traders, American travellers, and French voyageurs. They had come from a very widely-spread country, and were all much-travelled and intelligent men, from whom I could obtain explanations as to what I saw among the Indians. As I had also attracted to my side an excellent and experienced Canadian Frenchman, I succeeded in discovering all sorts of novelties, and understanding many strange matters.

Although so much has been said and written about the North American Indians since the days of Columbus, they still are in many respects a riddle, and though I had read nearly all already published about them, they seemed to me utter strangers when I went among them, and I fancied there was still a good deal to say about them. Hence I trust that my information about a race of men dying out so rapidly and irrevocably may prove to a certain extent acceptable.

My first care was to settle in the midst of this strange people, and I therefore built my own wigwam and kindled my own fire in one of their villages. Hence I will commence my narrative with the Indian lodge-building.

For this purpose I engaged an Indian woman, the squaw of a sensible and much-travelled Voyageur, who had offered to act as my interpreter to his relations and the other Indians. The first thing in building a wigwam is preparing the carcase and felling the young trees required for that purpose in the adjoining wood. This is the business of the women, like all the

work, heavy or light, always with the exception of
hunting.

My Indian woman went into the wood with an axe,
felled the trees, and dragged them out. Her old
mother and young sister and her daughters helped her
in the job. Martin, an unlucky, half-lame Indian
youth, who is of no use either to hunt or to paddle,
and hence remains in the house with the squaws,
very readily lends them a hand now and then.

The women are also obliged to procure and cut up
the firewood in the forest. This is one of their chief
daily tasks, and in the neighbourhood of the Indian
encampments round me I always hear at a certain
hour in the evening the axes of the women and girls
sounding as they prepare the logs for the next day,
and emerge heavily laden from the scrub. Usually,
too, I notice several young fellows idling about under
the trees, serenely watching the toiling women, and
conversing affably with them. As I am told, this
wood-cutting hour is the grand love-making time for
the young men.

It may be easily supposed that these squaws, owing
to their performing all the work of joiners, carpenters,
and masons, have corned and blistered hands. In
fact, their hands are much harder to the touch than
those of the men; and, indeed, their entire muscular
system is far more developed, and they are propor-
tionately stronger in the arm, for the men do not do
much to bring out the muscle. It is a general remark
that the male Indians have a soft, aristocratic hand,
which is an evidence of their freedom from toil. I
was also told that there was another distinction
between the Indian men and women: the former,
in walking, plant the foot quite straight, while the

women turn their toes in slightly. This is produced by the heavy weights they are obliged to carry, for a bent and heavily-laden body always produces an in-turn of the feet.

With their short tobacco-pipes in their mouths, and their children in wooden cradles on their backs, my women dragged the young trees from the wood, and thrust them into the ground at equal distances, so as to form a quadrangle. On this occasion they employed birch-trees, though they prefer the tamarack or larch for building. The quadrangle is a parallelogram, the longest side running from the entrance to the back of the hut; two trees were planted in front, where the door was to be, a little beyond the line of the qua-drangle, and the same behind, where the seat of honour is raised.

When the tall young trees are fixed in the ground, and stand perpendicular, like the basket-maker's frame-work, the side branches are bent down and fastened together two and two, when their ends are twisted round each other and secured with bast. For this purpose the extremely tough bast of the Canadian cedar-tree is used. Thus a species of arbour is formed. The two trees before and behind are somewhat longer, and are bent down and fastened together over the arbour in a similar fashion.

Thus the carcase is completed; but to give it greater firmness, and allow the covering to be put on, cross-bars are added. These are also young trees or branches, laid horizontally along the trellis-work, and firmly tied at all the points of intersection. The whole then resembles a widely interlaced basket of a semi-oval form.

Although my women were busy enough after their

fashion, I had no occasion to warn them against injuring their health by excessive toil. Besides building, they had many other matters to attend to; at times the old woman's pipe would go out, and she ran into the nearest hut to re-light it. Then a small boy came up, whose shirt was unfastened, and his clothes had to be tied up with a bit of the same bast employed on my mansion. Then they must look tenderly at their children, whom they had propped up against the trees, run up and kiss them, put their hands, ribbons, or caps straight, or sit down for a minute on the grass, lost in admiration of the little one.

Indian mothers are devotedly attached to their children, although they may possess no attraction for Europeans. They prepare them in their wooden cradles (although they seem to us a rack) such an exquisitely soft and well-arranged bed, that it is plain they must have thought most attentively on the subject.

One of the squaws was kind enough to untie her pappoose, and explain to me the Indian system of managing infants. I may be permitted to inlet here a slight episode in my wigwam building, for the "tiki-nagan" (the name of the Indian cradle among the Ojibbeways) is a little house within a house. Indeed, it is almost more carefully decorated and prepared than the dwelling of grown-up people.

The principal factor in this infant's house is a flat board. For this purpose poplar wood is selected; in the first place, because it is light; and, secondly, because it does not crack and splinter. On this board a small frame of thin peeled wood is fastened, much after the shape of the child's body, and stands up from the board, like the sides of a violin from the sounding-board. It is fastened on with bast, because the Indians never use nails, screws, or glue.

The cavity is filled and stuffed with very soft substances for the reception of the child. They prepare for this purpose a mixture composed of very fine dry moss, rotted cedar wood, and a species of tender wool found in the seed vessels of a species of reed. This wool was recommended to me as a most useful ingredient in the stuffing, for it sucks up all moisture as greedily as a sponge; and hence, then, there is no need to inspect the baby continually. In those houses where infants are an annual necessity, I saw casks filled with this soft stuff, so that I presume the mothers frequently re-line the nest.

In this bed the little beings nestle up to the armpits: so far they are wrapped up tightly with bandages and coverings, but the head and arms are free. At a convenient distance above the head is a stiff circle of wood, also fastened to the cradle with bast. It serves as a protection to the head, and if the cradle happen to fall over, it rests on this arch. In fact, you may roll an Indian tikinagan over as much as you please, but the child cannot be injured.

There is a special name for every part, however small, of the cradle; thus, for instance, the bow over the head is called agwin-gweon. It also serves as a receptacle for all the playthings and presents, which hang down from it, and are within reach of the infant's hands. I could write an entire chapter about the countless articles to be seen on the cradles of Indian pappooses: among them are a multitude which no European child would know what to do with. One can understand a rattle or bells, but what is an infant to do with carefully worked little mocassins hanging down over its nose; or a miniature imitation of a bow and arrows; or a wooden ring, over which leathern thongs are drawn; or a round piece of cariboo leather, from which small pieces of stag's horn are suspended? But I suspect that all these things are placed there more for a good omen than as playthings: the mocassins, that the boy may be a good runner; the bow, arrows, and bones, that he may become a famous hunter; that strange ring, with the network of leather, I am told, is good against illness. " Yes, very good! oh, excellent!" my women said. But how so, I never rightly comprehended.

The squaws at times display extraordinary luxury in the gaily embroidered coverlid which they throw over the whole cradle. I saw one woman use as a covering a wide sky-blue cloth, on which glistened at least a couple of pounds of pearl beads. She told me she had paid her neighbour ten dollars for it (half her yearly income). The apikan, or band, on which the mother carries infant and cradle, is also often richly ornamented.

Immediately after birth the little being is stretched out on the board, and its tender limbs laid straight; they drag and pull at it, make its back and legs as straight as possible, and place the feet exactly perpendicular, parallel, and close together, before packing it up. Thus, even in the cradle, care is taken that the Indian's feet should not turn outwards. A Canadian Voyageur assured me that the Indians, at every step, covered an inch more ground than the Europeans who turn their feet out. In winter it is impossible to use the snow-shoes if the European fashion of walking is followed. But, besides the feet, the Indian mothers play tricks with other parts of the infant's body.

Thus, for instance, they pay great attention to the nose, and try to pull it out so long as the cartilage remains soft, for a large nose is an ornament among the Indians.

While I was considering all this, the apakwas had arrived, and my house-skeleton was about to be clothed. This is the name given to the rolls of birch bark, which are generally kept in readiness to cover the wigwams or repair the roofs. These consist of a number of large quadrangular pieces of birch bark sewn together. Each piece is about a yard square, for a larger piece of good elastic bark, free from flaws and branch-holes, is rarely met with. Six or seven such pieces are sewn firmly together with cedar bast, and then formed into rolls resembling the cloth in our tailors' shops. That these rolls may acquire greater stiffness, thin laths are sewn into each end of the strip, on which they can be comfortably rolled, while the end most exposed to contact is reinforced with a double piece of bark, and the roll tied round, so as to be easier of carriage.

The women have always some of these rolls ready to hand, and hence I was enabled to purchase the nine or ten I required, or the bark of some sixty trees, from my neighbours. The women began covering the hut from the bottom, and bound a couple of long apakwas round it to the branches: the second row hung down over the first, so that the rain could run off it: a third and fourth row completed the whole, and a couple of apakwas were thrown crossways over the hut, leaving a smoke-hole in the centre. A mat was hung over the space left as a doorway.

In order that the wind might not disturb the apak-was, long cords of cedar bast were thrown across, with

heavy stones fastened to the ends. In this way the
semi-conical wigwam was completed, and received the
due amount of firmness.

When the Indians quit their place of residence,
they remove the valuable cords and apakwas, and
carefully roll them up. The poles and skeleton are
left standing, because those can be found everywhere;
at least the forest Indians can do so, but in the barren
prairies of the Far West the poles must also be
dragged hundreds of miles. The apakwas are so arranged that every woman has two to carry, in addition
to the other " plunder." Every little girl has also one
to carry, just as each Roman soldier carried his pali-
sade pole. These Indian girls begin to work when
six years of age, while their haughty brothers walk
along merely encumbered with bow and arrow.

My wigwam was hardly finished, and I proceeded
to enter it, than I found denizens already in it. An
Indian dog had settled very cozily in it, and a couple
of children had crawled through the door and were
grovelling on the new mat in great delight.

These mats, with which the Ojibbeways cover the
walls of their wigwams, and which also serve as
carpets, beds, and sofas, are the handiwork of the
women, and are excellently made. They employ for
the purpose a species of thick reed, which they call
Kitchi Gami-washk (Great Lake bulrush), and form of
it very soft and lasting mats. The mode of working is
extremely complicated, and the result of considerable
thought. The reeds must only be cut at one period
of the year, when they have attained a certain ripe-
ness. They are fastened up in small bundles, each of
which is boiled in hot water separately for about
three-quarters of an hour. Without this process the

reeds would become harsh and brittle. Bleaching is necessary to prepare them for colouring, and the women manage to produce really very pretty patterns.

In plaiting them they take various precautions, like those of the Belgian flax-spinners, who carry on their work in damp cellars in order to give the threads the required toughness. The Indians told me they did not plait these mats in dry and cheerful weather, but on damp and rainy days, else the reeds would become brittle. I lived once in the house of a very industrious mat-plaiter; every night she laid her work out in the dew. The next morning she brought it in, and plaited a bit more, till the sun rose too high. I asked her why she did not pour water on it during the day, but she said that would turn the reeds black.

I confess such a new, clean wigwam, with its gay matting, looks very comfortable, especially when a fire is crackling in the centre, and such a house would amply satisfy a Diogenes. Many Indians keep them in excellent order, but others soon make them dirty, do not mind the holes in the apakwas, but let the bark flutter in strips round the wigwam. If the wind carries off a strip, they will sooner crawl out of the rain than take the trouble to repair the damage. So much is certain, however, that there are poor peasants in Lithuania and Ireland, and wretched Jews in the Polish towns, housed no better or no worse than many of these savages. And the tents which the gipsies put up in Southern Russia and Wallachia are many of them less artistic and comfortable than the wigwams of the Ojibbeways.

I have described here only one variety of hut, namely, the ordinary winter abode of the Ojibbeways, which, indeed, is used by many of them the whole year round. They are somewhat narrower, and thence warmer; they are also easier to repair, for it only needs to throw an apakwa over any hole, and fasten it down by a cord. As they are externally round, without any angles, they offer a better resistance to storms, rain, or snow.

Still, some of them have more spacious, lofty, and airy summer wigwams. These are four-sided, with an oblique roof, and are covered with shingles. Then they are not called wigwams, a name exclusively belonging to the round birch-bark house. This word comes from "wigwass," which means the birch-tree, or its bark. The correct Ojibbeway form of the word is "wigiwam." It is employed, like many words of the Algonquin dialects, by the English to designate every Indian hut, although it may not be made of birch bark.

CHAPTER II.

I HAD scarcely settled comfortably on my island ere
one of the great steamers that now traverse Lake
Superior arrived, bringing several influential persons,
among others, the chief commissioner of Indian affairs.

The Indians call him their "Great Father *from*
Washington," as they call the President their "Great
Father *in* Washington." They call everybody at all
connected with government, Father, and, judging from
the great number of fathers these children of the
desert possess, they must be excellently taken care of.
During the whole period of our payment the number of
fathers, great and small, was astounding.

No sooner had the news of the Great Father's
arrival spread around, than the Indians prepared to
welcome him with a solemn full-dress procession, a

war-dance, and the presentation of the calumet of peace. The preparations for the ceremony began in various tents at an early hour, and the drum could be heard in the tent of a great chief, and his flagstaff, adorned with many gay feathers, was erected.

I wandered from tent to tent and looked at the preparations, and, as I already boasted of several acquaintances, I could step in here and there and watch the toilet of a warrior.

It is to a European a most comical sight to notice a savage before a looking-glass. Vanity and self-admiration are as visible in him as in a Parisian coquette. He even outvies her; for while she changes the fashion of her bonnet and the colour of her dress three or four times a year, the Indian alters the colour on his face —for his attention is confined to this portion of his person—daily.

I have watched three or four handsome young Indians here, and saw them every day wearing a different pattern on their faces. They belonged to the aristocracy of their band, and were evidently dandies. I saw them lounging along very seriously and with great dignity, with green or yellow stripes on their noses, their long pipes under their arms, and wrapped up in their wide blanket-cloaks. They were always together, and evidently formed a clique.

Daily, when I had the opportunity, I drew the pattern their faces displayed, and at length obtained a collection, whose variety even astonished myself. The strange combinations produced in the kaleidoscope may be termed weak when compared to what an Indian's imagination produces on his forehead, nose, and cheeks. I will try to give some account of them, as far as words will reach.

Two things struck me most in their arrangement of colours. First, the fact that they did not trouble themselves at all about the natural divisions of the face; and, secondly, the extraordinary mixture of the graceful and the grotesque.

At times, it is true, they did observe those natural divisions produced by nose, eyes, mouth, &c. The eyes were surrounded with regular coloured circles; yellow or black stripes issued harmoniously and equidistant from the mouth. Over the cheeks ran a semicircle of green dots, the ears forming the centre. At times, too, the forehead was traversed by lines running parallel to the natural contour of that feature. This always looked somewhat human, so to speak, because the fundamental character of the face was unaltered.

Usually, however, these regular patterns do not suit the taste of the Indians. They like contrasts, and frequently divide the face into two halves, which undergo different treatment. One will be dark—say black or blue—but the other quite light, yellow, bright red, or white. One will be crossed by thick lines made by the five fingers, while the other is arabesqued with oxtromely fine lines produced by the aid of a brush.

This division is produced in two different ways. The line of demarcation sometimes runs down the nose, so that the right cheek and side are buried in gloom, while the left looks like a flower-bed in the sunshine. At times, though, they draw the line across the nose, so that the eyes glisten out of the dark colour, while all beneath the nose is bright and lustrous. It seems as if they wished to represent on their faces the different phases of the moon.

I frequently inquired whether there was any significance in these various patterns, but was assured it was a mere matter of taste. They were simple arabesques, like their squaws work on the mocassins, girdles, tobacco-pouches, &c.

Still, there is a certain symbolism in the use of the colours. Thus, red generally typifies joy and festivity; black, mourning. When any very melancholy death takes place, they rub a handful of charcoal over the entire face. If the deceased is only a distant relative, a mere trellis-work of black lines is painted on the face. They have also a half-mourning, and only paint half the face black, when a certain time has elapsed.

Red is not only their joy, but also their favourite colour. They generally cover the face with a coating of bright red, on which the other colours are laid. For this purpose they employ vermilion, which comes from China, and is brought them by the Indian traders. However, this red is by no means *de rigueur*. Frequently the ground colour is a bright yellow, for which they employ chrome yellow, also obtained from the traders.

They are also very partial to Prussian blue, and employ this colour not only on their faces, but as a type of peace on their pipes, and as the hue of the sky on their graves. It is a very curious fact, by the way, that hardly any Indians can distinguish blue from green. I have seen the sky, which they represent on their graves by a round arch, as frequently of one colour as the other. In the Sioux language, "toya" signifies both green and blue, and a much-travelled Jesuit father told me that among many Indian tribes the same confusion prevails.

I have also been told that tribes have their favourite colours, and I am inclined to believe it, although I was not able to recognise any such rule. Generally,

all Indians seem to hold their own native copper skin
in special affection, and heighten it with vermilion
when it does not seem to them sufficiently red.

I discovered, during a journey I took among the
Sioux, that there is a certain national style in this
face painting. They were talking of a poor Indian
who had gone mad; and when I asked some of his
countrymen then present in what way he displayed his
insanity, they said, " Oh! he dresses himself up so
funnily with feathers and shells, and paints his face
so comically, that it is enough to make one die of
laughing." This was said to me by persons so over-
laden with feathers, shells, green, vermilion, Prussian
blue, and chrome yellow, that I could hardly refrain
from smiling. Still, I drew the conclusion from it
that there must be something conventional and typical
in their variegated style, which might be easily in-
fringed.

I was enabled, from my drawings, to make a grand
discovery, some time after, at an American state fair.
A gigantic Indian was shown, and though he had
painted his face, I insisted that his painting was false.
I certainly had only a general impression, and could
not prove in what lines the error consisted, but I felt
quite certain in the matter. And all the world asserted that he was a false Indian; nothing but a stout
Anglo-Saxon clumsily dressed up as a savage.

And yet, after living for some time among these
gaily painted fellows, you would feel sorry to see
the paint removed. I have heard this asserted by
many Europeans who have lived a long time among
them. Whenever my Indians washed themselves,
they seemed to me insignificant and uglier. Everything is habit, and my readers can easily imagine how

paltry the pale faces must appear to these dazzling
Indians.

The young men, the dandies, are the sole victims
of their painting mania. When they grow old, and
nature draws wrinkles in their faces, they do not
bestow such pains on their paint. Then, they no
longer pluck out their beards, which would be an
obstacle in painting. In their old age they leave
everything standing, and the hairs are usually scanty
and scrubby. Nor do the women, even the prettiest
among them, paint themselves. The only exception
is at any religious ceremony, when all appear gaily
painted, old men, women, and girls; but not to the
extent practised by the young warriors.

Such matters, then, I observed, while lounging from
tent to tent, and watching the preparations for the
war-dance. By the afternoon all were ready, and the
grand pipe of peace they intended to hand to the
" Great Father" was properly adorned with red feathers, blue drawings, strings of wampum, &c.

It occurred to me that, although it was, after all,
but a ceremony, the Indians regarded the matter very
solemnly and earnestly. According to traditional custom, the pipe of peace passed from tent to tent, and
from mouth to mouth, among the warriors. When
each had smoked, the procession started, and marched
with drums beating, fluttering feather flags, and flying
otter, fox, and skunk tails, through the village, to the
open space before the old fort of the North-West
Company, which was now converted into a sort of
central hotel. Here they put up a wooden post, and
close to it their war-flag, after which the dances,
speeches, and songs began.

A circle of brown-skinned dancers was formed, with

the musicians and singers in the centre. The musicians, a few young fellows, cowered down on the ground, beat a drum, and shook a calabash and some other instruments, which were very primitive. One had only a board, which he hammered with a big knife, while holding his hollow hand beneath it as a species of sounding-board. The principal singers were a half-dozen women, wrapped up in dark cloaks, who muttered a monotonous and melancholy chant, while keeping their eyes steadily fixed on the ground. The singing resembled the sound of a storm growling in the distance. To the music the warriors hopped round in a circle, shaking the otter, fox, and beaver tails, attached to their arms, feet, and heads.

At times the singing and dancing were interrupted: with flying hair and skins a warrior walked into the circle, raised his tomahawk, and struck the post a smart blow, as a signal that he was going to describe his hero deeds. Then he began to narrate in a loud voice and very fluently some horrible story in which he had played the chief part. He swung the tomahawk and pointed to the scars and wounds on his naked body, in confirmation of his story, giving the post a heavy blow now and then. Many had painted their scars a blood-red colour, and their gesticulations were most striking when they described the glorious moment of scalping.

Although surrounded by many kind interpreters, who translated all that was said at once into English or French, I fear it would lead me too far were I to write down all that was said. Here is a specimen, however.

Many speeches were begun in a humorous fashion. One little fellow bounded into the circle, and, after striking the post, went on: "My friends, that I am little you can all see, and I require no witnesses to that. But to believe that I, little as I am, once killed a giant of a Sioux, you will need witnesses." And then he plucked two witnesses out of the circle. "You and you, you were present." And then he told the story just as it had occurred.

Another, with a long rattlesnake's skin round his head, and leaning on his lance, told his story objectively, just as a picture would be described. "Once we Ojibbeways set out against the Sioux. We were one hundred. One of ours, a courageous man, a man of the right stamp, impatient for distinction, separated from the others, and crept onward into the enemy's country. The man discovered a party of the foe, two men, two women, and three children. He crept round them like a wolf, he crawled up to them like a snake, he fell upon them like lightning, cut down the two men, and scalped them. The screaming women and children he seized by the arm, and threw them as prisoners to his friends, who had hastened up at his war yell; and this lightning, this snake, this wolf, this man, my friends, that was—I. I have spoken!"

In most of the stories told us, however, I could trace very little that was heroic. Many of them, in fact, appeared a description of the way in which a cunning wolf attacked and murdered a lamb. One of the fellows—with one eye painted white, the other coal-black—was not ashamed to tell loudly, and with a beaming face, how he once fell upon a poor solitary Sioux girl and scalped her. He gave us the minutest details of this atrocity, and yet, at the end of his harangue, he was applauded, or at least behowled, like the other orators. That is to say, all the Indians stamped and uttered their war yell as a sign of applause, by holding their hands to their mouths trumpet fashion. At the moment the man appeared to me a blood-dripping tiger, and yet, when I formed his acquaintance at a later date, he talked most reasonably and calmly, like any honest farmer's lad. Such are what are called the contradictions in human nature.

Very remarkable in all these harangues was the unconcealed and vain self-laudation each employed about himself. Every speaker considered his deed the best and most useful for the whole nation. Each began by saying that what his predecessors had told them was very fine, but a trifle when compared with what he had to say about himself. It was his intention to astonish them once for all. His totem was the first in the whole land, and the greatest deeds had always been achieved by the "Spotted Weasels" (or as the case may be), and so he, the youngest Weasel, not wishing to be inferior to his forefathers, had gone forth and performed deeds the description of which would make their hair stand on end, &c.

The others listen to all this with considerable patience, and give their yell of applause. Each warrior has the right to make himself as big as he can, and no one takes it upon him to interrupt or contradict him. If the narrator, however, is guilty of any deception as regards facts, and the deception is of consequence, any man may get up and contradict him. But this is a rare case, and becomes a very serious matter, for any man convicted of falsehood at the solemnity of a war-dance is ruined for life. A liar can hardly ever regain the confidence of his countrymen.

"Oui, oui, monsieur," an excellent old Canadian Voyageur said to me on this subject, "ils sont tous comme ça. Etre trop modeste, de se croire faible, ce n'est pas leur faible côté. Chacun d'eux sé croit fort et bon. Chacun pense et dit, ' C'est moi qui ai le plus d'esprit. Je suis le plus courageux de tous.' " Walk through the whole camp, from hut to hut, and every one will say so to you. Yes, if you visit the poorest and last of them—even if he should be a cripple—if he can still speak, he will assert that he is " sans peur et sans reproche," and that he knows no one in camp he will allow superior to himself.

All the " heroes" present did not take part in the ceremony, and several sat or stood among the spectators. On sitting down on a bench to rest, I noticed a man at my side, who sat looking on and smoking his pipe. He was evidently a renowned warrior, for his head was covered with eagle feathers and other insignia, and he carried a tomahawk and other murderous weapons in his belt. There was a degree of calmness and freshness in his expressive features that pleased me. I remembered that I had once seen him gambling, and he had been the chief winner, and I observed the liberality with which he gave the shirts, pieces of calico, arms, ear-rings, &c., he had won to his friends. I now counted the large blood-red feathers on his head, saw there were seven, and asked him: " Tell me, Wattab, hast thou killed seven Sioux ?"

" Ho, ho!" he replied, nodding and smiling, " that is a good number. Ho, ho! But," he added, correcting himself, "I only killed four really; but I scalped three others who had been shot by my friends, and they were not quick or bold enough to scalp them."

While talking of scalping, he thrust his hand thrice

into the grass, and twisted a tuft, to make his meaning clearer.

"Hast thou the scalps still?"

"Here are some," he said, pointing to his long hair. He then pulled out two thick black locks. "Those are Sioux hair locks, not mine," he said. And I then noticed a piece of dried skin at the end of them, which he had secured to his head with the feathers. Another piece of skin and hair was attached to the back of his tomahawk. "This scalp," he went on, "I nailed separately, because I took it under curious circumstances, and like to recal it to memory. I went on the war-trail, just ten years ago, against the Sioux band of the chief Wabasha. There were eighty of us Ojibbeways, and we went down the Chippeway River in canoes. When we found ourselves close to the enemy we turned into an arm of water, which we thought was the main channel, but it was only a bayou, which lost itself in swamp and rushes, and on attempting to push through, all our canoes stuck in the mud. The Sioux fleet was coming up to cut us off in our hole, and we left our canoes and went on foot up the river bank. The Sioux fired on us from the water, and we replied from land; but the distance was too great, and no one was wounded. One of the boldest and bravest of the Sioux, however, pushed on far in advance, in order to cut us off. He came too near the bank, and was shot by one of our men; and he fell back in his canoe, which began drifting down the stream. His long hair hung over the side of the boat into the water. I saw this, and, feeling desirous to have this scalp, I leaped into the water and swam after the canoe. There was plenty of risk, for the other Sioux were now paddling up; besides, it was not at all certain the man was really dead. I did not care, though, but swam on, seized the canoe and the man, and had his scalp with a couple of cuts. Ha, ha! I waved it once to the Sioux, pushed the canoe with the half-dead quivering fellow towards them, and soon joined my party again. We all escaped, and only our enemies had cause to lament. He was their best warrior, and so I nailed his scalp—the only one taken that time—here on my hatchet, which I carry about with me."

" Hast thou already killed an enemy?" I asked another young man, who had seated himself by us to hear the story.

" Not yet," he replied, half smiling, half sighing. " I am no better than a woman."

After the doughty deeds had been all described, the blue feather-adorned pipe of peace was produced, the hot coal laid on it, the chiefs took a few puffs, and it was then handed to some of the European Fathers standing round. A few words were spoken which I did not understand, and several of the gentlemen puffed away lustily. At last, the pipe was passed to the " Great Father from Washington," but when the chiefs tried to hold the pipe to his lips he assumed a very stern look, and refused to smoke. " How! what! is it possible?" Yes, he refused to smoke, merely saying he did not like things of that sort, and then withdrew.

General interruption—universal dissatisfaction! inexplicable event! But, as the fact was patent and must be accepted, the Indians struck their flag on the moment, and one of the chieftains announced the circumstance in a stentorian voice. What he said was translated to me thus:

"My friends! our Father from Washington has refused to smoke the pipe of peace with us. He has rejected and despised it. My friends! it is of no consequence to us! Let him go his road, and we will go ours!"

The assembly was immediately dissolved, the musicians and singing women sprang on one side, and the warriors marched off at full speed without chant or drum, dispersed among their tents, held a council, and discussed the unwelcome circumstance—the open insult which they fancied had been offered them. I found it highly interesting to watch these angry countenances; for though it was merely the wrath of the chained lion, they behaved precisely as in olden times, if a friendly tribe had refused the pipe of peace.

The next day the Indians sent a deputation to their Great Father, and questioned him as to his behaviour.

"We came here to form a treaty of peace with thee, and as thou refusest to smoke the pipe of peace, there is war," they said.

"This is not the proper place," was the reply, "to speak of war between the Ojibbeways and the United States. But I did not mean it in that light," their Father added. "You must know, in the first place, that I am no friend of dancing. When my white friends invite me to a dance, I refuse, and do not go. And then the dances of my red children! they are perfectly barbarous, and I should like you to abolish them. See! I wish you to become like the white men, and quite give up your old pagan and bloody ceremonies. I will refuse every pipe of peace you offer me in connexion with such ceremonies, and have always done so among the other tribes of your red brethren. I wish to civilise you, and give you a lesson and an example. But if you want to smoke with me and talk about serious matters, I am quite ready. See! here you have each a pipe. I invite you. Take them, and let us talk about the cultivation of your land, the affairs of your villages, and the improvements in your household."

The good children of the forests gradually calmed down, and asserted afterwards that they had a capital hour's smoke with their Great Father.

It was all over, however, with our " war, scalp, and buaffalo-dances," and the Indian ball play and other matters which generally delight the visitors to an Indian payment, but to which the commissioner was opposed. I was most vexed at the loss of the discovery-dance (la dance de la découverte), which had been promised me, for it is said to be a masterpiece of Indian mimic. It is performed by one dancer, and there are but few men able to execute it. The dancer or actor begins at the moment when he is lying in his hut and hears the war yell. Then he goes through all the usual preparations. He beats the drum, paints his face, seizes his weapons, prays, sings the death-song, and marches off. Accompanying the performance with singing and music, he shows all the varieties of the march—the snake-like creeping, the listening and spying—and the whole terminates with the surprise, the battle, the scalping, and the yell of triumph.

CHAPTER III.

THE word "canoe," the title given by the Europeans to the various kinds of clumsy boats employed by the American aborigines, is derived from the West Indies. The Spaniards were the first to learn the word and bring it into currency. One of the oldest Spanish writers on the Indians, Peter Martyr, a contemporary of Columbus, says that the Indians called their boats, hollowed out of trees, canoas. From the Spaniards the word passed into all European languages, though altered by the French into canot, by the English into canoe. It is now generally employed in this country, although none of the Indian tribes here recognise the word, and have all a distinct name for their boats.

The form and material of the canoe differ as much as its name. Some hollow out the trunk of a tree, others make their canoes of leather or seal-skins, while others, again, employ bark, especially that of the birch. The latter, owing to their lightness and other good qualities, are in most general use. They are found among all the tribes of Canada and the Hudson's Bay territory far to the north wherever the birch grows, especially among the wandering, fishing, and hunting tribes of the great Algic nation, who constantly employ canoes, as other nomadic races do horses or camels.

Although it is conceded that the English and French Canadians build the Indian canoe better than the Indians themselves do, and many believe that the latter have improved since the introduction of iron tools among them, the invention is indubitably of great antiquity. We find birch-bark boats mentioned in the oldest reports of the French discoverers of Canada. The Indians came from the most remote regions, whither no Frenchman had yet penetrated, to the European settlements in these canoes, and the intruders employed the same vehicle in their voyage through the interior, while making several improvements upon it. It is a pity that Champlain, Marquette, Charlevoix, and other old writers on Canada, did not take the trouble to give us a detailed account of this Indian boat, so that we might be able to judge of the advantage of iron over stone-headed axes.

I have had a famous opportunity to watch the present procedure, for new canoes are being constantly built around me, or old ones repaired, and I saw them in every stage of perfection. The Indians expend as many bark canoes as we do hunting-boots, and, regarding the stuff of which they are made, we can imagine they must be constantly under repair.

In the first place, the Indian canoe-builder appeals
to the birch-tree, not exactly in the words of Hiawatha—

> Lay aside your cloak, O birch-tree!
> Lay aside your white-skin wrapper—

but with a good axe and sharp knife. The largest
and smoothest trees are selected, so that the pieces of
bark may be as large as possible, and prevent too
much sewing. The inner side of the fresh bark is
cleansed and scraped with knives (just as our tanners
treat leather), and is then handed over to the squaws,
who sew them together, and form a large cloak, which
can be wrapped round the whole of the canoe. While
the women are thus engaged, the men prepare the
carcase or framework of the boat, for which they
employ the elastic branches of the Canadian cedar-
tree.

They have usually a sort of model, or a frame of
the figure and size of a canoe, round which the
branches or ribs are bent. In the centre the arches
are larger, growing smaller towards either end. They
are of a semi-circular form, or nearly so, so that at last
the canoe has the shape of a sausage cut in half.
These ribs are peeled wonderfully thin, because lightness and easy carriage are the chief qualities of a
canoe. The Canadians call them " les varangues,"
which they pronounce " varengles." I may remark
here, that there is not a single part of the canoe to
which the Canadians do not give a distinct name.

Between the upper end of the varangues a thin
cross piece is fastened, to keep the ribs in a horizontal
position. At the first glance you are apt to take
them for seats, but they merely serve to give strength
to the sides. The Canadians call them " les barres,"

and each pair of ribs with its bar resembles a bow and its string.

In our boats the ribs are supported by the keel, from which they stand out like the branches on a tree. But as these canoes have no keel, the varangues and barres are necessarily tied to a piece of wood at the top. This wood, called "le maître," runs round the gunwale of the boat, and receives the ends of all the ribs and bars. Probably the French gave it this name because it acts as the backbone of the canoe in lieu of a keel.

It must be noticed here, too, that the Indians make no use of nails and screws, but everything is sewn and tied together. But the seams, stitches, and knots are so regular, firm, and artistic, that nothing better could be asked for. For binding they employ the bast of the cedar-wood, which the Canadians call "bois blanc."

When the framework has been made in this way, the bark covering is spread out on the ground, and laid over the wood. It then looks for all the world like a cobbler making a gigantic shoe, with his leather wrapped round the huge last. The bark is drawn as tightly as possible round the frame, and the edges are turned down over the "maître," and firmly bound to it. Finally, a reinforce is placed all along the edge, called the "faux maître," which protects the bark, in some measure, from the injuries to which it is necessarily exposed.

The interior of the canoe is then lined with thin boards, laid across the ribs, which the Canadians call "les lisses." These protect the bottom from the feet of the passengers, and injury from the bales. They are remarkably thin and light, and not much stouter than the sides of a cigar-box. Of course these canoes are not suited for the nailed boots of a European, or the transport of iron-shod boxes, but only for the soft mocassined feet of the Indians, and the still softer bundles of furs.

All the wood-work in the canoe is derived from the cèdre blanc, for this wood is very elastic, does not split, has but slight specific gravity, and is easily cut with a knife. The material for the cords and strings is also obtained from the same tree, though they also use the bast taken from the roots of the epinette blanche (a species of spruce). All this is prepared by the women, who are always busy in twisting "watab," owing to the large quantities used. They can make either twine or stout cords out of it, and for their fishing-nets the ropes often reach a length of fifty yards. These cords last a long time, and resist the influence of water, and they can be laid up for two years without deteriorating. If damped, they become as supple as leather.

The people here give them a preference over hemp ropes. "Our bast cords," they say, "are always rather greasy in the water, and slip more easily through our hands. Nor do they cut the skin, like the ropes of the Europeans, when anything has to be pulled. Lastly, they feel rather warmer in winter."

The canoe is sharp, front and back, and the ends stand up a little. These ends are often gaily decorated in the larger canoes, and the French give them the name of "les pinces." A small piece of wood is inserted in either end, to give it increased strength, which the Canadians call "le petit bonhomme." This, too, is often carved and painted into the shape of a queer-looking mannikin.

After the canoe is completed, the material is left
to dry. For this purpose pieces of wood are inserted
in every part to keep it well extended, and it is then
hung up in the air. Pitching all the little holes,
seams, and stitches, is the final process. For this
purpose the rosin of the pine or fir is used, and is
laid on in thick patches wherever a hole would allow
the water entrance. The weak parts of the bark, or
the holes of branches, are also covered with this rosin,
and the Canadians call this process "chauffer le
canot."

It might be supposed that this task at least should
fall on the men, as they employ the canoe almost
exclusively in hunting, fishing, and fighting, and, as it
were, live in it, just as the squaws do in the wigwam.
But the lazy fellows compel their wives to help them
in this job. I often saw girls, women, and men, all
engaged in hammering and pitching the canoes. Of
course, all the sewing and tying—nearly one half the
labour—is left solely to the women. The men, however, undertake the paddling, although the squaws
understand it perfectly, and, indeed, are generally more
skilful in every respect than the men. When the
whole family is moving about, man and wife paddle
side by side.

The old Indian fashion of paddling is the same as
we can see on the Greek bas-reliefs, in Charon's bark
and other classical oarsmen. They use a short broad
paddle, with which the boat is propelled. The French
call it "aller à l'aviron." Many Indians have, however, taken to use oars like ours, and made the proper
arrangements for them in their canoes. In the old
fashion one paddler sits at the stern, another at the
bow, particularly if the voyage be dangerous, and

there are any rapids to contend against. I may here remark in a parenthesis, that the canoe has really a bow and stern, although the ends, at the first glance, appear precisely similar. All canoes are slightly broader in front, though this is not so perceptible as in the body of a fish, which the Indians evidently selected as their model.

The paddler in the bow the French call "le devant du canot," the man behind "le gouvernail du canot." The bowman keeps his eye on the water, and looks out for any shallows, rocks, or rapids which might prove dangerous. He makes signals to the gouvernail, who undertakes the principal part in propelling the canoe. He paddles on in the course on which he started, until there is a necessity for any change of direction.

As the canoes have no keel, and are, besides, built of such light materials—even large boats do not weigh a couple of hundred-weight, and small ones a man can carry on his head—they lie very lightly on the water—

> Like a yellow leaf of autumn,
> Like a yellow water-lily.

They are, too, very handy for crossing dangerous places, and, if you take proper caution, you need not positively be upset. The Indians have extraordinary command over them, and they seem to fly over the surface of the water. Hence it is not surprising that the poets impart mysterious and magic powers to the bark canoe:

> And the forest's life was in it,
> All its mystery and magic,
> All the lightness of the birch-tree,
> All the toughness of the cedar,
> All the larch's supple sinews.

Even the Indians seem to honour their own inven-

tion greatly, and impart to it a divine origin. They
say that Menaboju (their Prometheus, or Hercules)
invented the canoe. They even point to some half-
dozen lumps of stone, on the shore of one of these
Apostle Islands, and say that Menaboju built his canoe
between them, and hung it to dry upon them.

There are of course considerable variations in the
size and build of the canoes. The principal distinction I heard the Voyageurs make was between canots
à lège and canots de charge. The first signifies the
light, unladen canoes, employed as post or express
boats, and are also known by the name of " canots
Rabasca." The canots de charge are their large heavy
goods canoes.

It is surprising how the Indians manage to employ
the limited space in their "jimans"—so they call their
canoes—and how much they manage to carry in them.
I recently saw an Indian family arrive here from the
interior, or, as they term it, Les Grandes Terres, and
looked with admiration on the infinity of objects which
they produced from their small bark-trough. The
scene is worth describing.

The family came from Geté-Kitigan, an Indian
village and lake in the heart of Wisconsin, and one
hundred and fifty miles off. The French call the
place Le Vieux Désert. I watched the nut-shell come
floating up like a duck for a long way, and the people
on the shore shouted: "Ho! there comes Antoine
Gendron with his family from Vieux Désert."

The said Gendron had relatives here, who ran down
to the beach to welcome their friends. " Antoine "—
so I was told—" was a French Canadian, but had lived
from his youth among the Indians, was a pagan, and
pire que les Indiens, plus sauvage que les autres, et

grand magicien, but much respected among the people up the country."

Gendron was the gouvernail, and one of his boys acted as devant. Very quietly and steadily did they glide into the little inlet. The wife, with her other children, two boys and two girls, was buried beneath a pile of parcels and boxes. Among them lay a dog, with three pups, and on the top of all the plunder was a large cage, with two tamed falcons in it. The gun-wale of the boat was only a few inches above the water, and in this way all these beings, and animals, and lumber, had made a seven days' voyage.

When they stepped on land, where Gendron's brother-in-law, his wife's sister, and his old grand-mother, several other persons, and an infinity of children were awaiting them, their behaviour was re-markably quiet. There was no waving of handker-chiefs, no shouts of greeting, no laughing and gesticu-lation. They quietly stepped out of the boat one after the other, and the relatives stood there just as quietly, and waited till their guests had crawled out of their nests. Still the welcome was not the less hearty: the women kissed, and asked each other all sorts of ques-tions. The children were all kissed, and kissed each other. The dogs—especially the young ones—were also taken great care of by the children. Idem, the cage with the falcons. The Indians frequently tame wild animals, and I have seen various instances of it. I was told that they also tamed eagles, mews, ravens, and magpies, sometimes as playthings, but also to fatten and then eat them. In the same way they are said to treat deer, foxes, and even bears, and they lug the latter along after them by a rope or chain. A Voyageur told me that he once met an Indian carrying his bear on his back, because the brute was very tired, and its whining had moved his tender heart.

The quantity of packages, and bags, and bark boxes (makaks) which the people handed out was interminable. First came a clean little makak filled with brown maple sugar, which was presented to grandmamma; then a bag of black boucaned venison, the greater portion of which had, however, been consumed on the voyage. The children, too, had all sorts of playthings. Generally, when an Indian travels with his family, it is " omnia mecum porto," and he drags everything after him, if he has no one to leave in his lodge, and fears a visit from the Sioux.

The principal goods came last, consisting of several large bales, containing deer and beaver skins, the result of Gendron's shooting expeditions. " My boys," he told me afterwards, " shot those deer; yes, and I my share too." As the wild Gendron interested me no little as the countryman of Mme. de Staël and Lamartine, I paid the family a visit at their birchbark lodge, to see how the long-separated relatives got on together.

I found more than twenty persons collected in the limited space, Gendron, le grand magicien et le grand chasseur, in the centre. The grandmother had her present in her lap, which had been brought a hundred and fifty miles from the Grandes Terres, over various portages and cataracts, in a dry and healthy condition. The countryman of Mme. de Genlis, " le Français sauvage" (they often call themselves so, and I remember one of these wild Europeans telling me he was a savage Englishman) held his medicine-bag in his hand, and, as he invited me to take a seat by his side, he soon began showing me a quantity of "medicine" and charms, whose virtues he explained to me. He also talked about some sort of worm, which gets under the skin, and which he could expel. Everything was very quiet and peaceable in the lodge, and each person was engaged in a whispered conversation with his neighbour. The children crawled about among the grown-up people, and, in a word, it was *tout comme chez nous*.

It struck me as very curious that even the dogs, both those they had brought with them and the countless ones attached to the wigwam, seemed to share in the general satisfaction at the meeting of the relatives. They all lay round the fire at their masters' feet, and, on this occasion, were left at peace, for usually they are kicked out of the wigwam. At the first sight of the way in which the Indians treat the dogs in their villages, one is apt to regard their behaviour to this faithful comrade as very heartless. The whole day through the poor brutes are heard yelping, and, altogether, they have a very seedy appearance. Their great object of life is to crawl into the huts and carry off something eatable, but they are continually driven out by the women and children, and recommended, by a smart blow, to satisfy themselves with the fish and beaver bones thrown out for them. But they soon detect some convenient hole, and, presto! a dozen of them creep into the hut again. For a while they may be left in peace, but then one gets in the way, when the kicks and blows begin again, and the dogs bolt with the most heartrending whines. So it goes on all the livelong day. If you attempt to pat one of these dogs, and speak kindly to him, he does

not understand what you mean; he tucks his tail
between his legs and slinks off to a convenient distance, where he begins growling.

In truth, the Indians seem not merely unloving, but
even cruel to their dogs. A short time back I wit-
nessed the following scene: An Indian shot one of
his dogs, a handsome black animal, in order to offer
it as a sacrifice at a coming festival. The dog was
lying half dead in the grass, in a pool of its own
blood, and howling most pitifully; but the Indians
stood round it quite callous, and watched its death-
struggle. The little cannibal boys, however, came up
and shot their blunted arrows at the poor brute, which
was suffering enough already, and thrust their feet
into the gaping wounds. The dog could no longer
bite them, as they most richly deserved. "Thou
wretched brute," one yelled, "why dost thou howl
so?" as if meaning to say to it, as they do to their
martyred prisoners, "Shame on thee! die like a
brave!" They are, at times, equally merciless and
barbarous to their horses; and, indeed, the sight of
wounds, suffering, and blood seems to render them
more hard-hearted than usual.

From all this, as I said before, one is apt, at the
first glance, to regard the Indians as fit subjects for
the Society for preventing Cruelty to Animals. Yet,
after all, the matter is not so bad as all that. What
contradictions exist in their ideas will be seen from
the fact that the dog is regarded by them as unclean,
and yet as, in some respects, holy. If a dog is unlucky enough to thrust his muzzle into a lodge or
a temple where a religious rite is being performed, the
lodge is considered to be disturbed and profaned, and
the animal pays for the intrusion with its life; and yet,

on the other hand, they cannot offer their deities and
spirits a finer sacrifice than a dog; though it might
be thought that the gods would prefer an innocent
deer or lamb. An Indian, of whom I inquired the
cause of this sanctity of the dog sacrifice, answered
me: " The dog was created in heaven itself, and sent
down expressly for the Indians. It is so useful to us
that, when we sacrifice it, this must be considered as
a grand sign of piety and devotion." In the same way
the Indians can never make up their minds to kill any
of the pups: they are divided among the family, and
each boy and girl selects one as a pet. I also repeatedly heard Indian hunters say they had their favourite
dogs, which they valued and paid great attention to.
On the other hand, there are many stories of the
fidelity of these dogs to their Indian masters. Thus,
an American gentleman told me how he was once
witness at Detroit of the affecting grief of a dog for
its Indian master. Indians had come into the town,
and, by an accident, had left one of their dogs behind.
The animal grew terribly uncomfortable, and ran sniff-
ing about the streets for the whole of the day, while
keeping carefully aloof from every white man. At
length, when evening set in, and the dog had not found
its master, it sat down, wearied and despairing, in the
market-place, and began addressing such a lamentable
howl to heaven, that all the neighbours ran up to
see what the matter could be. The poor brute would
not touch any of the food offered it, and was evidently
suffering deep grief. I trust the faithful beast at
length hit on the trail of its master, and made its way
from the stony-hearted town to the happy hunting-
grounds.

CHAPTER IV.

THE TEMPLE WIGWAM—THE ORDER OF THE MIDÉS—AN INDIAN CHRISTEN-
ING—THE HIGH PRIEST—THE BIG DRUM—THE EVIL SPIRIT—THE MEDI-
CINE BAG—LIFE AND DEATH—THE MUSIC—THE BEHAVIOUR OF THE
INDIANS—PRESENTATION OF THE CHILD—THE DANCES—THE MYSTERIOUS
SHELLS—WAMPUM—TOBACCO—RECEIVING THE PRESENTS—MAGIC AND
MYSTERY—MAIZE BROTH—FINALE.

HEARING that the Indians had built a temple wigwam on the beach, about two miles off, and that a
grand festival was coming off, in which a father would
present his boy for reception into the order of the
Midés, we started at an early hour, in order to
see as much as we could of the solemnity.

We walked through the woods, and at length
reached a steep path leading down to the beach. A
sandy promontory jutted out here far into the lake;
it was the point that protects our little haven, from
which the island derives its name.

A number of wigwams had been erected here under
the tall cliff, and a little further on we noticed, at the
edge of the declivity, the temple lodge, or, as the
Indians call it, the " midewi-gamig."

Midewiwin is the Indian term for what the Canadians call "la grande médecine," that is, the great fraternity among the Indians for religious purposes. "Midé" is a member of the fraternity, while "gamig" is a corruption of wigiwam, always used in composition. Hence, "midewi-gamig" may be translated "temple wigwam," or, "house of the brethren."

Our temple wigwam reminded me of the bowers built by the Jews for their Feast of Tabernacles. But it was forty feet in length, running from east to west. The entrance was to the east, and a similar door for exit at the western end. It was composed of young trees and branches, and cut a very respectable figure, when we bear in mind that it was merely erected to receive an infant into the Midé order, or, as we should say, to christen it. The unending succession of ceremonies which were performed during the day also proved to me that the Indians regarded such an affair as highly important.

As the branches were very loosely interlaced, I was enabled to take a peep before entering. On one side, with their backs resting against the posts, sat the great Midés, the chief brothers of the order, the high-priests, or the faculty. They were about half a dozen, among them being several of the chiefs whose acquaintance I had formed at La Pointe. I recognised one by the silver ring he wore in his nose, and a couple of pounds' weight of plated earrings, which hung from his distended lobes, like bunches of grapes. He appeared to occupy the first place, and play the principal part.

Opposite to him cowered the father of the little novice. The latter, firmly tied on his board, lay in the grass, as quiet and well-behaved as Indian pap-

pooses usually are. The little one caused no un-
pleasant interruption the whole day through, and
endured all the ceremonies performed on him or
around him with an equanimity that proved to me
fully that he belonged to that race who, when grown
up, endure martyrdom without a groan.

On either side the father was a row of god-parents
and witnesses, men, women, and children, all in their
Sunday state—*i.e.* with their faces painted a fiery red,
like fresh-boiled lobsters. Before the east entrance
the presents hung on tall posts, which the father had
brought for the priesthood, the chief one being a
quantity of gaily-flowered calico, which fluttered in
the breeze.

In the middle of the temple was the big drum,
which in religious ceremonies is beaten with a small
wooden hammer fastened to a long wand. It is
slightly different in form from the ordinary drum:
it is longer, produces a more hollow sound, and has a
special name, "Midéguakik,"—the temple drum.

A large stone lay in the grass, also in the central
line of the lodge, but nearer the east door. I cannot
exactly explain the significance of this stone, which
was left untouched during the entire ceremony. One
of the Midés I cross-questioned on the subject gave
me the following account: "See," he said, pointing
with his finger to heaven, "the Good Spirit is up
there, and the Evil Spirit," he added, pointing down
to the earth, "is there under us. The stone is put
there for him." Hence I conjecture that rough masses
of stone, as being the coarsest and commonest portion
of the elements of the earth, represent the Evil Spirit,
who plays a certain part in the ceremonies, and that
the stone was laid there as a sort of lightning con-
ductor against the spirits of the nether world.

At length we walked in, and, after laying a pile of pressed tobacco-leaves before the Kitchi-Midé, received a tacit permission to take our places among the spectators.

Any critical description of all that took place I am unable to give, as I could not understand all that was said, and even my interpreters broke down now and then. A high degree of initiation is necessary to understand the whole how and why of Indian mysteries. And though these ceremonies may all possess their history, origin, and meaning, they are only performed by the majority as something got by heart, and they understand as little of them as our choristers and singing men of the history and meaning of the various parts of the mass.

What I saw, heard, and understood, then, was about so much :

In the first place, my old prophet with the ring in his nose, who wore a very solemn aspect during the whole ceremony as a true pillar of the temple, made a speech. I noticed that he spoke very glibly, and now and then pointed to the heavens, and then fixed his eyes on the audience. He also made a movement several times over their heads, as if blessing them, just as priests do in all nations and churches. His speech was translated to me much in this way. He had addressed a prayer to the Great Spirit ; then he shortly explained why they were assembled, and that a member of the tribe wished his infant to be received into the order of the Midés. He concluded by welcoming all the assembly, the high Midés and brothers, all the " aunts and uncles," the " sisters and cousins," and giving them his blessing.*

* The members of the order regard each other as related, and call themselves in the convocation uncle, aunt, &c.

After this address a procession was formed of all the Midés, while the father of the child and the guests rose and leaned against the sides of the wigwam. The priests walked one after the other, with their medicine-bag in the right hand.

These medicine-bags, called "pindjigossan" in the Ojibbeway language, were made of the skins of the most varying animals: one of the wild cat, another of the bear, a third of the otter, a fourth of the skin of a snake; and all retained more or less the shape of these wild beasts, as head and tail, and in some cases the feet, were left on. They were all filled with valuable and sacred matters, of course not visible. The Indians imagine that a spirit or breath is exhaled from these varied contents of the skin-bag possessing the power to blow down and kill a person, as well as to restore him to life and strength again.

The proceedings of the procession were based on this supposition. The Midés held their bags at charge, like Cossacks hold their lances in attacking, and trotted up at a sharp pace to the victim they had selected. The drum was beaten powerfully the while, and the rattle of the calabashes, filled with peas, was incessant. The Midés also accompanied their steps by a species of war-yell, which increased in noise in proportion to their speed, and grew quicker in time the nearer they drew to the victim, much after this style: Ho! ho!—hohohoho!—o! o! o! o! o!

On approaching one of the guests, a Midé made a stab at him with the bag, and the person assailed fell back immediately, and lay on the ground. The French Canadians, who have generally best translated the Indian terms, call this operation "tirer," or "souffler."

So soon as a Midé had blown down his patient, he relaxed his speed and his " hoho !" and walked round the lodge to a slower time, turned back, and trotted to his place, to start once more as soon as the bag had collected sufficient strength to upset another patient. As the seven or eight priests ran about continually, before long all the spectators lay on the ground, like a house of cards blown down by the wind.

It was a very comical sight, and some behaved with considerable drollery. I shall never forget the behaviour of a strangely bedizened old man, who rushed upon the guest with a wild yell, took a prodigious bound, and puffed out his cheeks, as if aiding his medicine-bag.

The girls, too, as they lay in a heap, nudged each other and giggled, as if conscious of the comical effect the scene must produce upon an impartial witness. But all this smiling and tittering was in secret, and the ceremony generally proceeded in a very reputable manner; and though it lasted so long, everybody appeared to know the part he had to play so accurately that no mistake occurred, and all went on with the regularity of our military manœuvres.

Many regarded the affair very seriously, among them being my friend Nose-ring. He leaped on his prey like a lion, and held a very critical examination of the person he blew down, as if convincing himself that all was done properly. I also saw a girl, whose every movement I followed, extremely zealous. When blown upon by the magic animal, she fell in a heap at once and did not stir. When restored to life by the same medicine-bag, she sprang up like a champagne cork, and was all life and fun. When the dancing came off, she went through the various figures with

the precision of a puppet, and if there was anything to
be sung or said, she was the first to join in with the
leader. In short, she knew her catechism by heart,
and always kept a most pious countenance.

After the destructive power of the medicine-bags
had been proved in this way, their holy and reviving
strength had to be displayed. This was effected precisely in the same fashion, but no one ventured to stir
hand or foot till breathed on by the enchanted animal.
I even noticed this among the merry tittering girls.
One of them had been overlooked by the priest, and
though she was indulging in a quiet grin, she did not
dare rise of her own accord. One of the girls timidly
recalled the priest and pointed out his oversight. He
came back, held his otter-bag to her, and up she
jumped.

This trial of the bag was repeated the whole day
through, as a species of interlude between all the
greater ceremonies.

After this ceremony had been once performed, the
father walked forward with his child. He stood with
his face turned to the faculty, holding his baby on the
board in his hands, and presented it to the priests, just
as the godfathers do in our christening. Five or six
women stood behind him in a row : they were the witnesses. At first I conjectured it was really an imitation of our baptismal service with pagan additions, but
the Indians asserted that it was a primitive custom.

The father was dressed in his full war panoply. His
head was covered with a quantity of eagle, hawk, and
raven feathers, which, like our orders, bore the
evidence of his bravery and services. The rough-
haired skin of that dauntless beast the Americans call
a skunk was bound turban-wise round his head, the

long parti-coloured tail hanging down behind like a queue. Similar skins were fastened round his feet, and the tails dragged after him like long spurs. In his hand he held a fox's skin, filled with relics, as his medicine-sack, and his fire-red face shone out of all these skins, and tails, and feathers, like the sun from clouds.

He was most attentive in performing all the duties his position laid upon him. At times he looked very lovingly at his child, which he was presenting to the order, and it seemed to me as if he were most anxious the infant should enjoy all the benefits and good results of the initiation in their fullest extent.

The presentation of the child was naturally accompanied by a short speech from the father, long speeches from the priests, as well as drum-beating, calabash-rattling, and dancing. This time the five women behind the father performed the dance, which consisted in taking two quick leaps to the right and then to the left, with a movement of the whole body. They did this with a degree of precision, as if they were all pulled by one string. At times the father danced too, with his child in his arms, and all his tails shook about as if restored to life.

After the presentation and its concomitants, a general procession, a general bag trial, and alternate blowing down were repeated. As nearly everybody present shook in his hand a different quadrupedal, reptile, or amphibious animal (in addition to those I have mentioned, I saw large owls, little weasels, bears' paws full of claws, red foxes, grey foxes, young wolves, and varieties of snakes), the scene was very picturesque. Nor was there any want of noise, for most of the skins were covered with bells, pieces of metal, and shells, fastened to the feet and tails. More than half the contents of Noah's ark was carried in procession before me. With this the morning's performance terminated.

When we took our places again, in the afternoon, we saw a pile of branches in the middle of the temple, covered with a cloth. They lay exactly in front of the large stone, which I said had something to do with the Evil Spirit. A very strange ceremony now commenced, which is, however, never omitted in Ojibbeway solemnities.

In the first place, the high priest held another discourse, beginning, "All ye that are initiated and belong to the great Midé! friends! brothers! colleagues! this is a day of grace." The rest I did not exactly understand.

Then followed a general procession of all the priests, guests, men, women, and children, one after the other. On first walking round, each stooped down once over the cloth, and looked in. There was nothing to be seen, so they danced on. The second time they stooped closer, and looked in more sharply, as if expecting something to appear there. The third time they seemed to be attacked with involuntary spasms on approaching the cloth. The next time their movements grew convulsive, and it was plain that they were trying to expel something from their mouths; but nothing came. This lasted a long time. All at once, on looking at the cloth, I noticed two little yellow shells lying upon it, like eggs in a nest. The number rapidly increased, and, at last, every participator dropped a shell on the cloth. The old Midés took extraordinary pains, and regarded the product of their exertions very thoughtfully; but the young people and girls did not treat the matter so seriously. They looked at the cloth carelessly, and sent out the shells as easily as a smoker does a puff of smoke, and paid no further attention to them.

When the shells were all produced they appeared very contented, and began to recover. Afterwards, each person returned, took a shell from the cloth, and placed it in his medicine-bag.

I was informed that these shells typify the illness and wickedness which is in man, which he is enabled to expel by zealous exertions, and due attention to his religious duties. The Indians attach great value to these shells, and pay long prices for them. In their symbolic writing they also play a great part. Their wampums, or peace strings of beads, are made of lacustrine shells, and they bear reference to the shores of the ocean whence their religious doctrines and rites came to them from the East.

As this shell-production took place near the stone placed for the Evil Spirit, I fancied I could detect the meaning of the ceremony. Still, though I listened most attentively, I did not once hear the name of the Matchi-Manitou in any of the songs or speeches. The name of the Kitchi-Manitou (the Great or Good Spirit) was, on the other hand, repeatedly heard, and constant allusions made to his "mercies and gifts." Several times my interpreter nudged me, and said, "The speaker is now mentioning the unbounded mercy and generosity of God." Hence I believe that the first Europeans who visited America were mistaken in stating that the Indians worshipped and sacrificed to the devil.

What took place after the expulsion of the shells seemed to me in some respects a consecration, a prayer, or short separate worship performed by each

person. It consisted in the following: each individual stepped forward in turn, seized the drum-stick,
and accompanied his song by a sedulous tapping.
The first words of the song, repeated by each, were
translated to me thus:

"God hath given us this Midé order, and I rejoice
that I am a member. Hohohoho! o! o! o! o! o!"
The rest of the public, scattered in groups through
the temple, at times fell in with a ho! ho! It was,
probably, a confirmation, a species of Amen! so
be it!

The men smoked their pipes comfortably the while,
for among the Indians smoking is a consecration. It
forms part of every solemn rite, and is allowed even
in the temple-wigwam. Some even did not lay down
their pipes during the dance.

I also saw several persons, who did not appear to
belong to the society, come in, beat the drum, hold a
short speech, and then walk out again. This was,
probably, a sort of compliment they paid to the
society on the important affair of the day.

After all had finished their private prayers, towards
evening more practical matters were begun, and the
child and its father, who had been kept some time in
the background, regained their importance.

At sunset a huge kettle, full of steaming maize broth,
was dragged in, and placed in the centre of the hut.
Then the high-priests proceeded to the eastern end,
and received the presents which the giver of the feast
(who bore all the expenses of the day) offered them.
They hung the gay calico over their shoulders, the
tobacco was shared among them, and, thus adorned,
there was another procession and dance round the

kettle, to the sound of the drums and calabashes. After which all returned to their places.

Then the priests rose again one after the other, and offered their valuable gifts and amulets to the father of the child in trust ; and the priests received such rich presents solely to obtain these things from them in return. In the eyes of the father this set the crown on the whole affair.

As I sat close to him I could see what the priests brought him. One came with a paper parcel, which he carefully undid: after removing several coverings, a pinch of snow-white powder was visible, which the priest showed the father, and delivered to him, while explaining the virtues of the powder in the minutest detail. The father listened with open mouth, and carefully hid the recipe in his medicine-bag. We could not, however, understand any of the directions, for the priest spoke in a mysterious whisper. Another priest brought a small bundle of dried roots, fastened together with a red ribbon. He hung it on the child's wooden cradle, and said, in a loud voice, what was translated to me thus: " This shall guide him through life." Then, of course, followed a long muttered explanation, which no one was able to translate to me. All sorts of things were then suspended from the cradle; a thimble, some shells, &c. The number of presents was considerable, among them being several useful matters, such as a little bag of fine wheat flour, and another filled with the grain of the wild rice. The father, the shaggy old brave, sat, half pleased and half ashamed, as all these fine things collected around him.

Last of all, the high-priest held a parting address

near the kettle, in which he referred again to the
bountiful mercy of God, and then all was still. The
maize broth was served out to all the guests, who first
began to feed their children, before taking a mouthful
themselves. Even the apples, sugar-plums, and other
dainties we gave the squaws, were reserved for the
children; at the most the father and mother would
only take a bite at the apple.

The maize was simply boiled in water, without
meat, milk, or salt. It was, indeed, an unpretending
banquet, which the good people had fairly earned by
a whole day of fatiguing ceremony.

CHAPTER V.

A PALAVER—A KNOTTY POINT—RED AND WHITE—GOLD CHAINS AND RAGS—
A BAD BARGAIN—ARGUMENTUM AD HOMINEM—PLEASANT EVENINGS—
INDIAN SUPERSTITIONS—PROTECTING SPIRITS—DRYADS AND OREADS—
THE GREAT SPIRIT—THE POSES—OTAMIGAN SACRIFICES—REVERENCE
SHOWN TO COPPER—THE STORY OF KEATANANG.

THE political discussions between the American
agents and the Indians have commenced on our island.
Every day we have public assemblies in the open air,
in which many chiefs distinguish themselves as orators,
and much that is instructing and characteristic may be
noticed.

As everything said by the speakers was translated
by the government interpreter sentence by sentence,
I had no difficulty in following them. Although I
could describe accurately many of the speeches in
which the Red Skins expressed their wishes and complaints, I will confine myself to one political harangue
as a specimen, which I have written down word for
word, as it will furnish a parallel to the already given
instances of the Indians' warlike and religious elo-
quence.

At the outset, I must remark that the speaker had

risen to express his opinion about a point in dispute, whether the debts of all the Indians should be collectively deducted from the tribute, or whether each should receive his specified sum, and settle his own personal debts. Two opposite parties had formed on this matter, and my orator, it will be seen, was against the deduction *en bloc,* and took advantage of the occasion to bring forward a variety of complaints against the white men, which, indeed, none of the speakers neglected.

" There is a Great Spirit," he began, " from whom all good things here on earth come. He has given them to mankind—to the white as to the red men; for He sees no distinction of colour. They must settle among themselves the possession of these things given by God.

" When the white men first came into this country and discovered us, we received them hospitably, and if they were hungry, we fed them, and went hunting for them. At first the white men only asked for furs and skins. I have heard from our old men that they never asked for anything else. These we gave them gladly, and received from them their iron goods, guns, and powder.

" But for some years they have been asking land from us. For ten years they have asked from us nothing but land, and ever more land. We give unwillingly the land in which the graves of our fathers rest. But for all that we have given land in our generosity. We knew not that we were giving so much for so little. We did not know that such great treasures of copper were hidden in our land.

" The white men have grown rich by the bargain. When I look round me in this assembly, I notice' rich

golden watch-chains and golden rings on the clothes
and fingers of many men ; and when I look in the
faces of the people who are so richly adorned, I
always see that their colour is white, and not red.
Among the red men I never see anything of the sort !
they are all so poorly clad! they are miserably poor.!
How poor they are, I must request you to judge by
personal inspection. I have brought some of our poor
sufferers here, that you may see them. There they
come! there they are! How wretched do they look !"

(At this passage of the speech a number of old
wrinkled squaws and children clothed in rags pressed
forward to heighten the effect. They certainly looked
wretched enough; but, although we could all see this,
the speaker described their scanty clothing, their thin
and bowed forms copiously, and then proceeded :)

" And through whom have they fallen into this
lamentable condition? You have become rich through
us, and these have grown poor through you. Your
golden chains, your dollars, and all you brag of, have
been taken from them and from us. We promised
thee"—the speaker here turned to the chief American
official—" that we would open our ears to what thou
wouldst say to us, and keep it in our heads; but now
thou shouldst hear what we say to thee, and keep it
in thy head!

" We are not only poor, but we have also debts.
At least, people say that we have debts. On the
former treaty and payment we also paid debts. I
fancied then we paid them all. But now the old
question is addressed to us. A number of old things
are brought against us from an old bag. Where these
debts come from, I know not. Perhaps from the
water!" (I must here remind the reader that the

Ojibbeways transfer the evil principle to the depths of the lake.)

"But you say we have debts. It may be that we have them. We must pay these debts. The just and recognised debts we will pay. But the question is, how? On other treaties and payments the whole of our debts were taken in a lump from the moneys coming to us, and the rest divided among us. This is not good. I say, it is better and more just that each man should receive his full payment, and settle for himself with his creditors. Each knows best for himself what he owes. I know exactly what I owe, and will pay it. But I do not wish that the innocent, and these our poor, should suffer by the deduction of these debts from the total sums belonging to the tribe. That is my opinion. And I speak not only for myself, but also for the majority of the chiefs and for the young men, and for these poor widows, orphans, and sick!

"Our debts we will pay. But our land we will keep. As we have already given away so much, we will, at least, keep that land you have left us, and which is reserved for us. Answer us, if thou canst, this question. Assure us, if thou canst, that this piece of land, reserved for us, will really always be left to us. Tell me if you and we shall live in friendship near each other, and that you will never ask this land from us. Canst thou promise this? That is what I wished to ask of thee. That is all I have to say. But no! I have still one thing. The chiefs, my brothers, have commisisoned me to mention one point more, and lay another question before thee. It would be unjust of me not to speak it out openly. If I kept it to myself, it would be a heavy burden upon me. It would weigh on my breast. It would terrify me in my dreams. Father, thou knowest we are glad to see thee here. We salute thee with joy. Thou hast said that thou camest to us in friendship and kindness. We received thee here in the same way. We wish, therefore, to place confidence in thee, and not to speak to thee with a forked tongue. We will speak to thee with a simple tongue. We wish to lay before thee not only our thanks but our grievances.

" Father, the point is this. In our former treaties —yes, in all former treaties—it was settled that a certain sum should be deducted from our tribute for blacksmiths' shops, schools, and other establishments among us. We have *heard* of those moneys. But we have *seen* nothing of these works. They have not come to us. We know not where those moneys are gone, or where they went off in smoke. We beg thee, examine into this closely. This we beg thee much. I could say much more on this point. But I will now sit down. For I am not accustomed to wear these new European trousers which have been given me, or to stand long in them. They annoy me. Hence I will cease to speak and seat myself."

With this comical turn he gave his address, the speaker broke off, and sat down in the grass, under the applauding laughter of the whole assembly.

I have now arranged my mode of life most satisfactorily. By day I wander about the island among the people, who interest me so greatly, and observe everything that happens. In the evening I return to my little wigwam, and talk over the events of the day with the guests who assemble round my fire. I produce abundance of tobacco, sweetmeats, and other Indian delicacies, and thus it is an easy task for my zealous

interpreter to attract here his relatives and friends.
Nearly every evening a new guest is introduced to me.

They speak to me about their affairs—they willingly
explain to me what I did not understand—they tell
me their life-histories, and they impart to me the
fables and traditions of their nation. The hours pass
away in such an instructive and pleasant manner that
I ever do all in my power to lengthen the sederunt.
In truth, all I hear and see excites me so much, that I
watch, the preparations for putting out the fire with
great grief. Even at midnight the evening seems to
me to have been too short.

As is usually the case at such soirées, the conversation turns from one subject to another. Recently we
discussed a theme, which possessed considerable interest for me, on the superstitions of the Indians.

Although the American Indians are frequently
praised for their belief in one Great Spirit, and though
they mention him so repeatedly at their festivals, the
question whether they are really monotheists is a very
moot one. Their Kitchi-Manitou does not fare much
better than the "Optimus Maximus" of the Romans.
He presides in heaven, but is at times unheeded here
on earth, where coarse natural strength and terrestrial
objects are deified.

Nearly every Indian has discovered such an object,
in which he places special confidence, of which he
more frequently thinks, and to which he sacrifices
more zealously than to the Great Spirit. They call
these things their "Manitou personnel," but the proper
Ojibbeway word is said to be "Nigouimes," which
means so much as "my hope." One calls a tree,
another a stone or rock, "his hope."

Thus, for instance, on the mainland opposite La

Pointe, there is an isolated boulder and huge erratic block, which the Voyageurs call "le rocher," or "la pose de Otamigan."

The Voyageurs and Indians have little stations or resting-places along their savage paths in the forests, where they are wont to rest a moment from their fatiguing journey. They call such resting-places "des poses," probably because they lay off, or "posent," their burdens there for a short time. This rocher de Otamigan is in a swamp close to one of these poses. Otamigan is a young Indian well known here, who once travelled along that road. When he sat down at the resting-place, and regarded the rock opposite him, it seemed as if it were oscillating, then advanced to him, made a bow, and went back again to its old place. This phenomenon, which may be, perchance, explained by Otamigan's excessive exertion and a transient giddiness, seemed to him so remarkable, that he straightway felt the greatest veneration for the rock, and ever after considered it his "protecting god." Now, I am told, he never goes past it without laying some tobacco on the rock as a sacrifice, and often goes expressly to pay worship to it.

There is another Indian here who once fancied he heard a very remarkable rustling in a tamarak-tree (the Canadian larch). Since then he has taken this tree as his protector, and often leads his friends to it, and says, "Voilà l'arbre en qui j'ai confiance."

It seems to me as if they employ the word Kitchi-Manitou at times not as the proper name of a single Great Being, but as the appellative of an entire class of Great Spirits. As they have no schools or orthodox churches, the ideas they form in their minds on this subject are very various and confused. An old Indian,

with whom I once talked, told me there were six
Kitchi-Manitous. One lived in the heavens, one in
the water, and the other four, north, south, east, and
west. They were all great; but the two in heaven
and the water were the most powerful, and the water
god was also spiteful. This seems a tolerably extended view.

The two most usual sacrifices the Indians offer to
Divinity, or the Great Spirits, are a dog and tobacco.
Tobacco they sacrifice and strew everywhere: on all
stones, boulders, masses of copper, graves, or other
places to which they attach a holy significance. The
dog, however, is the great sacrifice. " The dog is our
domestic companion, our dearest and most useful
animal," an Indian said to me. " It is almost like
sacrificing ourselves." The bear is honoured, but
does not serve as a sacrifice; nor do they offer plants,
corn, flowers, or things of that nature.

Among the dead stuffs of nature, the dwellers on
Lake Superior seem to feel the most superstitious
reverence for copper, which is so often found on the
surface-soil in a remarkable state of purity. They
frequently carry small pieces of copper ore about
with them in their medicine-bags; they are carefully
wrapped up in paper, handed down from father to
son, and wonderful power is ascribed to them.

Large masses of metallic copper are found at times
in their forests. They lie like erratic blocks among
the other rocks, and were probably, at first, regarded
as common stones, until an Indian hit on the idea of
trying their weight, or giving them a blow with a
hammer, by which the unusual weight, firmness, and
toughness of the ore were detected. Admiration leads
the savage to adoration, and thus these masses of

copper began to be regarded by nearly all the Ojibbeways as something highly mysterious, and were
raised to the dignity of idols.

One of my acquaintances here, an ex-Indian fur-
trader, a man of considerable intelligence and great
experience among the savages, told me the following
characteristic story of one of these lumps of copper:

"In the year 1827," he said to me, "I was trading
at the mouth of the Ontonagon river, when the pleasant
little town now existing was not thought of. The old
Ojibbeway tribe, now known as the Ontonagon Band,
lived there almost entirely independent, and Keatanang
was the name of their chief.

"Keatanang, from whom I purchased many skins,
and paid him fair prices, was well disposed towards
me. He was often wont to say to me, ' I wish I could
do thee some good. I would gladly give thee one of
my daughters.' Once, when he spoke so kindly to
me, and renewed his offer of his daughter, I said to
him, ' Keatanang, thou knowest I cannot marry thy
daughter, as I have a wife already, and the law forbids us Christians marrying several wives. But listen!
Thou hast often told me of another treasure which
thou possessest in thy family, a great lump of metal,
which lies in thy forests. If thou really wishest me
so well as thou sayest, and wouldst do me good,
show me this lump of copper, and let me take it to
my house. I will carry it to my countrymen, and if
they find it good they will surely seek for other pieces
of ore in thy country, and thou wilt soon have many
lumps instead of one. If thou wilt show it to me
I will pay thee any price thou mayst ask for it.'

"Keatanang was silent for a long time after hearing
my proposition. At length he began: ' Thou askest

much from me, far more than if thou hadst demanded one of my daughters. The lump of copper in the forest is a great treasure for me. It was so to my father and grandfather. It is our hope and our protection. Through it I have caught many beavers, killed many bears. Through its magic assistance I have been victorious in all my battles, and with it I have killed our foes. Through it, too, I have always remained healthy, and reached that great age in which thou now findest me. But I love thee, and wish to prove my love. I cannot give thee a greater proof of my friendship than by showing thee the path to that treasure, and allowing thee to carry it away.'

" 'What dost thou ask for it, Keatanang?'

" After long bargaining, we agreed that I was to give him two yards of scarlet cloth, four yards of blue cloth, two yards of every colour in silk ribbons, thirty pairs of silver earrings, two new white blankets, and ten pounds of tobacco; and that when I had all this in readiness, he would show me the next night the road to the copper, and allow me to carry it off in my canoe. Still he made it a condition that this must be done very secretly, and neither any of his people nor of mine should hear a word of it. He proposed to come to me at midnight, and I would be ready for him.

" The next night, exactly at the appointed time, while lying in my tent, I heard a man creeping up gently through the grass, and felt his fingers touch my head. It was Keatanang.

" 'Art thou awake,' he said, 'and hast thou the goods ready?' I gave him all the articles one after the other. He examined them carefully, packed them together, fastened the bundle up with the silk ribbons, placed half the tobacco on the top, and the rest in his

belt. He took the packet under his arm, and off we
started.

"We crossed a little meadow on the river bank,
and reached a rock, behind which Keatanang's canoe
lay in readiness.

"I offered to help him in paddling, but he would
not allow it. He ordered me to sit with my back
against the bow of the boat, and paddled along so
noiselessly, never once lifting the paddle from the
water, that we glided along the bank almost, I may
say, like Manitous.

"In two hours we reached the spot we call the
High Bluffs. From this point our path trended land-
wards. Keatanang took up the bundle, and when we
had climbed the bluffs he turned quite silent, raised
his eyes to the starry heavens, and prayed to the Great
Spirit.

"'Thou hast ever been kind to me,' he then said,
in so loud a voice that I could plainly hear him.
'Thou hast given me a great present, which I ever
valued highly, which has brought me much good fortune during my life, and which I still reverence. Be
not wroth that I now surrender it to my friend, who
desires it. I bring thee a great sacrifice for it!'

"Here he seized the heavy bale of goods with both
hands, and hurled it into the river, where it soon
sank.

"'Now come,' he then said to me, 'my mind is at
rest.' We walked to a tree which stood on a projecting space of the slope. 'Stay,' Keatanang said, 'here
it is. Look down, thou art standing on its head.'

"We both commenced clearing away from between
the roots the rotten leaves and earth, and the fresh
herbs and flowers that had just sprung up, for we

were then in spring. At length we came to several large pieces of birch bark. These, too, were removed, and I discovered under them a handsome lump of pure copper, about the size and shape of a hat. I tried to lift it, and it weighed a little more than half a hundred. I carried it out into the moonlight, and saw that the copper was streaked with a thick vein of silver.

"While I was examining the copper, Keatanang, who was evidently excited, and was trembling and quivering, laid the other five pounds of tobacco he had thrust in his belt as a conciliatory sacrifice in the place of the copper, and then covered it again with bark, leaves, and roots. I wrapped my lump in a blanket, and dragged it down to the canoe. We paddled down the river as noiselessly though more rapidly than we went up. Keatanang did not say a word, and, as we found everybody asleep in the encampment, we stepped into our tents again as unnoticed as we left them.

"The next day I loaded my treasure on my canoe, and set out. My specimen was ultimately sent to the authorities of the United States, and was one of the first objects to draw public attention to the metallic treasures of this remarkable district.

"Old Keatanang bitterly repented afterwards the deal he had with me, and ascribed many pieces of misfortune that fell on him to it. Still I always remained on a friendly footing with him, and gave him my support whenever I had an opportunity. Afterwards he became a Christian, and found peace."

CHAPTER VI.

INDIAN GENEROSITY—BEHAVIOUR OF THE CHIEFS—CHARACTER OF THE
WARS—THE PILLAGERS—SAFETY OF EUROPEANS—LIFE AT LA POINTE—
COMMUNISM—APPEALS TO THE GREAT SPIRIT—HOSPITALITY—THE INDIAN
SQUAW—THE BREAD WINNER—CURIOUS CEREMONY—GRACE BEFORE
MEAT—THE SWIFT RUNNER—THE LAND SURVEYOR—AN INDIAN PASS—
THE SAUVAGES DES TERRES—THE TRADERS—ADVANCES TO THE INDIANS
—A NOBLE RETURN—THE CHIPPEWAY CHIEF—FIVE HUNDRED DOLLARS
IN JEOPARDY—A HARD WINTER—FRESH ADVANCES—CONFIDENCE FOR
CONFIDENCE—CIVILISATION RETARDED.

WE Christians regard the law to love our neighbour,
and the pressing recommendation of charity, as the
most material feature of our morality, and as some
thing which distinguishes it from all other religious
dogmas.

In a certain sense, and to a certain degree, this may
be true; but we must be cautious not to exalt ourselves too much, and deny the natural goodness of the
rest of humanity.

Charity and liberality, as regards the goods given
by God, and noble hospitality, are praised as the principal virtues among non-Christian nations equally as
with us. Among the Indians this reaches such a pitch,
that it is one of the chief obstacles to their conversion.

I will presently show the meaning to be attached to this, but first adduce some facts suited to verify my general assertion.

As a universal rule, next to the liar, no one is so despised by the Indians as the narrow-hearted egotist and greedy miser.   The Indians might possibly give a murderer or other sinner the seat of honour in their lodges, but a man known as a " sassagis " (mean man) must sit at the doorway.   As long as a man has anything, according to the moral law of the Indians, he must share it with those who want; and no one can attain any degree of respect among them who does not do so most liberally.   They are almost communists, and hence there are no rich men among them.   Their chiefs and warriors live and behave much like the first barefooted kalifs, and they bestow all their gains on their followers.   "Those vain scamps," a man said to me, " whom you see here parading their silver medals and other European presents, are not the influential chiefs and great men among the Indians.   They ridicule them. The right men conceal themselves, and are worse clothed than the others."   They give to the tribe not only what they obtain by the chase, but also all the presents they get from the Europeans, even to their tribute-money.   Frequently, when a chief receives very handsome goods, either in exchange for his peltry, or as a recognition of his high position, he will throw them all in a heap, call his followers, and divide all among them.   If he grow very zealous, he will pull off his shirt, give it away, and say, " So, you see, I have now nothing more to give; I am poorer than any one of you, and commend myself to your charity."

A man who lays up such capital in the hearts of his

followers is thence much richer than if he had all the wares under lock and key. In case of need, all his followers blindly obey his orders.

How little the Indians are prone to cupidity is seen in the character of their wars. The forays of the wild predatory Beduin tribes are nearly all for plunder, but the Indian wars solely for revenge. When a young Indian prepares an expedition, he never dreams, like the thievish comrades of Ulysses, about the plunder he can obtain, but only of the relations he can avenge and the blood-foes he can punish. On the battle-field his first and most important business is to take the scalp of the enemy he has killed. Having this, he is satisfied, and leaves the ornaments on the corpse, which a predatory Arab or Affghan would fall upon first.

In the enemy's camp they destroy more than they plunder. In order to injure him, they will, perhaps, burn all he possesses, but, once holding the scalps, they do not burden themselves with much booty. Indeed, each of the warriors will leave something of his own behind, as proof positive that he has been there. At times, too, they leave tobacco or other matters in the enemy's encampment, as a conciliatory sacrifice for the spirits.

These wars—even the successful and victorious ones —are so far from being a source of profit to them, that they often entail heavy expenses on them. A chief who designs war will ruin himself, and give his last farthing to equip his followers for the war-trail. And when they return from the wars their clothes are torn, their mocassins worn out, perhaps their entire flotilla expended. But if they bring scalps with them, the whole camp is drunk with joy, and the women work

gladly and patiently for a couple of months to set
matters in order again, and repair deficiencies.

The Voyageurs and traders assure me that they
generally consider their wares perfectly safe among
the Indians, although they travel among them frequently with valuable stores and full purses. Though
there are no police or soldiers, it has very rarely happened, since Europeans have traversed the country,
that any trader has been attacked for the mere sake
of plunder. The robberies which have been committed now and then have been effected by Europeans,
or at their instigation, especially at that period when
the two great rival fur companies—the Hudson's Bay
and North-West—existed here side by side. The
agents of these companies often plundered each other's
posts, and employed the Indians for that purpose.

It is only an exception to the rule that there is an
Ojibbeway tribe, near Lake Superior, known by the
name of "the Pillagers." They have obtained their
name, as it happens, from an isolated fact, and not
from any disposition to plunder. They once attacked
an American trader who lived among them, and robbed
him of his goods. Although there was a valid excuse
that this trader was a harsh man and bad paymaster,
the matter caused so much excitement that the tribe
has henceforth received the name of Pillagers, both
from Europeans and Indians, as a punishment.

It seems to me that I may quote our own unusual
situation on this small island as a proof that love of
plunder and avarice are not the prominent or dangerous passions of the Indians. We are here a handful of Europeans, surrounded by more than a thousand
Indians armed with tomahawks, knives, and guns, and
yet not one of us feels the slightest alarm. Hardly

one of us Europeans possesses a weapon; only the Indians are armed. There is not a trace of any precautionary measure, as in the towns of Austrian Illyria, where the Montenegrins and other mountaineers are compelled to deposit their arms at the gate before being allowed to enter the town, nor is there a single soldier or armed policeman on the whole island. And yet, for miles round, every bush conceals an Indian, and the wooden booths of the Europeans are filled with the most handsome and desired articles. A whole ship-load of wares has just arrived, and the blockhouse in which they are packed could be broken open with a hatchet. The sum of ready money on the island, in handsome new coinage, amounts to several thousand dollars, and yet we sleep with open windows and doors, and not one of us thinks of locking a door or bolting a window.

To this it may be replied, I grant, that the Indians, for their own sake, would soon detect and give up a single thief, and that they are well aware a robbery *en masse* would be eventually avenged on the whole nation. But to this I answer, first, that these reasons are equally valid in Illyria and Spain, but in neither of those countries could money or men be so exposed without a company of gendarmes; and, secondly, it is universally and justly asserted that the Indians are as thoughtless as children, and as careless of consequences. Were, then, cupidity a powerful passion among them, they would easily give way to it, and we should all be probably plundered and scalped, and it would be left to others to avenge us.

How strict the views and habits of the Indians are to the principle that a man must first share with others and then think of himself, is revealed in a

hundred instances. It often happens that a poor
hunter, in spite of all his incantations, is unable to
shoot anything of value. He fasts, his wife fasts, his
children cry for hunger. At length he shoots a deer.
What would be more natural than that they should
all fall on it, like hungry wolves, and satisfy themselves, after putting aside one or two good lumps, so
that they might have something for the morrow and
the day after? The Indian is far from devoting his
sole attention to these precautionary measures. His
feeling of honour insists that he must first of all consult with his wife how the deer is to be divided among
his neighbours and friends. Of course he reserves a
portion for himself and his children, but he reduces
their portions, so as to send larger pieces to his relations and neighbours. And thus none of the deer is
left for "to-morrow, or the day after;" the coming
day must take care of itself. It is true the hunter
profits by the occasion to recommend himself to the
charity of his friends and patrons. "I give you," he
says, "the last and only thing I have. Be so good,
on your side, to interpose for me with the Great
Spirit, so that He may allow me to kill more game.
Stand by me with your dreams, and help me by your
fasts." On such an occasion, one of those who have
received a present steps forth, and replies that, " he
will exert himself on behalf of his friend, and remember all the most important dreams he ever had in his
life, and help him by his thoughts of those dreams. He
will also fast for him afresh, and implore the Master
of Life to have mercy on him, and give him future
luck in hunting."*

* Although I did not hear a speech of this character, my description is
after nature, second-hand. A French Voyageur told me he had once been

An educated American told me a circumstance, proving, in a most affecting manner, how capable the Indians are of liberal charity, even in their own poverty. About twenty years back, he said that he was travelling in the savage north of Wisconsin. He and his two comrades had expended all their provisions. It was winter, and deep snow covered forest and plain, so that they found difficulty in advancing, and could not possibly kill any game. They marched on for three days without sustenance, and were in a state of deep distress. At length, to their delight, they discovered an Indian lodge, entered it, and begged some food. Unfortunately, the Indians had nothing to offer, and replied to their guests' complaints with others even worse : " We," they said, " have been fasting nearly so many weeks as you have days. The deep snow has prevented us killing anything. Our two sons have gone out to day, but they will return as usual, with empty hands. Other Indians, however, live twenty miles to the north, and it is possible they are better provided than we are."

The American and his comrades, tortured by hunger, set out at once on snow-shoes to try their luck with their neighbours; but they had scarce gone four or five miles, when they heard a yell behind them, and saw an Indian hurrying after them on snow-shoes. " Hi! halloh! you men, stop! Come back!"— " What's the matter?"—" Our lads have returned. They have shot a deer, and brought it home. We have now a supply, and I have hastened to tell you

present at such an affair, and that the grateful recipient had promised, " qu'il voulait se servir en faveur de son ami de ses rêves les plus pesants, qu'il voulait jeûner pour lui, et qu'il voulait dire au Maître de la Vie : " Faites-lui la charité."

of it." The European travellers turned back, and were stuffed with food, though the deer was small and the family large.

I have, I confess, never seen any starving Indians reduced to extremities, but all the Voyageurs here present have experienced it, for the satisfaction of hunger is here the standing question the year through. They are almost always in a state of want. All the Voyageurs I questioned were unanimous in their verdict that the Indians, even when starving, never lose their desire to share, but do not easily give up their courage, hope, and, so to speak, their confidence in God. " We Voyageurs," one of them said, " when times are bad, grow quite de mauvaise humeur: we curse and growl, while the Indian laughs and jests. Even the Indian squaw does not complain or lament if her husband comes home to-day, as yesterday, empty-handed. She does not even ask him, ' Didst thou not shoot anything to-day ?' When he enters, she pretends as if she did not notice it. He, too, says nothing, but she sees at once, in the way he comes in, the colour of his hands, and the drops of blood on his shirt, whether a deer is lying outside or not. If he bring nothing home, and when there is scarce any-thing in the lodge, still she sets his supper before him. She has always put something aside for the man, the hunter of the house, the support of the family, and, for his sake, has starved with the children. He must, above all, remain healthy and strong, so that he may go to work again to-morrow."

It was once the custom here on the Lake, and the more savage and pious Indians of the Far West still keep it up, that every morning an old chief, or great orator of the tribe, should step forth and hold a species of morning prayer. This prayer they never omit, however badly off they may be. "Hoho, hoho!" the man shouts through the village. "Ye friends, brothers, cousins, and uncles, I need not announce to you that we have hunger, want, and misery in our village. Our wives are starving, our children are fasting, you yourselves have nothing to chew. We have nothing, nothing at all. But courage, comrades! it is the deer season. I saw in my dream the hoof marks of the deer in every direction. Let us set out. Perhaps the Great Spirit will have mercy on us!"

I write this literally from the mouth of a Voyageur, who often heard such addresses. Educated Americans have also assured me that the grace before meat, uttered by these pagan Indians when they place the good gifts of God before honoured guests, is most edifying and reverent.

"Once," a man told me, "I was travelling in the interior of the country, and camped one evening on a lake in the heart of the desert, and, as we fancied, far from all human abode. As it had been raining for several days, and was now pouring down heavens hard, we were unable to kindle a fire, and sat in melancholy mood and very hungry under the trees, wrapped in our blankets, and exchanged precious few words. All at once we heard steps approaching, and my name was uttered.

"An Indian of the name of Kisaiasch (the Swift Runner), an old chief, advanced to me with some of his companions, and saluted me as an old acquaintance. I had once stayed with him for six weeks in the forest where he was hunting, and had made him a present of an old compass and a lantern. He lived on an island in the very lake on whose bank we were

now encamped, though I was unaware of the fact.
As he had noticed through the twilight some movement in the forest, he had come over with his followers to see what it was. They had landed from
the canoe at a distant spot, and, while creeping round
our camp, he had recognised my voice as that of an
old acquaintance, in the dark, although six long years
had passed since I last saw him. He invited us immediately to his lodge, and we spent the night dry and
warm beneath his roof. The next morning, when we
woke, we found his squaws had prepared a famous
breakfast. For this purpose they had built a spacious
hut, and hung it with clean mats. A capital bean
soup, with fresh venison, steamed in the centre, with
berries and other sweets; while my presents, the compass and the lantern, were hung up in good condition
in the hut. Here our host welcomed us in a short
and very proper speech, told all present how he had
met me formerly, and how he had received those presents as signs of my friendly feeling. Then he expressed his delight that chance enabled him to repay
me. After which he uttered a prayer, in which he
thanked the Giver of all good gifts for placing him in
a position to refresh the hungry, and, finally, implored
a grace upon the meal as well as any preacher could
have done it.

"We enjoyed it, and one of the Indians who accompanied me, unable to devour the whole of his
soup, but thinking his family would like it, was permitted to take it with him if he could carry it without
the plate. ' As for carrying it,' the recipient said,
' that was his least care;' and he ran out into the
forest with his knife, and soon returned with a piece
of fresh bark, which he speedily formed into a sort of

bottle. Into this he poured the bean soup, fastened it to his waist, and let it hang there till he reached his lodge, which we should pass during our travels.

"The white Americans were, at that period, a very new appearance in this country, and, as I proposed to undertake certain operations, against which the Indians even now entertain prejudices—namely, geodetic experiments, or a preliminary land survey—the protection of my host, the influential chieftain Kisaiasch, was not without value. Hence I asked him for a letter, or pass, to those persons of his tribe I might happen to meet. I wrote it myself in the Indian language, and explained in it my friendly views. Kisaiasch placed his mark under it, a St. Andrew's cross with a flying bird to the right of it. The pass, I may here remark, did me excellent service at a later date; for, stumbling over a party of seventeen Indians, who regarded my mathematical instruments with great mistrust, and at first were anything but friendly, I read them my pass, and they looked at it, and fancied their old chief was speaking to them out of it. They also saw his mark, and totem sign under it, passed it from hand to hand, said it was good, and were henceforth at my service. At that time, it is true, a chief was held in greater respect than at present."

A Canadian Voyageur once described to me a similar instance of Indian hospitality. "I and two other Canadians," he said, "were once travelling to the west of the Mississippi with a small herd of cattle. One evening we camped on a river, on the opposite bank of which stood an Indian lodge. We had scarce kindled our fire ere the male inhabitants came across, an Indian and his son, attracted by the bells of our animals. On noticing that we were rather short of food, they told us there was abundance over in their wigwam, and began counting in the most open manner all the deer, and ducks, and prairie hens they had recently shot, and to which they invited us. We crossed over, and the squaws, who prepared the supper, were not disposed to contradict their husbands, for they served up all the game mentioned in succession, adding to it many sorts of fish. We ate, talked, and slept famously, and the next morning took off our silk handkerchiefs and gave them to the women. But lest they might fancy we gave them at all as a requital for their hospitality, we turned it off with a jest. ' We could not bear the handkerchiefs,' we said; 'they were too hot for us. We could not endure their colour. They were only intended for squaws. They were not worth a rap to us men. And if the squaws would not accept them we would fling them into the water.' Then they were not ashamed to accept so worthless a gift."

But I should never end were I to narrate all the stories I heard of Indian hospitality. Enough to say, that everybody seems agreed that an unfortunate man rarely knocks in vain at an Indian door, and the latter is always ready to share his last meal with the starving stranger.

" Eh!" a Canadian Voyageur said to me, with whom I conversed on this subject—" eh bien, monsieur, donnez-moi les sauvages des Terres.* Ce sont des gens d'un cœur grand, tout-à-fait comme il faut." Among them a man is always welcome. If the weather is bad, or your feet sore, you can live with one of them for eight or ten days, choose the best

---

* Les sauvages des Terres, or des Grandes Terres, is the name given to the Indians of the interior, who live far from white settlements.

piece of meat, and dare not speak about payment.
And if you have once done a service to a "sauvage
des Terres," he will repay you when he has it in his
power, en grand seigneur. I once asked one of these
fellows to supper with me; he drank a couple of cups
of tea, and as he was beggared I gave him twenty-five
cents to get a good meal the next day. He went
away, and, as I heard nothing of him for a whole year,
I supposed he had forgotten me. In autumn, at payment time, he came down, however, from the interior
to receive his tribute in money and provisions. On
this occasion he paid me a visit, but I gave him
nothing particular, not through any ill feeling, but
because I was myself very queerly off. Without my
saying a word, he soon noticed my state, returned
the next day, and told me (though not making the
slightest reference to my poverty) that he had received at the payment, for himself and family, five
casks of flour. It seemed very good flour, and I had
better bring a vessel along and carry home some as a
specimen.

I went the next day with a pan, and my Indian
said, "There is the flour, take it."

"But, my uncle," I remarked, "thy cask is not yet
opened, and I have no hammer with me."

"Well," he replied, "if the cask is not opened, and
thou hast forgotten thy hammer, I have no hammer
for thee. Thou must, therefore, take the whole cask.
And now that thou hast so much, thou wilt require
a forkful of bacon as a change. There, take that
with it!"

With these words he took two sides of bacon, hap-
hazard, and threw them on my cask. I tried to protest, and make him understand that he was robbing

his family; and then I began offering him my hearty
thanks.

"Let that be," he said; "thou art a good fellow.
Thou didst think of me when I was poor, it is right
that I should now think of thee when thou art
hungering." And then he thrust me, and the flour,
and the bacon, out of the lodge.

The Canadian traders also told me many pleasing
stories of the Indians, which go to prove that they are
frequently capable of feelings of gratitude and confidence, and how little cold calculation exists in their
character. These traders often give the Indians credit
for large supplies, and rarely find any difficulty in
getting their accounts settled. Although the Indians
carry the state of the ledger entirely in their heads,
they generally remember all the advances made them,
and their own payments on account so accurately, that
both statements are usually found unanimous. At
times the Indians, when they have no reason to doubt
their trader, will accept his reckoning without any
examination, and say it is all right. A trader told me
the following little anecdote of the way in which an
Indian squared up with him:

He, the trader, had made his debtor—a chief from
the Chippeway river — considerable advances for
blankets, guns, powder, flour, and other house provisions, and it was arranged to be paid off the next
year in peltry. But the times were very bad: a hard
winter set in, with such an unusual snow-fall, that no
game could be killed, and the poor Indians lacked the
little they did shoot for their own sustenance and
clothing. The Sioux, too, during the spring, repeatedly
invaded the country along the Chippeway, and half
the hunting season was spent in war and skirmishes

with them. Instead of bringing skins, therefore, the Indians, and among them their chief, came down to their traders with complaints and requests for further advances. These took pity on the Indians, and gave them food for the next year. My trader even provided his chief with a dozen new beaver traps, and sent him well equipped into the forest, although he felt some apprehension on account of his outlay, which now amounted to upwards of five hundred dollars, for the chief and his family. The next year, however, was more productive, and it also happened that the Indians sold a tract of country to the United States government, and had a considerable payment to receive. At such payments, when the traders expect to find their debtors in funds, they usually lay their detailed account before the government pay-agent, and, if the Indian agree to the items, the amount is deducted from the sum he has to receive and handed to the trader.

The payment had been going on some time, and all the Indians and traders assembled for weeks; but the indebted Chippeway chief had not yet presented himself before his creditor, as is the rule, in order to go through the accounts. They met at times, it is true, bowed distantly, but the Indian seemed to take no notice of the trader, so that the latter began to grow horribly suspicious that his debtor had treacherous designs. The hour was approaching when the chief was to receive his share, the shining dollars already lay on the pay-table, and yet the long-detailed account, which filled several pages, had not yet been gone through or accepted by the Indian. At length, when the chief's name had been called, and the trader had made up his mind to protest, the Indian came to him

and asked for his account. The trader gave him the
sheets of paper, on which all the items, with the dates
written out, amounted to hundreds. The creditor
wished to run through it with him, but the Indian
said, "Let it be! Hast thou calculated the interest
of my old debt? I thank thee for having given me so
long credit, and confidence deserves confidence. And
it would be improper for me to reckon and wrangle
with thee now. Nor do I wish that the gentlemen
should see thy account. Show me—where is the
total?" He then tore it off, handed back the rest of
the bill, with a hint that it should be employed for
pipe-lights, and went straight to the paymaster, begging
him to pay the trader the five hundred dollars he
owed him. Very little of the tribute was left for the
chief.

As a natural consequence, this generosity among the
Indians has grown into a species of communism, and
has a very prejudicial effect on their civilisation. As
the hunter—no matter how clever and successful he
may be—is forced to give all his spoil away, industry
is never rewarded, and the hard-working man toils for
the lazy. The indefatigable hunter is always accompanied by a couple of idle fellows, who live upon him.
If he do not give abundantly, he runs the risk of being
branded a miser. The whole tribe will set to work
annoying and injuring him. They tear his nets, pull
down his hut, and kill his horse. In this way, then,
no one is able to retain the fruits of his toil, and no
rich and prosperous families can spring up among the
Indians.

CHAPTER VII.

INDIAN SPORTS AND PASTIMES—THE GAME OF THE BOWL—THE PIECES AND
PAWNS—MODE OF PLAYING—AN ANGRY NATIVE—THE GAME OF PINS—
TOPS—SAUVAGERIE—SOCIABILITY OF THE NATIVES—A FUMERIE—SMOKE
INCENSE—THE FIRST BIRD—A MEDICINE FEAST—INDIAN SING-SONGS—
STORY-TELLERS—CURIOUS LEGENDS—HIAWATHA—BALL PLAY—RAQUETS
AND BALLS—PRAIRIE DE LA CROSSE—CONSPIRACIES—THE THROWING
GAME—SPORTS ON THE ICE.

THE remark which Tacitus makes of our old Germanic ancestors, that they spent one half their life in
hunting and war, the other half in idleness and play,
is equally referable to these savage Indians. It is
really incredible what a variety of games they have
invented, not merely games of pure chance, but also
those in which the brain and the muscle are exercised,
and time passed in a pleasant way. I have paid much
attention to this matter, and yet I daily detect some
new variety of Indian amusement.

The young men have their games, the young women
theirs, and so have the children. For summer and
spring they have special games, and they have others,
too, on the winter ice. And the most curious thing
is that I find all these Indian games, as far as I can
understand them, very ingenious and amusing, and,
at any rate, much less monotonous than that stupid

European game of Montè, which the entire Hispano-
American race, down to the Straits of Patagonia, is so
passionately fond of.

In proof of this assertion, I may here allude to the
game called by the Indians " pagessan," and which I
frequently saw played. The Canadians call it " le
jeu au plat" (the game of the bowl). It is a game of
hazard, but skill plays a considerable part in it. It is
played with a wooden bowl, and a number of small
figures bearing some resemblance to our chessmen.
They are usually carved very neatly out of bones,
wood, or plum-stones, and represent various things:
a fish, a hand, a door, a man, a canoe, a half moon,
&c. They call these figures "pagessanag"(carved plum-
stones), and the game has received its name from them.
Each figure has a foot on which it can stand upright.
They are all thrown into a wooden bowl (in Indian
" onagan"), whence the French name is derived. The
players make a hole in the ground, and thrust the
bowl with the figures into it, while giving it a slight
shake. The more figures stand upright on the smooth
bottom of the bowl through this shake all the better
for the player. Each figure has its value, and some of
them represent to a certain extent the pieces in the
game of chess. There are also other figures, which
may similarly be called the pawns. The latter, carved
into small round stars, are all alike, have no pedestal,
but are red on one side and plain on the other, and
are counted as plus or minus, according to the side
uppermost. With the pawns it is perfect chance
which side is up, but with the pieces much depends
on the skill with which the bowl is shaken. The
other rules and mode of calculation are said to be
very complicated, and the game is played with great

attention and passion. My Indians here will lie half
the night through round the bowl, and watch the
variations of the game. It is played with slight
divergences by nearly all the Indian tribes, and in
many both men and women practise it.

How seriously they regard the game, and how
excited they grow over it, I had an opportunity of
noticing. Some time ago I seated myself by some
Indians who were playing at pagessan. One of them
was a very handsome young fellow, wearing broad
silver rings on his arms, the carving of which I was
anxious to inspect. On turning to him with a question, however, he grew very impatient and angry at
this interruption of the game, considered my question
extremely impertinent, and commenced such a threatening speech that my interpreter could not be induced to translate it to me. He merely said it was
most improper, and then began, for his part, abusing
the Indian, so that I had great difficulty in appeasing
him. All I understood was that an Indian must not
be disturbed when gambling.

In many of their games they exercise the skill of
their fingers and senses, which is so necessary for them
in hunting, fishing, &c. Thus, the children here play
a very clever little game with pins. They beg as
many as they can from their mothers and sisters, and
then lie down on the grass. The game is played in
this way: after a piece of grass has been smoothed
down, one lad throws on it a pin; another then gives
his pin a fillip with his finger, and tries to make his
pin cross the other; if he succeed, he gains the pin.
Delicate fingers and wrists are required for this, and
many of the lads aim as surely with the pins as with
bow and arrow.

The Indian boys manage to make tops out of acorns and nuts as cleverly as our boys do. They also collect the oval stones which are found on the banks of the rivers and lakes, and use them on the ice in winter. Barefooted and active, they run over the ice, and drive the stones against each other with whips and sticks. The stone that upsets the other is the victor.

The social French seem to regard unsociableness as a quality of barbarism, for they call it sarcastically "sauvagerie," and distinguish a man who keeps aloof from society by the name of "sauvage." These American savages, I hardly think, can have given the French cause to form such an opinion, for they seem to me to evince great partiality for social amusements and sports. I always see them lying together in their tents and chattering away, and, whenever I peep into their confined keeping-rooms, I find them as crowded as coffee-houses among us. Only when an Indian is sorrowful does he retire into solitude, and sigh out his grief in the forest. If he is merry, and disposed for sport and fun, he likes to assemble as many of his friends as possible. In their ball games many hundreds collect; the same in their dances and songs. Every game in which only two persons are engaged attracts a band of helpers and spectators. I may almost say that the savage knows no other than social sports. How should he amuse himself in his solitude—by playing the violin to himself, like Paganini in prison?

It is true that most of their formal meetings have another motive and tendency beside the mere enjoyment of social intercourse and conversation. Their dances are nearly all religious ceremonies, and their dinners, to which they send out invitations, have a motive. A chief wishes to gain his friends for a certain plan, or a warrior desires to secure the assistance of a great "jossakid" (magician), or else it is a christening feast, a funebral banquet, or something of that sort.

What are termed by the Canadians "fumeries" (invitations to a smoke) have frequently a political 'or serious object. The chief who sends out an invitation wishes to discuss some question of peace or war, and to smoke it over with his friends. Still they at times arrange these fumeries merely for the sake of society. When, for instance, game is very scarce, and there is nothing else to set before a guest, a man will invite his friends to tobacco, and gossip with them over the hard times, and try to dispel their ennui. But even at such a purposeless fumerie there is always a degree of ceremony and a trace of religion. The chief who receives the company generally holds a short address to his guests, in which he tells them he thought it would be well in these bad times to meet for once in a way and send up the smoke in the air " pour le Maître de la Vie." The guest who arrives last, and has taken his place near the door, or the youngest man present, usually utters a few words in reply, thanks the host in the name of the other guests for his politeness, and says he was quite right in his suggestion. Generally on such occasions the host has his " skabewis " (assistant), or " dresseur," as the Canadians call such a person, whose duty it is to fill the pipes of the guests and light them. That these smoke societies have a religious tendency is proved by the thanks the guests give the pipe-lighter or the host; for they do not employ the ordinary phrase : " I thank thee !" or " Migouesh !" but the solemn expression, or shout of applause, " Ho, ho !"

The Indians are never at a want for an excuse for a
social meeting. I have been assured that they mark
every at all important event in their lodge by a little
festivity. Thus, for instance, the grandfather or grandmother gives a little party when the grandson shoots
his first bird. In the same way a feast is prepared
when a youth of the lodge kills his first bear, or elk, or
other large game. The latter festivities are also more
or less accompanied by religious or mysterious rites.

I also heard of feasts which an Indian hunter would
give "pour sa propre médecine;" that is to say, for his
own fortune or protecting spirit. They probably bear
some affinity to the solemnities the Russian mujiks
hold for their guardian angels, when, in addition to
the feasts they give their relatives, they pay for a
special mass to be read on their behalf in the church.

But of all the Indian social meetings, I was most interested by those at which songs were sung and stories
told. Before I had any opportunity of witnessing these,
I had often heard them spoken of by the Voyageurs and
traders. It is a frequent occurrence that the members
of a family or the neighbours will assemble on the long
winter evenings, when nothing else can be done, and
request a clever story-teller to tell them old legends
and fables. "These stories," I was assured, "are not
at all inferior to the 'Arabian Nights.' They are just
as amusing, various, and fantastic. They are, too,
almost in the same style." Some persons have even
conjectured that our "Arabian Nights" were borrowed
from the American Indians, while several appealed to
the resemblance of the stories as a proof of the Asiatic
origin of the Indians!

The Canadian Voyageurs, traders, and " coureurs
des bois" are as delighted with these stories as the

Indians themselves. But it says little for the poetic feeling and literary taste of the old missionaries, and the other innumerable travellers who have described these countries, that the outer public has only learned so little, and at so recent a date, of this memorable treasure among these savage tribes. Of the old authors, hardly one alludes to this subject, which the missionaries probably thought too unholy for them to handle, and which other travellers overlooked through their ignorance of the language and want of leisure. Mr. Schoolcraft was the first, in his " Algic Researches," to make an attempt to collect the fables and stories of the Indians; and Longfellow, in his "Hiawatha," has submitted some graceful specimens to the European world of letters.

I was naturally very curious to acquire some experience of the narrative talent of the Indians as well as of the contents of their stories, and, as I had some opportunities for doing so, I was no little surprised at finding how greatly this talent was spread, and was, as it were, peculiar to all. After hearing some old Indians tell stories, it seemed to me as if they all belonged to the same school. They all spoke and narrated very fluently, without the slightest affectation, or any peculiar animation. The life was in the story, in their original remarks and inventive parentheses. They usually spoke low and uniformly, without much pathos or gesticulation. It was like listening to the continued rustling of a stream or the murmurs of the wind. I never heard them stammer or repeat themselves, and the thread was spun off the reel as if they had the story by heart. The monotonous metre Longfellow chose for his Hiawatha is, therefore, a very good imitation of the Indian uncadenced delivery.

I have often heard it stated that men are the only story-tellers, and that men and boys are alone permitted to listen to them. I know not if this be the case, though it may be so with some sort of stories, but it is a fact that I found many old women equally eloquent and inventive.

It is difficult to form any idea how these stories, some of which are very old, attained their present shape, and were handed down from generation to generation. It would be very interesting could one compare a collection made in the time of Columbus with one made to-day, and see how much is permanent and how much changeable. It was clear to me, though, that every narrator added much of his own, and altered a good deal according to his taste. The same story has been told me by two different persons, and I have noticed considerable variations, although the groundwork and style of composition remained the same. But I will return to this subject presently.

Of all the Indian social sports the finest and grandest is the ball play. I might call it a noble game, and I am surprised how these savages attained such perfection in it. Nowhere in the world, excepting, perhaps, among the English and some of the Italian races, is the graceful and manly game of ball played so passionately and on so large a scale. They often play village against village, or tribe against tribe. Hundreds of players assemble, and the wares and goods offered as prizes often reach a value of a thousand dollars and more. On our island we made a vain attempt to get up a game, for though the chiefs were ready enough, and all were cutting their raquets and balls in the bushes, the chief American authorities forbade this innocent amusement. Hence, on this occasion, I was only enabled to inspect the instruments. They were made with great care, and well adapted for the purpose, and it is to be desired that the Indians would display the same attention to more important matters.

The raquets are two and a half feet in length, carved very gracefully out of a white tough wood, and provided with a handle. The upper end is formed into a ring four or five inches in diameter, worked very firmly and regularly, and covered by a network of leather bands. The balls are made of white willow, and cut perfectly round with the hand: crosses, stars, and circles are carved upon them. The care devoted to the balls is sufficient to show how highly they estimate the game. The French call it "jeu de crosse." Great ball-players, who can send the ball so high that it is out of sight, attain the same renown among the Indians as celebrated runners, hunters, or warriors.

The name of the ball play is immortalised both in the geography and history of the country. There is a prairie, and now a town, on the Mississippi known as the "Prairie de la Crosse." In history it is immortalised by more than one ball-play conspiracy—a peculiar sort of conspiracy among the Indians. On one occasion the natives combined to seize a British fort during peace, and the conspirators arranged a grand and solemn ball-play in honour of the British officers, who suspected nothing, and were less on their guard than usual. The merry shouting band of players approached the gates of the fort, and suddenly the ball flew over the walls. The Indians, as if carried away by excitement, rushed over the palisades after it, and made themselves masters of the fort. On another occasion, a British officer, who was disliked, was suddenly surrounded by the Indian ball players, knocked down with the raquets, and trampled under foot, as if accidentally, in the frenzy of the game.

Another description of ball play, especially practised by the women, is what is called the "papassi kawan," which means literally "the throwing game." It is played by two large bands, who collect round two opposite poles, and try to throw the object over their opponents' pole. In the place of a ball, they have two leathern bags filled with sand, and attached by a thong. They throw them in the air by means of a staff excellently shaped for the purpose, and catch it again very cleverly. The stick is sharp and slightly bent at the end, and adorned like the raquets.

I once saw a very neat model of these instruments for the women's throwing game suspended to the cradle of a little girl.

The Indians are also said to have many capital games on the ice, and I had opportunity, at any rate, to inspect the instruments employed in them, which they called "shoshiman" (slipping-sticks). These are elegantly carved and prepared; at the end they are slightly bent, like the iron of a skate, and form a heavy knob, while gradually tapering down in the handle. They cast these sticks with considerable skill over the smooth ice. In order to give them greater impulsion, a small, gently-rising incline of frozen snow is formed on the ice, over which the "gliding sticks" bound. In this way they gain greater impetus, and dart from the edge of the snow mound like arrows.

So much for the present about the games and social amusements of my islanders. I shall, probably, return to this subject again.

CHAPTER VIII.

AN INDIAN SHEHERAZADE—THE STORY OF OTTER-HEART AND HIS TWO WIVES, WHICH SUFFERS THE SAME FATE AS THAT OF THE BEAR AND THE FIDDLE.

An old insignificant squaw often came into our hut, and sat in a corner, smoking her pipe, without our paying much attention to her. She never had mingled in the conversation of the others, and I had hardly heard half a dozen words from her lips.

One evening she crept in as usual, and, as we had no visitors, and were alone with her, my interpreter requested her to tell us one of her pretty stories. "Does she know any?" I asked, somewhat doubtingly; and though my Canadian friend insisted she did, the old woman protested very zealously against it. "She did not know any stories," she said; "she was much too simple for that, and even if she had known stories once, her head was now too weak and her memory entirely gone."

But see there! After the old woman had once opened her mouth, she began to talk away fluently, like the ticking of a watch which will not require winding up again in a hurry.

The first story she told us was about "the wicked

and the good squaw," and was the first poetic legend
I had ever heard from Indian lips, and, as I find it
thoroughly Indian in its development, motive, and
delivery, I will repeat it here after my old woman.

THE GOOD AND BAD SQUAW.

Far away in a remote forest, on the shore of a
solitary lake, there once lived a maiden of fourteen
years of age. She had no one in this world but
a little brother, whom she took care of, dressed, and
gave the requisite food to. The little one could string
a bow, and shot in the forest the birds and the hares,
which he brought to his sister, and she cooked for
both.

" Sister, how comes it," the brother asked one day,
when he brought birds home again, " that we live so
alone ?   Are there no other beings besides us ?   And
where are our parents—our father and our mother ?"

" Our parents were killed by cruel magicians.
Whether there are any Indians besides us I know
not."

When the brother grew older, and gained his
youth's strength, he also shot deer and other large
animals, which he brought to his sister. But the
thought continually occupied him, whether there were
other Indians in the world besides him and his sister.
And one evening he said to the latter, " Sister, tan
the deer-skins I brought thee, and make me ten pairs
of mocassins of them."

The sister did as her brother ordered, though she
was very sorrowful.

" Wilt thou depart, oh my brother ?" she asked him.

" Yes, sister! I must go.   I wish to see if there are
not other Indians in the world."

The following morning the youth seized bow and arrow, stuck the ten pairs of mocassins in his belt, and, after taking leave of his good sister, wandered forth into the forest.

He marched the whole day through thickets and deserts without noticing anything remarkable. He passed the night under a tree, on which he hung up the next morning, before starting, a pair of mocassins, so that he might find the place again if he ever wished to return to his sister.

On the evening of the second day he noticed near his camping-ground the stumps of two felled trees. "Ah!" he said to himself, "that is an Indian sign. But," he added, as he gave the stumps a kick, "these blocks are rotten, quite soft, and covered with moss. It must be very long since people were here, and I shall have to go far yet before I find them." The next morning he hung up another pair of mocassins, and continued his journey.

The evening of the third day he found other stumps, less covered with moss, and not so rotten.

In this way he journeyed ten long days, and found at each camping-ground the signs better, the clearings larger, the tree-stumps harder. At length, on the eleventh day, he found trees only just cut down. He was so full of good spirits and anxious expectation, that on the last night he could not close an eye for excitement.

The next day he came upon a little footpath. He followed it—he heard human voices—he saw smoke and lodges from afar, and soon, to his great delight, he was among the inhabitants of a village.

He found them engaged at ball play. And as they seemed pleased at the appearance of the unknown

guest, and found him very agreeable and handsome,
they bade him welcome, and invited him to play at
ball with them.   This he did with the greatest zeal,
and so distinguished himself by activity and quickness,
that he gained the general applause.   After the end of
the game, they led him in triumph to the village and
to a wigwam, before which the " ogima-wateg " (tree
of honour) was erected.   He at once saw that it was
the lodge of the king, and it was a very long house,
full of men.   The Ogima received him very hospitably,
and gave him a seat of honour between his two
daughters.

But the names of the two maidens seemed to the
young man very ominous, and gave him much to think
of.   For one was called Matchi-Kouè (the wicked),
and the other Ochki-Kouè (the good).

He saw at once the meaning of this, and formed an
unfavourable opinion of Matchi-Kouè.   During the
feast he always turned to Ochki-Kouè, and declared
himself ready to marry her.   But the king and the
others made it a special condition that he must marry
both at once.

This did not please him, and he fell into a state of
sorrow.   When the feast was at an end, and the time
for sleeping came, he excused himself for a moment,
and said he wished first to pay a visit to one of the
young men with whom he had played ball.   He seized
his bow and arrows, hung his mirror on his belt, like
a man going to pay a visit, and after assuring the two
maidens he would return directly, he retired from the
palace.

The good and bad princesses sat for a long time
over the fire, awaiting the return of their beloved.
But he came not. At length they grew weary of wait-

ing, thought he might have fled, and set out to seek
him.

At least a dozen footpaths led in various directions
from the village. They followed them all to the point
where they entered the desert, and the trail of every
wanderer could be noticed. At length, after close inspection they came on the fresh trail of their flying
friend, and they followed it with the quickness of the
wind.

Oshige-Wàkon (Otter-heart)—for such was the name
of our hero, I will not conceal it longer—had walked
bravely the whole day, and when he fancied himself in
the evening far enough to rest a little, he suddenly
heard human voices and loud laughter behind him.
The two maidens were rejoicing because they had discovered him. He was frightened, and climbed up the
nearest fir-tree. He clambered up to the top, and
would not listen to the maidens' offer, that he should
come down and go home with them to the wedding.

Ochki-Kouè and Matchi-Kouè were, however, firmly
determined on having him. They had brought their
hatchets with them, and soon set to work cutting down
the tree. They struck as quickly as they had walked,
and the fir soon began to shake. At the last moment
Otter-heart thought of a good way of escape and magic.
He plucked the topmost cone of the fir-tree, threw it
in the air in the direction of the wind, and rode off on
it. The wind carried him half a mile off, and he ran
away again at full speed.

I here interrupted my old story-teller, and asked
her whence Otter-heart had obtained this recipe. She
explained it to the interpreter, who told me, " qu'il
était inspiré par les Manitous, et qu'il avait eu dans

sa jeunesse beaucoup de visions, qui le mettaient en
état de faire de telles choses."

"Bien," I said, "je comprends; c'était un génie.
Continuez."

The tree fell down, and the maidens were much
surprised that their beloved, whom they had not seen
fly away while at work, did not fall with it. They
carefully examined the whole tree to find the direction in which Otter-heart had taken his leap. At
length they saw the little cone was gone from the
top. "Stay," they said, "what is the meaning of
this — a fir cone is missing. Without doubt, he
escaped by its assistance." As they were equally
well inspired by the Manitous, they guessed the
whole affair, and so they set out in pursuit of Otter-
heart in the direction of the wind.

As they had lost some time in examining all the fir
cones, Otter-heart had a good start, and in the evening
of the next day, fancying himself safe, he prepared to
rest. Suddenly he again heard the voices and laughter
behind him: the two mad girls were still pursuing him.
"Oho, Otter-heart!" he heard them say, with a laugh,
"thou imaginest thou canst hide thyself from us.
Give up, give up! The earth is not large enough for
thee to escape from us!"

This time Otter-heart avoided the firs, and chose a
tall, thick, and hollow maple-tree. The wood of this
tree, when dead and exposed for any time to wind
and weather, becomes as hard as stone. "They cannot fell this so easily, their hatchets will break," he
thought to himself, and let himself down from the top
into the cavity.

The two maidens, who had not exactly perceived

which tree the fugitive had chosen, went round and tapped each tree with their hatchets to find out which was hollow, and cried, at the same time, "Thou handsome friend, art thou here?" At length they came to the right tree, and set to work at once to cut it down. But their hatchets made hardly any impression on the tough wood.

Resting from their hard work for a moment the bad squaw said to the good one, " Let us see, sister, if there is not a little split in the tree." They examined it, really found a split, and looked in. On seeing their beloved sitting inside, they set to work more eagerly than ever. They struck away bravely, but Otter-heart silently uttered a wish to the spirits that one of their hatchets might break. And he had scarce wished it than the bad one shrieked, " Woe, woe, sister, my hatchet is broken!" — " Courage courage," the other called to her, " my hatchet is still whole; let us not despair." But Otter-heart now made a second wish that this hatchet might break too, and it really happened.

Now the maidens saw clearly that they could do nothing by force. They, therefore, began praying him again, and cried together, in a friendly voice, " Oshige-Wakon, my handsome husband, whom our father, the mighty Ogima, gave us, come out—come here to me."

But though they sang this so frequently, the young man within did not stir. " It is of no use," the wicked sister whispered to the other, " we shall not get him out in that way; we must think of other arts. We will separate, and each try her best after her own fashion; and as he will only marry one of us, let it be the one who can catch him."

The good maiden was contented, and the sisters

soon separated, and went through the forest in different directions.

When Otter-heart heard that all around was quiet, he looked out of his hollow tree, got down, and continued his journey. He had grown very hungry by this time, and as he discovered a beaver-pond at midday, he determined on spending the night here, and catching a beaver for his supper. He laid his blanket under a tree, which seemed a good place for camping, then set to work piercing the dam and letting the water off. A fine fat beaver remained on the dry ground, and he killed it.

How great was his surprise, though, on returning to his camping-ground, at finding a beautiful birch-bark lodge where he had left his blanket. "Ah!" he thought immediately, "it is those two unlucky squaws again;" and he was about to fly, but he was so tired and hungry, and the lodge looked so comfortable, and the fire sparkled so pleasantly in the gloom! Besides, he was curious to see whether he were not deceived.

He walked round the lodge, and, on looking through a split in the bark covering, he saw only one maiden, engaged in cleaning and adorning the interior.

"Perhaps," he thought, "it is the good Ochki-Kouè." She seemed to him pretty, but very tall, and rather thin and pale. He walked in as a guest, and laid his beaver before the door. "Ah!" the maiden said, "you are surely a traveller. Surely you are tired and hungry. I will prepare your beaver and your bed."

She quickly skinned the animal, cut it in pieces, and prepared his supper. But while stirring the meat in the kettle, she tasted some of it. Otter-heart even noticed that she ate a great deal of it, and greedily looked out the best pieces, as if she could not conquer her evil nature. Hence he nearly lost his appetite, and ate very little. And as he did not find the tidbits which an Indian hunter is wont to look for in his squaw's plate, this put him in a very bad humour. He manfully resisted her hypocritical caresses, wrapped himself in his blanket, and retired to rest in a corner of the lodge, after ordering her to remain in the other.

In the morning, when about to start, there was not the slightest trace of breakfast in the kettle, though it is the regular custom of all good Indian housewives to put a couple of pieces of meat overnight in the kettle, so that the hunter, when he rises early, and goes out to the chase, may refresh himself before starting : his squaw had eaten it all. This made him furious, and he scolded her so violently that she turned pale, her features changed, her long figure sank in, and at last she was converted into a long-haired she-wolf, who sprang out of the lodge with a couple of bounds, and disappeared in the forest, probably to escape the righteous wrath of her angry husband.

When Otter-heart saw this, he could explain everything. It was evidently the bad sister, Matchi-Kouè. She had on the previous evening assumed a changed and attractive form, although, with all her magic art, she could not remove a certain lean pallor. She had caressed and flattered him, but her greedy nature had been more powerful than her love, and induced her to swallow the best pieces of his beaver. And when he attacked her for it, she showed herself in her true form as a wolf. He was no little pleased that he had entered into no closer connexion with her, and he continued his journey in all haste.

In the evening he again rested by a beaver pond, and laid his blanket under a tree, which seemed to him suited for his camp : then he proceeded to kill a beaver. When the water all flowed out, the beavers tried to escape through the hole, but he waited for them and killed three.

How great was his surprise, when, on returning with his booty to the steep bank, he again saw a pleasant lodge built, and a female form moving round the fire. " Ah!" he thought, " who will it be this time ? Perhaps it is Ochki-Kouè, the good one! I will go into the lodge and see where she has laid my blanket: if I find it near her own bed, it is she, and she is intended for my wife." He went in, found everything very clean and neatly arranged, and his blanket lay near the deer-skin she had laid out for herself. " Good!" he muttered to himself, " this is my wife."

She was little, but very pretty and graceful, and she did not move so hurriedly about in the lodge as the squaw of the previous evening, but cautiously and thoughtfully, which pleased him very much. She prepared him a famous supper of the beavers, and placed the best pieces before him. He enjoyed them, and told her to eat with him. " No," she said, modestly, " there is time enough for me: I will eat presently my usual food."

" But, Ochki-Kouè," he said, " I do not like to eat alone what I shot for myself—and my wife."

But she adhered to what she had once said. " I will," she repeated, modestly, " eat, presently, what I am accustomed to take."

He left her at peace, but, during the night a noise aroused him as if mice or beavers were gnawing wood. "Krch, krch, krch!" such was the rustling in the lodge. To his surprise, he fancied he saw, by the glimmer of the fire, his wife gnawing the bark of the little birch twigs with which he had tied up the beavers. He supposed it was only a dream, and slept again till morning. When he awoke, his breakfast was ready, and his little wife stood by his side, and handed it to him.

He told her of his dream, but she did not laugh at it so much as he had expected. "Halloa!" he thought, "was it really no dream, but the truth? Listen, Ochki-Kouè!" he said; "come hither: tell me, yesterday, when I brought thee home the beavers, why didst thou examine them so seriously, and look at every limb closely when thou didst cut them up? Speak, why didst thou this?"

"Oh!" she spoke, sighing, "have I not reason to look on them seriously? I know them all. They are my relations. One was my cousin, the other my aunt, and the third my great-uncle."

"What! thou belongest to the Beaver family?"

"Yes, that is my family."

Who was happier than Otter-heart? For the Otters and the Beavers have ever been related. The character and way of the Beavers pleased him greatly. And then his young wife was so modest and attentive to him; and that she had sacrificed her relations was a striking proof of her love. Still, he promised to respect her well-founded scruples, and, in future, only shoot roebuck, and birds, and other animals, but leave the beavers at rest, so that he and his wife might enjoy their meals in common. And she, for her part,

left the birch-twigs at peace, disturbed him no longer
at night by her nibbling, and accustomed herself to
flesh food.

Thus they lived very agreeably the winter through.
He was a bold hunter, and she a quiet, careful housewife, busy and peaceful, after the manner of the
Beavers. They were a happy pair. When the spring
came, and with it the merry time of sugar-making,
they went out into the sugar camp, and she bore him
a son there. He heard of it on the evening of the
same day on which he returned from the hunt with a
large bear he had shot. At once he made a great
feast, to which he invited all his neighbours, and each
received a chosen piece of the delicate game as a
present.

He regarded it as a very good omen that his son
was born on the same day when he killed so large
a beast in the hunt. And the next day he sat down
and began cutting bow and arrows for the little one.
His wife laughed, and said it would be long before
the child could use bow and arrow. "Thou art
right," he said, and broke up his handiwork. But it
was not long ere he had another bow and arrows
ready. He was so impatient to educate his son as a
distinguished hunter. He pictured to himself how he
would presently go with him to hunt, and how he
would instruct his boy in all things necessary for
hunting, and how he should become a great hunter,
renowned far and wide. He built castles in the air,
one above the other. But how rarely do such fine
dreams meet with accomplishment! How little is
wanting to destroy the most perfect happiness! A
breath of envious fate, the slightest accident, suffice !

Oshige-Wakon and Ochki-Kouè had spent their
fairest days. Fate caught them up on their return

from the sugar camp. As it was now quite spring, and all the streams and fountains full of water, his wife begged Otter-heart to build her a bridge over every river and stream, so that she might cross dry-footed. And he was obliged to promise this solemnly. " For," she said, " if my feet were wetted, this would at once cause thee great sorrow."

Otter-heart did, too, what he promised. At each river, each bubbling fountain, he built a bridge for his squaw. At length, though, he came to a small conduit, which was only six inches broad. Now, he was either tired of the constant bridge-building, or lost in thoughts and pleasant schemes—in short, he crossed the trumpery stream, and did not think of the bridge. But when he had gone on some distance, and his squaw and child did not follow him, he turned back to the streamlet, which he now found, to his terror swollen to a mighty and roaring river. A foreboding of what had occurred struck him like lightning, and he repented, too late, his forgetfulness.

Ochki-Kouè, with her son on her back, had tripped after him with short steps. At the six-inch conduit, which she found unbridged, she stopped, and called her husband to her assistance; but as he did not hear her, in the terror of her heart she ventured the leap. She stepped short, stumbled into the water, and, so soon as her foot was wet, it was all over with her. She was immediately changed into a beaver, and her son into a beaverling, and both swam down to the beaver-dam along the stream, which had now grown mighty.

In despair, Otter-heart, who, as I said, at once guessed what had happened, followed the course of the wild stream, and, after three long and fatiguing days' journey, reached the beaver pond. Here he

saw a "wisch," or beaver house.* He saw his wife
sitting on the roof. She was plaiting a bag of the
bark of the white wood (bois blanc), and had her
beaverling bound to her by a cord of white wood bark.

Otter-heart was out of his mind at the sight. From
the bank he implored her to return to him. But she
replied that she could not do so. "I sacrificed to
thee my relatives and all, and I only asked of thee to
build me bridges and help me dry-footed over the
waters. Thou didst cruelly neglect this. Now, I
must remain for ever with my relations." Her husband begged her, at least, to loosen the white wood
rope, and let him kiss his little son; but this she was
obliged to refuse him. She remained where she was.

And, with this, my old lady's story ended.

" But what became of poor Otter-heart, after all ?"
I asked her, not being fully satisfied. " Did he con-
vert himself into an otter, and live at any rate on the
bank of the same water to which his squaw now belonged ? or did he return to his sister, and seek solace
in his old days by talking of his happiness, that had
melted away with the winter ice ?"

But my old woman would give me no further information. She kept to her text, " the story was
ended." The deserted sister, with whom the story
began, and of whom I reminded her, was forgotten.
And the unhappy Oshige-Wakon remained at the end
unsatisfied, and like a pillar of salt.

Such are the conclusions Indian stories often have;
they pulse for a time like an Æolian harp, and are
then suddenly silent.

---

* Wisch is the pure Ojibbeway orthography and pronunciation of the
word. The French voyageurs have accepted it in their language, and
turned it into " wasch" or " waschi."

CHAPTER IX.

THE drum had been beaten two evenings in succession in a lodge about half a mile from mine, in which a young couple lived. There was a sick and dying child there, which the doctors attended daily. One evening, passing near the wigwam, I could not resist the temptation to peep in, and so lifted one of the loose apakwas. I had chosen the right spot, for I was opposite the doctor and his little patient.

The poor little being lay in its father's arms, who looked remarkably sorrowful and grieved. Before him knelt the doctor, who crawled first up and then back again. He gazed fixedly on the suffering child, and kept his eye fixed on it as on his prey. It was much like a cat playing with a mouse, except that in this case the illness and not the child represented the mouse to be captured.

The doctor's chief instrument was a hollow, very white, and carefully polished bone. This bone, which was about two and a half inches long, and of the thickness of a little finger, the doctor repeatedly swallowed, then brought it up again, blew on the child through it, sucked up the skin through the tube, and then ejected the illness he had drawn out into a basin with many strange and terrible convulsions. All this was accompanied by incessant drumming, rattling, and singing by an assistant of the doctor, and many sighs from the mother of the child. But for all that the poor little thing was hurrying rapidly to the grave.

The next morning, when I arrived at an early hour, and walked into the lodge as a sympathising neighbour, the doctor was no longer present. But the child still lay in its father's lap wrapped in a thick blanket. He held it most tenderly. The mother seemed utterly exhausted by the exertions of the past night, and lay on the ground with her face concealed in skins. All were perfectly still, and took no more notice of me than on the previous evening. The suffering patient was at the last gasp.

On the evening of the same day I again passed, but could not find the lodge. At length I convinced myself, at least, that I had found the right spot. But the hut itself had been utterly removed, the inhabitants had disappeared, the fire extinguished, and all their property carried away. The little being was dead, and already buried, and the mourning parents, after the Ojibbeway fashion, had broken up their lodge, and put out their fire, and gone to live temporarily with some relations.*

* "Les Indiens craignent la mortalité," my Canadians repeatedly said to me. Hence they bury their deceased as soon as possible. They do not

I was guided to the house where they were, and found them sitting very thoughtfully and mournfully among their friends. There were, though, a great many persons present, and extraordinary noise and confusion. Singing and drumming were going on, and they seemed to me like corybantes trying to expel sorrow.

"So it is," my Canadian companion said; "these drummers and singers are 'consolateurs,' whom our Indians engage on such occasions and pay handsomely. Usually they choose a 'vieillard parleur' like our Vieux Espagnol. (This was an old chattering Indian who at times visited us.) "But these consolateurs make no allusion to the event that has occured: ils chantent les chansons les plus récréatives, et racontent des histoires pour leur faire oublier leur chagrin."

Such a consolation lasts a considerable time, for I heard the drums for several evenings while passing the house where my young mourners were residing.

Both among the Ojibbeways and other Indian tribes it is a very general custom to cut off a lock of hair in remembrance of their deceased children, especially those still at the breast, and wrap it up in paper and gay ribbons. Round it they lay the playthings, clothes, and amulets of the little departed. These form a tolerably long and thick parcel, which is fastened up crosswise with strings, and can be carried like a doll.

carry them out of the doorway, but cut a hole in the bark of the lodge and thrust the body out. They fear lest the dead person, by remaining any time among them, might carry off other living beings. Hence they not only pull down the whole house and put out the fire, but are very careful not even to light the new fire in the new house with a spark or sticks from the old one. A new fire and new wood must be taken. Nor do they build the new lodge on the old spot, but choose another place as far from it as possible.

They give this doll a name, signifying "misery" or
"misfortune," and which may be best translated "the
doll of sorrow." This lifeless object takes the place
of the deceased child. The mourning mother carries
it about for a whole year: she places it near her at
the fire, and sighs often enough when gazing on it.
She also takes it on her excursions and travels, like a
living child. The leading idea, so I was told, was,
that the little, helpless, dead creature, as it did not
know how to walk, could not find its way into paradise. The mother could help its soul on the journey
by continually carrying about its representation. This
they bear about till they fancy the spirit of the child
has grown sufficiently to be able to help itself along.

At public festivals these dolls are also presented,
and, at times, presents and sacrificial gifts made to
them. When, for instance, a war-dance is executed,
and the unhappy mother sits weeping with her doll, a
warrior will cut off a lock of hair and throw it on the
doll, "pour faire plaisir à la pauvre mère et à son
enfant."

When the year of grief is ended, a family feast is
prepared, the bundle unfastened, the clothes and
other articles given away, but the lock of hair buried.

I had an opportunity of seeing one of these dolls on
my island, among some Indians from Lake Vermilion.
They had made a foot journey of ten days, and the
mother had dragged the doll along with all her plunder
on her back.

When I first saw it, one of the boys had it in his
arms. He was sitting with it by the fire, and playing
with it, just as he had done with his living sister. After
some time he laid it by his mother's side. I was permitted to inspect it, and found it very carefully and

firmly made. At the head end, some feathers and twigs from the *arbor vitæ* were fastened as ornaments; on the breast was also fastened the spoon with which the dead child used to be fed.

The Indians frequently regard the smaller and greater accidents of life and melancholy events with much philosophy and admirable resignation. This was perceptible in the following instance:

A young man sat down with several others to the game of paguessing. He had placed his loaded gun behind him, and paid no further attention to it. His younger brother, a lad of thirteen, took up the gun and began playing with the hammer. All at once it exploded, and the charge went through his brother's head. The young warrior, adorned with his feathers and paint, lay dead amid the counters.

When his death was found to be certain, a general yell of lament was raised, and all prepared for the burial. Women, men, and children gave way to the most violent grief. The women shrieked and moaned till late in the night, loosened their hair, and poured ashes over their heads. The men blacked their faces, and stuck knives, and needles, and thorns through their skin and flesh, and principally through the fattest parts of the chest and the muscles of the arm.

At the burial an old Indian stepped forth, took his place opposite a great fir-tree, and held a most affecting discourse to the weeping assembly. In this discourse the most curious thing was, that the speaker did not describe the catastrophe directly, but went a roundabout way to work.

The main argument was, that a tall, graceful fir had stood upright, like the one before him. Suddenly, however, by command of the Great Spirit, the lightning struck the fir-tree and levelled it with the ground. Not the slightest allusion was made to the young brother, the innocent cause of the sad accident. So soon as the deed was done, the latter fled, under the influence of terror, into the forest; but his other relatives hurried after him, spoke to him kindly, and brought him back. Not a word of reproach was addressed to him, nor was the affair ever again mentioned in the family, although many a mournful thought might be devoted to the departed.

If two Indians go on a journey, they ask each other a multitude of questions as to the state of health of their respective families. Each relative is mentioned separately, and his present condition described. "How is your wife? What are your children doing —are they all well and fat? Is your old mother in good health?" "No! she is rather unwell." "What is the matter with her?" "She has caught a bad cold, and is down with a fever." "Have you a powerful medicine for that? if not, will you try this? Take some of it." "Well, how is your uncle? and are your aunt's bad feet better?" "Her feet are better, but she has begun to suffer in her eyes." With such questions and answers the whole family is passed in review, and all their sufferings and illnesses closely investigated.

If the Indians generally neglect their old folk, as they are accused of doing, it is, at any rate, not always the case. Lately I saw, in front of a wigwam, great affection displayed towards a very aged woman, who was lame, blind, and half dead, who longed for the sunshine. The way in which the daughters and daughters-in-law prepared her bed in the fine warm sunshine, and then led her carefully out—to notice all this did me good. They told me they had brought their grandmother one hundred and thirty miles in a canoe, because there was no one at home to take care of her.

A well-known writer on the Indians is of opinion that it is not considered exactly honourable and respectable among the Ojibbeways to have several wives. This view my people here contradict point-blank. They assert that, on the contrary, it is considered highly honourable to be in a position to support several wives. The cleverer and more fortunate a hunter is, the more wives does he have. A distinguished and celebrated hunter has no occasion to look after wives—he can scarcely keep them at bay. A man who can support several squaws gains influence; he is regarded as a man of great gifts and powerful character, and parents offer him their daughters. Usually they take their wives from one family—frequently a whole row of sisters.* The first wife, however, always remains at the head of affairs : elle est la régnante. Her place in the lodge is usually by her husband's side. The hunter also entrusts the game he has killed to her for distribution. The several squaws have also their special Indian names; that of the first meaning " la femme de sa droite ;" that of the second, " la suivante;" the third, " la petite femme." They, however, rarely have more than three wives.

When they lose a squaw by death their grief is very deep. They paint the whole face raven black, lay aside their silver or brass armlets, and tie a blackened strip of leather round the arm. A similar strip is worn round the neck instead of the wampum strings. They also

---

* A valuable fact I beg to present to the society for marriage with a deceased wife's sister.—L. W.

cut off their hair, and do not comb it. But in such
cases the sister of the deceased often has compassion
on the mourner, comes into his house to take care of
the children, and usually remains as her sister's successor. The women are not so strict, or, as a Canadian
said to me, so "correct" in their mourning for a deceased husband; and, indeed, among the Indians the
finery and fashions are all on the side of the men.

I had recently an opportunity of noticing a peculiar
specimen of Indian arithmetic.

The people, on arriving from the interior, immediately report themselves to the American agent, in
order to prove their claims to a share in the payment
of tribute. The agent, with his clerks, sits in a room,
or barn, and another tribe is called forward every day.
Before beginning, he assembles round him the chiefs
and aldermen, who are acquainted with the family
circumstances, number of wives and children belonging to each member, and can verify their statements.

The tribute is mainly paid per head. Children,
wives, and men are all equally privileged; and so the
more children and wives a man has, the more payment
does he receive. According to the letter of the law,
every claimant should appear in person, and hence the
majority come in with their whole families. Still it is
impossible to carry out this law strictly, and there
always are plenty of old people, and sick, who cannot
undertake the journey. In many districts the women
are engaged with the rice harvest, or some other important affair at the time of the payment, and if they
had to be absent for weeks, their housekeeping might
fall into disorder. Hence excuses are not looked into
too closely, and many heads of families are allowed to
receive the entire sum for their members, after the lists

have been confirmed by the chiefs. Those, too, who
live a great distance off are dispensed from appearing
personally.

If the turn has arrived of a tribe whose members have
not all come in yet, the statistics are temporarily com-
piled from the memory of the elders. It is most interesting to see what good memories they have. They
possess no other registers and parish books than those
they carry in their heads, and yet they always know
exactly who of the tribe has had a child born, who
has taken a second or third squaw, or if a girl has
married into another tribe, and the reason for doing
so. They can also state whether a man is a half-breed,
in what degree he is related to the tribe, and how far
he has a claim to share in the tribute.

Any man who has an opportunity to be present at
such discussions as these about every family and its
members, can take many a glance at the internal life
of these races, and hear many a curious history.

A man who came from the heart of Wisconsin, and
was unable to bring his family along with him, brought
in their stead a little bundle of wooden pegs into the
registration office. When his name was called, and
he was questioned as to the size of his family, he laid
the bundle on the table, and said these were all his
people—they could count them. The pegs were very
neatly cut, and fastened together with a scarlet thread
of wool. There were two larger ones for his squaws
and seven smaller for his children, each peg being
longer, according to the height of the child intended.
He produced the bundle from a cloth, in which he had
carefully carried it on his long journey from home.
The members of the family, it was plain, had sat to
him, and had their portraits taken.

In the Indians' eyes this was a perfectly valid document, and far more certain than if he had merely written the number of his people on a piece of paper, or given the number *vivâ voce*.

During the payment of the tribute-money, I also noticed many peculiar and characteristic scenes, which, were I to describe them all, would fill a chapter.

It is very interesting to see the poor men and women, when summoned, walk up to the pay-table, and to watch how each receives the money.

One comes with a furry bag to receive the silver stream, another has only a piece of cloth, while a poor widow has but her apron, in which she knots it up. When a handful of shining coin fell in, she thought it was enough, and was going to fasten it up. " Stop," said the paymaster, " here's more." And he shook in another couple of handfuls, over which she was lost in amazement.

Of course the Indians never attempt to count the money ; they trust entirely to the Indian paymasters, and very often are ignorant of the relative value of the large and small coins thrust over to them in piles. They sign the receipt perfectly *bonâ fide*.

The mode of receipting is the most laconic I ever saw. As none of the Indians can write, the American secretary inscribes their name for them. Still they are obliged to touch the pen while the secretary writes, or a slight touch before he begins writing suffices. Many even cannot do this quick enough, so the clerk hits them over the knuckles with the pen. But they must always come into some contact with the pen, so that the matter may be stamped on the Indian's memory.*

* In Norway there is an equally laconic mode of payment, I may remind Mr. Kohl. When a peasant takes his wood into the crown yards, an

As, unhappily, there is no lack of dram-shops in our little village, some of the Indians came up to the pay-table in a state most unfavourable for the settlement of money matters. I noticed an Indian woman who had a drop too much, and rent the air with her disgusting shrieks. She was accompanied by her daughter, a child of twelve years of age, who observed her mother's condition with the greatest apprehension and sorrow. The girl had put the money her mother had received into her mouth, in order to have her hands free to support the staggering woman. As it was time to proceed to the other offices, where implements, food, and other matters were given to the Indians, she was trying to drag her mother there. At last, as she could not manage her, the little one left her drunken mother on a stone, and ran crying to the officials, and received the share intended for her family. I was delighted to see that her claim was allowed, and she came back to her now sleeping mother with as many things as she could carry. She then sat down quietly by her side, and waited for her to awake.

There were many comical scenes at the distribution among the Indians of the tools, provisions, and clothing. They received new beaver hats, blue coats with brass buttons, and very handy grey caps. They put on everything at once, and in a short time the whole assembly was metamorphosed. Many wrapped the fox and skunk tails they had hitherto worn on their heads round their hats, while some who received a cap as well as a hat put them both on at once in a

official writes on his back in chalk how much he is to receive. As he goes out again, another official pays him the sum, and gives him a smart rap on the back, which effectually settles the bill.—L. W.

very ridiculous fashion. One man who did not understand the use of the caps, or, perhaps, did not desire
anything on his head, filled it with tobacco, and hung
it to his waist-belt. In another case the mark or
address of the American manufacturer was left by
mistake on a coat. The recipient fancied this gilt
mark was a portion of his coat. He would not, on
any consideration, have it taken off, and I saw him
walking about for several days proud of this mark of
distinction, till the rain washed it away.

CHAPTER X.

INDIAN GEOGRAPHY—ASTRONOMY—THE POLAR STAR—A NATURAL CLOCK—
THE MONTHS—INDIAN TRAVELLERS—RUNNING—HUNTING DOWN GAME—
THE OLD MAN OF THE SKY—A BEAR BAFFLED—FEMALE RUNNERS—THE
MAID'S REVENGE—A FRESH SCALP—INDIAN TRADERS—THE FUR TRADE—
HINTS ON ETIQUETTE—STOICISM—JEWISH DESCENT OF THE INDIANS—
THE SHELL TRADE—WAMPUM FACTORIES—INDIAN KNOWLEDGE OF THE
OCEAN—CURIOUS TRADITION.

ANY map of the United States will show us that
the districts round about Lake Superior have the
names of Wisconsin, Michigan, &c. Here, however,
in the country itself, Canadians and Indians employ
very different names. I will mention some of them
to make my readers better acquainted with my Indian
locality.

The north shore of the lake is usually called here
"l'autre bord," in Indian, Agamkitchigamig; the country
to the south of the lake is called by the Canadians
"le pays de la folle avoine," in Indian, Manominikan,
or Manomin (the wild rice). This plant is very prevalent in the southern part of the lake.

The French Canadians often call these southern
lands, shortly, "les terres folles," and I frequently
heard them say, "In les terres folles, so-and-so is

done." At times, too, they will call the country "la folle avoine," as, "Je veux hiverner à la folle avoine."

In the same way they call the land where the Ottawa Indians live, or the upper peninsula of Michigan, "chez les Courtes Oreilles," for that is the Canadian name of those Indians.

The lands to the west, near the sources of the Mississippi, are usually called here "les bois forts." The name is the same in Indian, and the Indian name of the tribes living there may be translated "forest-men."

I took great trouble to discover a primeval Ojibbeway name for the river St. Lawrence, or the whole of the water system, but I could not find anything of the sort. At present—and for many years back, probably —the Indians call it the Montreal river, as the Canadians say, "la rivière de Montreal." As the Ojibbeways cannot pronounce the letter "r," this word is corrupted into Moneang, and the St. Lawrence is known among them as the "Moneangssebi." The broad St. Mary's River, running from the south of Lake Superior, they call "Kitchi Gami Ssebi," or the river of the great lake.

The Ojibbeways have paid some attention to the heavens. They all know the polar star, have noticed its fixedness, and call it "Giwe danang," or the star of the north. A much-travelled Voyageur assured me that even the most savage Indians know the star by this name.

In the same way they all know the morning star, which they call "Wabanang." I often sat with them before my hut, and they pointed out to me the planets they knew. They showed me the following: the "Bear's-head" (Makosh-tigwan), the "Bear's-cross"

(Mako-jigan), and the "three travelling kings" (Ada-womog). Unfortunately, I am not able to say which of our constellations these signify, for the Indians seemed to form theirs of different stars from ours.

The Pleiades they called Madodisson, or the "sweating stones." In their vapour-baths they employ red-hot stones arranged in a circle nearly in the shape of the Pleiades.

Not far from the polar star they showed me three stars, which they called Noadji-manguet, or the "man who walks behind the loon-bird."

They have also various expressions for the phases of the moon, or, as they term it, the night sun. The full moon they call the round night sun, and they employ phrases similar to ours to express the crescent and decrescent moon. They have also special terms for a halo, double suns, and other apparitions in the sky, which proves that they have paid considerable attention to the firmament.

Nearly every at all intelligent Indian can throughout the year tell the time of day, when the sun will cross the meridian, and mid-day. For the other hours they have expressions like this: "It is half-way to mid-day," or, "It is now one half from mid-day to sunset."

But they tell the time even better at night if the stars are bright. They appoint the time for a nocturnal foray most accurately, and they will arrange to meet after the declension of this or that planet, or when that star is at such or such a point.

Like all nations in the world they regulate the greater division of the years and the months by the movements of the sun and moon.

I have heard the Ojibbeways speak of the moon, where they throw off vice (la lune, où ils rejettent le vice). The first time persons, especially young men, see the moon in February, they say: " Je rejette ma mauvaise manière de vivre." This was, unluckily, all I could learn on this interesting subject. Many assured me the commencement of the year was typified by this.

They also divide the year into twelve moons, and have their regular names for them. It is hence probable that this division is very ancient among them, for they add every now and then a thirteenth nameless moon in order to get right with the sun again.

Among the Ojibbeways on Lake Superior the months have the following names:

JANUARY—The moon of the spirits.

FEBRUARY—The moon of the suckers, because those fish begin going up the rivers then.

MARCH—The moon of the snow-crust, because then the sun covers the top of the snow with a firm crust, and it is a good time to travel.

APRIL—The moon for breaking the snow-shoes, because then the snow disappears and the snow-shoes are often broken.

MAY—The flower moon.

JUNE—Strawberry moon.

JULY—Raspberry moon.

AUGUST—Whortleberry moon.

SEPTEMBER—The moon of the wild rice.

OCTOBER—The moon of the falling leaf.

NOVEMBER—The freezing moon.

DECEMBER—The moon of little spirits.

I grant that all the Indians cannot divide the months with equal correctness; and it is often comical to listen to the old men disputing as to what moon they are in.

The title "odgidjida" (a brave, or hero) is to the Indians the highest on earth. In order to gain it, they will run to the end of the world.

War and murder expeditions are not the sole means of attaining this predicate. Many Indians have employed other ways; among them, the accomplishment of long and dangerous journeys, to which curiosity, as well as thirst for glory and distinction, often incites them.

We find curious Indian travellers, who came a great distance, mentioned in the first European reports about Indians. The Choctas preserve the memory of a celebrated traveller of their tribe, who undertook a long journey to the west, in order to find the sea in which the sun disappeared on setting.

Similar traditions about great journeys and travellers are found among other tribes. I was told here of an Indian who had come all the way from the Rocky Mountains (one of the northern spurs) and appeared on Lake Superior. He spoke a language resembling the Ojibbeway, examined very curiously everything here, and then returned home.

But the appearance of a young Sioux, who came to the lake a few years back, caused even greater excitement than that traveller. He was the son of a Sioux chief, who, greedy for distinction and also curious to see how the Ojibbeways, the arch-foes of his tribe, lived, determined on making a friendly tour through their country. He travelled alone, only armed with his gun, from one Ojibbeway village to another, round the lake. They were astonished at his bravery; and though many assembled and said they must kill this enemy of their blood, others interposed and took charge of him, praising his boldness, and saying it

ought to be respected.   Such views as these gained
the day, and the young Sioux manœuvred so cleverly,
that he lived a whole winter among the Ojibbeways
unassailed.

When spring came, " au temps des sucres," as the
Canadians say, he started home again, and the Ojibbeways took leave of him with marks of honour.

Canadian Voyageurs assured me they had found such
travelling and adventurous Ojibbeways also among the
Sioux.   The matter is in so far interesting, as it
serves to explain to us how we Europeans, on our first
entry into the New World, found geographical knowledge of remote regions so prevalent among the natives
—for instance, the existence of the ocean known to
Indians living far in the interior.

I often had an opportunity of noticing that the
Indians value speed of foot as highly among their
people as the Greeks did in their Achilles, and that
they can cover an extraordinary space of ground by
their persistent and steady trot.

Many remarkable performances of the Indian runners, whom the fur companies employed as postmen,
are generally known; but here I learned much new
and interesting matter on this point.

As the sparse population of the country is scattered
over wide distances, cases frequently occur in which a
swift runner can save a family from destruction; and
this is a sufficient reason why the savages honour him
as greatly as a bold hunter or warrior.

Before they possessed horses, speed of foot must have
been even more highly prized.   As they were compelled to hunt all their game on foot, what is called
"running down the game" was quite ordinary; and
even now they perform it at times.   They frequently

do so, for instance, with the elk, especially in winter, when that animal has difficulty in getting over the snow, and breaks through, while the Indian easily glides over it on his snow-shoes.

A hunter residing here told me the following anecdote about running down an elk. He had been running for half a day behind an elk, and several times he had nearly caught it. But, he said, he did not wish to kill it, in order to save the trouble of dragging it home. Hence he sat down several times at some distance from the exhausted brute, gave it time to collect its strength, and regained his own wind also. After a few minutes he would begin his extraordinary chase again, and arranged it so, that the brute was driven nearer and nearer to his hut. At nightfall he had it near enough to his camp, so he went up, drew his knife, and killed it.

I at first thought this a rodomontade dressed up *à la chasseur*, till I heard other similar stories of driving wild beasts home. The most remarkable and best described I found in an American journal, *The Friend of Dakota*, and as it confirms my own notes, I will repeat it here:

A Sioux Indian, called the Man of the Sky, seated himself, on returning from a day of unsuccessful hunting, on a mound at the edge of a flat prairie to smoke a pipe. (The Indians always prefer an elevation to rest and smoke, when the weather permits it, and their summer paths usually run over the highest ground, where they sit down now and then and observe the country.)

While Master Skyman was sitting there, smoking, looking about, and thinking, his watchful eye suddenly fell on a black bear, which was trotting very com-

fortably straight up to his hillock. A young Indian
who can boast of having "run down" a bear is as
proud of it as an English boxer of a victory; and Skyman, who had long desired an opportunity for distinguishing himself in this way, now thought that the
time had arrived. If he had merely cared about
killing the bear, he could have concealed himself and
shot it from an ambush, but any one could do that
who knew how to pull a trigger. Hence he decided
on having a bold race with Master Bruin. The blood
began to course through his veins as he silently removed all his clothes and other encumbrances, and
laid them on one side, with the exception of his mocassins, pipe, and rifle. The bear came up, and Skyman
rose: at the sight of his enemy, Bruin made a bolt to
the side, and was soon a long distance ahead. But his
increased speed was only momentary. After a while
his movements grew slower, and the Indian felt his
courage increase the more the distance between them
decreased. When he drew close up to the waddling
bear, the latter did his best to get away, but he gave
in more quickly this time, and in a few moments the
long, steady trot of the Indian brought him once more
alongside his victim.

By constant repetition of the same experiments, the
extraordinary exertions and sudden spurts of the bear
grew weaker, and the hunter saw plainly that the
animal was beginning to "sweat"—the term the
Indians apply to any one who grows tired. But at the
same time he noticed, to his alarm, that the wide, flat
prairie was giving out, and that a thick wood and
scrub was close at hand. The matter must be decided
at once. Bruin put out his best speed in order to reach
the scrub in a straight line, and if he were successful

the chase would be over, for he would soon find a hollow tree, or a "renversi," impenetrable by any but a quadruped. Skyman could have easily stopped the animal by a shot, but that he did not wish, as he would thus lose the renown of running a bear down. He put forth his utmost strength, managed to head the bear before reaching the scrub, and drove him back into the open prairie.

For a minute he stopped, took a long, deep breath, and then said, "And now, my black friend, show thy mettle. Two legs against four! thou must now sweat, or I, before we part." Both now coursed over the prairie like two race-horses. But it was soon evident that Bruin would have to beg quarter before long, for his hesitating zig-zag course gave the hunter a decided superiority. The race was as good as over; Bruin was lame and beaten, his opponent hearty and active. He could almost clutch the animal's wool; hence he now raised his rifle and took the poor hunted beast's life. After enjoying a comforting pipe, he threw the shaggy carcase over his shoulder and carried it to the neighbouring village, where the most delicate parts were eaten at a festival, and the usual religious rites paid to the spirit of the bear.

Old Man of the Sky, who was, at the time this story was written in the above-mentioned American journal, seventy years of age, often told this running story of his youthful years with great gusto.

Even the Indian girls dream at times that they will become mighty runners, and evince a pride in excelling in this art, like the men. A case occurred during my stay at La Pointe. A warlike maiden suddenly appeared, who boasted of having taken a Sioux scalp, and she was led in triumph from lodge to lodge. I

was told that a supernatural female had appeared to
this girl, who was now nineteen, during the period of
her great fasts and dreams of life, who prophesied to
her that she would become the greatest runner of her
tribe, and thus gain the mightiest warrior for husband.
I must remark here, as indeed every reader will easily
conjecture, that the fasting dreams of the Indian girls
chiefly allude to the subject of marriage.   Thrice—so
said the prophetic voice—she would join in an expedition against the Sioux, and thrice save herself victo-
riously by her speed of foot.   In running home the
warriors of her tribe would try to outstrip her, but she
would, in the two first campaigns, beat everybody.
(Notice here that, even on the return from the field,
speed of foot is considered an honour among the
Indians.)   On the return from the third campaign,
however, a young Ojibbeway would race with her, and
conquer her, and she would then be married to him.

The girl had made her first war expedition this
year.   She had proceeded with the warriors of her
tribe into the enemy's camp, raised the scalp of a
wounded Sioux on the battle-field, and had run
straight home for several days, thus bringing the first
news of the victory, which greatly augmented her
renown.

At La Pointe she walked in procession through the
village, the scalp being borne before her as a banner.
She was pointed out to everybody as the heroine of
the day and of the island, and probably long ere this
some young warrior has run a race with her, in which
she was only too ready to be defeated.

It is, by the way, no rarity here for the women and
girls to take part in the employments of the men, and
even in their wars.   That the " mulier taceat in ec-

clesiâ" is not so strictly observed, as, for instance, among the Jews, I showed while describing the great medicine dance. The women become full members of the Midé order, dance with the men in the temples, sing with them, have like them the mysterious bag, and perform miracles. There have also been celebrated prophetesses and enchantresses among the Indians. The women also take a certain part in the war dances by accompanying them with singing. One of the strangest warlike exploits of an Indian girl was told me here.

A poor woman lived a miserable life with her children and her sickly husband. Her only hope was in her eldest son, a lad who had already begun to go hunting for his mother and relatives, and was becoming the head of the family and bread-gainer.

Hence it was a crushing blow to these poor people when this hopeful youth was attacked on a distant hunting expedition by treacherous Sioux, murdered, and scalped. The whole family fell into a state of melancholy, and blackened their faces: they were utterly helpless, but, before all, thirsted for revenge. The poor sickly father sang, the life-long day, mourning songs for his murdered son, and complained of his own impotent condition, which prevented him from going on the war-trail, and taking vengeance on the enemies of his tribe and family. He was nearly alone in the world, and had but few relations who would take compassion on him. There was nought in his house but mourning, grief, and a vain cry for vengeance.

At length the grown-up daughter, a girl of seventeen, began to beat the war-drum, mutter wild songs, and question destiny, or, as they term it, "dream."

She had a dream, in which it was revealed to her that the only method by which to obtain consolation and cheerfulness—that is, revenge—for her family, was by sacrificing her own lover.

This beloved of her heart was a youth of the Sioux tribe, whose acquaintance she had formed in happier and more peaceful times, and whom she loved fervently, in spite of the blood-feud between the two tribes. They had often met in secret, and were enabled to do so with ease as their villages lay on the frontier of the two hunting-grounds. He belonged to the band which had murdered her brother, and as the revengeful girl did not know how to get hold of any other warrior, she determined to act in obedience to her dream, and choose her beloved as the victim. These Indians regard their enemies as responsible *en masse* for the excesses committed, and their revenge is hence satiated when it falls on one of the relatives of the culprit.

The girl marched across mountain and forest to the neighbouring territory of the Sioux. In the night she made her way into their encampment, and crept up noiselessly and unnoticed to her lover's lodge. She gave him a love-signal, whispered to him through the cracks of the airy branch-hut, and invited him to come out. The young man, filled with longing, went into the forest with the maiden of his heart to spend an hour in converse sweet. While in her embraces, she was suddenly converted into the angel of death; she thrust a knife through his heart, scalped him, and hurried home, where she was regarded as a benefactress of her family and a great heroine.

A report spread that a fresh Buanich-Tigwan (a

Sioux scalp) had arrived on the island, and as I
wished to see it, I set out in search.

Some Ojibbeways had a fight a few hundred miles
off in the interior, and raised the hair of a Sioux.
They had decorated it in the traditional manner,
and handed it to some acquaintances who were
going to La Pointe, so that they might show it to
the collected relatives and friends of the fortunate
heroes.

We asked the people we met where the scalp might
be. They showed us a lodge in which it had been,
to their knowledge, during the morning; but when
we asked after it there, it was gone. They directed
us to another outlying lodge, whither they had
carried it. But there, too, it had gone away again;
and it was not till evening, and after a long search,
that we found it.

A boy, seated with several other persons of various
ages round the fire, was holding it on a long stick.
On looking more closely at the disgusting object, I
was surprised that it did not appear so repugnant as
I had imagined. The scalp was carefully extended
on a wooden ring, and so copiously adorned with
feathers, gay ribbons, tinkling bells, fox and other
tails, that the bloody skin and hair were nearly entirely covered. The boy held it in his arms, as little
girls do a doll, while the grown-up people were discussing the events of the war and the mode of capture. The trophy was fetched during our presence
by other parties, who also wished to enjoy the happiness of fondling it for a while at their fire, and listen
to the accurate account of the foray.

Among the men collected here, and with whom I
principally associate, I have already alluded to the

Indian traders.   They form one of the most important classes among the persons who live on an intimate footing with the Indians.   They are far more highly educated than the trappers and Voyageurs, and even form a better judgment of the Indian character than the missionaries do; and as I learned much interesting matter from them about the aborigines, I shall often have occasion to allude to them.

Many of these traders have carried on the fur trade for generations, and thus acquired great influence over several tribes.   The terms on which they stand to the Indians resemble those of master and men among us.   The Indian trader is generally a capitalist, at whose expense, or on whose advances, the Indian hunter lives.   He provides the latter with guns, powder, provisions, and articles of various descriptions, with which he debits him.   Well equipped, and tolerably free from care as to the support of his family, the debtor goes off hunting, frequently for many hundred miles into the prairies and forests. Once a year he has a meeting with the trader, to deliver his skins, pay his debts, and obtain fresh advances.

At times the traders will make a commercial treaty with the chiefs, and thus enter into a debtor and creditor account with an entire village or tribe. Hence they frequently acquire great political influence, and, as they risk very considerable sums, it may be conjectured that a trader can only be successful through caution and the exercise of tact.   I have been told, and have indeed remarked it, that association and difficult negotiations with the Indians have produced famous diplomatists among these traders, who carry on the " ars rerum gerendarum" with great cleverness and tact, and can form an excellent judgment of the character of these savages.

For instance, a friend of mine, a missionary, who had gained much experience during his intercourse with the Indians, showed me once a small code of rules for dealing with them, drawn up by a trader in French. I translated this interesting document, and will quote it here, as being equally characteristic of the Indians and their employers. The principles and views of this diplomatic fur dealer were as follow:

1. Respect everything in their customs which deserves respect, for there are here and there very excellent things among all of them.

2. Always praise whatever really deserves praise: for the savage is as accessible to flattery as are other men.

3. In your presents to them take into consideration their tastes and wants. Only give where there is a chance of a return, and never squander your presents.

4. If you wish to introduce a custom among them point-blank opposed to their habits, wait till they begin to see the necessity of it, and gain sufficient strength and inclination to accept the innovation. Never employ direct pressure, for you will meet with opposition; but smoothe the road and remove obstacles.

5. If you are anxious to abolish any religious or superstitious practices, always prepare them for it by instruction harmonising with their views.

6. If you lower their great men, chiefs, and priests, as regards their powers in Indian magic arts, always offer them a compensation in the increased personal respect you pay them.

7. Do not trouble yourself much about the crowd, but apply yourself to several influential and prominent men. Obtain, through the mediation of the chiefs, all that you can. Let them decide on the arrangements, and make the speeches. This flatters their vanity; and even the greatest men still believe that by holding a speech they not only net honour, but also obtain profit.

8. Any present of value you may make to a chief, exercises more influence than a hundred small gifts which you waste on the lower classes. The savage measures the kindness and value of a man according to his generosity, which, again, he measures by the size of the presents. In addition, public opinion entirely depends on the views of the chiefs. A chief is either better educated, or braver, or more liberal than the others.

9. When a savage accompanies you, does you a service, or works for you, be careful, above all things, that he be so fed and treated as he wishes or requires. You give him tenfold the value of the food by offering it when he needs it, and is hungry. And if you give him anything he dislikes, you only render him dissatisfied.

10. Never defer your payments or your rewards. Among savages, " a bird in the hand is always worth two in the bush."

11. Never ask of an Indian any humiliating service. But if you have any honourable commission for him, apply to him, and he will serve you faithfully. Never suffer him to eat with you as your equal, and, as a general rule, play the great man with the natives. They also wish to appear as great gentlemen. Whatever bargain you may close with them, always add a small present of your own accord, as a sign of your satisfaction and a proof of your generosity.

12. Never try to gain anything by force, but all through persuasion, reasoning, and presents.

13. Never promise them anything you are not quite certain of fulfilling. Never deceive, delude, or lead them astray; and, as far as is possible, make sure you are never mistaken. Breaking a promise is regarded by the Indians in the same light as a lie. And if you once appear to them a liar, mutual confidence is irrevocably lost.

14. They most esteem truth and kindness of heart. But just as they cannot comprehend the latter quality, unless allied with generosity, so truth cannot exist without a decided and sure judgment.

15. If you say to one of them "I love thee," have a present ready to hand, to prove your love clearly. You will lose in their sight if a present, or some tangible politeness, does not follow on such an assurance. But it is often sufficient to hand them the plate from which you have been eating, and on which you have left a fragment for them.

I fancied I recognised in these lines a Machiavelli discoursing on diplomatic intercourse with mankind. Still, I was surprised at not finding in this excellent code a rule which I have often heard praised as being of the highest value:

"Be always patient and equanimous with the Indians. Display no anger, or violent and passionate gestures. Never be prone to notice insults, for if you do so you are soon ruined in their estimation."

They say of a calm and patient man, "he is brave; he has a strong and sound heart." But if you passionately take up an insult, or say, for instance, violently, "That is not true," the Indians will immediately whisper to each other, "There is no danger with that man." "Nil admirari" is another great

principle with them.   Even though the admiration be
directed to themselves, and flatter their vanity, they
are but little pleased with a man who possesses to an
extreme degree the organ of enthusiasm.   I recently
saw here a hunter who had returned from the hunting-grounds in the upper peninsula with an extraordinary quantity of game.   In six weeks he had killed
to his own gun no less than fifty-five deer.   I exclaimed, "Thou art a distinguished hunter," and then
asked him how many shots he had missed.   He told me
he had expended sixty bullets on the fifty-five deer.
I made him a special compliment on his skill, and
called him a Nimrod; but he hardly listened to me,
made no reply, and seemed, in fact, to despise my
enthusiastic applause.

It is very curious that I meet so many persons here
still adhering to the belief in the Jewish descent of
the Indians, not merely among the American clergy,
but also among the traders and agents.   Many cannot
be persuaded out of this curious idea, though it seems
to me to be more deeply-rooted among the Anglo-
Saxon Protestants than the French Catholics.   Perhaps
this arises from the fact that the former employ themselves so much more in reading the Old Testament,
the history of the Jews, and, above all, the final fate
of the lost ten tribes.   The latter they insist on finding here in America, and detect all sorts of Jewish
customs among the Indians, which are, in truth, no
more than the resemblances they bear to all other
peoples that live in a similar nomadic state.   A trader
recently told me that there was a passage in Isaiah in
which America is clearly alluded to and pointed out
as the refuge for the expulsed Jews.   The passage, he
said, was : "O thou land, shadowed with wings like
an eagle !" which he interpreted much in this way:

" Oh. thou land, that casteth the shadow of thy wings far like an eagle!" By these wings, he said, the prophet typified North and South America, which are fastened together in the centre like eagles' wings. He also wished clearly to indicate that the Jews would emigrate to this fair country. I confess I could not find this passage in the English Bible, but, on the contrary, one that denounced " woe to the land shadowing with wings." (Isaiah xviii. v. 1.) But my trader's opinion, as well as several others I could add, show what interpretation the people here like to give of the Biblical prophecies.

The traders tell me wonderful stories about the trade in shells which was formerly carried on with the Indians, and the high value the savages placed on them. If the traders brought a large handsome periwinkle and held it to the Indians' ears, the latter were astounded, and said they could hear the sea beating in it, and would pay, for such a miraculous shell, peltry to the value of forty or fifty dollars. There were also varieties of shells which they held in special repute: thus there was a long shell of the size of a finger, which in the Indian trade was worth more than its weight in silver.

Now-a-days this has ceased, and the Indians will not pay so much for a single shell. Still, they are held in high respect even in the present day, and I have already alluded to the small shells which play so great a part in all the religious ceremonies not only of the Ojibbeways but of the Sioux residing in the interior.

The most valued ornament they have, what is known by the name of " wampum," is also made of shells. It consists of small pieces of tubing carved or turned out of certain shells. There are said to be several factories in Jersey city, near New York, where wampum shells are prepared for the Indians principally by German workmen. There is a variety of bluish or grey wampum exclusively employed for ornaments. Influential and respected chiefs, or jossa-kids, wear at times heavy masses of these shells round the neck. The strings of white shells are chiefly used in peace negotiations, and by holding one end of the chain and giving the other to the adversary, they typify that the future intercourse between them shall be as smooth, white, and regular as this wampum necklace. All these shells have been found since the earliest period among the Indians. The Europeans did not introduce them, but merely followed a trade which had existed for years among the Indians. We find no Indian tribe, however deep it might dwell in the interior, of which the first Europeans do not mention their high respect for sea-shells. There is no doubt, I think, that historic reminiscences are connected with this shell worship—recollections of that great water from which the ancestors of the Indians and the founders of their religion probably stepped on shore. These Indians appear to have been as well acquainted with the fact that America was surrounded by an ocean, as the Greeks were in their small country. For instance, it is very customary among the Ojibbe-ways to call America an island, and it seems that this idea was not imported by the Europeans. Among the Choctaws and other Mississippi tribes the fable is prevalent, that once a youth felt a longing to see the water into which the sun dips at setting, and that he consequently took a fatiguing journey that lasted a year, wandering from tribe to tribe towards the west until he discovered the Pacific Ocean.

CHAPTER XI.

THE LANGUAGE OF SIGNS—SYMBOLIC WRITING—SPECIMENS OF SIGNS—THE NOMADIC AND SETTLED TRIBES—UNIVERSALITY OF SIGNS—A GRAMMAR OF SIGNS—ADMIRATION—ORIGIN OF PICTURE-WRITING—THE ENGLISH ALPHA-BET—TENTS AND BLANKETS—HIEROGLYPHICS—BIRCH-BARK BOOKS—LOON-FOOT—A FAMILY TREE—ANTIQUITY OF THE CRANES—THE MEDICINE LODGE—THE PATH OF LIFE—A SONG OF THE SEASONS—AN INDIAN TOMB-STONE—FOOD FOR THE DEAD—A COUPLE OF PILLAGERS—TOBACCO AT A DISCOUNT—VALUE OF BIRCH-BARK BOOKS—A TRIAL OF GENEROSITY.

ONE of the most interesting subjects to which an ethnographer travelling among the Indians can direct his attention, is undoubtedly the language of signs and symbolic writing so extended through these tribes. I may say with Shakspeare,

I cannot too much muse
Such shapes, such gesture, and such sound expression
(Although they want the use of tongue), a kind
Of excellent dumb discourse.

This matter is connected with so many other re-markable questions, that I should have to write a comprehensive work if I wished to exhaust it. I will confine myself, then, to explaining clearly and fully my own little stock of knowledge on the subject ac-quired among the Ojibbeways.

The commencement of the symbolic writing must

probably be sought in the language of signs. The
Indians first represented their meaning with fingers
and hands, adopted in conversation certain repeated
signs and gestures, and then tried to imitate these and
give them a permanent character by marks on the
birch bark (their paper).

I will, therefore, begin with the sign-language, but
only make a few remarks, as it is not so much practised among the inhabitants on Lake Superior as
among the wandering tribes of the prairies further to
the west. The Ojibbeways living on their lake as fishermen and forest hunters do not come so often into contact with strange races and languages as the western
nomadic and buffalo hunters, who traverse enormous
districts. Among the former the sign-language is,
therefore, less cultivated than among the latter, who
can make themselves understood by means of it everywhere.

Still, among the Ojibbeways, and then among the
Sioux on St. Peter's River, I had opportunity for ad-
miring the natural, thoughtful, and symbolic mimic
with which these Indians accompany their conversation. Even among persons of the same tribe this
language is employed, either to save their lazy tongues,
or to heighten by gestures the effect produced by their
words.

Although the Indians do not use very animated
gesticulations, these are very natural, characteristic,
and easy of comprehension.

When speaking, for instance, of the Great Spirit,
they usually direct a reverential or timid glance upwards, or point the forefinger perpendicularly but
gently to the sky.

When alluding to the sun or to the time, which is

much the same thing, as the sun is their clock, and indicating the spot at which the sun stood when the event to which they are alluding occurred, they point fixedly to that point, and hold their arm in that position for several moments.

When speaking of a day, they pass the finger slowly along the entire vault of heaven, commencing at the east, and terminating in the west. This is the sign for "one day."

If a shot has to be mentioned in the story, they usually strike the palm of the left hand with the back of the right, so as to produce a slight sound.

If describing a journey on horseback, the two first fingers of the right are placed astride of the forefinger of the left hand, and both represent the galloping movements of a horse. If it is a foot journey, they wave the two fingers several times through the air.

In counting, the ten fingers are naturally used, and the number is not only held up, but mentioned.

In this manner, and by many hundred similar gestures, they supplement and support their oral remarks. And it will be seen, from the gestures I have described, that the tongue can be frequently allowed a rest, and the meaning perfectly conveyed by the signs.

Suppose an Indian wished to tell another that he had ridden for three days over the prairie, he first points to his own worthy person. That will indicate " I." Then he sets his fingers a galloping as I have described. This perfects the idea: "I travelled on horseback." Next he passes his hand once athwart the sky, which furnishes the notion of " day;" and finally holds up three fingers before his friend's eyes, to show he spent " three" days.

It is a curious fact that, though Indian dialects differ

so greatly, this language of signs is the same for enormous distances. All travellers who had crossed the prairies told me that there was only *one* sign-language, which all the Indians comprehended, and any one who had learned it could travel with it from one end of America to the other.

For such signs as those of which I have given specimens, such as the sun, a day, a number, a horseman, &c., when nothing better or more natural could be chosen, this is easily to be understood. But the sign-language developed itself to a fuller extent, and undertook a visible representation of abstract ideas. Hence much must naturally become conventional. Thus, for instance, if desirous to express the idea of "beauty," this could not be imitated like the explosion of a gun. Still, some sign to express this idea could be agreed on. Most curiously, the Indian races were unanimous in accepting the same sign. When they wish to explain that they saw a "beautiful" woman, they pass the flat hand gently and slowly through the air as if imitating the wave-line. Even the sex is described unanimously. When speaking of a woman, the Indians pass the palm once down the face and the whole body, as if wishing to indicate the long waving dresses or the graceful contour of the female body. This smoothing of the face universally means "a member of the fair sex."

A copious grammar of this language of signs could be written. How rich it would be, may be drawn from the fact that Indians of two different tribes, who do not understand a word of each other's spoken language, will sit for half a day on one spot, talking and chattering, and telling each other all sorts of stories, with movements of their fingers, heads, and feet. They may be frequently seen to laugh loudly, or to look very serious and sad, and it seems as if they can equally produce a comic or a melodramatic effect with their fingers.

I have no space here to draw up the plan of such a grammar, but I may be permitted to describe a few general signs I have collected, as throwing further light on this interesting subject.

When "speaking" is specially referred to, the gestures by which it is described are made close to the mouth. If the hand is passed several times across the lips, it means addressing the people (haranguer).

If the fingers of both hands are crossed before the mouth like a pair of scissors, it means a dialogue (causer).

If the flat hand is pressed to the lips, and thence moved upwards to the heavens, it indicates a prayer or address to Deity.

If one finger is thrust forward in a straight line from the mouth, it means a straight speech, or speaking the truth.

If the two forefingers are parted and moved from the mouth, like the split tongue of a snake, it signifies lying. This sign is adopted in the sign-language of all the Indians, as well as the figure from which it is derived: "Speak with a forked tongue"—*i. e.* "lie."

If the speaker point with his forefinger to his ear, it means, "I have heard and understood." If he move the flat hand quickly past the ears, it means, "I have not heard," or "understood." With the same motion he can, however, indicate that he *will* not understand, or that the request passes his ears unheeded. According to circumstances, it may also mean that it passes by his ears because he considers it untrue. Slightly modified, this sign will indicate, "You are trying to take me in."

A hollow hand, with the motion of drawing water signifies water. When the finger traces serpentine lines on the ground, it is a river. A hand moved up and down in the air signifies a mountain.

The several beasts have naturally their special signs. Usually only some characteristic portion of the animal is imitated—for instance, the horns. The horns of the buffalo differ from those of the elk, and thus the entire animal is indicated.

The idea of a large number, or "many," is described by clutching at the air several times with both hands. The motion greatly resembles that of danseuses playing the castagnettes.

"Little," or "nothing," is signified by passing one hand over the other.

Very curious, but quite universal, is the sign for admiration among the American Indians. They hold the hollow hand for some time before the mouth. This is, however, I suspect, a species of quiproquo, and the real sign—namely, the mouth widely opened in amazement—is concealed behind it. They carry the hand to the mouth and conceal the face behind it, because it is improper to display emotion or admiration.

The gestures and mimic, as I said, were first invented for conversation, and thence transferred to the symbolic writing, which is partly only a copy of the sign-language. The undulating lines, which the finger drew in the air to imitate water, were afterwards drawn in colour by the same hand on paper, and it thus became a hieroglyphic meaning "river." The semicircle which the sign-speaker described with his hand in the sky, was put down on the paper in the same shape, where it means "sky," or "day."

It does not appear to us to require any peculiar power of mind to make such a transition, but history teaches us that this, apparently so easy, step has always been very difficult to nations, and many have not yet taken it. Probably our Indians conversed for many a long day mouth to mouth and eye to eye in a very ingenious manner ere they made the discovery that they could fix their rapidly-disappearing signs by a slight addition of paint, and could hand them down to their posterity through symbolic writing.

There are various materials and subjects employed by the Indians in their symbolic writing.

The whole affair began with trunks of trees in the forest, on which they carved or hacked the first rough signs. Probably, at first, they were no better than those which a hunter still makes in the forest, in order to find his way back, or give a comrade a sign in what direction he has gone.

Afterwards they cut different signs in the trees, longer messages, or what may be termed letters. Large trees have been found covered with symbolic writing of every description, magic incantations, or, if you like it better, sacred hieroglyphics. It is well known that they covered large rocks and blocks of stone with inscriptions, especially the walls of caves, which appeared to them, as to other nations, something wonderful and sacred, and which were usually composed of a soft stone, on which a picture could be easily carved. Hence nearly all the numerous sandstone caves on the banks of the Mississippi are filled with pictorial inscriptions.

From very natural reasons, however, the inscriptions are more frequent on their productions, vessels, clothing, &c., than in the open air. On the western prairies the chiefs frequently have the exterior of their tents covered with pictures and writing, containing representations of their doughty deeds, their family arms, or references to their pagan belief and magic recipes.

They have also picture-writing on their clothes, the leather side of their buffalo robes, or the blankets in which they wrap themselves. We find among them cloaks entirely covered with figures and hieroglyphics, like the dress of a magician. At times their heroic deeds are again described on these furs; and on the buffalo skins, which are softer to sit on than the blankets, there will be found long stories. The blankets are usually only decorated with their totems, or special personal signs. Thus, for instance, one will have on his back the figure of the sun drawn in clumsy red marks. Another has the awkward figure of a bear or a bird sewn with blue thread in the selvage of his cloak, and is as proud of it as a Roman patrician would be of the purple edging of his senatorial toga.

Of their instruments, those most highly decorated are generally their pipes and the handles of their tomahawks, the important emblems and instruments of peace and war. Rarely do you find either of these articles in the possession of an Indian which has not some story on it, either his " dreams of life," or the number of war expeditions in which he has joined, or of the foes he has killed.

Sometimes they have accepted our European alphabet into the catalogue of their patterns. I saw an Indian whose squaws had worked the whole of the English alphabet along the edge of his cloak, and another who had painted the same alphabet, though horribly disfigured, round his hunting-pouch. This was, however,

I feel certain, something more than mere ornament, and meant to be ominous and magical.

The principal writing material, however (among our Ojibbeways, and all the northern savages who do not live on the desolate prairies), is the stuff so useful to the Indians for a hundred matters, and which supplies to them the place of our leather, cardboard, and canvas —the birch bark. It is probably the very best writing material nature has produced unaided by art. You need only to take the bark from the tree, cut it a little into shape, and the page is ready. The inner side of the bark is covered with a white silky membrane, which receives the slightest mark made on it with a bone, a thorn, or a needle.

The Indians call a piece of birch bark to be employed for writing "masinaigan." The word is derived from the verb "nin masinaige" (I make signs), and means a thing on which signs are made. They also give our paper and books the same name.

The form of these masinaigans varies greatly. At times I saw mere quadrangular plates, at others they made a species of pouch of it. Usually, however, it is a long strip, which they fold in the middle, and looks like the cover of one of our books from which the contents have been removed. The writing is inside, and the rough bark outwards.

I exerted myself while on the island in purchasing, copying, and collecting as many of these Indian birch-bark books as I possibly could. Sometimes I had them explained to me by the owners, and I will now proceed to give some specimens of my collection, while accurately describing all I heard about them from my Indians. And even if the documents I secured may not appear in themselves very important, still I trust that the reader will find in the explanation much that is characteristic of the Indians.

One of the chiefs with whom I associated here was known by the name of " Loon-foot."

This man very readily showed me all his documents, papers, and birch bark. Among others, he possessed a certificate, signed by two government officials, installing him as chief of the Ojibbeway band at Fond du Lac. It ran as follows:

"This is to certify, that the chief Shingoop, the speaker Nanganop, the headman, and warriors of the Fond du Lac band of Chippeways, have this day requested that Mangusid* be hereafter recognised as their chief pacificator, and they have solemnly promised to refer to him all difficulties that may arise hereafter between them, and to abide by his decision."

Loon-foot told me that his ancestors had frequently held such high offices. He knew their names for eight or nine generations upwards. And he produced an old, venerable, smoky, and dirty birch bark, on which a number of strokes, crosses, and points were engraved, as thus:

---

* In the Ojibbeway, Mangusid is composed of " Mang," the Loon-bird, and " usid," his foot. Mangusid is therefore, literally, Loon-his-foot.

Loon-foot told me the names of all the men indicated by these strokes:

No. 1, he said, was his father, Kadawibida (l'homme qui a les dents percées).

No. 2. His grandfather, Bajasswa (l'homme qui fait sécher.

No. 3. Father of the last, Matchiwaijan (l'homme qui porte une grande peau—the Great Skin). He was a mighty hunter, Loon-foot added.

No. 4. His father, Wajawadajkoa (à cause qu'il avait la peau bien rouge).

No. 5. His father, Wajki. I received from Loon-foot no explanation of this word, but Wajki means so much as " the young man," or " the beginner."

No. 6. Father of No. 5, Schawanagijik (le ciel du sud).

No. 7. His father, Mitiguakosh (le bec de bois).

No. 8. His father, Miskwandibagan (l'homme à la tête rouge).

No. 9. Father of No. 8, Gijigossekot. Of this name Loon-foot gave me the extraordinary explanation, " le ciel qui a peur de l'homme." He must have been a species of Titan. I cannot give the derivation of the word, but I find in it, certainly, traces of gijig—heaven, and agoski—fear.

With the name of the last, Loon-foot's genealogical tree was lost in the clouds.

I asked my chief whence he obtained the names, and how he could read them from the bark. He said that his grandfather had been a great "jossakid" (magician). Once his squaw had been quite paralysed, nearly dead, but his grandfather had brought her to life with his breath (en soufflant). This grandfather of his had told him all the names, and although

they were not written on the bark, he could remember
every one accurately by looking at the signs, crosses,
and dots. The cross reminded him of the person, and
the points and strokes of the age he reached.

As neither the dots nor the strokes on the bark ex-
ceed ten in number, and the latter precede the former,
I suspect that the dots signify the years, and the
strokes decades. Possibly a European aided in drawing up the family tree, by indicating the figures on
the decimal system. It was clear that Loon-foot regarded the document as extremely important, and
that he knew the names of his ancestors thoroughly
by heart, I learned both with eyes and ears.

It was an interesting fact to me, in itself, that an
Indian family should carry back its genealogy to the
ninth link, or, at least, believe that it could do so.

Loon-foot spoke to me on this occasion so highly of
the totem of the Loons, and told me so many great
things about it, that I at the time believed the Loon
totem to be the eldest and noblest in the land.

I had opportunity, however, afterwards to notice
how proudly the Indians always talk of the totem to
which they or their wives belong, and I was astounded
at seeing how deeply the aristocratic element is rooted
in them. Thus I formed at La Pointe the acquaintance of a half-breed, who spoke a little French, and
possessed considerable knowledge of the language and
customs of the Indians. He had even been employed
in compiling an Ojibbeway dictionary; but for all
that, he belonged, in his mode of life, more to the red
than the white race.

He lived entirely like a forester, and had erected his
lodge about two miles from our fort, on one of the
promontories of our island. I frequently visited him

there, partly on account of the pleasant walk through the woods, and the magnificent prospect over the lake, and partly for the sake of the information I derived from him on Indian matters. His wife, an Indian woman, belonged to the totem of the Cranes, and his mother had come from the same clan. On one occasion he drew for me on paper all the coats of arms, or, as the French Canadians call them, " les marques des totems," of all the best known families and chiefs of the Ojibbeways.

When we came to the arms of the Cranes (la marque des Grues), my friend spoke of this family as follows: " La marque des Grues est la plus noble et la plus grande marque parmi les Ojibbeways. Les Grues montent jusqu'au Déluge. On trouve leurs noms déjà dans les livres des Romains."

As he saw I was disposed to smile, he remarked, very earnestly, " Non, non, monsieur, sérieusement on a trouvé déjà à la destruction de la Tour de Babel tous les noms qui sont à présent parmi nous."

" You are jesting."

"Monsieur," he replied, still more earnestly, "je suis tout-à-fait sérieux. Les Grues ont pris possession de ces terres après le Déluge. C'est bien connu. Pour des siècles les Grues avaient le nom le plus haut. Ils sont écrits dans les grands et les plus anciens livres. Ma mère était une Grue. Ma femme est une Grue. Dans les derniers temps ils sont un peu timbés.* Mais il y a encore des Grues—1, à La Pointe; 2, au Sault de Sainte Marie; 3, à la Folle Avoine; 4, près de Détroit; 5, à la baie de Hudson. Enfin, monsieur, les Grues ont été et sont encore partout les hommes les plus remarquables du monde !"

* Canadian for tombés.

In Loon-foot's lodge I also saw two other drawings
engraved on the two sides of a birch-bark pouch, and
of which I here give a faithful copy:

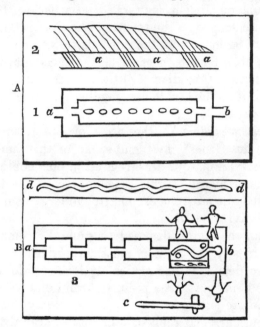

" A" was one side, " B" the other, of the pouch.

I will repeat the explanations given me by my jossakid as clearly and fully as possible, but, of course, I
did not understand it all, partly through the laconic
manner of my Mentor, who had no desire to reveal all
the mysteries, and partly because the affair cannot be
rendered perfectly clear. I believe, however, that the
little I caught is sufficiently interesting to claim space
here.

On asking Loon-foot what No. 1 was, he naturally
first told me the history of the creation of the world,
and when I brought him back to the real point, he

then explained : " That is the big water, Kitchi-Gami, or Lake Superior. This sea, and the lands round it, form a great wigwam. The broad square round the sea represents the path of life, on which men have to travel." (Probably no more than the daily path of duty, the scene of the joy and suffering of the Ojibbeways ?) "The outlets or holes at either side at a and b are the gates leading from the great wigwam into the world." (Perhaps to the right St. Mary's River, leading to Lake Huron, and to the left the river St. Louis, which runs across from Fond du Lac to the Mississippi ?) "The dots or circles in the middle of the water are the foot-steps of the great Otter, which soon after the creation of the world ran through the water and across the world. At the first movement it stepped on ice, at the second into the swamp, at the third into the water, while at the fourth flowers sprang up." (Loon-foot also said a good deal about the other footsteps in the drawing, which I could not understand.)

For No. 2, Loon-foot gave me no further explana-tion than this : " The strokes represented the cold breath of the spirits of the north. In the north there lived," he went on, " four great spirits, which looked down on the earth, and that there were four of them was indicated several times by the repetition of the strokes at a a a." (Assuming that No. 1 is Lake Superior, with its length running from west to east, then the strokes in No. 2 would run from the north-west ; and if they indicated, as Loon-foot said, the " breath from the north," they might bear reference to the north-west wind, so celebrated among the Ojib-beways under the name of the homeward wind.)

On the other side of the bark pouch (at "B"), Loon-foot said, a Manitou wigwam or spirit lodge, in other

words, an Ojibbeway temple, was represented. The
entrance was to the left (at *a*). The various little
squares represented the divisions which the brother of
the Midé order must go through, or the several grades
of consecration he received. The last square to the
right (at *b*), a species of sanctuary, indicated the last,
or highest grade. (I must here remind my readers
that the Ojibbeways have various degrees of initiation
in their Midé order. There are ordinary members,
chief and supreme Midés. The whole drawing is,
therefore, symbolical, and the large square enclosing
the smaller squares is not *a* temple but *the* temple, or
the whole ecclesiastical edifice in the sense we use the
word Church, when we say, for instance, "The Church
has various degrees of ordination.")

"The four human figures at the sides of the sanctuary are the four great spirits sitting to the north,
south, west, and east." (These four great spirits,
which govern the world, are very often repeated in
the pictures, speeches, incantations, myths, and prayers
of the Indians. I cannot venture to assert whether
the four principal winds are personified and adored in
them. Nothing further can be said with certainty
than that they recognise four quarters of the world,
and place a great and powerful spirit in each of
them.)

The three small marks below the Holy of Holies I
at first took for birds, but Loon-foot told me they
were the paws of the Great Lion. (What a great lion
has to do with the matter, I cannot see, however.)

The figure below (at *c*) looks like the drumstick
with which the Midés beat the great drum in their
temple ceremonies. Loon-foot said, though, that it
was not a drumstick, but an "emblem of life;" the tree

of human life was intended by it. "Like trees," he said, "we grow up, and like trees we pass away again." I remembered having noticed that when the people in the temple seized the drumstick, they had also made some references to the tree of life. As everything among these Indians is emblematical or symbolic, it is very possible they attach such a meaning to the drumstick. The serpentine double line (at *d*), running parallel, near and over the temple square, Loon-foot said was an allusion to speech. "It is the river of words," he said. And in truth, at their religious ceremonies there is no lack of words, speeches, or, if you like to call them so, sermons.

Among the bark papers of another chief, or jossakid, I found a drawing bearing some affinity to those of Loon-foot's I have just described. The owner allowed me to make a copy of it, but, when asked for an explanation, he was more laconic and retiring than Loonfoot. Although he explained very little to me, and the figures are in the highest sense mysteries to me, I will nevertheless insert them here. Perhaps some other person can use them, and explain what I could not understand.

On one side of the book was the drawing No. 1; on the other, No. 2.

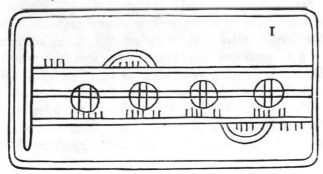

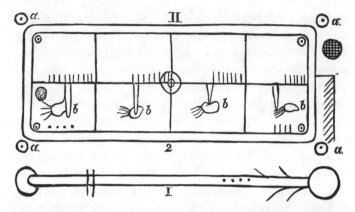

The fragments of explanation which the Indian let fall while I was drawing, amounted to no more than the following:

"The whole," he said, "was a representation of 'la grande médecine,' or a symbolic representation of the religious system of the Indians, their ceremonies, order of Midés, and also their hierarchy to a certain extent. The drawing at 1 in No. 2, is the road we wander along before we enter." (I was obliged to content myself with learning that there was a species of preparatory school or disciplining of the novices. I did not learn in what consisted the trials of this road, probably referred to in the dots and cross strokes.)

Figure 2 is once again the great temple wigwam, with the divisions of the degrees of consecration. The four small rules and dots at the four corners, *a a a a*, represent the four quarters of the world. Here, then, circles were used to describe what had been drawn in figures on the last picture.

My Mentor would not lead me into the interior of the temple. He merely said, "I saw there the grades, and at *b b b b* were the bear's claws, marking these degrees. The first caused an outlay of ten dollars; the second cost twice as much; and the third and fourth even more. Few, however," he added, "had sufficient 'butin' to reach and pay for the highest degree. It cost a pile of property. He had, however, once in his life taken this degree; but only once." (Hence, I suspect that a man can be initiated several times.)

I could not learn the meaning of the circles, divisions, and little strokes in No. 1.

Though I obtained at this sitting no more than a confirmation of what I had conjectured before, that the religious and hierarchical system of the Indians is tolerably complicated, still, what I did learn, amply repaid me. In fact, the Indians are not merely simple, naked, and ignorant savages; in many respects they know, unfortunately, too much. If they had nothing in their heads, if their minds were a blank piece of paper, our religion and civilisation might be more easily introduced among them. But we see clearly that they have all sorts of things to unlearn, and hence their conversion probably becomes so difficult.

As I heard that Indians had arrived from Vermilion Lake and "les bois forts," perfect savages and great magicians, who also had birch bark and picture writing, I sought out their lodge, which was very long, and filled with some twenty half-naked people. They received me kindly, in their fashion, and one of the hunters to whom I was introduced, and to whom I gave a heap of tobacco, sat down on a mat which was in a corner, produced his birch barks, and showed me the drawings they contained.

As, in spite of all the trouble I took, I understood

hardly any of his explanations, nor the connexion between the pictures, I might almost save myself the
trouble of registering them here.   But, as the whole
matter appeared to me so interesting, as the signs,
though partly arbitrary and individual, are for the
other part typical, and in use to the frontiers of Mexico,
I will copy here the symbols I found on this occasion,
and give the Indian's explanation.   The written language of the North-American savages is still a very
new subject, and even the symbols that may be regarded as typical, symbolical, and of universal comprehension, are not yet all collected and examined.
Perchance my drawing may contain a few new letters
of this great and widely extended language?

In the first place I must remark, that my man had
his characters arranged from right to left, and read
them in this order, while others read them to me from
left to right, and others, again, in a circle round the
entire leaf.   Perhaps this point, as to where the reading begins, is one of the secrets of their art, which they
keep hidden, so that the uninitiated cannot so easily
employ their magic incantation.

The hunter told me that he paid four handsome
bear-skins for the song.   He called it a " chanson
magicale" (wabana-nagamunam).   I fancied I could
trace in it a song to the seasons; at any rate, I recognised a series of references to winter, spring, and summer.   But let the reader judge for himself.   He must
picture to himself my Indian, who was to explain the
matter to me, but who was either ignorant or indisposed, holding the birch bark in both hands, and
singing each verse belonging to the hieroglyphic as
he had learned it by heart.

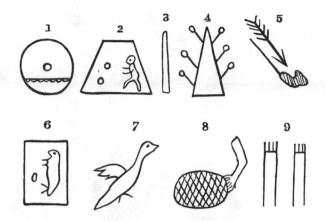

To No. 1 he sang: L'hiver est venu du nord.

To No. 2: L'enfant qui court dans le wigwam. (Winter joys ?)

To No. 3: Il a une belle voix, le tonnerre de l'Orient. (Perhaps the figure is a species of thunderbolt, and refers to the first spring storm.)

To No. 4: L'Esprit nous donnera des fruits. The sign represents a tree with fruit. (Summer ?)

To No. 5: L'homme qui fume la pipe et l'enfant qui tire la flèche. (A pipe for the man and arrow for the boy.)

To No. 6 : L'ours qui cherche une place où la rivière n'est pas profonde. (Return of the bear in autumn from the prairies to the northern forests?)

To No. 7: L'oiseau s'envole pour chercher sa pâture. (Return of the migratory birds from the north to seek food in the south ?)

To No. 8: La femme a préparé le plat pour son mari et le lui présente. (Return of the hunter to his squaw ?)

To No. 9 : L'Esprit a inspiré le sauvage avec cette invention, pour devenir plus poli.

I said that I fancied I traced some song of the seasons in the whole, but I cannot make head or tail of the last sign or verse.

On one of the graves in the Indian cemetery here I saw the following drawings:

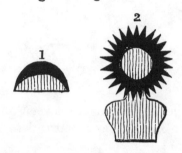

No. 1 was a representation of the sky.

No. 2 a picture of the sun. The lower part of the sky was, as usual, blue or green, the framework above, black.

The sun was painted red in the centre, but the beams were black. I was told—and this was certainly plain enough—that this was done as a sign of mourning. The idea of a sky covered with mourning, and a sun toned down to a solemn hue, is really remarkable—I might say grand—for an Indian. The idea can be regarded in two lights. Either we may suppose that it is intended to describe how sun and sky became gloomy to the deceased, as his eye closed in death, or, with reference to the survivors, that, after their loss, the sun seems to have lost its radiancy, and even the entire sky is set in a framework of mourning.

All the gravé coverings, made of wood, have a

small hole cut in the side. The relations place food in it for their dead. A friend or a relative, in passing, will put in some tobacco, and, on some occasions, a gun, so that the deceased may be able to shoot something and support himself on his long journey to Paradise. It is true that people help themselves to these articles, but this is not looked into strictly. So long as the food and tobacco are left there a certain time they are quite satisfied. But the deceased do not even enjoy these things, but only their smell or emanation, and these can easily reach them in a few days in the kingdom of spirits.

I found also a tombstone, or rather board, with a drawing, of which the following cut gives a faithful copy:

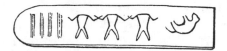

The three strokes cut into the board, painted of a red colour, were explained to me to be the three bloody hero deeds the deceased had performed, or three enemies he had killed.

The three figures holding each other's hands were his relatives mourning his loss or celebrating his funeral feast, and the inverted animal—a bear—was his family sign or name.

Reading this, it would run in our fashion: " Here lies the chief of the Bear clan. His relatives and friends mourn for him. But he was a hero, for he killed three of our mortal enemies."

An American author who has travelled in Egypt and Arabia, and who made a comparison between the half-savage Bedouins and the Indians of the New

World, remarked, not without reason, that the Arab
will do nothing for any one without baksheesh. The
American Indians, though so poor, are not yet tainted
with this craving for money : they rarely beg for it,
and will do many things without a reward.

Only on one point, as it seems to me, do they make
an exception from this rule. All their information
about religious matters, every exchange of magic
remedies, every copy and explanation of a picture-
writing, must be paid for, and they ask enormous
prices. They will often give a horse, a handsome
fowling-piece, or a packet of beaver skins, for a piece
of bark that has figures scratched on it. For how
little is a packet of skins in comparison with a magic
song, to which all the beavers in the world listen, and
must go into the traps on hearing it ?

It even seems as if they dare not be liberal in this
matter. "We must," they say, "insist on payment,
and high payment, for our religious mysteries. The
Great Spirit would be angry were we to squander his
gifts." They think that the Great Spirit, the source of
all mysteries, secrets, and miraculous powers, would
regard it as an insult if they betrayed these secrets for
a trifle. It is not always the Great Spirit whose wrath
they fear in such cases, but other spirits, to whom they
ascribe the magic formulas. An Indian whom I asked
for such a formula, replied: "I dare not; it belongs
to the Bear." "To the bear ?" I said, in surprise;
"how so ?" "Yes," he went on ; "I cannot explain
that to thee any further. But it belongs to the Bear,
and the Bear would be very angry with me if I gave
thee the bark. The only way is, that thou shouldst
give me a large present, and we could then offer the
Bear a grand sacrifice."

In a word, it is often possible to receive as a present from an Indian a richly decorated pipe without any return; you can eat your fill in his lodge, and, in some cases, he will refuse to take anything for it. He will run ten miles for you for a trifle, but if you try to get from him a piece of written bark and the requisite explanation of the hieroglyphics, you must pay its weight in silver. Brother keeps such secrets hidden from brother, son from father, and will only surrender them for payment.

I gained a little tragi-comic experience on this head, which I will describe as affording a further character-istic of the Indians. I had heard that a strange Indian had arrived from the heart of the Backwoods, the Bois Forts, as the Canadians call them, on the Upper Mississippi, who was not only a great hunter and warrior, but also a great medicine man. He belonged to the savage tribe of the Pillagers, and a mulatto of the name of Williams, who visited me now and then, said that this man was full of magic knowledge, and had undoubtedly many of the written birch barks after which I was so greedy. A present of a little tobacco or sugar would open his mouth.

Hence, I begged Williams to ask the man most politely to our fire that evening, and explain to him that I was fond of looking at birch bark, and if the Pillager chief had any, he might bring them along with them, I would pay him for his trouble.

At the appointed time the curtain of my wigwam was pulled aside, and in walked Williams with the Pillager chief from the Bois Forts. But the latter was not alone, he was accompanied by a countryman of his own. The Indians rarely visit another person's wigwam alone, and the chiefs, more especially, usually

take with them their "skabewis," adjutant or speaker,
whom they allow to speak for them and send on
errands when themselves too lazy, or when they consider it beneath their dignity to go in person.

Silent, and without wishing us " Good evening," or
awaiting our invitation to sit down, they seated themselves on a mat opposite to me. I offered them
tobacco directly, and they began smoking. The
flickering fire lighted up two figures, which, indeed,
looked savage enough. Their faces were blacker than
that of our mulatto, and they had probably had a
death recently in their tribe, for they were covered
with charcoal ash. And, as if this had not been
enough, their long, bushy, black hair hung down on
their foreheads, and their eyes only sparkled at intervals through the dense matting of hair. Wrapped up
closely in their blankets, they sat like two masked
associates of the Vehm-gericht. Only the clouds of
tobacco that emerged from their thick lips showed
that there were still breath and life in these statues of
flesh.

I had bought a pound of tobacco and another of
sugar, and laid them as an offering on the mat before
them, just as the grocer handed them to me.

At length I interrupted the silence, and spoke: " It
is good that you have come, and I rejoice that you
will take part of our fire and our evening meeting.
You are welcome ! What my lodge offers in tobacco,
apples, and sweetmeats, is at your service. And,
then, I have also bought tobacco and sugar, which I
offer you as a slight present. I expected only one
visitor. I am glad that there are two of you, but
had I known beforehand that I should have the

honour of receiving you both, I would have bought
two pounds of tobacco and two of sugar."

No reply, no sign of applause, no movement. Only
tobacco-smoke, and the unchangeable faces carved out
of wood! After ten minutes the chief, who appeared
to be rather deaf, turned to his adjutant, and asked
what I had said. The latter muttered something to
him, and the chief uttered a slightly intoned "Ho!"
(a sort of shout of applause).

After allowing the proper time to pass, I again
spoke. "I hear that you possess some pictured birch
barks. I am curious to be instructed in the fashion of
your writing. Could you show me the bark and
explain the symbols? If you have brought them in
your bags, be kind enough to show them to us."

General silence and immobility, as in a museum of
statues or of smoking automata.

At length, suddenly, after the couple had held a
whispered conversation, the adjutant laid his pipe
aside and held a lengthy harangue. It lasted, with the
interpreter's translation, a good half-hour. He began
with Adam and Eve and the creation of the world, and
then told me, circumstantially, how the Great Spirit
founded their Midé order, and that their religion had
come to them from the far East. Then he spoke
further of the principles and sanctity of this religion,
and of Menaboju (the Indian Prometheus), and of
Matchi-Manitou (the Evil Spirit), and of the spirits in
the air, water, and plants, of roots, and herbs, and
shells, and the efficacy of the magic drums and rattle
calabashes.

Although I had heard all this often enough before,
I listened to it this time patiently, in the hope that it

would prove an introduction to the aforesaid birch
barks, and that they would be finally produced. It
struck me with surprise that my little packets of
tobacco and sugar remained untouched, and apparently
unnoticed. The Indians had not touched them, nor
seemed to have looked at them. In the latter respect
I soon found I was deceived: they had not merely
looked at them through their bushy hair, but correctly
estimated their value.

My Indian began speaking again after a short time,
and I thought we should at length come to the point.
This occurred too, but it was not the point I expected.
Instead of taking his medicine-sack and producing the
birch-bark writing it contained, he stooped and lifted
the packet of tobacco. He held it merely with two
fingers, as if unwilling to touch it, by the string the
grocer had fastened round it. Then he held a short
speech over it, and laid it carefully back in the old
place. After this he took up the packet of sugar in
the same way, and held a speech over that before he
laid it down again.

This appeared to me rather suspicious, and I was
curious what translation I should receive from my interpreter. He told me at length that "the Indian had
spoken a good deal of double-barrelled guns, little
black-and-white striped horses, pieces of flowered
calico, each sufficient for a dozen shirts, woollen red-
striped blankets, and many other fine things, which
the superstitious Indian gentlemen are accustomed to
give when they desire to obtain powerful magic songs.
But, on entering my wigwam, they had seen at the first
glance that such things would not be found here, and
that they had not come to the right place. As regarded my tobacco and sugar, by holding them to the

fire's light he had given us to understand that a present
of that sort was very mean and pitiful, in comparison
with magic songs and charms, with which so many
beavers, deers, elks, birds, bears, and fishes as one
wanted could be trapped."

My other Indian acquaintances and friends at La
Pointe, I may here remark parenthetically, had
hitherto been quite satisfied and grateful when I gave
them what I now offered the two Pillagers, and
allowed me to copy their birch bark while giving me
a friendly explanation. But it appears that the denser
the woods from which people come, the higher is the
value they place on their superstition, and the less do
they understand why a European, who can catch no
beavers, is unable to give so much for it as one of their
countrymen, who not merely increases his knowledge
by its acquisition, but also his household stores. I
should have thought of this beforehand, and could
thus have avoided the downsetting I endured, but as
I wished to draw back from the affair as well as I
could, I said to the two Pillagers :

"Do not be annoyed with me. When I offered
you this small present in exchange for a birch bark,
I had no intention to decrease their value. I must
confess I did not know how valuable they might be to
you. The Little Magpie, Loon-foot, the Grey Cloud,
and several other chiefs whom you know well, have
hitherto accepted such presents from me, and given
me birch-bark books for them. You will not ? It is
well. I will not persuade you. I have nothing more
to say to you than that you can leave my hut or remain the whole evening at the fumerie, as you please.
Take these two packets or let them lie, as you please.
Show me your birch barks in return or not, as you

will. It is all right, and you are welcome to everything. Do as you are inclined."

With these words I turned to my other guests, and changed the conversation. Our two darkies, who were too stiff to give in, and did not know how to make the best of a bad job, felt themselves thrust upon one side, and knew not how to better their position than by suddenly rising and marching out of the lodge, without a word of salutation or thanks. Still, they afforded me a slight triumph by stooping and picking up the two parcels, which they pouched. It was evident that my medicine, after all, was stronger than theirs, for they had displayed more greediness and less magnanimity than I did, and I have no doubt this annoyed them excessively when they came to think it over in cool blood.

CHAPTER XII.

IT was four o'clock on a lovely September morning,
when one of the elegant steamers which now traverse
Lake Superior by the side of the Indian canoes and
the old brown "Mackinac barks," put us ashore on
the sandy beach of the great peninsula of Keweena.

We landed here with the intention of crossing this
wild country, and reaching the Indian missions at the
south end of the great pointed bay which, with the
continent, forms the said peninsula, and which the Canadians named l'Anse.   The English give it the pleo-
nastic name of l'Anse Bay, or, as they pronounce it,
Leonce Bay.   Sometimes it is called after the peninsula, Keweena Bay.

The point of the bay runs so deep into the interior
of the land, and is so remote from the great lake

routes, that a large vessel rarely finds it worth while (only once a year) to visit the missions there. Hence, any one who wishes to go to them at other times is obliged to cross the peninsula à la Voyageur, partly on foot and partly in a bark canoe on some lakes and rivers.

The American pedlars who had settled at our little landing-place, Eagle River, could afford us no assistance, and we therefore proceeded to the bark lodge of the Canadian Voyageur Du Roy, who, though settled at the Upper Mission, had come down to the coast for the sake of the fishing. He landed almost simultaneously with us: we from our nocturnal steam voyage, he from his nocturnal fishing expedition. He brought home a quantity of handsome white fish, and while his Indian wife was getting these ready for our breakfast, he immediately prepared for the journey, when we begged him to be our voyageur and interpreter in our journey of inspection to the missions on the Anse.

In order to make our good Du Roy's "paqueton"— thus the Voyageurs call their knapsack—as small and light as possible, we calculated every piece of paper, every pair of stockings we could possibly do without, and left the rest of our traps "en cache" with his squaw and half-breed children. She assured us that everything was as safe in her rickety wigwam as if locked up in a cellar, and did not deceive us, for when we returned in ten days she counted over every article with the utmost scrupulousness.

Du Roy thrust all our indispensable articles into his blue woollen "couverte," tied it round with his leathern "collier," and hung the whole on his back, while fastening the broad band of the "paqueton"

round his head, for the Voyageurs carry with their
foreheads and backs, like our oxen drag with their
heads. The weight only half lies on the back.

Du Roy, although married to a brown Indian
squaw, who looked like his grandmother, was still a
young and almost handsome man. He was powerfully built, and walked before us swinging a knotted
stake, with a light and elastic step, although, after all,
we had fastened a considerable load to his forehead.
The weights these Voyageurs can carry are surprising;
one hundred and fifty pounds is the ordinary and
almost legal weight packed on every Voyageur in
these lands, and is the rule throughout the Hudson's
Bay territory. Still, they frequently carry a heavier
load, and walk along paths on which any European
animal, unless it could borrow the qualities of the
squirrels or birds, would have quite sufficient trouble
in dragging itself along. The canoes have often heavy
loads of poultry, provisions, flour, salted meat, and
other heavy goods, and owing to the complicated
water system of these countries, portages are frequently reached, or places, where the cargo as well
as the boat itself has to be carried through the forests
and over the rocks for ten or twenty miles. Then the
question is who can carry the most, for the strongest
porter receives the highest praise. The Voyageurs
elevate a strong, powerful porter to the proportions of
a hero, while making a virtue of necessity, just as the
Indians, who have to fast so frequently, reckon as a
hero a man who can go ten days without food and not
complain. "Ha, monsieur," Du Roy said to me, "I
knew Jean Pierre Roquille. That was a Voyageur!
He was strong, leste, de bonne constitution! and a
porter of the first calibre. When others were worn

out, and he had a chance of distinguishing himself, he would set to work and put a double load on his shoulders. Et, pourtant, il ricanait toujours; il n'y a personne qui avait tant de qualités pour la gaîté que lui. Il était le plus fameux Voyageur entre le Lac Supérieur et la Baie de Hudson." Unluckily, these heroic porters overwork themselves in their zeal, grow old prematurely, suffer in the chest, and bring on peculiar diseases of the muscles, much like that perceptible among our Tyrolese and Styrian mountaineers.

We were soon in the heart of the forest, and walked in a southern direction in the hope of reaching by the evening the Lac du Flambeau, where we intended to take boat for the mission. Although our road was highly praised as a great improvement of modern times, and a kindness owing to the copper miners, who had cut it through the forest in order to have a central communication through the peninsula, we had often a difficulty in recognising a road at all in all the watery knee-deep mud through which we waded, and between the half-rotten and wholly rotten stumps over which we clambered. But it is true that when we came to a wild stream or swamp, and found huge branching logs laid down in succession, and were able to leap from one to the other without risk of life, then we felt that the improvement committee of the copper miners deserved our thanks.

We were soon mud up to our waists, and I could not look without envy at the pretty, clean, gaily-plumaged forest pheasants, which every now and then ran along the same road close in front of us. They had such an elegant, almost haughty carriage, moved their necks so gracefully, raised their feet as

high as peacocks, and walked, without wetting their
toes, from one stump to the other, or tripped over
deep pools of mud which we clumsy mortals were
obliged to sound with our feet. At the same time,
they were so tame, came so close to us, and regarded
us so impudently. These birds are called here the
Canadian partridge, but they are as large and handsome as a pheasant. When they rise a short distance
from you they produce a whirring sound, exactly like
hollow distant thunder. The resemblance is so great,
that when I heard it for the first time I could not
help believing a storm was raging in the distance;
but our people insisted it was no other thunder than
that produced by the wings of these pheasants. If
this be correct, I can understand how the Indians, in
their mythology, came to ascribe the existence of
thunder to the flapping of a mighty bird's wings. At
the first blush this idea had appeared to me very
strange.

At mid-day we reached the huts of a couple of Irish
squatters, who lived in a small clearing, and received
us most hospitably. They also refreshed us with a
peculiar forest drink, which they honoured with the
name of beer. Spruce-beer they called it. The French,
concealing its origin, call it, even more politely, "la
petite bière." The Indians, who probably invented it,
call it, very prosaically, by its right name, "jingo-
babo," or fir-branch water. This drink appears to be
common through the whole of Canada, Newfoundland, and New Brunswick, or what they still call,
after the old fashion, "the Lower Provinces." For
one of our Irish women, who regaled us with it, had
come here from Newfoundland, and told me she
brought with her a much better receipt for preparing

this beverage than the people had here. She led me
into a little store-room, and showed me a quantity of
freshly-cut twigs pickled in a brown sauce, and explained to me the entire system of brewing. But I
must not betray the process, for the good Irishwoman
forbade it. " To be sure, your honour," she said to
me, " I am very glad, indeed, to show it to you, but I
wouldn't show it to anybody else. They are so clumsy
here, and as they find my spruce-beer so much better
than their own, they pay me a couple of cents
more."

Southwards from these good spruce-beer brewers,
we found no trace of men till we reached our Torch
Lake. But on this lake, which is about as large as
that of the Four Cantons, there live again three men :
Beazley, a Briton; Richard, a Canadian; and le petit
François, an Indian. They are all three unmarried,
and live miles apart, like hermits in block-houses.
We had a perfectly free choice with which of them
to spend the night. As it was not very late in the
day, we decided for the Indian, who lived fifteen
miles further down the lake, and, while still in the
heart of the forest, sent our swift-footed Voyageur
before us to announce us at Beazley's, and engage a
canoe for us.

After forcing our way through the primeval forest,
and reaching the clearing where the lake was said to
be, we heard, in the distance, busy hammering and
carpentering. I stood for a moment leaning on my
stick, and inquired what the noise could be, when Du
Roy came up and told us our boat was being pitched
and repaired, and was almost ready. When we drew
nearer we found our canoe suspended over a fire, and
everybody engaged in stopping up the holes and patch-

ing the birch bark together with pitch, tar, and resin, lest greedy death might break in upon us in the form of water.

This was very consoling to look upon, and as Beazley told me he was a great bear-hunter, and had set several traps in the vicinity, in which he expected before long to catch some of these animals, I employed the interval in making a small excursion into the forest, and examining these arrangements. We clambered or stumbled over a chaos of trees six thousand years old, which the Canadians call a " renversi," and through various bottomless swamps and "honeypots," until we reached a thicket far from the road, where I found a cage prepared for dainty Bruin in the following fashion:

A piece of meat was nailed to the foot of a stout pine, as bait, and formed the attractive point de vue of a narrow, small corridor or apartment, whose walls were made of posts rammed into the ground. The entrance to this apartment is free and open, and the affair must appear peculiarly inviting to hungry Master Bruin. It looks as if a breakfast had been prepared for him expressly. He creeps in, for the height of the entrance is carefully calculated for his build; he needs only to stoop a little and stretch himself. But so soon as he seizes the meat, and tries to drag it away, as if by magic a very sudden change of scenery, quite ruinous for the poor brute, takes place. Over the entrance of the hole a very long and heavy fir-tree is balanced, which is rendered still heavier by laying cross-beams and lumps of stone upon it. The Canadians call it "l'assommeur." It lies apparently perfectly firm over the entrance, and no bear-sense could detect any connexion with the piece of meat.

Still, this is produced by pieces of string in so artistic
a way, that the bear need only pull the meat about a
little with its paw or muzzle to bring the tremendous assommeur plump on its back. The thoughtful
bear-trappers arrange the size of the cage so cleverly
to the structure of the bear, that his spine is just
under the assommeur when paw and snout are pushed
out towards the meat. The irresistible pressure thus
crushes the principal seat of the animal's muscular
strength. It is said that the yell of the poor bear,
when crushed beneath this merciless weight, is frequently heartrending, and very like the cry of a
suffering man. The brute must certainly have a foreboding of the fate that awaits it, and a species of contest must go on before the trap between its timidity
and its hungry passion, for it will only go into the
main hole when there is no other possible chance of
reaching the meat. A quantity of branches and thorns
are, consequently, laid over the whole apparatus, that
the bear cannot possibly reach through, and only the
deceitful entrance is left free. All the parts of these
Canadian bear-traps have also Indian names, and
hence, I believe, that it is an Indian invention adopted
by the Europeans.

At length our canoe, freshly patched and pitched,
floated on the water

> Like a yellow autumn leaf,
> Like a yellow water-lily.

Remarkably pleasant for a butterfly, I grant; but
when a trio of human bodies are stretched out on the
wooden ribs of such a wretched fragile "water-lily,"
made of thin birch bark, without the slightest com-
fort, no bench or support, not even a bundle of hay

or straw, such inconveniences are extremely un-
poetical.

Beazley lent us a canoe (for money and fair words).
Then we called at Richard's, and he lent us (for
money and fair words) a blanket, to protect us slightly
from the damp; and as, finally, we begged le petit
François for a night's shelter (for money and fair
words), we had thus laid the entire population of this
great lake under contribution, or they us.

The fifteen miles' trip to petit François was, however, glorious for any admirer of such things. The
entire lake was framed in by dense primeval forests.
Here and there an arm branched off, and was lost
in other dense forests. At some places the forests
marched like hostile battalions, with levelled bayonets,
against each other, narrowing the lake to a river,
while at others it was a mirrored blue expanse.

The name Lac du Flambeau is repeatedly found in
the geography of these districts. I conjecture it was
introduced by the discoverers on finding the Indians
spearing fish by torchlight. Several lakes which I
saw thus illuminated on my travels float across my
mind as torch-lakes.

The Lac du Flambeau passes through a narrow
stream into what is called the Portage lake. This is
also a very common name for lakes in this country,
for all the lakes are in connexion with some portage,
as they are gladly used by the Voyageurs. This
Portage lake, which branches off for a long distance
through the Keweena peninsula, has been used from
the earliest period by travellers on Lake Superior, in
order to cut across this huge peninsula, and avoid the
tedious and dangerous navigation round it. Indeed,
the whole of this peninsula, now known by the name

of the Copper region, received its Indian name from
this circumstance.   It was, and is, really called Kaki-
weonan,* or a country traversed by a cross-water
communication and a portage.   On the banks of this
lake resided our Indian, le petit François.   He was
still up, and we saw his light glimmering for a long
distance through the reeds and bushes that lined the
shore.

Le petit François was making fish-nets when we
entered and claimed his hospitality.   Nets he had, it
was true, but no fish, and he was ready enough to
offer us hospitality, but nothing else.   He had nothing
to eat or drink, no beds, no straw, no hay; in fact,
nothing at all by which hospitality is generally evinced.
But this did not lead him astray, and he begged us in
the most friendly manner to lie down and extend our
wearied limbs—if possible for balmy sleep—on the
wooden floor of his cabin, which was neither dry, nor
warm, nor even, but as hard as a stone.

The most curious and annoying thing to me was
always that in this country you might offer a kingdom
and not be able to procure for it even a bundle of hay
or straw.   No straw, because they grow no grain; no
hay, because the six cows along the twelve hundred
miles of lake-board devour all the hay that is mown.
Ah, misère!

I naturally mention all this not to obtain personal
compassion, but on account of the country and the
Voyageurs, as well as to throw a light on their
favourite expression, "Ah, misère!" which has become in this helpless country such a permanent inter-
jection, that it supplies the place of all others.   As regards myself, I ended by feeling much amused at the

* From "nin kakiwe"—*i. e.* I march across a country.

affair. For I seated myself at the fire to dry and
smoke; while le petit François and Du Roy gave me
an interesting account of a voyage, which seemed to
me a contribution to literature, and which contained a
piece of bibliographical history which concerned me
very closely, as the work alluded to was constantly in
my pocket, and its honoured author, my travelling
companion, had long before gone to sleep gently and
piously on the hard floor.

" You have already twice uttered the word ' misère,'
monsieur "—thus my two story-tellers began, mutually
confirming each other's story—" but you are mistaken.
It is now summer, and there is a superabundance in
the country, and nought but joy and festivity. You
ought to travel here once in winter, and then you
might use the word. You ought, for instance, to have
travelled, like your reverend friend did once, whom
the angel of sleep now holds so gently in its arms.
Look ye! when he was living, some few years back, at
his church in Anse Bay, and was busily writing that
book you always have in your hand—the Ojibbeway
lexicon—which he collected as busily and gladly as the
bee does honey, he was all at once torn from his peaceful avocations and quiet home in the midst of winter.
Business compelled him to make a long voyage to a
distant Indian parish, which was also under his
management.

" He was away for two months over ice and snow.
At length he returned to this forest land of Keweena,
which he regarded in some degree as his home, for
he had baptised nearly every one here who turned
Christian, and had collected all the wild Indians
living round the mission that he established at his
own expense on the Anse, as a good shepherd

does his sheep. He had scarce reached the shore of
our peninsula ere he at once buckled on his snow-
shoes and ran through the forests and over the mountains, which you crossed to-day with such difficulty,
for he longed to be back at his church, his writing-
desk, and his half-finished lexicon. Like you, he
reached Beazley's hermitage at nightfall, but Beazley
was not living there during the winter. It is true your
friend could have driven out the bats and martens,
and made himself tolerably comfortable in Voyageur
fashion, were he able to kindle a fire. But he reckoned
that if he did not cross the lake during the night and
reach my hut, he could not sit the next day over his
lexicon. The lake was covered with ice, and, unfortunately, with deep snow, while a cold snow-storm
blew in his face from the south.

"Everything seemed to advise him to stay and
spend the night at Beazley's lonely hut. But his
burning zeal urged him to continue his journey and
face wind and storm.

"Ah, misère, monsieur! now, I tell you, it is no
trifle to make these fifteen miles of lake journey to my
hut, which you traversed to-day so pleasantly in a
canoe, under twenty degrees of cold, through loose
snow, and with a stiff wind in your teeth. Even for
an Indian it is a hazardous feat, especially if he has no
compass, and, besides, has not eaten a morsel or drunk
a drop the whole day through. The worst was that
the snow-shoes would not glide along properly, as the
snow was very deep, granular, and shifting. A traveller
will endure any fatigue so long as he sees he is advancing; but when you are working so with your feet,
slipping and stumbling, and the snow sinks in like
wool and piles up before you like the sand of the

desert, and you try in vain to steer a zig-zag course to
get out of the holes and drifts, oh! then matters are
really bad.   The air is gloomy and thick, not a star
shines in the sky, the whole atmosphere is filled with
piercing ice-needles.   Ah! c'est de valeur, monsieur!
O misère!

"Then you fall into a strange and feverish state;
your head grows heavy, and your thoughts are confused.   There is a glimmer before your eyes, and they
begin to swell—at last you can see nothing.   Your
feet and your body wander onwards mechanically, as
if of themselves.   It seems as if they are so excited by
over-exertion, that they can do nothing but walk and
walk.   You have no other means of directing them,
save the cold wind.   You notice at starting that it
blows from the south, the quarter you wish to reach,
and straight in your face.   So soon as you perceive
that one of your cheeks is not so cold as the other, you
see that you are going false, and turn your full face to
the wind, which you cut through with the keel of
your nose.

"Thus you go on, no longer master of yourself, like
an excited automaton, and so I saw here, in my hut,
the next morning, while sitting at breakfast, your
friend covered with ice and snow, with swollen eyes,
stiff hands, and wearied limbs, walk in.   'Where am
I?' he asked.   'Is it thou, petit François?'

"I had work enough in restoring him a little to
himself, for he had cruised about the lake the whole
night through for twelve hours.   And the most wonderful thing was, that he would not believe that he
had already reached my hut, and almost doubted it
was really the sunlight which glimmered through the
foggy atmosphere.   He said it was as easy for him to

think he had spent only a few minutes on the lake as a much longer time. It was all to him as a dream.

"Yes, monsieur, I believe it was time to have him among us. Such snow-storm dreams are followed close by death. It seemed to him most unendurable that he could not reach his church and lexicon the same evening, but must wait till the morrow. We were obliged to nurse him a little during the night."

Du Roy: "Do you know the summer voyage our most reverend friend, your companion, once made in a birch-bark canoe right across Lake Superior? Ah! that is a celebrated voyage, which everybody round the lake is acquainted with. Indeed, there is hardly a locality on the lake which is not connected with the history of his life, either because he built a chapel there, or wrote a pious book, or founded an Indian parish, or else underwent danger and adventures there, in which he felt that Heaven was protecting him.

"The aforesaid summer voyage, which I will tell you here as companion to his winter journey, was as follows:

"He was staying at that time on one of the Islands of the Apostles, and heard that his immediate presence was required at one of the little Indian missions or stations on the northern shore of the lake. As he is always ready to start at a moment, he walked with his breviary in his hand, dressed in his black robe, and with his gold cross fastened on his breast—he always travels in this solemn garb, on foot or on horseback, on snow-shoes or in a canoe—he walked, I say, with his breviary in his hand and his three-cornered hat on his head, into the hut of my cousin, a well-known Voyageur, and said to him: 'Dubois, I must cross the lake, direct from here to the northern shore. Hast thou a boat ready?'

" 'My boat is here,' said my cousin, ' but how can I venture to go with you straight across the lake? It is seventy miles, and the weather does not look very promising. No one ever yet attempted this " traverse" in small boats. Our passage to the north shore is made along the coast, and we usually employ eight days in it.'

" 'Dubois, that is too long; it cannot be. I repeat it to thee. I am called. I must go straight across the lake. Take thy paddle and " couverte," and come!' And our reverend friend took his seat in the canoe, and waited patiently till my obedient cousin (who, I grant, opened his eyes very wide, and shook his head at times) packed up his traps, sprang after him, and pushed the canoe on the lake.

"Now you are aware, monsieur, that we Indians and Voyageurs rarely make greater traverses across the lake than fifteen miles from cape to cape, so that we may be easily able to pull our boats ashore in the annoying caprices of our weather and water. A passage of twenty-five or thirty miles we call a ' grande traverse,' and one of seventy miles is an impossibility. Such a traverse was never made before, and only performed this once. My cousin, however, worked away obediently and cheerfully, and they were soon floating in their nutshell in the middle of the lake like a loon, without compass and out of sight of land. Very soon, too, they had bad weather.

"It began to grow stormy, and the water rose in high waves. My cousin remarked that he had prophesied this, but his pious, earnest passenger read on in his breviary quietly, and only now and then ad-

dressed a kind word of encouragement to my cousin,
saying that he had not doubted his prophecy about
the weather, but he replied to it that he was called
across the lake, and God would guide them both to
land.

"They toiled all night through the storm and
waves, and, as the wind was fortunately with them,
they moved along very rapidly, although their little
bark danced like a feather on the waters. The next
morning they sighted the opposite shore. But how?
With a threatening front. Long rows of dark rocks
on either side, and at their base a white stripe, the
dashing surf of the terribly excited waves. There
was no opening in them, no haven, no salvation.

" 'We are lost, your reverence,' my cousin said, 'for
it is impossible for me to keep the canoe balanced in
those double and triple breakers; and a return is
equally impossible, owing to the wind blowing so
stiffly against us.'

" 'Paddle on, dear Dubois—straight on. We must
get through, and a way will offer itself.'

"My cousin shrugged his shoulder, made his last
prayers, and paddled straight on, he hardly knew
how. Already they heard the surf dashing near
them; they could no longer understand what they
said to each other, owing to the deafening noise, and
my cousin slipped his couverte from his shoulders, so
as to be ready for a swim, when, all at once, a dark
spot opened out in the white edge of the surf, which
soon widened. At the same time the violent heaving
of the canoe relaxed, it glided on more tranquilly,
and entered in perfect safety the broad mouth of a
stream, which they had not seen in the distance, owing
to the rocks that concealed it.

'" 'Did I not say, Dubois, that I was called across, that I must go, and that thou wouldst be saved with me? Let us pray!' So the man of God spoke to the Voyageur after they had stepped ashore, and drawn their canoe comfortably on the beach. They then went into the forest, cut down a couple of trees, and erected a cross on the spot where they landed, as a sign of their gratitude.

"Then they went on their way to perform their other duties. Later, however, a rich merchant, a fur trader, came along the same road, and hearing of this traverse, which had become celebrated, he set his men to work, and erected at his own expense, on the same spot, but on a higher rock, a larger and more substantial cross, which now can be seen a long distance on the lake, and which the people call 'the Cross of ——'s Traverse.'"

I, for my part, after listening to these stories, laid myself down on the knotted flooring, by the side of this excellent, gently slumbering man, and though I did not find much sleep, I had pleasant thoughts, and at an early hour the next morning we took to our boat again, and were soon dancing on the lakes and rivers amid the wild meadows and forests.

I found plenty of interesting things to observe *en route*, especially when we landed in the forests. Once I was fortunate enough to see the Indian food and sugar bowls growing in a state of nature, and made a drawing of them. These were sickly, semicircular excrescences on a maple-tree, about a foot in diameter. These excrescences, which are also found on other varieties of trees, are externally as perfectly round as half a bomb-shell. They have a hard shell, but are internally soft. The Indians cut them from the trees,

scoop them out, and as the natives suffer from a defi-
ciency of good turners and potters, they employ these
lusus naturæ as soup-plates.   At times these natural
dishes are said to be as large as umbrellas, and then
the Indians employ them for their sugar boiling, and
stir up the maple syrup in them and leave it to
crystallise.   The Canadians call these excrescences
" loupes."

Now and then Du Roy pointed out to me spots in
the forest where the bears had been scratching for
the " makopin."   This is a small tuber, which the
Canadians call the bear's potato, nearly a translation
of the Indian term.   We dug some, and I tasted
them, but found them marvellously bitter.   But man
digs after them just as greedily as the bear, and, indeed,
this shaggy bourgeois—as the Canadians often call the
bear, like the Ojibbeways give him the title of the
Forest-man—digs after, and is fond of, many things
which men also like.   " Ah !" said Du Roy, " this
bourgeois often works in his potato-fields like a trea-
sure-seeker.   He is a dainty gentleman, and eats the
bitter fruit with as much enjoyment as an American
chews tobacco.   Lately, I disturbed one eating makopin as I went through the forest.   He only went
a little out of my way, and sat down on a large log,
where he smacked his lips and yawned, like a man
picking his teeth after dinner.   Unfortunately I had
no gun with me, and went on my way.   He let me
pass, and looked after me.   ' Ah, oui! il est bon enfant, ce bourgeois-là !' "   As the bear is no less a
gourmand than the Indian, and as it tries all the
edible productions of the forest, and has a number of
favourite articles of food among them, the Indians
have named at least a dozen plants after the bear:

" bear potatoes," " bear roots," " bear nuts," " bear berries," &c. The latter we frequently found growing in the wood ; the English call it " service," and also " bear-berry," which is the translation of the Indian word " makwimin." It is a variety of the lotetree, and grows very handsomely. At this time we found it covered entirely with splendidly glistening red berries, and our Canadian told us that the bears bend down the whole tree with their paws, and then eat off the berries, like children do with a blackberry-bush.

In the thick reed-beds by which our canoe at times passed, I noticed now and then very curious excavations, holes, or little bays. I was told that the musk-rat produces this phenomena when getting in its harvest. We saw the nests or hay piles of these interesting animals all around us, and it is, indeed, one of the most common creatures in North America. The Canadians told me that the loon (the great northern diver) lived here in a species of community with the musk-rat, in the same way as the owl with the little prairie dog. The loon lays its eggs in these " loges de rat d'eau," as the Canadians call them, and they run no risk from the excellent teeth of its little friend. I had, however, no opportunity of verifying this fact in any of the musk-rat dwellings I frequently inspected. Still I had the pleasure at any rate, which I had not yet enjoyed, of seeing a heavy loon flying far above my head. Hitherto I had only seen the loon swim and dive, and almost doubted whether it could fly. In fact, flying causes it some difficulty ; at least, rising in the air does. People say it requires wind for the purpose, and can hardly do it in calm weather. But, when once under way, it flies not only high but for a long

distance, and makes great journeys both in spring and
autumn. The loon we saw was quite alone, and soared
like an eagle. I also heard here, for the first time, its
clear, loud, and harmonious cry. Our Canadian replied to it from the canoe, " Vol! vol! vol!" He said
he could entice the loons down with it.

Notre voiture—so the Canadians call their canoe or
transport boat—at length floated through what is
termed the Portage Entry, or the mouth of the whole
internal water system of the Keweena peninsula, into
l'Anse Bay, the greatest gulf on Lake Superior, and
the end of our voyage. Long before this took place
we had repeatedly discussed the question whether we
should find a " vent de terre" or a " vent du large"
on the main body of water. We desired the former,
for as these small voitures always glide along near the
shore, like timid ducks, the wind blowing off shore is
preferable for them. As it has to cross the steep shore
cliffs and the forest, it strikes the lake some distance off,
and leaves along the coast a perfectly smooth patch of
water, over which the canoe glides rapidly. The
" vent du large," on the other hand, sends up high
waves, produces a violent surf, and renders a canoe
voyage often impossible.

We fortunately found the desired wind, and paddled
most pleasantly and safely along the lofty wall of
rocks which here begird the western side of the bay.
These walls, like the celebrated " pictured rocks" of
Lake Superior, were composed of the reddish striped
and spotted sandstone, which is so constantly found on
this lake that it has been called after it " Lake Superior sandstone." At times it has a most peculiar appearance, as if a blood-red and a perfectly white clay
had been kneaded together. The red and white strata

form a sharp contrast, and are generally very thin, some not half an inch in thickness, others not thicker than cardboard. The dissevered blocks which the surf has rounded are very picturesque: red balls with a white stripe in the centre, white ones with several red stripes, &c.

The rocks here are as picturesquely undermined and formed as at the " pictured rocks." We found caves and arches, and, at one spot, an entire portico of pillars. The neatest specimens may be found, like objects of virtù, formed by nature. I made a drawing, for instance, of a small natural flower table. A small pillar, composed of several columns, stood up from the water: it sprang from a broad pedestal, and on the top of it rested a still broader and perfectly round tablet of stone, on the surface of which all sorts of mosses, flowers, and graceful little shrubs were growing. Such imitations of art produce a delightful effect in these solitudes.

The stone disintegrates in a very peculiar manner, for the several thin strata fall asunder in the shape of boards. And wherever the rifts are at all numerous, it looks for all the world like a carpenter's shop, great heaps of red and white stone boards and shavings and chips lying in picturesque confusion.

An artist could fill his sketch-book here most pleasantly, though he must not expect to find anything grand, but many pretty miniature effects. Thus, for instance, I found in a small sequestered nook an old tree floating in the water, and riding at anchor by its tough roots. The latter were still firm and uninjured, but the tree itself was perfectly rotten, and along its entire length covered with a multitude of beautiful flowers and weeds.

Trees hung on the walls of rock in bolder positions.
As the forest grows close up to the edge of the rocks,
now and then a gigantic pine will tip over when the
soil gives way, and it hangs suspended by a tough root,
as if attached to a rope, and oscillating in the wind.
It is not utterly unimportant to mention such things
here, for the popular mind has noticed them, and has
referred to them at times in its poetry, fables, and
myths, as I shall have occasion to show.

In the distance a far larger field for artistic studies
lay expanded before us. Opposite to us, on the other
side of the bay, stretched out the Montagnes des
Hurons—hills, we might call them more correctly—
and then, twenty miles further to the north, glistened
the broad expanse of the great lake at the entrance of
the bay. There lay a tall, bluish island, with which
the mirage played in an infinity of ways during our
voyage. At times the island rose in the air to a
spectral height, then sank again and faded away,
while at another moment we saw these islands hovering over one another in the air. That the watchful
Indians not only observe this optical delusion, but
also form a correct idea of its cause, is proved by the
name they give to the mirage. They call it "omba-
nitewin," a word meaning so much as this, " something
that swells and rises in the air." They also make of
it a very convenient and excellent verb, "ombanite"—
i. e. " there is a mirage around," to express which the
French and English require considerable circumlocu-
tion.

We turned our back on this broad and deceptive
gateway of the lake, and paddled still deeper into the
purse-end of the gulf, until we sighted the little
Catholic mission, with the Protestant mission lying on

the other side of the bay, where it is only three miles
in width.

The former was our destination, and we soon saw
the brown population collected on the shore—men,
women, children, and a countless pack of dogs. The
bell of the little wooden church, built in the centre of
the village on a mound, began ringing lustily as soon
as we came in sight. A flag was hoisted on a tall fir-
pole, and the guns of the young men were repeatedly
discharged. When we landed, they all fell on their
knees and received the blessing of their spiritual
father. After this we proceeded to our quarters, some
in a division of the log chapel, Du Roy and myself in
a room which a half-breed belonging to the village
gave up to us. Although our host, by way of an
excuse, said "qu'il n'avait qu'un très petit peu de
quoi—ah, misère!"—still, as regards mental food, I
have rarely spent more interesting and richer travelling
and rest days than those I passed in the little missions
on the Anse.

My reverend companion was engaged during the
day with the affairs of the church, and I had the canoe
and the Voyageur at my disposal. Daily I made small
excursions, visited every nook of our village, looked
at the life in this drop of water, and collected the
stories and fables which I shall immediately attempt
to narrate here for the edification of my readers. At
the same time, I will not omit describing all the circumstances and interludes amidst which these stories were
told me.

CHAPTER XIII.

CATHOLIC missionaries made their appearance in the
country round Lake Superior some two hundred years
ago. The Bible stories and Christian legends rather
pleased the savages, and excited their fancy. Had the
missionaries remained permanently among them, the
work so well begun might have prospered. But as the
labours of the Christian missions have often been given
up and then recommenced, the whole resembles a
garden that has been laid out and then left to itself.
The winds and currents of intercourse have wafted
some of the seed a long distance, and it has at times
taken root at spots remote from the mission in the
heart of the desert. But it has there grown up a
peculiar forest plant, which only in a few features
reveals that it originally grew in the Christian garden.
  Such a production, half Christian and half Indian,

is, I fancy, the story of the first human pair, which was told me on my Anse Bay by an old Indian of the name of Kagagengs.

He is the oldest man in our mission, and, as is usual in such cases of extreme age among the Indians, he is said to be a hundred years old. He believes this himself. " Si je peux attraper encore deux ans," he said to me, " j'aurai cent ans." His name means the Little Raven, and the French Canadians call him the same.

Kagagengs's birthplace and home is on the Lac du Flambeau (not the one we traversed). This lake is far to the southward of Lake Superior, in the interior of the country, and seems to have been from old times an Indian chief town. Even at the present day an influential chief, whose acquaintance I formed at La Pointe, resides there. Kagagengs spent the greater part of his life on that lake as a pagan, but when the Catholic mission was founded here on the Anse, and several of his relatives were baptised and removed hither, the old man came with them, and became—at least nominally—a Christian. People had prophesied in his youth that he would live to a great age.

The following curious circumstance happened to him, as he himself told me, shortly after his birth : It was the custom among the people on Torch Lake to carry a new-born child, if a boy, round from lodge to lodge and show him. The squaws inspected him, the men smoked the pipe of peace over him, and spoke some words of welcome and health to the little being. No sooner was Little Raven born than his father laid him on a deer-skin, and carried him, according to custom, round the village. All the women stared at the child, all the men smoked over him, during all which the babe remained remarkably quiet, and stared about him with his bright eyes.

The little stupid sucklings generally forget what happened on such occasions, or pay no attention to it, but Kagagengs, from his birth, was a chosen vessel. All that took place at this presentation remained faithfully imprinted on his memory, and he did not even forget one of the words spoken, although he did not understand them at once. So long as he was unable to speak, he could not tell this to any one, but he had hardly learned to speak in his second year than he frequently repeated to himself the words he had heard. Mother and father could not at first comprehend the child's extraordinary sayings, but at length he told them they were the words spoken by the neighbours at his " presentation," and he reminded them of all the events that took place, so that every one was amazed at the lad. " That will be a clever man," they said, and also prophesied " he would live to be a hundred years old."

Many persons in the village, I grant, assert that Kagagengs is a humbug, and invented the whole story for his own laudation: he was fond of telling many similar stories about himself. Thus he assured everybody that in his time he had been the best hunter of his tribe, and once killed eleven hopping squirrels at one shot. Not a soul believed this, but he was a curious old fellow, and it was quite certain he was a good story-teller, and knew a quantity of capital histories.

I was conducted to his cabin. We found it deserted, but, by dint of several inquiries among his neighbours, we came on his trail from the village, and at length found him at the water's edge, amidst the plants and saplings fringing the high bank. He was a little old man, bowed by age, with a wrinkled face and dark brown complexion, but his eyes were still bright. Wrapped up in a blanket also displaying its age, and which had equally assumed a dingy hue, he was walking slowly along among the stones and bushes and scattered logs.

"Bojo, Kagagengs!" we shouted to him, some distance off.

"Bojo, bojo!"* he muttered in reply, and scarcely looked at us.

"What are you doing here all alone, old man?" we asked, when we walked nearer and sat down on a log.

"What I am doing?" he said. "What does the bird do when it hops in the branches? What does the toad do when it creeps in the sand?"

"He is constantly crawling about in this way in the open air," my interpreter remarked; "by day he is always out. He is also a great collector of herbs. In the evening he sits in his hut over the fire."

We invited him to sit by our side on the log, and the pipes were soon lighted, which are alway requisite to place you on a footing of peace and confidence with an Indian.

Then I commenced: "Kagagengs, I hear that thy head is full of old stories, as an egg is of meat, and as I am so eagerly collecting the stories of the old time, as thou dost the herbs, I have come to thee to beg thee and to ask thee if thou art disposed to tell me some tradition of thy tribe?"

Naturally enough, such a request, which startled the

* "Bojo" is the customary salutation of the Indians here—a corruption of "bonjour."

old man like a gun-shot at his ear, rendered him quite
silent and confused. He wrapped himself more closely
in his blanket and the cloud of smoke, looked down
on the ground, and said not a word for a long time.
We, for our part, sat smoking, and were equally silent,
waiting for the result. At length he said that he was
not conscious of knowing any stories, and if he did,
they were not worth hearing; and, besides, there were
so many stories in the world, that he did not know
where to begin.

"Ah!" we said, "Kagagengs, if that is all, we can
soon help thee. See! we sit here in the very midst of
free nature. The broad lake before us, the shores
stretching out so far, the hills and forests behind us,
the sun and sky above us, and we little beings here on
the log in the midst of it all. Hence I propose that
we shall begin with the commencement of all things.
Tell us of the creation of the world, and of men, and
what thou hast heard about this from the old men on
thy Torch Lake. Hast thou any such story?"

"Oh yes, of course. The Indians think as much of
all the things that surround them as the white men
do, and there is no creature about which they do not
possess a story."

"Well, then, tell us the first story of all stories.
Wilt thou?"

Kagagengs assented, but first filled a pipe, and, while
doing so, remarked: "When I tell thee this story,
thou must not believe that I invented it. The old
men handed it down to us, and the story is very old—
much older than I."

"I can quite believe it," I said; and the Little
Raven now fell into a state of calm reflection while
surrounding himself with a cloud of smoke. We dared

not disturb him ; so, after having taken his last puffs,
he carefully tapped the pipe out, placed it by his side.
and began the story of

THE FIRST MAN AND WOMAN.

See ! on Torch Lake, it is said that Kitchi-Manitou
(the Good Spirit) first made the coast of our lake.
He strewed the sand, and formed a fine flat dry beach,
a road round the lake. He found that it was splendid walking upon it, and often wandered along the
beach. One day he saw something lying on the white
sand. He picked it up. It was a very little root.
He wondered whether it would grow if planted in the
ground, and made the trial. He planted it close to
the edge of the water in the sand, and when he came
again the next day a thick and large reed-bed had
grown out of it, through which the wind rustled.
This pleased him, and he sought for and collected
more little roots, and other seeds from the sand, and
spread them around, so that they soon covered the
rocks and land with grass and fine forests, in which
the birds and other animals came to live. Every day
he added something new to the creation, and did not
forget to place fish and other creatures in the water.

One day, when Kitchi-Manitou was again walking
along the sand, he saw something moving in the reeds,
and noticed a being coming out of the water entirely
covered with silver-glistening scales like a fish, but
otherwise formed like a man. Kitchi-Manitou was
curious to see on what the being lived, and whether
it ate herbs, and rightly, he saw it constantly stooping
and plucking herbs, which it swallowed. The man
could not speak, but at times, when he stooped, he
sighed and groaned.

The sight moved Kitchi-Manitou with compassion in the highest degree, and as a good thought occurred to him, he immediately stepped into his canoe, and paddled across to the island which still lies in the centre of our Lac du Flambeau. Here he set to work providing the man the company of a squaw. He formed her nearly like what he had seen the man to be, and also covered her body with silver-glistening scales. Then he breathed life into her, and carried her across in his canoe to the other bank of the lake, telling her that if she wandered busily along the lake and looked about her, she would, perhaps, find something to please her.

For days the squaw wandered about one shore of the lake, while the man was seeking herbs for food on the other. One day, the latter went a little further in his excursions round the lake, and discovered, to his great surprise, footsteps in the sand much like those he himself made.

At once he gave up seeking herbs, and followed these footsteps, as he hoped there were other beings like himself on the lake. The squaw, during her long search, had left so many footsteps, that the man at first feared they might belong to a number of Indians, and they might, perhaps, be hostile. Hence, he crept along carefully in the bush, but always kept an eye on the trail in the sand.

At last, at last, he found the being he sought sitting on a log near the shore. Through great fatigue she had fallen asleep. He looked around to the right and left, but she was quite alone. At length, he ventured to come out of the bushes. He approached her with uncertain and hesitating steps. He seized her, and she opened her eyes.

"Who art thou?" he said, for he could now suddenly speak. " Who art thou, what is thy name, and whither dost thou come ?"

" My name is Mani,* she replied, " and Kitchi-Manitou brought me here from that island, and told me I should find something here I liked. I think that thou art the promised one."

" On what dost thou live ?" the man asked the woman.

" Up to this time I have eaten nothing, for I was looking for thee. But now I feel very hungry—hast thou anything to eat ?"

Straightway the man ran into the bushes and collected some roots and herbs he had found good to eat, and brought them to the squaw, who greedily devoured them.

The sight of this moved Kitchi-Manitou, who had watched the whole scene from his lodge. He immediately came over in his canoe, and invited the couple to his island. Here they found a handsome large house prepared for them, and a splendid garden round it. In the house were glass windows, and in the rooms tables and chairs, and beds and conveniences of every description. In the garden grew every possible sort of useful and nourishing fruits, potatoes, strawberries, apple-trees, cherry and plum-trees ; and close by were large fine fields planted with Indian corn and beans.†

* Mani is the Indian name for Mary. As they have not the letter "r" in their language, and cannot pronounce it, they always substitute "n" for it. Without doubt this is a reference to the Virgin Mary. I have already hinted that the tradition I am narrating is a strange mixture of Christian and Indian. The mother of the human race, Eve, is here confounded with the mother of the Saviour. For Adam, Kagagengs gave me no name.

† This decoration of Paradise with European comforts and plants, after the fashion of a French settlement in Canada, is very natural when we reflect that the Indians obtained half this story, and especially the idea of this Paradise, from the European missionaries.

They ate and lived here for days and years in pleasure and happiness, and Kitchi-Manitou often came
to them and conversed with them. "One thing," he
said, "I must warn you against. Come hither! see!
this tree in the middle of the garden is not good. I
did not plant it, but Matchi-Manitou planted it. In
a short time this tree will blossom and bear fruits,
which look very fine and taste very sweet. But do
not eat of them, for if ye do so ye will die!" They
paid attention to this, and kept the command a long
time, even when the tree had blossomed and the fruit
had set.

One day, however, when Mani went walking in
the garden, she heard a very friendly and sweet voice
say to her, "Mani, Mani, why dost thou not eat of
this beautiful fruit? It tastes splendidly." She saw
no one, but she was certain the voice did not come
either from Kitchi-Manitou or her husband. She was
afraid, and went into the house.

The next day, though, she again went into the
garden, and was rather curious whether the same pleasant voice would speak to her again. She had hardly
approached the forbidden tree, when the voice was
heard once more: "Mani, Mani, why dost thou not
taste this splendid fruit: it will make thy heart glad!"
And with these words a young, handsome Indian
came out of the bushes, plucked a fruit, and placed it
in her hand. "Thou canst make famous preserves of
it for thy household!" the friendly Indian added.

The fruit smelled pleasantly, and Mani licked it a
little. At length she swallowed it entirely, and felt as
if drunk. When her husband came to her soon after,
she persuaded him also to eat of it. He did so, and
also felt as if drunk. But this had scarce happened,

ere the silver scales with which their bodies had been covered fell off; only twenty of these scales remained on, but lost their brilliancy, ten on the fingers and ten on the toes. They saw themselves to be quite uncovered, and began to be ashamed, and withdrew timidly into the bushes of the garden.

The young Indian had disappeared, but the angry Kitchi-Manitou soon came to them, and said: "It is done. Ye have eaten of Matchi-Manitou's fruit, and must now die. Hence it is necessary that I should marry you, lest the whole human race might die out with you. Ye must perish, but shall live on in your children and children's children."

Matchi-Manitou banished them also from the happy isle, which immediately grew wild, and bore them in his canoe to the shores of the Lac du Flambeau. But he had mercy upon them still. He gave the man bow and arrow, and told him he would find animals which were called deer. These he was to shoot, and Mani would get ready the meat for him, and make mocassins and clothing of the hide.

When they reached the other shore, Mani's husband tried first of all this bow and the arrows. He shot into the sand, and the arrows went three inches deep into the ground.

When Kagagengs told me this, he thrust his knife, which he constantly held in his hand, into the earth, and showed me, with his thumb on the knife, how deep the arrows had gone in. He showed it to each of us separately, and said: "See, so far." We looked at it carefully, and said: "Good, now go on!"

Mani's husband, then, went for the first time to

hunt, and saw in the reeds on the lake an animal moving, which he recognised for a deer, as Kitchi-Manitou had described it to him. He shot his arrow, and, see! the animal straightway leaped from the water on shore, sank on its knees, and died. He ran up and drew his arrow from the wound, examined it, found that it was quite uninjured, and placed it again in his quiver, as he thought he could use it again.

When he brought the deer to his squaw, she cut it into pieces, washed them, and laid the hide aside for shoes and clothing, but soon saw that they, as Indians, could not possibly eat the meat raw, as the barbarous Eskimos in the north do. She must cook it, and for that purpose have fire.

This demand embarrassed the man for a moment, as he had never yet seen any meat boiling or roasting before the fire. But he soon knew how to help himself. He took two different descriptions of wood, rubbed them against each other, and soon made a bright fire for his squaw.

The squaw, in the mean while, had prepared a piece of wood as a spit, placed a lump of meat on it, and held it in the fire. They both tasted it, and found it excellent. "As this is so good, the rest will be famous," she said, and cut it all up in the kettle, and then they ate nearly all the deer that same evening. This gave Mani's husband strength and courage, and he went out hunting again the next morning, and shot a deer, and so he did every day, while his squaw built a lodge for him, and sewed clothes and mocassins.

One day when he went a hunting again, the man found a book lying under a tree. He stopped, and looked at it. The book began speaking to him, and told him what he was to do, and what to leave un-

done. It gave him a whole series of orders and pro-
hibitions. He found this curious, did not much like
it, but he took it home to his squaw.

"I found this book under a tree," he said to her,
"which tells me to do all sorts of things, and forbids
me doing others. I find this hard, and I will carry it
back to where I found it." And this he did, too,
although his squaw begged him to keep it. "No,"
he said, "it is too thick; how could I drag it about
with me in my medicine-bag?" And he laid the book
again the next day under the tree where he had taken
it up, and so soon as he laid it down, it disappeared.
The earth swallowed it up.*

Instead of it, however, another book appeared in
the grass. That was easy and light, and only written
on a couple of pieces of birch bark. It also spoke to
him in the clear and pure Ojibbeway language, forbade him nothing and ordered him nothing, and only
taught him the use and advantage of the plants in the
forest and on the prairie.†

This pleased him much, and he put the book at
once in his hunting-bag, and went into the forest and
collected all the plants, roots, flowers, and herbs
which it pointed out to him.

Quite covered with herbs of fifty different sorts, he
returned to his squaw Mani. He sorted them, and
found they were all medicine, good in every accident
of life. As he had in this way become a great medicine man, as well as a mighty hunter, he wanted but
little more to satisfy his earthly wants. The children
his wife bore him he brought up as good hunters,

* It is easy to see that by this book the Bible, or the Christian teaching,
is meant.

† It is evident that with this birch-bark book the magic teaching of the
pagans is alluded to, which pleases the superstitious Indian better.

taught them the use of the bow, explained to them
the medicine-book, and told them, shortly before his
and Mani's death, the history of their creation and
their former mode of life on the Torch Lake island
with Kitchi-Manitou, who now, after so much suffering and sorrow, was graciously pleased to receive
them again.   And in this way the story of the first
human pair has been kept up among our tribe on the
Lac du Flambeau.

We thanked Kagagengs much for his pretty story,
and declared ourselves perfectly satisfied. We begged,
also, to be allowed to be his guests that evening, and
said we would bring with us tobacco and the other
matters essential for an Indian soirée. He was to
make a good fire, and sweep out the lodge, so that we
could sit comfortably together. This he promised us,
and hurried home: we, however, entered our canoe,
and made a pleasant trip in the mean while.

In the evening, " le Petit Corbeau" had swept his
floor; a huge log, with branches and knots, glistened
and crackled on his hearth, and he sat very quietly in
a corner, nor did he rise when we entered and saluted
him with a " Bojo!"   He did not even thank us when
we laid a packet of tobacco by his side, as well as a
couple of yards of flowered calico for a new shirt, such
as he had wished for, although he regarded the latter
with a smile of satisfaction, hurriedly put it aside, and
said " it was good."

We lit our pipes, and proposed to Kagagengs, as the
subject for the evening's entertainment, his own dream
of life.   " As thou hast told us such a fine story this
morning of the first couple, what would be more suitable now, when we sit round the fire, than that thou

shouldst describe the most important event of thy life—the dream of thy youth?"

When I had made the old man understand this, he became perfectly dumb, and sat there like a statue. He did not utter a word in reply, and my interpreter remarked to me that I asked too much from him. These dreams are always kept very secret by the Indians. They think about them their whole life through, as a mighty mystery. Only on their dying bed would they speak about them, and describe the dream to their relations. It was true that le Petit Corbeau had turned Christian, but it was only nominally, and the old pagan customs and views were still deeply rooted in his mind. As a Christian, he probably had two reasons for hesitating to speak about his dreams of youth. In the first place, an avowed reason, because he was supposed to be ashamed of such superstition, and was well aware that the Christian priests reproached him for such things; and, secondly—a secret reason—because he still believed in such things, and fancied he would commit treason by revealing them, and that they would be requited by misfortune.

Hence I said to the old man, "Kagagengs! if thou believest that thou wilt bring evil on thyself by telling thy dream, I will desist from my demand. However, we are here by ourselves. Thou mayest be sure that I will not speak about it to thy people here in the village, and what I may, perhaps, tell my people about it across the big water must be a matter of indifference to thee. It will not affect thee. If thou believest, then, that under these circumstances thou canst do it, I repeat my request, tell me thy dream."

"Hem!" the old man said, "thou art the first man who asked me about my dreams."

Then he filled his pipe, and smoked it to the very
end without saying a word. A pipe quite smoked
out, according to the Indians' idea, conciliates everything, even the jealousy and revenge of the spirits.
And so, after he had collected his thoughts, he put his
pipe in the corner, stretched out his brown long legs
before the fire, and began the following story :

THE DREAM OF THE LITTLE RAVEN.

I was a boy so tall, that when I was standing, and
my father was seated on the mat, we were both of
one height. It was autumn, and harvest time. We
had gone to gather the manomin, or wild rice.

One day when we were hard at work, and all busy
husking the grain and filling our canoes, I heard gun-
shots in the distance. These shots came from our
village, and were replied to from the neighbouring
village. They were mourning shots, which are heard
from village to village when any one is dead.*

When I heard these shots, I quickly left off working, and became solemn and very mournful, for the
thought at once crossed my head that my mother was
dead. Soon, too, the messengers of sorrow came,
hurrying to the lake where we were collecting our
harvest, and brought us the sorrowful intelligence
that my mother was dead. We buried her with
many sighs. I wished, however, to weep out my
heavy grief all alone, and I longed to go out into the
forest. But my father, uncle, and sisters would not
let me go, and watched me closely when they noticed
my melancholy and disturbed manner.

---

* I was told at Anse that the people in the Catholic mission fire a salvo
when a death takes place among them, and it is replied to from the Protestant mission, and *vice versâ*.

Once, however, my father and uncle were invited to a fumerie. Then I sprang away from my sisters, and ran into the forest so far and so quickly as I could. When I was far enough from the village, I began weeping and calling loudly on my mother. But as I cried I ran ever further and further. At last I climbed a tall tree, where I wept myself out, and being quite exhausted by pain and weariness, I remained hanging in the branches of the tree.

All at once I heard a voice near me, and perceived a black form hovering over me. "Who art thou? —why dost thou weep?" the form asked me.

"I am an Indian lad," I replied, "and I weep for my mother."

"Come, follow me," the black figure said, and took me by the hand. It walked with me through the air with one step to the next tree. It was an épinette blanche. When we stepped on the top of this shaking tree it trembled and bent, and I feared it would give way under us. "Fear not," the stranger said, "but tread firmly. The tree will bear us." Then she put out the other foot, and we reached with the second step the top of a tall young birch. This tree also shook greatly, and bent down, and I feared that it would let us fall to the ground. "Fear not," my black companion said again, "step firmly. The tree will bear." And thus we stepped out again, and with the third step came to the foot of a tall mountain. But what appeared to me three steps were, in reality, three days' journeys: during the nights we had rested on the tops of the trees, and many forests and prairies already lay behind us.

When we stood on the top of the mountain, she said to me, "Knowest thou the mountain?" and when I said I did not, she replied, "It is the Mountain of the Stag's Heart."* She waved her hand. Then the mountain opened, and we saw, through a long narrow ravine, the sunlight shining brightly at the other end. We went through the rift in the rock. My black conductress glided along before me. At the other end we walked out into the light and sunshine. In the centre of the brilliancy there was a house.

"Go in there," said the black woman.

The door opened and I walked in, but my companion remained outside. I found a supernatural light inside, and covered my eyes with my robe. I trembled from fear and expectation. At length a person who sat in the back of the room began speaking, and said:

"Kagagengs, as I saw that thou wert sorrowful for the death of thy mother, I sent for thee. Thou art welcome. Come nearer. Look around thee. Thou canst now see how I live, and how things are with me."

After growing a little accustomed to the light, I looked round. I saw nothing at first but a lamp hanging in the middle of the hut, which gave a tremendous light. It was the Lamp of the Sun. The Sun itself was sitting behind, and spoke further to me:

"Look down!" Then I looked down through an opening in the floor, and saw the earth far beneath us, the trees and forests, the mountains, the Big Sea water, and the whole round of the world. "Now look up!" said the voice. I looked upwards through an opening

---

* A mountain, or chain of hills, bearing this name exists at the present day in Wisconsin, some days' journey from the Lac du Flambeau.

in the roof, and saw the whole vault of heaven above me, and the stars so close that I could grasp them.

Then again, after I had looked at all this above and below me, the voice of the Sun said, " Now look straight forward. What seest thou ? Knowest thou him ?"

I was terrified, for I saw my own image. " See," the Sun said, " thou art ever near me. I see thee every day, and watch over thee. I gaze on thee and know what thou doest, and whether thou art ill or well. Hence be of good cheer. Now look out to thy right and thy left. Dost thou know the four persons that surround thee? They are a present which I, the great source of life, make thee. These four are in thee. They will come from thee. They are thy four sons. Thy family shall be increased. But thou, thyself, shalt live long, and thy hair shall become like to mine in colour. Look at it." I then gazed on the white locks of the Sun Spirit. They shone like silver, and a feeling of joy came over me, that I should have so long and happy a life.

" In remembrance of thy visit to me," the Sun continued, " and for a good omen, I give thee this bird, which soars high above us, and this white bear with the brass collar."

Then the Sun dismissed me, after saying to me that the woman he had sent to me with his invitation was awaiting me, and would lead me back. The two presents, though, I received—the white bear and the eagle—have ever since been my protecting spirits.

" Didst thou really bring such presents home with thee from heaven, or from the forest?" I asked the Petit Corbeau.

" Not so," he replied.

" In Indian dreams," my interpreter explained to me, " it is not necessary that the presents which spirits make them should be really led away. The gift is rather a spiritual present. The idea or image of the thing is given them, and they then have permission afterwards to make the best use of it they can. Thus, Kagagengs in his late years caught a number of young eagles, which he brought up, and in memory of his dream let them free again. He also took the image of the white bear with the brass collar as his token, and has scratched it a hundred times on his pipes, or sewn it into his blankets, or carved it out of a piece of wood, which he carries about in his medicine-sack."

Kagagengs: When we again descended to the earth, the height seemed to me immeasurable; it now appeared far higher than when we climbed up it first. One tall pine-tree stood above the other. We spent the whole night in clambering down. When we at length reached the earth it was early in the morning, and one half the sun's disk had risen above the horizon. It was still dusk, but we could notice, as we stood on the last fir-tree, a black dog running past. " That thou wilt give me," my companion said, as she saw it, " next spring sacrifice this dog to me." I promised it to her, and, after letting me down from the tree, she said further: " Four persons will come directly to fetch thee, but do not follow them if they try to seize thee with naked hands. If they have leaves of the lime-tree in their hands, and seize thee with them, it is good—follow them. Farewell, Kagagengs."

On this, I heard voices under me: one said, " I am going here," and the other said, " I am going there, to seek him." But I felt too weak to turn round and see who it could be. Suddenly I heard a cry, and a general exclamation: "What is that up in the tree? A man? Yes, yes—it is he! Come here, sisters, we have found him!" They were my four sisters, who had come out to find me, after I had escaped from the lodge, in order to lament my mother's death. "But stay," they said further, "he dreams deep. Do not touch him with naked hands. Pluck leaves from the lime-tree, and cover your fingers with them, before you take him down."

This they did, and then they carried me home, laid me on a bed, and nursed me, and gave me to eat. But I was so weak and ill that I could take nothing for three days. Then, however, I began gradually to eat like the rest, and lived among men, but I often thought of my dream and my visit to the Sun. And all has been fulfilled that was then promised me. I married and brought up four sons, and my hair has grown white like the silver hair of the Sun Spirit. I am now a hundred years old.

As I was rather surprised he did not mention his mother again, I asked Kagagengs, "Hast thou not dreamed again of thy mother?" "Yes," he replied, "every autumn, at the time of the rice crop, I dream of her, that I am going on the path of the dead, and see her and speak with her. Except at that period, when I heard the shots that startled me, I never dream of her."

CHAPTER XIV.

THE Ojibbeways, and, indeed, nearly all the Northern American Indians, situate their paradise to the west.

Many European authors have offered the opinion that the Indians did this because to the far west are found the splendid flower-enamelled prairies, the wide hunting-grounds, on which the buffalo herds roam, and where there is an Elysian abundance of game and hunting adventures.

This opinion, however, does not appear to me tenable, and I consider, for various reasons, that the cause of transferring paradise to the west must, partly at least, be sought elsewhere and much higher.

In the first place, when the Ojibbeways ever spoke to me of paradise, they never added "the prairies." They did not say " westward in the prairies," but

"towards the sinking sun, at the extreme end of the
world, lies our home after death."

Those tribes which have grown up on the prairies
have accustomed themselves to the mode of life there,
and know how to use the resources the prairies offer,
may possibly love the prairie as their home. But it is
difficult to discover why all the tribes living in the
eastern forest lands should hold so high an opinion of
the prairies. The most valuable animals for peltry,
food, and trade—the bears, beavers, deer, stags, elks,
foxes, wild cats, martens, squirrels, &c.—generally
live in the forests. Not only the numerous animals,
but also the varieties of wood in their forests, are in
many cases indispensable for the Indians. They obtain their canoes, their wigwams, and nearly all their
utensils from them. In their sugar-tree plantations
they find the greater part of their best and most
nourishing food, and I can scarce imagine an Ojibbeway paradise without sugar-maple plantations, in
which they spend the merriest part of the year.

The prairies, though they may appear so flowery to
the European in spring, when he gallops over them
well provisioned, expose those who live on them the
whole year through to innumerable privations. They
are in winter the roughest and most unprotected portion of America. And as here in the north the
winter is at least six months long, I do not see why
an Ojibbeway, sitting by a good fire and under shelter-
ing trees, should feel any enthusiasm for the prairie
deserts over which the snow-storms howl.

The Americans have now banished all the remnants
of the eastern forest tribes to the prairies or their
vicinity. If the Indians were so enamoured of the
western prairies, they ought to be in some degree

thankful for this banishment to their old longed-for
paradise.   But when I visited the Sioux on St. Peter's
River, who had just surrendered their forest land, and
were now living on the skirt of the prairies, I soon
found that these men lamented nothing so much as
the loss of their forests, and that all their thoughts,
and often, too, their steps, were directed to what was
called the "Great Forests."

It seems to me that the same may be said of all the
other Eastern races now settled westward.   They feel
there all more or less uncomfortable; "the land that,"
like Iphigenia, "they seek with the soul"—at least,
the terrestrial land—lies for all of them, without exception, eastwards, on the branches of the Mississippi,
and on the great lakes and countless rivers of the
Alleghany Mountains.   And yet they all place their
celestial paradise in the west, at the end of the world.

At present, hunting may be more productive on the
prairie than in the forests, where the white man has
built his towns all around.   But this was certainly
not the case formerly, or at the time when the religious views and traditions of the Indians assumed a
form.   But, even if we wished to represent the buf-
falo-covered prairies as a paradise for the hunter, it is
still questionable to me whether hunting forms a material feature of the Indian paradise.   To us Europeans hunting is more or less an amusement, but to
the Indian it is a toil, and frequently a most fatiguing
mode of life.   In many Indian dialects the words
" hunter" and " hunting" are synonymous with
" work" and " working."   A good hunter is a clever
and industrious workman.   As, then, the idea enter-
tained by most nations of paradise is, that it will be
without toil or labour, it is to me more than doubtful

whether they regard the chase as an element of their paradisiac existence. Among the Ojibbeways I never heard that they held such a view. I once asked a man of their tribe, who was describing paradise to me, and did not at all allude to hunting, "And then you will go every day to hunt and kill a countless number of animals?" "Oh no!" he replied, dryly, "there is no hunting or labour in paradise."

Lastly, the fact is worth mentioning that the nations living in California, beyond the prairies, across the Rocky Mountains, equally place their paradise in the west. If the central prairies of the continent appeared to the indians so glorious, the magnet of attraction among the Californian Indians would necessarily point to the east. It seems to me, then, as I said, probable that the feelings of the whole American race in these ideas obey another and higher impulse; that they place their paradise far beyond the prairies, as they say "at the end of the world," and that their imagination seeks and finds it in following the brilliant course of the sun and planets. I fancy the whole idea has an astronomical origin, if I may be permitted to use the term, and this view is supported by the Indians calling the milky way "the path of the dead," or "the path of souls." Among the Ojibbeways, the milky way is called "Jibekana," which word has that meaning. They would scarcely place their path of souls so high if they merely wished their dead to reach the prairies, or if they did not rather wish them to hurry after the setting sun.

We Europeans have so accustomed ourselves to connect the idea of paradise with the east and the rising sun, that we have at first some difficulty in following the opposite reasoning of the American aborigines. We picture to ourselves the rosy-fingered Helios rising each morning fresh and renewed from the Gardens of Paradise; and, besides, all the roots of our history and primeval traditions lie in the east, the home of all the European races and their patriarchal progenitors. But the western tendency of the Indian fancy is no less beautiful and natural—and, perchance, like our longing for the east, based on history. They compare their life-day with that of the sun. As the sun, when dying out in the west, becomes transfigured on his departure, and wondrous regions seem to lie expanded there, so they let the souls of their departed flutter after him, and be submerged with him in ether in those Elysian Fields in which he sinks to rest.

"But let us leave these suppositions out of sight, and come to more special topics about your paradise, to which you may be able to give me a more certain answer." Thus I spoke one day to a half-breed and an entire Indian, with whom I was discussing these matters on the shore of the Anse, "Tell me, now, how do you Ojibbeways regard the matter, and what traditions you possess of the migration of your deceased to paradise, and of the things that happen to them along the road, as well as those that await them on entering?"

Here my friends began telling me of a great, straight path, and its branch and side roads, of a great strawberry that lay in the path of souls, of a river, and a serpent before the entrance to paradise. I did not readily understand it all, so the full-blood Indian at length said to me, "Hadst thou a pencil and a piece of paper, I could draw all this accurately for thee, and then explain it much better."

I gave him what he wanted, and my man began

drawing and measuring, as if he were preparing a map, very thoughtfully and silently. When he had finished, he laid the following sketch before me :

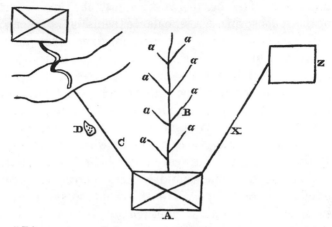

"Listen, now," he said, "and see. This is the earth (A, a rectangular parallelogram). On the earth God has planted his law, like a tree straight upwards, or like a path straight forward. Some wander the right path (B), but many get on to the side-paths of the lane (*a a a a*). These run into the desert.

"When men die, they all go, after death, along the path of souls (C). On the centre of this path (at D) thou seest the strawberry lying on one side. It is extraordinarily large, and is said to taste very sweet. A man stands by it, who invites all passers-by to taste it. But they must not accept it, for whatever soul does so is lost at once. Those that resist continue their journey prosperously till they come near paradise. It is altogether a journey of from three to four days. Then a large broad river bars the way. Over it there is no regular bridge. Something that looks like a great tree-stump lies across it. Its roots are firmly fastened on the opposite shore. On this side it raises its head, but it does not reach quite to the land. There is a small gap, over which the souls must hop. The log, too, is constantly shaking. Most of the souls spring across, balance themselves properly, and save themselves. Those, however, that jump short, or slip off the bridge, fall into the water, and are converted into toads or fishes. Hence it is not good when the deceased are bound to a board, for otherwise they might move freely, and, perchance, save themselves by swimming. If fastened to a board, they can be easily carried down with the stream. Little children, too, fare very badly here, because they are not good jumpers, and so they perish in great numbers at the bridge. Hence our mothers can never be consoled when their children die before the time when they could help themselves along the road to paradise.

"Paradise (Wakui, or Wakwi) was made by Menaboju.* He aided the Great Spirit in the creation of the world, and at first neither of them thought of a Paradise. Men, such was their decree, should be happy on this earth, and find a satisfaction in this life. But, as the Evil Spirit interfered, and produced wickedness, illness, death, and misfortunes of every description among them, the poor souls wandered about, deserted and hopeless. When the Great Spirit saw this, He grieved for them, and ordered Menaboju to prepare a paradise for them in the west, where they might assemble. Menaboju made it very beautiful, and he was himself appointed to receive them

---

* The same deity that Longfellow has apostrophised under the name of Hiawatha. Our author calls him the Indian Prometheus, but the legends he tells of him seem to give him higher attributes.

there. They are always merry, happy, and contented there, play the drum the whole day, and dance. They live on a variety of mushroom, and a species of wood that resembles the phosphorescent wood that is seen shining in our forests."

I. " Is there any hunting there ? "

My Indian. " No, war and hunting are at an end."

I. " But what are that path and quadrangle which thou hast drawn to the right (at X and Z)?"

With that the Indian told me he wished to designate the paradise of the Christians. They, he said, had also a paradise, into which no Indian, however, could enter. He knew nothing at all of its nature, but he had drawn it for the sake of giving me a perfect idea.

On seeing the two paradises, I remembered directly the double cemeteries so frequently seen at the mission villages on Lake Superior, one for the Christian, the other for the pagan, inhabitants of the village. I fancied my Indian had drawn the plan of such a village, the earth resembling the villages, the two paradises the two cemeteries, the paths of souls the two roads to the graveyards.

Probably, too, the tree of the law of the Great Spirit (B), with its branch roads, was derived from such a Christian mission, and was a Christian idea planted on pagan soil. It seemed to me to be rather isolated, and not bearing any reference to the rest.

As to the pagan part of the story, I may add the following remark :

The length of the journey which my Indian gave as three or four days I have heard confirmed by others, and it agrees in some respects with the length of the time of complaining and grieving, which the Indians

keep as a species of burying or death solemnity on the
loss of a relative. Still, according to the idea of
other persons, the journey must last longer, for they
often carry food and tobacco to the graves for weeks
or months, which the deceased can enjoy on his
migration. They also leave the gun, which they
give the deceased that he may kill some game to support him on his journey, for months in the grave, till
it is quite rusted, and thence they must at times presuppose a very long journey.

The tempting strawberry on the path of souls was
regularly described in all the accounts I heard from
the Ojibbeways of this migration. I was not told
who the tempter is who stands by the strawberry,
whether Matchi-Manitou or not. I also do not know
why the poor souls have to endure such trials on their
last journey. It might be assumed, that with the departure from this world each soul had closed its
account, and that it was by that time settled whether
it would be counted among the denizens of paradise
or not. Nor did I clearly learn what became of the
greedy souls which tasted the strawberry.

" After the strawberry," an Indian said, to whom I
read over the narrative as it was first told me, and
who added several corrections and emendations, "a
huge dog lies on the path. This dog, when sitting,
is as big as a house. He watches the path, allows
every one to pass unhindered westward, but does not
suffer any one to return from the world of souls to
the east."

The same Indian who added this dog to my picture, also made a remark as to the nature of the
bridge across the river. It was, he said, not really a
tree stump, but looked like one. In reality, it is a

great serpent, which has its tail on the opposite shore, and thrusts forth its head to this side. On this head the souls are obliged to leap. The movements of the wood were nothing but the constant windings of the snake's body, and hence it became so difficult to get across. As it seemed to me most uncharitable that the little innocent children should incur such danger at the Indian Styx, I mentioned this repeatedly to the Indians, but they were obstinate on this point, and would not allow that special arrangements were made for the children. Any one who could not help himself on the path of souls was badly off. Generally, however, they said the children met some charitable grown-up soul on the water or on the road, who helped them along. Hence it was good, that if a child died in a family, an uncle, cousin, or grown relative should go out of the world soon after, so as to help his little nephew or cousin. I was told of an Indian squaw whose child and husband died soon after each other, and that when the infant died the mother wept and yelled frightfully, but when her husband died directly after, she dried her tears, and appeared quite consoled. On being asked the reason of this extraordinary behaviour, she replied, " Yes, I am happy now, because my husband is close behind my child. He is strong, and a famous hunter. He will take care that the little one does not perish of hunger on the road. He will also surely carry it across the water. I am now free from care."

I never could rightly make out whether the souls that are lost at the strawberry, or step off the bridge and are converted into toads, are the souls of the wicked and evil doers; or if those which successfully dance the tight-rope into paradise are the good and virtuous; or whether, after the Indian fashion, all depends on skill and strength. I believe, however, that the last is the case, for I questioned Indians on the subject, and when they condescended to give me an answer at all, it was in this wise: "We know that you Christians make a distinction between good and bad persons, and have separate places for them at the end of the world. We have only one place for all, and we know not whether the Great Spirit makes such a distinction, or how and in what way he separates good and bad." I must confess I praised the Indians to a certain extent, because they pretended to no opinion on this subject, and left it an open question. Perhaps they think—indeed, they hinted so much to me—that what we praise and condemn here may be judged very differently by the Great Spirit. To this we must add, that among them the ideas of bad and good, lying and truth, evil deeds and heroic deeds, are more confused than among us.

"Do your deadly enemies, the Sioux, enter your paradise?"

"Yes," they replied, to my amazement; "we have already told thee that after death all war ceases. There is only one paradise for all savages and pagans. There the Indians are all related!"

If this be the correct view, and generally accepted, it is remarkable enough that these revengeful Indians are yet capable of forming the idea of a universal reconciliation after death.

"But how do you know all this about the nature of the path of life, as no one ever returned thence?"

"Oh!" they said, "many of our tribe have been there and returned. When a man dies, our jossakids make a feast, and in their convulsions the spirits carry them on the way of souls into paradise, They manage to deceive the attention of the great dog, and when they return they make a speech, and tell us all they have seen. Many a one of our hunters has been there too, when we fancied he was dead, but came to life again."

I. " Do you know exactly the history of any hunter who went into the other world while apparently dead ?"

They. " Oh yes; one lived among us, and often told us of it. He is still alive, and if he were here he could tell thee the story himself."

I. " What did he say to you—and how did it all happen ?"

They. " The hunter was sick—very sick. He was drawing nigh his end. He seemed to be dead, and his soul went on the great wandering. He marched straight to the west, towards the setting sun. At first he had to make his way through an extraordinary quantity of forest, scrub, and wilderness. There was no path there. At length he found a trail and narrow paths. These little paths came from every quarter. There were very many of them, the paths of all the dead souls from all the tribes and villages of the Indians, which at length formed into one great broad trail. Then he began to march along rapidly. Shortly before, his cousin and friend had died, and he hoped to catch him up. He knew that his cousin had taken with him neither a gun nor a cooking-kettle. He himself, however, had two guns and two kettles with him, and would gladly divide them with his cousin. Hence he hurried on.

" At length he arrived at the great strawberry. Near it stood a person, wrapped up in the black plumage of a raven. The raven spoke to him:

" ' Whither art thou going?'

" He replied, ' To the end of my path.'

" ' Thou art tired—stay a little while.'

" 'I will not.'

" ' Thou art hungry. Taste this. Take it.'

" ' No; I will wander on to the end of my path.'

"He went straight through. Without finding his cousin, he reached the great river that surrounds paradise. He wandered for a long time along the bank, and could not find the bridge. At last he heard a cry and a call, ' Viens icit! viens icit! viens icit!'

" He followed the call, and found that it was not a person, as he fancied, who shouted so, but the great log, which lay at anchor on its roots, and in its moving up and down produced such a creaking sound, just like the old trees in the forest, when the wind rattles them and they rub against other trees, are wont to utter, and which sounds exactly like ' Viens icit!' He succeeded in crossing, and entered the land of souls. It was a remarkably large village. Longways and broadways, as far as eye could see, huts and tents were erected closely together on the meadows and along the river. The end of the village could not be seen. A long distance off the murmur of the songs and the noise of the countless drums that were being beaten could be heard. On all sides were sports and amusements going on. On the meadows they were playing the ' jeu à la crosse.'

" The hunter sought his deceased parents in the throng, and though he at first fancied he should be unable to find them, they soon joined him. The mother was highly delighted, but the father was serious, frowned, and asked,

" ' What wilt thou here, my son ?' He tried to send

him back at once; but the mother prevented it, and held her son tightly, and led him to her wigwam. 'Thou art very sickly-looking, my son,' she said to him; 'but thou art not dead yet, as we are. Come in, refresh thyself, and eat.' And she gave him 'bellois séché' to eat. It is a little black fruit.* Then she gave him something that looked like dried meat, but it glistened like fungus, and he did not like it. 'What wilt thou here?' the father again interposed. 'Thou hast thy wife and thy children still at home. It will be a long time ere thou removest here for ever.' His two uncles, who had been dead a long period, also came up, and said: 'Why hast thou come hither? Go back, and take care of thy little ones!' And so he was obliged to go at last. The mother took a very sorrowful parting from him, and wrapped in paper something that looked like vermilion powder, put it in a box, and gave it to him, saying, 'That will do thee good.'

"The return was accompanied by much greater terrors. When he came to the river, he found its waters foaming and dashing as if in a storm. The banks were covered with many fragments of wood. These were the remains of many shipwrecked and broken children's cradles, which he had noticed on his arrival, nor did he hear the cry 'Viens icit!' as before. Instead of this he noticed a rattling and hissing, as if of serpents, and that the log was converted into a mighty serpent. It writhed and crested so that he began to feel rather frightened; still, he

---

* I do not know what sort of plant this may be. I cannot find the word in the Dictionary of the Academy, though it is possibly the plant I find there under the name of "la bellie" (the whortleberry). But I write it just as my Canadians spoke it. (Further on, Mr. Kohl will be found translating "bellois" as "whortleberry.")

must go across, as his father said, and return to his
little ones. Hence, he sprang forward, and reached
the opposite bank with great difficulty and trouble.

" When he arrived at the strawberry, that was also
changed. What seemed to him before a pink strawberry was now a red-hot mass" (" du fer rouge," my
interpreting Canadian said). " By its side no longer
stood a friendly inviting bird, but a great savage man,
who swung a heavy hammer in his hand, and menaced
him. Still, the hunter would not allow himself to be
frightened, and went on undisturbed.

" After some time he found his cousin on the road,
who must have marched very slowly, and whom he
had passed before, in his zeal, without noticing. He
tried at first to persuade him to turn back with him,
but his cousin would not. He was really dead, and
must go to the land of souls. So he gave him one of
his kettles and his guns, and some good advice in the
bargain, and let him go on.

" At last he lost his way. So long as the path was
broad, it was all right ; but when the little side-paths
began to branch off, he could no longer find the trail
of his village. He lost his way in the prairie, and
suddenly found himself encompassed by smoke and
flames, for the prairies were burning all around. At
first he was afraid he should never see his children
again, but he cast himself into the sea of flames.
Terror, however, agitated him so greatly, that he
drew a deep breath and—awoke.

" When he had opened his eyes a little, he heard
sobbing and weeping around him. It was his children and wife, who were standing round his bed, and
mourning him as one dead.

" ' I have been in the land of souls. I have seen my

mother, but have returned to you,' he said, to console them: and then, straightway remembering the charm his mother gave him, he begged his wife to feel if there were not something in his bag: he was too weak to do so himself. The squaw produced a small birch-bark box, and in it she found a piece of paper, in which was wrapped a pretty little blood-red sponge. He kept this receipt by him, ate some of it, and then lived for a long time with his squaw and children."

I repeat this story precisely as it was told to me. If we were, however, to take from it some coarse Indian additions, just as the Greek poets dressed up the dream of some Thracian boor, and converted it into the heroic descent of Orpheus into Hades in search of his Eurydice, we might fairly say that it contains a most affecting motive, and describes the following epos: how a hunter lies sick unto death; his mother appears to him in a dream; this apparition restores him to health. Love to his mother draws him to the other world, but the feeling of duty that attaches him to his children draws him home again, makes him conquer all the dangers on the road, and gives him back his strength, to enable him to live as an attentive father and husband.

I conversed afterwards with other Indians about their paradise. One of them spoke a little French, although not much more than the Upper Canadian "Français sauvage," as they often call it. I will here add his remarks and description of the Indian paradise. Though I know not what value I may attach to them, there is something in them that confirms the above. This was his account:

"Là, dans le paradis, il y a un chèfre le plus haut

de tous. Son nom est Omissa-Kamigokouè. Je ne peux pas bien traduire ce mot, mais ça veut casiment dire 'le maître de la terre.' Cette personne est toujours tranquille. Il ne parle jamais, excepté quand quelqu'un est né ici-bas. Il entend ça. Il entend ça comme un coup de canon, et alors il s'élève et crie le nom de cette personne, et dit combien de temps elle vivra—soixante ans, ou cinquante ans, ou deux jours. C'est son ouvrage. Et encore il a l'œuvre de recevoir toutes les personnes qui viennent au paradis. L'histoire est, qu'ils se trouvent plus riches là qu'icit. Il y a plus de quoi. Ils trouvent plus de chevreuils et encore de meilleurs animaux qu'ici-bas, et sans les chasser. Ils n'ont jamais chagrin, trouble, ni misère. Tout pousse sans travailler—les fraises, le pain, le ris, &c. Mais il y a là-dedans quelque chose de particulier. Quand quelqu'un est casiment mort icit, et quand il va sur le chemin du paradis, sans être réellement mort, il lui paraît que toutes les bonnes choses ne valent rien. Il pense que les fraises du paradis sont de bois, que le pain c'est du fer, et que les morceaux de viande sont des pierres. Mais quand il est réellement mort, il mange comme les autres, et trouve tout délicieux. Quant à l'enfer, je n'en sais rien du tout. Nous pensons que tous les hommes vont dans le même chemin."

CHAPTER XV.

THE PROTESTANT MISSION—THE GREAT FAST—THE DREAM OF LIFE—THE
INDIAN BLACKSMITH—THE WIGWAM—VISIT TO THE SHINING CLOUD—HIS
DREAM OF LIFE—THE FAILURE—THE BED IN THE TREE—EFFECT OF
FASTING—THE SPIRIT—MIGRATIONS OF THE SOUL—THE VISION—THE
GREAT COUNCIL—THE LADDER TO HEAVEN—RETURN TO LIFE—THE PRE-
DICTION FULFILLED.

WE paid a visit in our canoe to the Protestant mission, lying four miles off, on the other side of the
Anse. As this village was much older, and was
powerfully supported by the government of the United
States, we found everything here on a better footing.
The Indians had pretty, roomy houses, slept in excellent beds (such as I should like to introduce among
our German peasants, were it possible), and had small
kitchen gardens round their cabins. The most respected man in the village was the " Indian blacksmith," appointed by government. I found in him a
very interesting man, living with his large family in a
delightfully airy cabin; and he sheltered me for the
night, and allowed me to rest in a luxurious bed,
such as had not fallen to my lot for a considerable
time.

I formed here several peculiarly interesting acquaint-

ances among the Indians, with whom I continued my
conversations on several points affecting their countrymen. More especially I made deeper investigations
into their great fasts and dreams of life.

I found this subject most remarkable; in fact, could
it be possible to hear anything stranger, or, I might
say, more wonderful, than these stories of unheard-of
castigations and torments, to which young boys of
thirteen or fourteen subject themselves, merely for
the sake of an idea, a dream, or the fulfilment of a religious duty, or to ask a question of fate ?

When was it ever known, among us Europeans,
that boys or girls were able, at the tenderest age, to
fast for days on behalf of a higher motive, retire to
the most remote forests, defy all the claims of nature,
and fix their minds so exclusively on celestial matters,
that they fell into convulsions, and attained an increased power of perception, which they did not possess in ordinary life ? What courage! what self-
control! what power of enduring privations does this
presuppose!

I say such things would appear to me incredible,
did I not hear them spoken of everywhere as ordinary
occurrences. More surprising still is it when we remember that it is not merely some extraordinary
youth who is capable of this, but that every Indian,
without exception, displays such heroism.

Although, then, several had described to me their
dreams of life, I was still desirous to hear more. Besides, with every new story I discovered fresh accessories, and much was still unclear and doubtful to me.
Hence, when I made the acquaintance of old Agabe-
gijik, at the aforesaid Protestant mission, and had conversed for some time with him, I brought him to talk

about these dreams. And this old man promised to tell me his dream of life, with all its accompanying details, if I would visit him at his hut, where we could sit comfortably round the fire.

Agabe-gijik, translated literally, means "the end of the projecting cloud." At times such brilliantly-illumined cloud-edges appear in the sky, resembling beaming or snow-clad promontories. This name refers to such a manifestation, and, indeed, the Indians are usually close observers of the appearances in the sky, and especially of the frequently menacing and black, frequently bright and cheery, cloud formations. They have even many expressions, which may be almost called scientific, for frequently recurring forms of the clouds and the characteristic features of the sky physiognomy, which are quite untranslatable, and for which it is hopeless to seek an equivalent in European languages. Thus, the Ojibbeways, for instance, have a peculiar fixed name for the appearance of the sunshine between two clouds. In the same way they have a distinct appellation for the small blue oases which at times are seen in the sky between dark clouds. They will also derive the names of their heroes from the phenomena observable in the heavens. Thus, one of the best-known chiefs on the Upper Mississippi is called the " Blue Hole," or the " Bright Patch in the Dark Cloud Sky." The Indians render this with a single designative word, which the English have translated "hole in the day" (or hole in the sky, for sky and day are synonymous in the Indian language). Hole in the Day is a chief known far and wide. Another instance is my friend Agabe-gijik, whose name, according to the above, may be translated the "Brilliant Cloud-head." I need not stop to explain why such characteristic and poetic names are admirably adapted for prominent men of the nation.

Old Cloud-head was a pagan, but had several relatives at the Christian mission, and had come with some other members of the family, also heathens, to visit his Christian relatives in this village. He had been on a visit here for two years already, and had built his lodge a little away from the mission, on a clearing in the dense forest.

We started for his lodge one day after dinner in the canoe, for in this pathless country you progress better by water than on *terra firma*. I have a natural predilection for the land, because I can then see a little more of the interior of the country; but the people here have an opposite predilection to thrust me into a canoe on every possible occasion, to which they take as readily as we put on our walking-boots.

We shot onwards in our light bark as if borne on the back of a dolphin, coasted along the precipices and forests, and soon reached the clearing which had been pointed out to me as the residence of the " Shining Cloud." A young and handsome Indian was busy on the beach preparing his fishing materials and his canoe, in which his young squaw, our old man's daughter, was helping him. His name was the " Spotted Feather," and I mention him here, as I intend to say something about him presently.

The high beach formed a rather sharp incline towards the water. On the topmost edge I saw three white flags fluttering from tall poles: they marked the graves of those members of the family who had died during the two years' residence here. The graves were carefully tended, and made at equal distances from each other on the breezy cliff, so that the sea wind blew freshly over them, and kept the flags in a constant state of flutter. From one of the poles waved a Sioux scalp, which they had brought from the interior as a family trophy, and offered to one of their deceased.

When we reached the top, a little pleasant forest oasis opened before us, at the rear of which stood the cabin.

Small beginnings of potato culture, and attempts at garden-beds and bean patches, had been made amid the piles of timber and stone, while around all frowned the dense, gloomy forest, like a lofty wall.

The entire scene was very pleasant, and, at the same time, most peculiar. I was most pleased with the three graves in the front and the fluttering flags. How tender, to wish to have the memory of the dear departed so constantly before them! These ever-fluttering, ever-moving, flags over the graves are highly symbolical: they doubtlessly refer to an existence beyond the grave, the immortality of the living soul.

I had rarely seen so cleanly and carefully kept a wigwam as that of old Cloud. The flooring was raised above the damp earth, and we had to mount a couple of steps. Floor and walls, seats and beds, were covered with a quantity of fresh, gay-coloured mats, which gave the whole a very pleasing appearance. It was all so quiet around, as if the huts were uninhabited, that we were quite astounded, on entering, to see a number of persons collected in groups in the room. This stillness is usual in all Indian wigwams, when the fire-water has not made the denizens noisy. They never quarrel with each other, and cursing is a rarity among them. The old papa and grand-papa, a little, most intelligent-looking man, in spite of his bushy, uncombed hair, sat in the centre, smóking his pipe, and awaiting us at the appointed hour. An old woman was sewing shirts and squatting near the windows or light-holes. Some grown-up sons or sons-in-law, with their squaws, sat at the places belonging to them, and seemed to be resting from their fatigue, or busy with their medicine-bags or hunting-sacks. Only very rarely did they exchange a few whispered words.

We went up to our old man, and sat down as quickly as possible on his mat, while laying a couple of packets of tobacco in his lap as greeting. According to Indian habits, it is not proper or polite to remain standing any length of time in their lodges. If you do not sit down soon, or if you walk about, the squaws will soon make some sharp remarks, or you will hear from all sides the exclamation, " Sit down! pray sit down !" Indian guests, when they enter a hut—even that of a stranger—hence sit down at once. If he be a perfect stranger, or has some favour to ask, he will take a seat very modestly near the door, and remain silent, till the head of the family asks the cause of his visit. If, however, he has business with any person in the lodge, he walks straight up to his mat, and places himself at once under his protection by squatting down by his side.

The confined space in these wigwams, in which there is no room for walking about, causes this custom to appear founded on reason. As with every step you invade the territory of another family, and might see all sorts of things that a stranger ought not to see, respect demands that the guest should sit down directly, and fix his eyes on the ground. Indians, as a general rule, are not fond of restless people; little children and dogs have the sole privilege of disturbing the family, and in this hut swarms of both were crawling in and out.

"Well, then, Agabe-gijik, thou rememberest thy promise to us, yesterday, to tell us thy dream of life and thy great youth fast, with all the accompanying incidents. Wilt thou now keep thy promise?" So we spoke at once to our host, with whom we were as good as alone, for the rest of the company took no notice of us, but went on with their little amusements, as if living in so many different rooms.

"Ah!" the Cloud said, after a long silence and rumination, "when God cleaned and arranged His great wigwam, I was swept out like a useless grain of dust, cast into a corner like a patch of dirt. As the whole room was prepared for the great festival, I lay my whole life in the corner, poor and forgotten, while the others were dancing. I grew old in a night. What great story can a man like me tell?"

After the old man had thus spoken, he was again silent. What he said was a modest introduction to his story—a *captatio benevolentiæ*, after the Indian fashion.

"Thou speakest truly," we replied. "We men are all so. Nature is a great banqueting-hall, in which man appears forced to suffer more than all the other creatures. And especially when we grow older, it seems to us as if the human beings around entirely forget us. But we Christians say of the Great Spirit, that He even counts the hairs on our heads, and we are all numbered by him. Speak! Didst thou obtain in thy dream of youth a lesson of life—a revelation? Tell us what thou didst see in thy great fast."

"Kitchi-Manitou," the old man went on, after

another pause, " sent us our Midés from the east, and his prophets laid it down as a law that we should lead our children into the forest so soon as they approach man's estate, and show them how they must fast, and direct their thoughts to higher things; and in return it is promised us that a dream shall be then sent them as a revelation of their fate—a confirmation of their vocation—a consecration and devotion to Deity, and an eternal remembrance and good omen for their path of life.

" I remember that my grandfather, when I was a half-grown lad, frequently said to my father, in the course of the winter, ' Next spring it will be time for us to lead the lad into the forest and leave him to fast.' But nothing came of it that spring; but when the next spring arrived, my grandfather took me on one side, and said to me, ' It is now high time that I should lead thee to the forest, and that thou shouldst fast, that thy mind may be confirmed, something be done for thy health, and that thou mayst learn thy future and thy calling.'

" The grandfather then took me by the hand, and led me deep into the forest. Here he selected a lofty tree, a red pine, and prepared a bed for me in the branches, on which I should lie down to fast. We cut down the bushes, and twined them through the pine branches. Then I plucked moss, with which I covered the trellis-work, threw a mat my mother had made for the occasion over it, and myself on top of it. I was also permitted to fasten a few branches together over my head, as a sort of protection from wind and rain.

" Then my grandfather said to me that I must on no account take nourishment, neither eat nor drink, pluck no berries, nor even swallow the rain-water that

might fall. Nor must I rise from my bed, but lie quite
still day and night, keep by myself strictly, and await
patiently the things that would then happen.

"I promised my grandfather this, but, unfortunately, I did not keep my promise. For three days I
bore the lying, and hunger, and thirst; but when
I descended from the tree into the grass on the fourth
day I saw the acid and refreshing leaves of a little
herb growing near the tree. I could not resist it, but
plucked the leaves and ate them. And when I had
eaten them my craving grew so great that I walked
about the forest, sought all the edible sprigs, plants,
mosses, and herbs I could find, and ate my fill. Then
I crept home, and confessed all to my grandfather
and father."

"Wert thou not severely punished?" I interposed.

"Not further than that they reproved me, and told
me I had done wrong, at which I felt ashamed; and,
as I had broken my fast, it was all over with my
dream, and I must try again next spring. I might
now have been a man, but would remain for another
year a useless fellow, which was a disgrace at my
age."

I. "I pray thee stop a moment, and permit me to
ask some questions here, as we have a year before us.
Why did thy grandfather manage all this, and not thy
father?"

The Cloud. "My father was still young. My
grandfather was old. For all such affairs old men
have the most experience and knowledge. And they
also pay greater attention that the children shall be
instructed, and that all shall be done according to old
customs."

I. "Further tell me how high do you make your
dream-beds in the trees?"

The Cloud. " Generally from ten to twelve feet above the ground. Sometimes, though, they are more than twenty feet. The tallest and finest trees are selected."

I. "Why do you make this bed in the trees? Why do you not build a hut on the ground?"

The Cloud. " A cause du Matchi-Manitou." (On account of the Evil Spirit.)

The Cloud gave me no further explanation of this laconic reply, and left it to me to imagine that, in all probability, according to the Indian theory, the good spirits and salutary dream genii reside high in the air, while the Matchi-Manitou wanders about on the ground and annoys people. At any rate, the latter has his snakes, toads, and other animals, against which the dreamer, who is not prepared for hunting and defence, cannot protect himself.

I may here add another parenthetical remark, that if the entire operation of the dreaming is interrupted by the nightmare, or any bad dream, it is rendered impossible during that spring. The Ojibbeways have divided the dreams into various classes, and give each a special name. The excellent Bishop Baraga, in his lexicon of that language, has collected the Indian names for a bad dream, an impure dream, an ominous dream, as well as for a good or a happy dream.

I will not add the Indian names, as they would be highly unserviceable to my readers; but the fact itself may be interesting. My industrious lexicon, however, as its compiler assured me, has by no means exhausted all the classes of dreams.

The boys are warned, so soon as a nightmare or a bad dream oppresses them, to give up the affair at once, come down from the tree, and return home, and

try again and again till the right dream comes. But
I was unable to discover how they begin to recognise
a good or a bad dream.

The Cloud. " When the spring of the next year was
approaching, my grandfather told me, although a great
deal of ice and snow still lay in the forest, that it was
time for me to go out again to fast, and try my dream.
As, however, I was ashamed of my defeat in the last
year, and had determined on carrying out the affair
now, I begged him to let me go alone, as I knew what
I had to do, and would not return till my right dream
had come to me. I had already selected a place in
the forest I knew, where I intended to make my bed.
It was on a little island covered with trees, in the
centre of a forest lake. I described the place to my
friends, that they might come in search of me if anything happened to me, and set out."

I. " Why didst thou select that precise spot ?"

The Cloud. " Because I knew that one of my relations and friends was lying on his dream-bed in the
same locality."

I. " Didst thou intend, then, to communicate
with thy friend during the period of dreaming and
fasting ?"

The Cloud. " Not so; for he was some distance
from me—two or three miles. But though I could not
see or hear my friend, nor be allowed to speak with
him, there seemed to me some consolation in knowing
him near me and engaged in the same things to which
I was going to devote myself.

" There was ice still on the little lake, and I reached
my island across it. I prepared my bed, as on the
first time, in a tall, red pine, and laid myself on the
branches and moss.

" The first three or four fast-days were as terrible
to me as the first time, and I could not sleep at nights
for hunger and thirst. But I overcame it, and on the
fifth day I felt no more annoyance. I fell into a
dreamy and half paralysed state, and went to sleep.
But only my body slept; my soul was free and
awake.*

" In the first nights nothing appeared to me; all
was quiet: but on the eighth night I heard a rustling
and waving in the branches. It was like a heavy
bear or elk breaking through the shrubs and forest.
I was greatly afraid. I thought there were too many
of them, and I made preparations for flight. But the
man who approached me, whoever he may have been,
read my thoughts and saw my fear at a distance; so
he came towards me more and more gently, and rested,
quite noiselessly, on the branches over my head. Then
he began to speak to me, and asked me, ' Art thou
afraid, my son?' ' No,' I replied; ' I no longer fear.'
' Why art thou here in this tree?' ' To fast.' ' Why
dost thou fast?' ' To gain strength, and know my life.'
' That is good; for it agrees excellently with what is
now being done for thee elsewhere, and with the
message I bring thee. This very night a consultation
has been held about thee and thy welfare; and I have
come to tell thee that the decision was most favourable. I am ordered to invite thee to see and hear
this for thyself. Follow me.' "

I. " Did the spirit say this aloud?"

The Cloud. " No: it was no common conversation:
nor do I believe that I spoke aloud. We looked into
each other's hearts, and guessed and gazed on our

---

* " Mais ce n'était que mon corps qui dormait. Mon esprit était libre
et veillait." These were my interpreter's exact words.

mutual thoughts and sensations. When he ordered
me to follow him, I rose from my bed easily and of
my own accord, like a spirit rising from the grave,
and followed him through the air. The spirit floated
on before me to the east, and, though we were moving
through the air, I stepped as firmly as if I were on
the ground, and it seemed to me as if we were ascend-
ing a lofty mountain, ever higher and higher, eastward.

" When we reached the summit, after a long time,
I found a wigwam built there, into which we entered.
I at first saw nothing but a large white stone, that lay
in the middle of the hut; but, on looking round more
sharply, I saw four men sitting round the stone. They
invited me to take a seat on the white stone in the
midst of them. But I had hardly sat down than the
stone began sinking into the earth. ' Stay!' one of
the men said; ' wait a minute; we have forgotten the
foundation.' Thus speaking, he fetched a white
tanned deer-skin, and covered the stone with it; and
when I sat down on it again, it was as firm as a tree,
and I sat comfortably."

I. " What is the meaning of this deer-skin: who
was it that gave it to thee?"

The Cloud. " On that point I have remained in un-
certainty. A man does not learn everything in these
dreams. As I sat there and looked round me again,
I noticed a multitude of other faces. The wigwam
was very large, and filled with persons. It was an
extraordinary council assembly. One of the four took
the word, and ordered me to look down. When I
did so, I saw the whole earth beneath me, spread out
deep, deep, and wide, wide, before me."

I. " Did it appear to thee round?"

The Cloud. " No; it had four corners. Immediately another of the four took the word, and bade me look up. I looked up, and saw the whole sky over me quite near. I gazed a long, long time, and almost forgot where I was, for it was a glorious sight. Then a third took the word, and spoke: ' Thou hast gazed. Now say; whither wilt thou now — down below, whence thou camest, or up above? The choice is left thee.' ' Yes, yes,' I replied, ' I will go up; for that I have fasted.'

" The four men seemed pleased at my answer, and the fourth said to me, ' Ascend!' He pointed to the back of my stone seat, and I saw that it had grown, and went up an extraordinary height. There were holes cut in it, and I could climb up as if on a ladder. I climbed and clambered higher and higher, and at length came to a place where four white-haired old men were sitting, in the open air, round the pillar. A dazzling cupola was arched above them. I felt so light that I wished to go higher, but the four old men shouted ' Stop!' all at once. ' Thou must not go higher. We have not permission to allow thee to pass. But enough that is good and great is already decreed for thee. Look around thee. Thou seest here around us all the good gifts of God—health, and strength, and long life, and all the creatures of nature. Look on our white hair: thine shall become the same. And that thou mayst avoid illness, receive this box with medicine. Use it in case of need; and whenever thou art in difficulty, think of us, and all thou seest with us. When thou prayest to us, we will help thee, and intercede for thee with the Master of Life. Look around thee once more! Look, and forget it not! We give thee all the birds, and eagles, and wild beasts, and all the other animals thou seest fluttering and running in our wigwam. Thou shalt become a famous hunter, and shoot them all!'

"I gazed in amazement on the boundless abundance of game and birds which flocked together in this hall, and was quite lost at the sight. Then the four old men spoke to me. 'Thy time has expired, thou canst go no higher; so return.'

"I then quickly descended my long stone ladder. I was obliged to be careful, for I noticed it was beginning to disappear beneath my feet, and melted away like an icicle near the fire. When I got back to my white stone it returned to its former dimensions. The great council was still assembled, and the four men round the stone welcomed me, and said, 'It is good, Agabe-gijik. Thou hast done a brave deed, and hast gazed on what is beautiful and great. We will all testify for thee that thou didst perform the deed. Forget nothing of all that has been said to thee. And all who sit round here will remember thee, and pray for thee as thy guardian spirits.'

"After this I took my leave, and let myself down to my bed in the red pine. I found that three more days had passed away. During this time my body had lain there motionless as a corpse; only my soul had wandered so freely in the air. Then I breathed, sighed, and moved about like one waking from a deep sleep. When I opened my eyes and looked around me, I found the green branches of the tree gnawed and sucked, and guessed that my craving body during my absence had bitten off the bark and licked the sap of the pine-shoots. This was a sign to me of the wretched condition into which my body had fallen. I also felt myself so weak that I could not stir.

"All at once I heard a voice, a whistle, and my name called. It was my grandfather, who had come on the tenth day to seek me. 'Come down, my son,' he said, 'and join us here.' I could only reply to him in a weak voice that I was unable to stir, and that I could not return over the lake. I had walked across the ice ten days before, but the warm weather had melted it all, and I was cut off on my island. My grandfather ran home quickly, and returned with my uncle. They brought a canoe, took me down from the tree, and carried me across the lake. From there we were obliged to go on foot. At first I could hardly move, but by degrees I grew better.

"On the road home a bear met us. My uncle wished to shoot it, but both grandfather and myself said, 'Stay! that must not be! On his return from his dream and his great fasting, a man must not shed the blood of any creature, or even shoot any animal for three days after.' I then walked up to the bear, and said to it, 'Bear, my cousin, I have great strength. I have a powerful medicine. I come from the spirits. I could kill thee on the spot, but will not do so. Go thy way!' The bear listened to me, and ran away into the forest. Perhaps my miserable appearance terrified it, for I was thin, pale, and exhausted.

"At home they prepared for me a soft bed of moss, on which I lay down like a patient. It was not till the following day that I took any food, but three days later I was quite recovered, and strong. And from that time I was, and remained, a perfect man!"

CHAPTER XVI.

TRADITIONS ABOUT THE EUROPEANS—THE DREAM—THE DEPUTATION—
OJIBBEWAY SONGS—SPECIMENS—A MOURNING SONG—A LOVE STRAIN—
SONGS OF VENGEANCE—VOYAGEURS' SONGS—CHANSONS A L'AVIRON—THE
OAR AND THE PADDLE—SIR GEORGE SIMPSON—THE GOVERNOR'S CANOE—
THE SONG OF LA BELLE ROSE—COMPLAINTES—OVID'S "TRISTIA"—THE
HALF-BREEDS—THE STORY OF JEAN CAYEUX—INTERCESSION OF THE
VIRGIN—THE GREAT CALUMET FALL—PURSUIT—THE IROQUOIS—DEATH
OF CAYEUX—POPULARITY OF THE COMPLAINTE.

OUR historians have reported to us what effect was
produced on the inhabitants of Europe when Columbus
displayed the first red men among them, and took
some with him through the Spanish provinces and
towns on his triumphant procession from Seville to
Barcelona. On the other hand, we know very little
as to the effect which the sudden appearance of the
pale faces produced upon the Indians, how the news of
it ran from nation to nation, or what fables originated
touching this event among the aborigines. No one
was enabled to watch the development of these things,
for the report preceded the Europeans, and none
of the new comers understood the language of the
nations.

Hence, it afforded me great satisfaction to find at

Anse at least a trail of those traditions which bear
reference to the first appearance of Europeans in
America. I met at the Protestant mission, across the
bay, an Indian of the name of Peter Jones, who belonged to the totem of the Makwa, that is, the clan of
the Bear, a very old tribe on Lake Superior.

He told me that his father, grandfather, great-grand-
father—in short, all his ancestors—had lived here since
pre-historic times. Long before anything was known
of white men in these parts, his people had lived on
the small promontory of the bay now called the
Point of the old Village. In the same way, he added,
one of his ancestors had been the first to journey
down to the whites on the great Montreal river (St.
Lawrence). I begged Peter Jones to describe this to
me, and tell me who first brought information about
the whites, and how he described them.

No one, he said, had " brought" these news, and
no eye-witness had described the strangers to the
Ojibbeways, but when the white men—the French—
came up the Lower St. Lawrence, one of his forefathers, who was a great jossakid, immediately had a
dream, in which he saw something most highly astonishing—namely, the arrival of the white men.

The seer busied himself for days, and very earnestly,
with this dream. He fasted, took vapour baths, shut
himself up apart from the rest in his prophet lodge,
and did penance in such an unusual manner, that it
caused a general excitement in the tribe, and people
asked each other what would be the end of it all ?
Whether it meant a universal war with the Sioux, or
a great famine, a very productive hunting season, or
something else equally grand ?

At length, when the prophet had examined into

everything carefully, and had the whole story arranged, he summoned the other Jossakids, and Midés, and the Ogimas (chieftains) of the tribe together, and revealed to them that something most astounding had happened.

Then he told them that men of a perfectly strange race had come across the great water to their island (America). Their complexions were as white as snow, and their faces were surrounded by a long bushy beard. He also described to them exactly the wondrously large canoes in which they had sailed across the big sea, and the sails and masts of the ships, even their iron corslets, long knives, guns, and cannon, whose fire and tremendous explosion had filled him with terror even in his dreams and convulsions.

His clairvoyance entered into the smallest details, and he described exactly how the " boucan" (smoke) ascended from their long tubes into the air, just as it did from the Indian pipes.*

This story of the old jossakid, who spent a good half-day in telling it, was listened to by the others in dumb amazement, and they agreed on immediately preparing an expedition of several canoes, and sending a deputation along the lakes and the great river to the eastward, which could examine these matters on the spot, and make a report on them to the tribe.

This resolution was immediately carried out. The deputies voyaged for weeks and months through the lands of many friendly tribes, who knew nothing as yet of the arrival of the white men, probably because

* My French Canadians and interpreters here frequently employ the word "boucan" or "boucane" for smoke, although this meaning is not found in the Dictionary of the Academy. In the latter the word is explained to be " le lieu où l'on fume la viande."

they had not such clairvoyant prophets and dreamers among them as the gifted men on the Anse.

I may remind my readers here, that it is known from Cortes's History how Moctezuma continually asserted that the arrival of the Spaniards had been predicted and described long before by his prophets and priests. The affair seems to have the same bearing through all the Indian tribes. If indisposed to believe in the clairvoyance of the priests, we may imagine that the influential men of a tribe, perhaps, had secret information, first learned the event from eye-witnesses, and then, in the hope of maintaining or increasing their reputation, narrated the history, after the Indian fashion, as a revelation of their own.

When the deputies from the Anse at length came to the lower regions of the river, they found one evening a clearing in the forest, where the trees, even the largest, had been cut down quite smoothly. They camped here, and inspected the marvels more closely. They examined the stumps of the trees, which seemed to have been cut through by the teeth of a colossal beaver. They had never seen such a thing before, and their jossakid explained to them that this must have been a camping-place of the white men, and that the trees had been probably felled with the long knives he saw in his dream. This circumstance—the trees having been cut down with such ease and in such numbers—filled the poor savages with terror, and tremendous respect for the white men, and gave them the first tangible impression of their superiority. With their own stone-headed axes they could not achieve such feats.

They also found long, rolled-up shavings, which not

one of them was able to account for, and they thrust
them, as something most extraordinary, into their ears
and hair. They also examined very carefully the
pieces of gay calico and woollen rags the French had
left behind them at their camping-ground, and fastened
them round their heads, as if they were magical productions.

Thus bedizened, they at length came up with the
French, among whom they found everything: the
ships, the long knives, the thundering fire-tubes, the
bushy beards and pale faces, just as their prophet had
seen them in the dream and described them. They
were very kindly received, and dismissed with rich
presents of coloured cloth and pieces of calico.*

When they returned with these things to Lake
Superior and the Anse, the excitement was very great.
The people flocked in from all sides to hear the wondrous story. Hunters came down from the interior of
the forests to obtain a shaving, or one of the lumps of
wood, which had been cut off with such extraordinarily sharp tools. The cloths and calico were torn
into a thousand little pieces, so that each might have
one. In the same way as they sent the scalps of their
enemies, bound on long poles, through special messengers to each other, splinters of wood and coloured
strips of calico were attached to poles, and sent from
one chieftain and tribe to the other. They passed
from hand to hand round the whole lake, and in
this way the population of Lake Superior became first
adorned with European wares. In a very modest

---

* Unfortunately my reporter, or the tradition he narrated to me, was
not so circumstantial at this interesting period of the story as I should have
liked.

way, it is true, at that period, while now they wear on their bodies whole shirts of flowered stuffs and wide woollen cloaks.

The stories the Ojibbeways tell in natural prose are generally very long, in many cases interminable. And these stories may, in a certain sense, be called poetry; but so soon as the Indians rise into the actual territory of material poetry, accompanied by tune, they seem to grow remarkably laconic.

Their "songs" consist nearly always of only one verse, and one or two ideas. It is a versified sigh, or an exclamation of joy set to words, to which they give length and expression, by repeating it a countless number of times. I do not know whether they have any peculiar music, but that there must be a species of metrical rhythm is evident from the fact that they accompany such songs with music and chorus, or with drum-beating, and a regular strain of the voice.

The melodies appear to be singularly monotonous, and on first hearing them the European fancies he is listening to a murmuring cadence, apparently imitated from the roaring of the wind, no matter whether he be told that the subject of the song is elegiac or erotic, peaceful or martial. But the characteristic variations are traceable on repeated hearing.

Among the Dakotas (Sioux) I heard very pleasant tunes. A half-breed once sang to me there a series of songs, whose music, though very wild and melancholy, was so original that I wished I could have written it down. I found an extraordinary resemblance between this Dakota music and that of the Cossacks and Little Russians. I discovered not only isolated accords, but also regularly recurring cadences, almost exactly like those of the Cossacks, especially the shrill note accompanying the end of the melody. But, unluckily, I am speaking here of a subject which it is difficult to make persons understand with words.

It would be indeed strange if music had not assumed various forms among the Indians, for these tribes, according to the unanimous opinion of all who have attempted to give them musical instruction, not only, as a rule, possess a correct ear, a right feeling for harmony and discord, but also very good and plea-santly sounding voices.

Here, on the Anse, I also found a half-breed who knew many Ojibbeway songs by heart, and sang me several of them, which I will attempt to give here. I purposely say "attempt," for drawing from these Indians or half-breeds the real and precise meaning of their songs is a labour of such difficulty that no one could believe who had not tried it.

On regarding the produce of my exertions, it may be possibly considered very trifling; but among the Indians, when not speaking of their hunting and wars, it is ever "Excusez du peu." Besides, the main point is not so much the songs themselves as the circum-stances under which they are composed, and the manner in which they are applied. I always inquired carefully into this, and learnt in this way, if not valu-able poetry from the Ojibbeway Olympus, at any rate the situations of life in which they compose lyrics or employ them.

As a specimen of an Indian song of consolation, the following was offered me, sung by an Indian, who had marched into the field, for the purpose of com-forting his three sisters who were mourning him at home.

> Weep not, ye three sisters, for your brother!
>   For your brother is a brave!
> Weep not, ye three sisters, for your brother!
>   For your brother is a man!
> Weep not, ye three sisters, for your brother!
>   For he is returning as a victor!

There is no very great inventive faculty displayed in this; but how peculiar are the situations in which it is sung! The brother, aware how anxious his sisters are at home for him, sings it so soon as he has secured the enemy's scalp, and repeats it every night on his homeward march over the camp fire, his scalps being hung up around him the while. He believes that the song will have a consolatory effect on his sisters from a distance, just as it cheers himself.

But his sisters also know the song, which their brother made expressly for the occasion, and sang to them when he bade them farewell. They know it by heart, and sing it, too, for a consolation in the paternal lodge, till at length, on the approach of the brother to his home, their songs are harmoniously commingled.

> My son, my son, my young Wabasha!
>   Why hast thou left me to pine?
> Why art thou gone so soon to the land of shades?
> Oh! hadst thou let me, aged man, go with thee!

This verse, which an old Indian sang about the death of his son Wabasha, I will not pretend to assert is a very poetical elegy. But now listen to the way in which these mourning words were uttered, which my half-breed himself overheard, and described to me thus:

"I was voyaging with an uncle of young Wabasha —who had died two years back—a brother of his father. We were going to pay a visit to the latter and bargain for his furs, and we knew his hunting-camp was on the bank of our river.

"We paddled in our canoe a long way down the stream. At length, one evening, we came to a small lake, on which the evening mist had already settled.

"'This is, I believe, the lake on which my brother lives,' the Indian said: 'yes, listen; I hear his voice from the other bank.'

"'Ha!' I remarked; 'bravo! how merry he is; he is singing and shouting.'

"'No,' my Indian replied, motioning me to be silent; 'he is singing, I allow, but it is a mourning song. He is lamenting his son, who died two years agone. Hearest thou not how melancholy the sound pierces through the fog?'

"In truth, I soon noticed it. It was a death-song. The old man lamented in a trembling voice, which affected me deeply. As we had moved up near him, unnoticed, through the fog, I could at last clearly distinguish the words: 'My son, my son, my young Wabasha, why hast thou left me?' &c. But the Indian, his brother, considered my listening improper; so he plashed with the paddle, and the hunter heard it. Hush! his song ceased, and when we joined him on the bank, he had dried his tears, and seemed unaffected and careless. We pretended not to have heard anything, and only talked of hunting and the fur trade."

This scene reminded me of Landseer's solitary and lamenting stag on the Highland tarn. Perhaps my Indian, lamenting alone for his child who died two years back, is a less picturesque subject, but it is more affecting.

Many other songs imparted to me, and translated

with difficulty, had no other value than as indicating
the usually most prosaic, practical, and coarse fashion
of Indian thought and feeling. What else can we
say to such a verse as this, said to be the courting
song of an Indian lover:

> It is time, it is time, it is the autumn time,
> That is the right time for me to seek a squaw who will work for me!

How insignificant, too, appears the song given me as
the parting elegy of a maiden when her hero leaves
her. It was sung to me several times, just as the
lamenting lovers sing it. So long as I did not understand it, it seemed to have a trace of poetry; but, when
translated, it was no more than this:

> What will become of poor me
> If my Ninimoshin* leaves me perhaps for ever?

The following song was sung by an Indian girl residing in Sault de Sainte Marie, whose Ninimoshin,
the half-breed, Jean Paget, had gone to Lake Superior:

> Dear friend, worthy friend, look up, look up,
> Our Ninimoshin has promised that in three months he will be here again;
> The time has nearly expired, and the end is quickly approaching!
> To-morrow, perhaps, we shall see his red canoe in the white foam of the
> cataracts;
> To-morrow, perhaps, see him sitting in his red canoe, our sunburnt Nini-
> moshin!

The girl who composed this song, and sang it to
her friend some hundreds of times, was tremendously
in love with Jean Paget, and, perchance, believed
herself worthy of his love. Her friend listened to it
silently, and, while busily working mocassins for Jean
Paget, now and then joined in. She was secure of

---

* "Ninimoshi," or "Ninimoshin," originally means "cousin," or "friend"
generically. In the love-songs my Canadian always translated it "cava-
lier."

his love, and when she married him after his return, she often recited to him in jest the sighing strain of her " foolish friend." He remembered it, and translated it to me twenty-two years after.

An Indian girl is capable of singing a verse like the following the whole winter through:

How sad is the thought that my friend in autumn departed;
How sweet is the hope that with spring I shall see him returning!

She will sing these words, as I said, every day for six months. Still it shows how earnestly the Indians regard matters, and how entirely they devote themselves to one or two ideas. Verses expressive of revenge they will sing for a longer period, and these verses, like their revenge, they never forget. I heard of an Indian chief who sang to his drum hundreds of times the three words, " Thou wolf on the prairie! thou wolf on the prairie! thou wolf on the prairie!" Thus singing, he sat day after day by the fire. He gave to this extremely laconic verse a secret, and, as it seemed, serious meaning, though he told it to nobody until he showed it in the spring, when he made war upon an enemy among the Sioux.

In Canada, and, indeed, throughout North America, I had heard much said in praise of the Canadian Voyageurs' songs without rightly discovering what they really contained. Although I took great trouble, I could not discover any authentic collection of this interesting poetry. I certainly found several books which pretended to be such collections, but, as they did not satisfy me, I applied to actual life, and never allowed a song of this nature to escape me when I had a chance, and copied many of them in their entire length. I discovered, however, that these are not productions that can be easily collected and given out again. They very frequently resemble polypi and certain molluscs, which, while floating on the sea, have splendid colours and interesting forms, but which, when seized, prove to be a lump of jelly, and dissolve in the hand.

I grant that the old French Voyageurs brought many a pretty song from France into these remote countries, and you may hear on the Upper Mississippi, and in the bays and wild rivers of Lake Superior, even at the present day, an old chanson sung two hundred years ago in Normandy, but now forgotten there. But I am not speaking here of that class of songs. They interest an ethnographer least of all, although a French historical writer might be delighted with them. I here allude especially to the songs composed on the spot which are characteristic of the land and its inhabitants, as the people paint in them their daily adventures themselves, and the surrounding nature; and, among these poetic productions, there is much that makes no great figure in a book, although it produces its good effect in actual life.

The Voyageurs accompany and embroider with song nearly everything they do—their fishery, their heavy tugging at the oar, their social meetings at the camp fire; and many a jest, many a comic incident, many a moving strain, which, if regarded closely, will not endure criticism, *there* serves to dispel ennui. If even at times no more than a "tra-la-la-la!" it rejoices the human heart that is longing for song and melody. Besides, the temper of the social travellers in the open air gives a hearty welcome to much that, to the solitary reader, will seem scarce endurable.

Generally they designate their own most peculiar songs as "chansons de Voyageur," and exclude from them songs they have derived from France and else-where.

As the Voyageurs from here to the Rocky Moun-tains, to Hudson's Bay, and to the Arctic Sea, rarely travel otherwise than in canoes, the great majority of their songs are calculated for the paddling work which they are specially intended to accompany and enliven. Hence they are classified according to the nature of the work, and are divided into " chansons à l'aviron," " chansons à la rame," " chansons de canot à lège," and so on. But, as is natural enough, the difference is less in the character of the song than in the time and tact of the melody.

" L'aviron," or paddle, is a smaller and shorter in-strument than the " rame," or oar, and is used diffe-rently. They make so great a distinction between them, that they have two perfectly differing names for the manipulation. Paddling they term " nager," and the paddlers " nageurs," while the expressions " ramer" and " rameur" are confined to the rame, or oar. When there is a large crew they paddle, when a smaller one they take to the oar, as a rameur re-quires nearly twice as much space as a nageur. When there are only one or two persons they give the pre-ference to the oar, because it offers them more power against the current and rapids. The paddle, on the other hand, is employed principally when speed rather than strength is required. In paddling, the canoe is always lifted a little out of the water, and glides over the surface, while, on the other hand, the long heavy oar presses the canoe down, and gives it more firm-ness in wind or high waves. In fast voyages they all paddle, therefore, and the time of the chanson becomes much quicker.

For those express voyages, when only persons or messages have to be carried, and the canoes are not laden with goods, they employ the expression "aller à lège," and the post boat employed is called a "canot à lège."

In such quick voyages the paddling is very lively, and the song follows the example. The rapidity of the "light voyage" partly animates them with a desire to sing, and partly, too, they consider singing as specially necessary to give them fresh mental strength for the bodily exertion. They hence spoke to me of "chansons de canot à lège," and gave me two or three tunes under this title. They were remarkably long. But it must not be supposed that length is the exclusive characteristic of this class of songs.

The most celebrated canot à lège among my Voyageurs on Lake Superior is the "canot du gouverneur." This is Sir George Simpson, governor of the Hudson's Bay territories, who lives at La Chine, near Montreal, and makes annually a rapid voyage of inspection to Lake Superior and through a portion of the territories. The people on the southern or American shore of the lake told me marvellous stories of this canot à lège voyage of the governor, which almost seemed to me like a poem. "The great gentleman," they said, "is always in a terrible hurry. His canoe is very large and long, and remarkably pretty, and of light build. He has always a corps of twenty or twenty-four paddlers with him. These are very powerful, hardy, and experienced Voyageurs: 'Des hommes choisis! les plus beaux chanteurs du monde!' They sing the merriest songs, and work à l'aviron actively the whole day. The canot du gouverneur cuts through the waters as a bird the air—eight miles an hour! A steamer can scarce keep up with it. The men paddle eighteen or twenty hours a day. On reaching the camping-ground, they wrap themselves in their blankets and sleep four or five hours. Young men, however, who try it for the first time, are so excited that they can neither sleep nor eat. And yet, at sunrise, the signal for starting is given. All the transport operations are performed with the greatest order and energy. If they come, for instance, among the cataracts to a rock, where the navigation ceases, or to what is termed a portage, the governor's canoe is quickly pulled into its proper haven. At the word of command the paddles are unshipped. Each man knows the packages he has to carry, and away each trots with it over the portage. Ten others drag the canoe from the water, swing it in the air and on their shoulders, and away they trot with it. In ten minutes all is ready again, and, singing and paddling, the governor and the crew again dash through the waves."

How far this account agrees with the prosaic truth, the reader can judge for himself by consulting the account the said Governor Simpson has published of one of his trips.

To repeat here the chansons the good people dictated to me on the spot, I hold to be impossible—as impossible as it would be for a botanician to pack into his herbal the creeping plants six hundred feet in length that float in Magellan's Straits. The principal virtue of these songs appears to be their length. They must last, if possible, for a whole river, or at least a lake, and hence they have countless "bis." They pause upon every idea, repeat it with a certain degree of admiration, and break off into musical refrains and repetitions. They are like the murmur of the river

itself. The singers, so it seems, are satisfied when
they have found some pleasantly sounding word which
they can adapt to a favourite melody, or a refrain
which gives a good accompaniment to the paddling.
The refrain and its constant repetition occupy so much
time and place, that the contents of the song itself at
length appear to be a mere makeweight.

Thus, for instance, they sang me a long song, whose
refrain was, the first time, " Ma dondon, ma dondette,"
and the second time, " Ma luron, ma lurette."* After
each short line came these refrains, between which the
song itself twined like a monster creeping-plant.

Another time the singer happened on the words,
" La belle rose du rosier blanc." These words pleased
him on account of their pleasant sound. The allusion
contained in them to his sweetheart also seemed to
him proper, and hence he made this pleasing line the
theme of a song.

Of this endless chanson à l'aviron, the "White
Rose," I may cut off half a yard as a specimen, merely
to furnish an example how these Canadian poets spin
out such themes. In the first verses the poet describes
how he went walking in the forest in melancholy
mood.

> Mais je n'ai trouvé personne (*bis and pause*),
> Que le rossignol, chantant la belle rose,
>   La belle rose du rosier blanc !
> Qui me dit dans son langage (*bis and pause*),
> Marie-toi, car il est temps, à la belle rose,
>   A la belle rose du rosier blanc !
> Comment veux-tu que je me marie (*bis and pause*) avec la belle rose,
>   La belle rose du rosier blanc ?

* "Dondon" and "luron" are popular names for girls, sweethearts, &c.
In Dr. Bigsbey's amusing work, "The Shoe and the Canoe," I find a
Canadian boat song, the refrain of which is "La violette dandine, la violette
dondée.—L. W.

Mon père n'est pas content (*bis and pause*) de la belle rose,
  De la belle rose du rosier blanc!
Ni mon père nani ma mère (*bis and pause*);
Je m'en irai en service pour la belle rose,
  La belle rose du rosier blanc!
En service pour un an (*bis and pause*), pour ma belle rose,
  Ma belle rose du rosier blanc.

But, *sapienti sàt*, the song goes on in this way for
an endless period. A person reading it may think it
wearisome, but any one voyaging to its tune will think
otherwise. It is a slight variation for the ear that a
solo singer utters the few words, which give the story
a shove onwards, while the others join in chorus with
"La belle rose," &c.

The Voyageurs have, however, another sort of
songs, in which I discovered a deeper poetical feeling.
These are what are termed the "complaintes."

These "complaintes," in themselves, are not thoroughly Canadian, they are a species of popular and
elegiac romances, well known in French literature.
Still it is characteristic enough for land and people,
that of all the numerous varieties of French songs,
these "complaintes" should have found a local habita-
tion and a name in Canada and on Lake Superior.

I heard them speak of their "complaintes" everywhere, and I am bound to believe that at least one-
half of their songs consists of elegies. Indeed, it may
be fairly asserted that their entire music and poetry
have an under-current of elegy.

Nothing, I say, is more natural than this. They
regarded themselves as exiles—indeed, as doubly
banished, first from France, and then again from
Lower Canada. Their life is a very hard one, the
natives that surround them rough and wild. On hearing their songs, I often thought of the "Tristia" which

Ovid and many another expatriated Roman warrior
sang on the Danube, and which have an echo in the
songs of the Roumans in Wallachia and Moldavia.

Their mode of life exposes them to countless dangers
and wants, and though they all say that they will soon
return to Lower Canada, their real home, very few of
them carry this into effect. And there are whole families of Voyageurs here on Lake Superior, who, from
father to son, have sung of the "return to Canada,"
but who have all perished here.

"Où restez-vous?" I once asked a Voyageur, who
had taken a seat near us in a Canadian fishing-hut.
In Canadian French this means so much as, "Where
do you live?—where is your home?" "Où je reste?
je ne peux pas te le dire. Je suis Voyageur—je suis
Chicot, monsieur. Je reste partout. Mon grand-père
était Voyageur: il est mort en voyage. Mon père
était Voyageur: il est mort en voyage. Je mourrai
aussi en voyage, et un autre Chicot prendra ma place.
Such is our course of life." I must remark here, in
explanation, that my Canadian had some Indian blood
in his veins, either on the father or mother's side, and
hence, jestingly, called himself "Chicot." That is the
name given in Canada to the half-burnt stumps, and
has become a nickname for the half-breeds. They
also call themselves, at times, "Bois brûlés," or "Bois
grillés," in reference to the shades of colour that bronze
the face of a mixed breed.*

Frequently, too, pure-blooded French Voyageurs,
if they live entirely among the Indians, and inter-
marry with them, are counted among the Chicots.
How much these French Voyageurs identify them-

* In addition to half-breeds, there are also quarter-breeds, quadroons,
called in Canada "quarts."

selves with the Indians against the Anglo-Saxons, I
had often opportunity of seeing. When they spoke
of the irruption of the Americans into the country
round Lake Superior, they used nearly the same language as the Indians. A pure French Canadian, with
whom I spoke about the old Canadian songs, thus expressed himself on one occasion to me: "Depuis que
les blancs sont entrés dans le pays, nous n'usons plus
de ces chansons-là. Formerly," he added, "when the
white men were not so numerous here, we Voyageurs
were always entre nous. Then there was a pleasure
in singing, we knew that everybody was acquainted
with any song begun, and would join in. But now,
if a party of Voyageurs meet, there are often so many
Britons, and Scotch, and Irish, and Yankees among
them, that when one begins singing there is often
nobody who knows how to join in. Hence we prefer
remaining quiet. C'est bien triste à cette heure."

Complaintes are often made about tragical events,
especially shipwrecks and deadly accidents, which become universally known. One of the most celebrated
of these elegies is that in which the melancholy fate
of Jean Cayeux, an old Voyageur, is lamented. It
describes a thoroughly Canadian tragedy, and is characteristic of the Voyageurs and the country. This
complainte is very long, and unfortunately I met with
no one who knew it all by heart, though I took considerable trouble. But I heard many fragments at
different places, and nearly every Voyageur knew a
part of it, or was at least acquainted with its contents.

As, therefore, I cannot quote the entire song, I will
at least describe the story to which it refers. It will
serve as a type of many others.

Jean Cayeux (according to the story) was a great Canadian Voyageur, a hunter and fur-trader, beloved by the Europeans and friendly Indians, and known through the entire country of the St. Lawrence. He was once voyaging and hunting on the Ottawa River, and was stationed for a long time, with his wife and children and all his family, in the neighbourhood of the cataracts in that river, known as "le Grand Calumet."

It was in the old French time, when the Iroquois, the partisans of the British, were still powerful, and frequently made savage and extensive forays into the land. They crept along forest paths, and appeared quite unexpectedly, like lightning from a clear sky, attacked the French settlements, and those of their Indian allies, and if they were victorious, nothing escaped their merciless arms and fire.

One evening Cayeux saw his camp surrounded and threatened by such a suddenly appearing band of Iroquois. He had nothing to hand but a canoe, and in this his wife and children saved themselves, and his young son went to the stern to guide the boat.

"Généralement on ne saute pas le Grand Calumet," for they are too violent, rocky, and long. Hence a portage is usually made; but Cayeux's family ventured it, as there was no other way of safety left them.

Cayeux, himself, remained behind, fearing lest he might overload the canoe and thus expose his family to certain death, but promised to join them again by a circuitous route. Then he sprang on a rock in the centre of the river, and watched from it his family safely glide down the wild cataracts and float on the smooth water beneath. He saw them commit them-

selves to the mercy of God, and fold their hands in
prayer. He saw, too, that a white form appeared on
the bow of the canoe, and recognised in her the
blessed Virgin. At length he saw them saved from
the Indians, who had followed them like foxes along
the bank.

The pious family, under the protection of the Virgin,
soon reached a part of the river where was a
strong French post, which the Indians dared not
attack. Then Cayeux began thinking of his own
safety, for the Iroquois, who quickly returned when
their richer prey escaped them, were preparing to
pursue him. Cayeux rushed into the woods, but his
enemies soon cut off the road which would lead him
to his family, and drove him further northwards to the
upper deserts of the Ottawa River. They hunted him
like wolves do a startled roebuck. By day the fugitive managed cleverly to conceal himself in hollow
trees, and at night he hurried on through the thickest
scrub.

The chase lasted for days, and still poor Cayeux
heard the howling of the savages after him. His provisions gradually gave out, and his strength began
failing him. Hence, although the Iroquois at length
grew weary of the chase and returned to their own
country unsuccessful, it was all over with poor
Cayeux.

They had driven him into such a wild, swampy,
helpless, and remote desert, that he no longer possessed the strength to find his way back from it to the
inhabited parts of Canada and to his family.

As a protection against the rough weather, he built
him in his pathless desert a little hut of branches on
the shore of one of the uppermost confluents of

the Ottawa. This river was the only path that led to Canada, but he had no canoe to take advantage of it. Nor did he dare to venture forth from his hiding-place, for he feared that he might yet fall into the hands of his enemies. His only hope was that Frenchmen would pass along the river and save him.

> C'est donc ici, que le monde m'abandonne,
> Sainte Vierge, ne m'abandonnez pas !

So runs the complainte. But no one visited him save the beasts of the forest. A wolf walked one day yawning past his body. " Ha ! thou savage comrade, what wouldst thou ?" Cayeux, who was now ill, shouted to the animal. " I am not yet completely broken. Take to flight, or thou must wrestle for the prize with me!"

A croaking raven seated itself the next day near him, on the branch of a tree. " Eh! mangeur de chair humaine !" Cayeux addressed it. " Thou hast come to see how far I am gone. But see, I have still strength enough to drive thee away." And the raven flew off with a croak of disappointment.

But he grew weaker and weaker every hour, and when on the third day three little singing-birds came and sat twittering before his hut, he began to lament, and gave them a mournful message:

> Cher petit oiseau des érémites,*
> Va dire à ma maîtresse
> Que les érémites ne pensent plus à moi.

He now felt that his hour had arrived, and with the expenditure of his final strength dug himself a Christian grave. Over the grave he erected a cross, and he cut and carved on the wood his complainte, the entire

---

* The "hermits" stand here, as in many Canadian songs, for the "saints."

history of his tragic fate. (So, at least, my Canadians asserted. They believed they sang the very song composed by Cayeux on his death-bed, but I imagine they could only have been some short allusions to his end.)

As he lay there before his cross, and, dying, prayed, three French faces appeared before him.

"Mais ils me donnaient une courte joie." The delight was too great for him. He spread out his arms towards them. His eyes sparkled once more with delight, and then they closed for ever. He fell into the grave he had dug for himself, and his three countrymen, who read his complainte on the wood, buried him with tears.

The wooden cross soon rotted away, but the copy of his complainte is saved. And the cross has been repeatedly renewed up to the present time, and the Voyageurs still know the spot exactly.

As such Cayeux stories are frequent enough in this hard country—although the Iroquois who were the cause of this one have died out—a country where every Voyageur has been at least once in a position more or less resembling that of poor Cayeux, and wolves and ravens have often passed him, anxiously desirous to pick his bones—it may be easily imagined with what sympathy they listen to such complaintes.

CHAPTER XVII.

INDIAN GLUTTONY—A STORY WITH A MORAL—PUNISHMENT OF CRIMES—
AUTHORITY OF THE CHIEFS—CITIES OF REFUGE—FRIENDSHIP—INSULTS
REMEMBERED—INSOLENCE PUNISHED—CHOICE OF NAMES—EDUCATION
OF CHILDREN—A PATERNAL WARNING—AN INDIAN DREAM—THE CHRIS-
TIAN PARADISE—SPIRIT-RAPPING—POISONING—PIPESTONE QUARRIES—
THE PIPE-MAKER—KINNE-KANIK—INTRODUCTION OF TOBACCO.

THE Indians are generally supposed to be improvi-
dent beings, who have no thought for the morrow,
and this is in many respects true, although it is only
a further proof that there is no rule without its exception. Many Indians, I am told, are models of
economy. Nor is there any lack of customs and laws
among them; as, for instance, those which refer to the
careful division and regulation of the game. They
have also traditions, which evidently have the moral
design of preaching economy and condemning extravagance. Thus I was told the following story:

THE SPIRIT OF THE CORN.

Once a tribe of Indians had an extraordinary corn
year. On their small fields they had grown an un-
common quantity of maize. But this rendered them
very arrogant and extravagant. They devoured more

than they wanted; let the corn lie about and rot, or
gave it to the dogs. The children fought with the
stalks like sticks, and then threw them in the mud.

At length they grew so surfeited of the excellent
corn, of which they had so much, that they went off
hunting, after cacheing the remainder of their grain
stores. The stags, deer, elks, &c., were also in great
abundance. But see there! so soon as they began
hunting them, they could not catch one of them. The
whole hunting season was most unproductive—de-
sperately unfortunate. Their usually clever shots
seemed to be blind, and the animals endowed with
double speed. Very soon hunger and need broke out
among the hunters.

Then they remembered their dear corn, which they
had hidden at their home. They sent a party to
fetch it, but they found the whole store devoured by
the mice.

When they returned with this fearful news to camp
the sorrow was great, and they saw that a powerful
destiny had declared against them. They tried in
every possible way to discover the reason, in order to
appease their destiny, and performed much drum-
beating and holy songs.

One of their people, a serious man, who had taken
no part in the godless waste of the corn, the beautiful
gift of the Great Spirit, was walking alone and solitary in the forest, brooding over the melancholy fate
of his tribe.

Suddenly he came to a clearing in a perfectly wild
and rarely trodden district. He saw a small meadow,
and in the centre a mound, on which stood a birch-
bark lodge.

When he curiously approached the lodge he heard
cries and groans issuing from it, and when he walked

in he saw a sickly and miserable-looking mannikin
stretched out on dirty, much-worn hides.

" See," said the mannikin to him, in a mourning
voice, " what a wretched condition these men have
placed me in. They insulted me, their best friend, in
the most ungrateful manner. They dragged me about
in the mud and dirt. They allowed the dogs to tear
my garments. They ill-treated me in every possible
way. This is the cause of their own misfortune and
their present want. For friends cannot quarrel without inflicting mutual wounds. I am glad that thou
hast come to me, and hast seen how wretchedly I live.
I have no water in my jug, and no clothes; not even
a leaf to protect me from the cold. Weeds and wild
plants grow in my garden, and the savage beasts of
the forest prowl round me, and I shall soon become
their prey. Go back and tell this to thy people."

The good Indian, moved with compassion, promised
this, and hurried back to his tribe. He told them
immediately, in very animated language, in what a
state he had found the good Spirit of the Corn, and
how their culpable extravagance was the cause of all
their own misfortune.

His countrymen listened to the story in amazement,
and suddenly recognised their own injustice. They
soon hurried home to their uncultivated and weed-
choked fields. They sacrificed a dog to the Spirit of
the Corn, and set their houses in good order. A little
corn which the mice had not eaten served for a fresh
sowing. They managed to get on somehow till the
next summer, but then had a good harvest; they used
it more carefully, and, owing to their repentance, their
hunting luck returned to them.

The state of the law among them, and of those

institutions which might be called their criminal code, was a special object of my inquiries among the Indians.

I heard a good deal on this head, from which I may draw the conclusion that evil-doers are certainly punished among them, though in a peculiar manner, resulting from their slight political development.

Their chiefs, or civil authorities, hence usually play a less important part in the matter than the private revenge of those aggrieved by the culprit. In the case of a murder, for instance, there is usually an agreement between the members of the two families to which the murderer and his victim belong. Generally the murderer is regarded as the exclusive property of the injured family, and he is either surrendered to them, or they will take a sum of money instead of him. But if they can come to no agreement, a family feud is produced, and families belonging to the same tribe will regard each other as enemies, and demand as payment for the blood shed the sacrifice of some member of the opposing family. The following case was told me:

An Indian had murdered another, and straightway fled into hiding. The murderer's family declared its willingness to give him up without resistance, if the others would take the trouble to find him. On this, two members of the insulted family offered their services as trailers and hangmen, but asked, at the same time, that the next brother of the murderer should accompany them, and serve as a guarantee of their safety. This was conceded.

After a long search the murderer was found, and immediately stabbed by the two avengers. Indian murderers and criminals are said, in executions of this nature, to offer as little resistance as our police-guarded convicts. The brother was then set at liberty. Had

the real culprit not been found, he would have paid
the penalty for him with his life.

The so-called chiefs, as a general rule, are authorities possessing very little power, and rarely venture to
punish criminals seriously.   They fear the private
revenge of their young men.   But now and then it
happens that they will order a criminal's gun to be destroyed, or his horses shot.   The chiefs among the
Sioux and the prairie Indians have greater respect
shown them, partly because Europeans have not so
thoroughly undermined their authority, partly because
all the buffalo-hunting tribes usually live together in
large bands.   The buffalo hunt demands a concentra-
tion of strength, and hence an energetic commander.

Among the Ojibbeways, the old respect shown to
the chiefs has been weakened through many reasons.
First, because they are more dispersed.   Most of their
forest animals—the bear, the cariboo, the elk, the stag,
&c.—do not live in great herds, like the buffalo, but
must be chased separately.   Secondly, the lengthened
contact with Europeans has worked against the authority of the chiefs.   Formerly there were very large
captaincies ("cheferies," as the Canadians call them),
and I was told of several localities on the lake, where
chiefs once lived who wielded extensive power.   The
Europeans found it to their interest to break up these
cheferies.   They took advantage of the internal dis-
sensions of the tribes, and set up small chiefs.   The
French, British, Americans, all who have ever held
authority here, created many chiefs, and the fur companies followed the example. Indeed, many respected
European traders have given Indians diplomas as
chiefs, and often managed, through their influence,
that one of their favourites should hold his own as

chief by the side of the old hereditary chiefs; or, as
my Canadian interpreter always called them, "les
chefs naturels." Hence, such a confusion has been
introduced into the system of chiefs, that the Indians
frequently do not know whom they have to obey, and
the authority of the natural chief is gone.

I was told of various places of refuge which exist
among the Ojibbeways, and are said to be respected.
I heard there was such an asylum on Leech Lake, one
of the lakes of the Upper Mississippi. Thither, I was
told, any murderer could flee in safety, and it was the
general belief or superstition that no revenge could be
taken on him there. The murderer of a " governor of
the Hudson's Bay Company" from Red River was
said to be living there in perfect safety. I do not
know, however, what is the real condition of these
Indian asyla, and how far they must be regarded as
places of refuge, such as the ancients had. Perhaps
these so-called refuges are nothing more than places in
the desert protected by nature, or situated in the territory of perfectly independent tribes. Such an asylum
is said to exist among the Pillagers, an Indian band
living in the heart of the forest.

It frequently happens among the Ojibbeways, as
well as among the Sioux, that young men who take a
mutual fancy to each other form a bond of union
lasting for life. When a number have agreed to form
such a union, they first exchange their horses, guns,
pipes, and everything they possess, and then hold a
festival, smoke together, and take a vow that this
sharing of their property shall be repeated every time
a friend is in want.

They, from this moment, always assist each other
in war, and never refuse any request. I inquired

from several persons whether, owing to the fickleness
of the Indian temperament, these bonds of union were
not frequently broken, but I was assured that no instance of such a thing was known, and that it was
considered most sacred and lasting for life. Among
the Ojibbeways a friend who has taken such a vow is
called a "nidji-kiwesi." This word is derived from
"nidji," which means "as much as myself." They also
form of this word a verb, which signifies, "I have
him to my own self," or, "as a friend." Similar
bonds of union are also made among the young women
and girls.

The feeling of revenge appears to be impregnated
with the blood of even the youngest Indian children.

I was told the following anecdote in a school established for Indian children. A little girl of six years
of age, brought to this institution, was on one occasion very severely scolded and punished by the mis-
tress. The little one believed that great injustice
had been done her, and that she had been grossly
insulted.

Three years later the girl's father came to pay her
a visit, and sat down to have a confidential chat with
his daughter. How great was the surprise of the
schoolmistress at hearing afterwards that the first
thing the little one told her father, was the occurrence that had so deeply affected her three years before. She had never once alluded to the circumstance during the whole period, but she had not forgotten it, had constantly brooded over it, and so soon
as her father made his appearance, her lips overflowed
with what filled her heart. She made loud complaints to him, and appealed to him to procure her
satisfaction.

Like the women, young persons must observe a very modest silence in the Indian council assemblies.

The old people, in our meetings at La Pointe, always sat in the centre of the circle, close to the place where the American agents have their table, and where the speakers stand. Some of them, who were very old, were allowed chairs to sit on. The other old men sat together in the grass near them. Further out the young fellows lay about in groups. Among them were men of twenty and twenty-five years of age, but they never interfered in the discussions, save by now and then uttering a loud " Ho, ho !" or some other cry of applause.

The opinions of the Indians as to the long-lasting minority of the young men are very strict, and if the latter do not act in accordance with their views, they are very roughly reminded of their position. Once, I was told, a very old and celebrated speaker was interrupted by a young impudent fellow in a most improper manner. The old warrior was so incensed at it, that he drew his tomahawk, split the young man's skull open, and then quietly continued his harangue as if nothing had happened.

When a child is born in an Ojibbeway family, it remains for some time without a name, till an occasion offers, or the father has had " the right dream," and then he names his son after the object that appeared to him in his dream; for instance, " the Dark Cloud," or " the Grey Sky," or " the Black Bird," or the " Violent Rain," &c.

If the father cannot manage a dream to his satisfaction, or does not place entire confidence in the name he has found, he invites an influential friend to " dream" about his child's name. At times he does this also to secure the child the good influence of this friend's name, and he gives the child, consequently, a second name, for instance, "the man who runs," or "the white otter," or "the yellow fox," and so on. The forest animals are especially welcome in this selection of a name. In such cases the Indians descend to the smallest animals, as "the rat." I knew, myself, one woman, who was called "the Musk-Rat." Animals introduced from Europe, such as the horse, donkey, pig, &c., are never found among Indian names, though that of the ox is very frequent, for that animal has inhabited the deserts from the earliest period of history.

To these two names—those of the father and friend —a third is often added, which the child receives when presented in the temple and received into the great religious order. At this ceremony, which, as I have shown, resembles our christening, the child receives another name, generally that of a godfather especially invited. Which of all the three names gains the upper hand and becomes the permanent one through life depends on chance. Very frequently it is the one given at baptism.

I was assured that there is no peculiarity about the names given to women. Like the men, they receive the names of "Ox," "Fox," &c., but the word "ikwe" (squaw) is always added to the name. Still, I was given the following as names very frequently recurring among females: Miskogijik-ikwe, or "the woman of the red sky;" Niganigijik-ikwe, or "the woman who marches in front to heaven;" and Ogimangijik-ikwe, "the queen of heaven."

There is always some difficulty in finding out an Indian's real name, and if you are alone with an in-

dividual this is almost impossible, for they employ
every evasion to conceal it.   They are afraid to mention their own names; indeed, they will not answer a
question directly addressed to them on that subject.
When you want to know an Indian's name you must
always ask it of another.

The squaw of the unknown man is also usually
afraid to tell his name.   If you ask her, "To whom
does the gun belong?" and it is her husband's gun,
she will say, "It belongs to him."   If you ask, further,
whom she means by him, she will reply, "The man
who has his seat there," and point with her hand to
her husband's seat.

An Indian whom I once asked for his name hesitated for a long time.   At length he nudged a by-
stander, and said to him, "Dites donc mon nom."

Another old Indian, whom I once asked as to the
cause of this timidity, which is said to be common to
all Indian tribes, replied, "Nous croyons que ça dimi-
nue notre valeur;" in other words, they think it beneath their dignity.

These names are also occasionally altered or lengthened when they enter into a new relationship.   This
is frequently the case when they become members of
another family, as sons-in-law.   Usually the mother-
in-law gives her daughter's young husband a new
name.   This is derived from some remarkable circumstance that accompanied the son-in-law's first appearance in the family, or by some action he performed
at the time.   Thus, a son-in-law was called "the
Butler," because, on entering the lodge, he brought the
mother-in-law a beverage and poured it into a vessel
of very unusual form, which attracted all eyes.

Nor will the mother-in-law openly utter the son-in-

law's name.   She usually indicates him by periphrases
—for instance, thus: " The man who performs the part
of son-in-law in our house."

I had frequently heard that the Indians by no
means entirely neglected the education of their children, and that many of them even follow very decided
principles, though they are never severe and harsh.
On one occasion I had an instance of this.   We were
sitting with an Indian chief and smoking. The Indian's
son—a man, almost—was sitting by his side. As the
latter was not smoking I offered him tobacco, but he
declined, and his father—I must mention that he was
a perfectly wild pagan from the interior—said that his
son did not smoke yet, he did not allow it.   " My
father," he said, " brought me up so. Formerly, we
never allowed our sons to smoke till they were quite
grown up. Now they want all too much to imitate
the Americans, and begin too soon."

" What do you say to it ?" I asked my companion,
who translated the Indian's speech to me.   " Oh," he
replied, " matters are exactly as he states. Many
Indians, I can assure you, from my own experience,
bring up their children as strictly as the Presbyterian
families in the East, allow them no sort of extrava-
gances, and keep them—sometimes too severely—to
fasting, privation, and self-denial. Nor is there any
want of warnings and lessons of every description,
and it is frequently quite edifying to listen at evening
to the speeches which an old Indian will make to his
children and children's children. I knew an Indian
hunter, who was a most exemplary and amiable father
of a family. When he returned home in the evening
from the chase, his squaw had a warm dish in readiness for him. She wrung out his wet clothes and

mocassins, and hung them round the fire to dry. After he had supped he would lie down on his bed, and the children would nestle round him. He would joke and play with the little ones, called the elder children to him, questioned them as to their conduct, gave them good lessons and rules of life, and told them stories."

One of the Indians residing at Anse, of the name of Aganab, or, " the man who is in front of all," told me how he once committed a fault in his youth, and in what way his father punished him for it. The latter, he said, bound him to a post, and then felt him all over with his hands, first on the right, and then on the left side, till at length he found his heart. There he stopped, felt it, and said, " Aha, stay there! it beats! So, then, thou hast a heart! Come, I am glad of that; let us see further!" Then he felt him about the head till he found his ears. " Aha, stay there!" he said again; " I thought you had, perhaps, no ears. But I see that I was mistaken. Hence thou hast no excuse. Fie, be ashamed of thyself! Go away, and use thy ears better in future. Think of the heart that beats in thy bosom, and never do again what thou didst to-day !"

An Indian at Fond du Lac had formed a great predilection for the Christian religion, and was thinking about being baptised. He was, however, attacked by a fever, and in his hallucinations dreamed that he ascended by a ladder into heaven. He reached a lofty mountain, on which was a wide and beautiful plateau. He noticed in the grass countless trails, and the footsteps and traces of innumerable men. He examined them more closely, and found they were made by white men; he examined them all, and he

could not find the trace of a single mocassin among
them. Then he began to feel terrified in this beautiful meadow. He feared that he should meet none
of his countrymen in the Christian paradise, and that
they were all excluded. He hurried down the ladder
again, and when he reawoke he felt quite averse
from Christianity, and remained an obstinate pagan
as before.*

The Indians have for a lengthened period been
great spiritualists, ghost-seers, table-rappers, and perhaps, too, magnetisers, which we "educated" Europeans have only recently become, or returned to.
The lodge which their jossakids, or prophets, or, as
the Canadians term them, "jongleurs," erect for their
incantations, is composed of stout posts, connected
with basket-work, and covered with birch bark. It is
tall and narrow, and resembles a chimney. It is very
firmly built, and two men, even if exerting their utmost strength, would be unable to move, shake, or
bend it. It is so narrow that a man who crawls in
has but scanty space to move about in it.

"Thirty years ago," a gentleman told me who had
lived much among the Indians, and was even related
to them through his wife, " I was present at the incantation and performance of a jossakid in one of these
lodges. I saw the man creep into the hut, which was
about ten feet high, after swallowing a mysterious
potion made from a root. He immediately began singing and beating the drum in his basket-work chimney.
The entire case began gradually trembling and shaking, and oscillating slowly amidst great noise. The

---

* This story, told me on Lake Superior, reminds me of the inhabitant
of the Antilles mentioned by old Spanish writers, who refused to go to
heaven when he heard that Spaniards were admitted there.

more the necromancer sang and drummed, the more violent the oscillations of the long case became. It bent back and forwards, up and down, like the mast of a vessel caught in a storm and tossed on the waves. I could not understand how these movements could be produced by a man inside, as we could not have caused them from the exterior.

" The drum ceased, and the jossakid yelled that 'the spirits were coming over him.' We then heard through the noise, and cracking, and oscillations of the hut, two voices speaking inside, one above, the other below. The lower one asked questions, which the upper one answered.

" Both voices seemed entirely different, and I believed I could explain them by very clever ventriloquism. Some spiritualists among us, however, explained it through modern spiritualism, and asserted that the Indian jossakids had speaking media, in addition to those known to us, which tapped, wrote, and drew.

" I cannot remember the questions asked and answers given. Still much of the affair seemed to me strange, and when an opportunity offered, long after, to ask the jossakid about his behaviour on that occasion, under circumstances peculiarly favourable to the truth, I did so. Thirty years later he had become an old man and a Christian, and was lying on his deathbed, when accident again brought me to his side.

" 'Uncle,' I said to him, recalling that circumstance, and having nothing else to talk about—'uncle, dost thou remember prophesying to us in thy lodge thirty years ago, and astonishing us, not only by thy discourse, but also by the movements of thy prophet-lodge ? I was curious to know how it was done, and

thou saidst that thou hadst performed it by supernatural power, "through the spirits." Now thou art
old and hast become a Christian, thou art sick and
canst not live much longer. Now is the time to confess all truthfully. Tell me, then, how and through
what means thou didst deceive us ?'

("It may appear to you cruel," my friend here
turned to me and said parenthetically, "that I should
remind the old man of his rapidly approaching death,
but you need not be very courteous in this respect
with Indians. They always view death calmly, speak
very tranquilly about it, and hear others allude to it
without any fear.")

" 'I know it, my uncle,' my sick Indian replied. 'I
have become a Christian, I am old, I am sick, I cannot live much longer, and I can do no other than
speak the truth. Believe me, I did not deceive you
at that time. I did not move the lodge. It was
shaken by the power of the spirits. Nor did I speak
with a double tongue. I only repeated to you what
the spirits said to me. I heard their voices. The
top of the lodge was full of them, and before me the
sky and wide lands lay expanded. I could see a great
distance around me, and believed I could recognise
the most distant objects.' The old dying jossakid said
this with such an expression of simple truth and firm
conviction, that it seemed, to me, at least, that he did
not consider himself a deceiver, and believed in the
efficacy of his magic arts and the reality of his
visions."

Poisoning is also said to be by no means rare among
the Indians. Many persons have assured me that they
know how to prepare poisons from certain plants and
portions of animals—for instance, the heart and liver

of toads—or, at any rate, believe in the power of the poisons so prepared.

The Indian girls and women are accustomed to chew the gum of many trees, and the husbands and lovers bring them such gums as a present. It frequently happens that rejected and insulted lovers will poison such presents out of revenge.

"A lover burning with revenge," a Voyageur told me, "will sit alone in the forest and prepare his poisons and his gum, while singing gloomy songs. For instance, a verse like the following: 'Je me vengerai de cette femme! Je me vengerai de cette femme! Je lui ferai honte! J'entends bien ce qu'elle dit de moi. J'entends bien ce qu'elle pense de moi. Je lui ferai honte!' He will repeat verses of this description for entire evenings, and thus feed fat his revenge. When his poisoned gift is ready, he seeks a friend who will hand it to the girl. Frequently, though, the poison, which they are not so skilled in preparing as was the old Tofana, only produces a violent bleeding at the nose, or something of that sort."

Countless are the magic forms and spells by which they fancy they can hurt others. When they wish a neighbour grief, death, or anything unlucky, they have recourse to the following procedure: They make a small image of wood, which represents their enemy or victim, take a needle and pierce holes in the figure in the head or the region of the heart, or wherever they desire their foe to suffer. If he is to die of it, they bury the image with certain magic spells, and place four red pegs on the grave. At times they will burn the victim in effigy. If he really die, they boast of it afterwards, and say: "C'est moi qui l'ai tué par ma force surnaturelle!"

Just as they execute the sick persons they wish to injure in effigy, they will behave with the diseases themselves if they wish to help a sufferer. When no other curative process avails, they make a human figure, or phantom of clothes stuffed with straw, intended to represent the illness or evil spirit that torments the sick man. This figure they carry to a medicine-lodge, and shoot arrows at it in the presence of the sick man till it is reduced to tatters.

Such practices may be very frequently seen among the Pillagers, and other remote Ojibbeways, on the Upper Mississippi. Much the same sort of thing, however, is done on Lake Superior. Such a doll, with holes pierced in it, as I have just described, with the accessories, was shown me here on the Anse, and its use was described to me with a certain degree of secret timidity.

On one of my canoe excursions from our mission, I visited a small quarry on the shores of the lake, from which I was told the Indians obtained a soft dark stone for their pipe-heads. Hitherto, I had only heard of the celebrated quarries known as the Red Pipe-stone, situated half way between the Upper Mississippi and the Missouri. In those celebrated quarries, which have been visited by several travellers, the soft pretty red stone is dug out, of which the majority of Indian pipes, and especially their calumets of peace, is made. It has a dark flesh colour, can be easily cut, and the Indians form very graceful bowls out of it. They adorn the tube end of the bowl very prettily with all sorts of small carvings, animals, huntsmen, models of canoes, lodges, and other things.

Usually however, such a bowl is merely decorated

by inlaying tin or silver. On the outside of the bowl, rings, figures, &c., are engraved, and filled in with tin or silver, which forms a very pleasing contrast to the flesh colour of the stone. At times, too, they inlay the pipes with agates, onyxes, &c. The Red Pipe-stone Quarries are a species of sanctuary or asylum among the Indians, where war and murder cease, because they frequently meet here in fetching the stone for their calumets of peace.

The pipe, however, plays so great a part in Indian life, that they have sought the stone for it elsewhere. Thus I was told at La Pointe of another. celebrated Red Pipe-stone Quarry in the interior of Wisconsin, on the Chippeway River. I also heard afterwards of a Black Pipe-stone Quarry, known to the Indians on the north side of Lake Superior, near the Pointe au Tonnère. This black stone must be found in several places, for I have seen many pipes made of it.

Here, then, as I said, I found a small pipe-stone quarry of grey stone. This soft stone lay wedged in like a thick vein between two strata of the common sandstone, and the Indians had dug a considerable hole in it. The matter is for this reason remarkable, because these pipe-stone quarries are the only description of excavating which the Indians have practised from the earliest period. There are people among them very clever in carving pipe-bowls, and who carry on a trade in it.

I formed the acquaintance here of such a "faiseur de calumets," and visited him several times. He inlaid his bowls very neatly with stars and flowers, made of black and white stones. His work progressed very slowly, however, and he sold the bowls for four or five dollars a piece. The Indians, at times, pay much higher prices.

As Longfellow has introduced an arrow-head maker
in his " Hiawatha," and represented him as an artisan
living by trade, the discovery of this pipe-maker was
interesting to me, because it seemed to show that the
Indians really had some idea of the division of labour
and handicraft trades.

It was quite certain that the Indians here have
smoked since the earliest period of their history, for
pipes are found in their oldest graves; but whether
they smoked and cultivated tobacco, as the Mississippi
Indians are said to have done, appears to me very
doubtful. The Voyageurs and traders, at least, assured
me that the Indians had a tradition about the first
introduction of tobacco by the French, in consequence
of which their forefathers felt very queer after smoking
tobacco; or, as they say, were " drunk." They have,
however, a quantity of indigenous plants, whose bark
and leaves they smoke. They even smoke it at this
day, but mix tobacco with it, and call this mixture
"kinne-kanik." They have, in the first place, a creeping plant, called by the Canadians " bois tord;" then
a light red willow, called " bois rouge;" further,
another wood, " bois d'ourignal" (the elk bush), as
well as another called " bois de flèche." They smoke
the bark of all these bushes, and if there is a great
want of other smokable matters, they will fill their
pipes with maple-tree bark.

CHAPTER XVIII.

INDIAN MUSIC—THE SPOTTED FEATHER—PICTURE-WRITING—MYSTERIES—
THE SONG OF THE STEAM BATH—THE SONG OF INITIATION—DOUBTFUL
EXPLANATIONS — MUSIC UNDER DIFFICULTIES — BIRCH-BARK BOOKS —
HIEROGLYPHICS—RELIGIOUS SONGS—A TOMAHAWK—THE DREAM OF LIFE
—AN INDIAN WARRIOR—MEANING OF THE SYMBOLS—RETICENCE.

I HAD read that the Indians not only possessed
certain hieroglyphics for things and ideas, but that
they also had music notes to mark the modifications of
tune in their songs. Mr. Schoolcraft, in his large and
valuable work on the Indians, gives several specimens
of pictures and figures, which he considers to be
musical notes. I had been long desirous to gain some
information on this head, and I fancy I at length succeeded in unravelling something of the sort. I believe I can show, at least to my own satisfaction, that
the Indians have discovered something which may be
called notes.

But it is necessary that I should tell my story with
all the accompanying details. I have already mentioned that I formed the acquaintance of a young
Indian, old Agabe-gijik's son-in-law, at the Protestant
mission, whose name was Kitagiguan, or the Spotted
Feather.

I heard in Agabe-gijik's wigwam that the Spotted

Feather had several birch-bark books and songs, and, after some argumentation, we formed a contract, to the effect that he would show me his songs, not only explain, but also sing them to me, and also permit me to copy them, in return for which I promised to give him a certain quantity of tobacco. I was to return the next day for the purpose.

When I came, and reminded the Spotted Feather of his promise, he was quite ready to fulfil it. Still he hesitated, and at length said:

"It cannot be done in the wigwam. The others will hear it."

"Good," I replied; "let us go and sit outside."

We took our seats on a stone near the wigwam. Kitagiguan then produced his bark books, and showed me the picture-writing on the opposite page.

He then proceeded to an explanation of the symbols, with the aid of my Canadian boatman, and the interpreter of the Protestant mission, who was also present. This explanation was as barbarous as the drawings themselves. I will, however, attempt to repeat it here as accurately as possible, as I believe that the reader will be able to derive from it some further information about the Indians.

The Indian laid the birch bark on my lap, and said, as he pointed with his finger to it, at fig. 1 (in No. I.):

"This is a wigwam, and I sing at it the following words: 'I enter into the wigwam of the Midés, the temple, and bring, singing, a fine sacrifice.' (No. 2.)

"The sign No. 3 signifies that the same voice and the same tune continue." (A note, then, I thought to myself—a musical sign.)

I.

II.

"At No. 4 I sing the following words: 'I have come here to pray thee that thou wilt give me this animal, the bear. (No. 5.) I will walk on the right path for it, the path of life.' (No. 6.)

"Now I (No. 8) have walked along it, and my medicine-sack (No. 7) is strengthened with new power and fresh breath. Here I sing the following words:

'Give me now this animal, as thou didst promise me
to do when I go hunting in the backwoods. Thou
saidst to me: I bless thee with my abundance, and
thou shalt ever see thy table full—that is, there will
always be a beast there for thee!'

" This is a long song that I sing and often repeat,
and how I am to sing it is shown by the signs from
9 to 12.

" No. 9 is a kind of note that the voice shall go up.
Nos. 10, 11, 12 mean nothing further than that they
show me how I shall go on singing." (Notes, then!
I thought again.)

" No. 13 is a Midé shell. It does not look so, but
I know it is one. The man of whom I bought the
song told me so.

" No. 14 is my wigwam, to which I return after I
have sung."

The series of signs in No. II., so the Spotted
Feather told me, is a bathing song—that is, a magic
strain, with which the vapour-bath is consecrated,
which is not taken by the Indians solely for bodily
cure, but also to strengthen the mind, and is almost
a species of religious rite. The vapour-bath also
strengthens the hunter, mentally and bodily, for the
chase. The song contains at the same time, at least
to a certain extent, a description of the actions and
behaviour in taking the vapour-bath.

No. 1 is a person carrying a stone to the vapour-
bath.

No. 2 represents the stone itself, and the fire that
heats it.

No. 3 is the patient, or the man about to take the
bath.

No. 4 is the man who lays medicine on the stones,

or consecrates them and fills them with strength, and assists the bather. No. 5 is the door of the temple wigwam.

No. 6 is the temple wigwam itself. "At No. 7," so said the Spotted Feather, "I sing the verse: 'I will wander with the man who sits on the globe.'"

I asked him whether the sign (at No. 7) was not intended to represent a flower-pot.

"No!" he repeated, "it is the man who sits upon the globe."

"No. 8," he continued, "is my countenance refreshed by bathing and prayer. No. 9 is my medicine-bag, also strengthened by both. As a sign that it has received great force, and can wound and kill, an arrow (No. 10) is flying from it." (I have already frequently remarked that the Indians apparently consider their medicine-bag more important in hunting than their bow and arrow. The medicine-bag is supposed to give the arrows the new life, the right direction, and sharpness.)

"The arrow flies against a hollow tree" (No. 11). (The bears frequently sit hidden in hollow trees; hence such trees are often used in the picture-writing to typify the animals themselves.)

"In conclusion," my Indian said, "I stand there again" (No. 12).

"How so, then?" I asked; "that No. 12 looks like a great chafer, or, at any rate, it does not bear the slightest resemblance to thee or any other Indian."

"That is no consequence," the Indian replied. "It is intended to mean nothing else than myself, or the singing, bathing, and sacrificing Indian. No one knows it but I and the man who gave me the writing and explained it. If it were an easy matter for any of our friends to see or guess what the signs mean, they would soon steal our birch-bark books. Hence all our ideas, thoughts, and persons are represented in various mysterious disguises."

Up to this time my Indian had only spoken. Now I asked him to fulfil his part of the bargain and sing the song. He could only make up his mind to this with great difficulty; but though he was so timid, I was equally desirous to make the discovery that an Indian can sing to notes.

At length he asked me if I would be satisfied with the part (from 9 to 12) where the note signs were. I granted him this, and he commenced in a trembling voice. But he could not go on.

He told me that, if he were quite alone with me, he would do it. I, therefore, seated myself with him, far away from the others, on the edge of the cliff, where the graves lay in front of me, and the scalps fluttered in the breeze.

When we sat there alone, he began once more to sing, or rather to mutter. His voice trembled, and he seemed to be very frightened. I almost fancied his forehead was bathed in perspiration. He placed his mouth close to my ear, so that his hot breath blew on my cheek. His eye was every now and then turned timidly and wandering towards the gloomy forest, behind which the sun had already descended. It almost seemed as if the savage child of the forest were seeking protection in my breast. All this while, however, his finger pointed to the notes, and he raised and lowered his finger, and in accord with it his muttering voice. So much I saw, however, that there could not possibly be notes for every tone. "Good," I at length said. "Spotted Feather, I set thee free.

Cease thy song, and here thou hast a quantity of tobacco, so that if anybody wish thee harm for what thou hast betrayed to me, thou canst reconcile thyself again !"

The pictorial writing on the following page I copied as carefully as possible in the lodge of an Indian, who had arrived here from the interior of Northern Wisconsin.

I found this man, to whom I was introduced for the sake of his chansons, in a remarkably good humour. The previous evening, owing to some ailing, he had taken a steam bath, was now perfectly cured of his aches and pains, and was comfortably sitting on his bed, smoking his morning pipe. The stones he had employed in order to produce the steam were still lying before him. They were collected in a hole, and covered with green twigs of the *Arbor vitæ*, " en signe de gratitude et pour marquer son respect pour le Grand Esprit."

The book, or birch-bark cover, which he showed me, and on the inner side of which were the drawings, was about five inches wide, and consisted of two lids, each one inch and a quarter in length, so that the whole was two inches and a half.

My Indian told me that they were "nagamowin-ninin," or songs.

I first asked him who made the books and wrote the songs down. He said it was his brother-in-law, " un Indien de la folle avoine," or a " Menomeenee." His brother-in-law had kept possession of the book a long while, and only given it to him on his death-bed on his most earnest prayer. He added, that it had cost him much time till he had learned it all. He had studied and practised the songs for months.

When I asked him if he could teach me some of his knowledge, and explain the leading features, he replied that "it was very difficult to learn." I assured him that I should be satisfied if I could only reach so far with my weak understanding as to see how difficult it was, and why it was so; and he then condescended to give me a few explanations. I will repeat them exactly as I received them from him, and only interrupt them here and there with a parenthesis and marks of interrogation :

"The crooked sign at *a* is the sign that the song commences here.

"The bear (at *b*) begins the dance: 'Il marche là pour signe de la vie.'

"At *c* stand a boy and his teacher (father, uncle, or grandfather), who instructs him. You see the heart of the good teacher, and the stream of discourse which flows in a serpentine line from his heart through his mouth to the head of the boy, as well as the boy's answers, which flow back from his mouth to the heart of his teacher.

"*d* is the circle of the earth, with the sacred shells in it. (?)

"*e*, repetition of the couple, the teacher and boy." (The scholar appears to have made considerable progress, for his head is enclosed in the "circle of heaven," as if in a nimbus of sanctity.)

While pointing to the bear and his traces (at *f*), my Indian gave me the advice: "On doit suivre l'ours par ses pistes." I cannot say whether this was a material part of the song, or merely the insertion of a good and useful Indian proverb.

"*g* is a sign to pause. Up to that the song goes slowly. Afterwards a quicker time begins.

"At *h* a boy stands, watching a flying bird.

"*i*, two men, who expel shells from their mouths, as they are in the habit of doing at their ceremonies.

" *k*, the Midé priest, with his medicine-bag on his arm.

" *l* is not, as might be supposed, a flying eagle, but the medicine-bag of the man *k*." (As I have already said, the medicine-bags are sometimes made of birds' skins. And as these bags are supposed to be so full of life and spiritual strength, the artist has here represented the bag flying through the air with outspread wings, and to a certain extent symbolised its magic powers.)

" *m*, pause, or concluding bar of a division of the song. At this bar dancing and beating the drum commence.

" At *n* a new division commences." (It represents a couple exerting themselves to expel a shell.)

" At *o* a man is walking, not, as might be supposed, on a many-branched tree (*p*), but on the path of the life and the law (il marche sur le chemin de la vie et de la loi)." (This path, it will be seen, has many side paths. But over his head a bird (*q*) hovers, surrounded by a ring of small birds, like a cluster of stars. The man (*o*) appears to be looking up to this cluster as a reward or crown of victory.)

"Tibekana," the Indian said, "meant, in his language, ' the path of life.' A portion of the word simply means, in the Ojibbeway, 'trail,' or ' path.' And the whole means, ' the way of the dead,' ' the path leading into paradise,' or ' the path of life.'

" *s*, the ring of heaven.

"The bear (*t*), who, by the way, is no bear, but a man in the form of a bear, is marching towards this ring. He is trying to reach the opening to it, ' le centre du monde,' or ' le trou de bonheur.'

" *u*, the priest of the temple, or medicine wigwam,

(*v*), who makes an oration at the end of this division. The speech is depicted by the undulating line, which goes down from his mouth to the roof of the temple."

As a perfect conclusion of this part, there is a turn at eating and smoking, indicated by the pipe (*w*) and the dish (*x*).

1. " Great bar—grand pause. The main affair, the great ceremony of the reception of a new member into the order of the Midés, really terminates here.

"The man (at 2) is the new member just received. He emerges from the temple into the open air, with his powerful medicine-bag (3) in his hand. He tries its strength and consecration, and the animals, both bears and birds, appear to fly before him." (While blowing on them with his medicine-bag, he also seems to be snow-balling them with the sacred shell.)

Thus strengthened by magic arts, and initiated into the Midé order, he at length shoots (at 4) an arrow, and, like Max in the Freischütz, brings down a bird from the air. It falls at his feet (at 4). The Indian told me it was a kiniou (warrior-eagle).

For this he is obliged to offer a dog, as a sacrifice to the Great Spirit (5).

6. " Pause, or concluding bar of this division." (The pictures that now follow are so fantastic, and my Indian's explanations were so fragmentary, that I must give up all attempt at any continuous description.)

At 7, instructions about the constantly recurring vomiting of shells seems to be again represented.

" At 8," I was told, " a song is represented between the sun (9) and the earth (10). The song," my Indian said, " must be sung exactly at mid-day, because the sun is then floating perpendicularly over the earth."

The quadrangle (at 11) is meant for a piece of cloth, such as the priests receive as a reward and payment after their exertions. I cannot say, though, why this piece of cloth again hangs between the sun and earth.

The priest (at 12) sings, "Le voilà! le sacrifice, qui a été donné au grand-prêtre!"

With this figure the whole performance terminated.

I noticed, in the possession of one of the young warriors who came down from the interior to the bay, a tomahawk, richly decorated on both sides, or, as the Ojibbeways call this instrument, a "wagak wadongs." Some of the things represented on it were merely idle ornaments, but others had a meaning.

On one side was a drawing, of which I here present a copy:

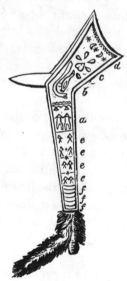

My friend told me it represented his dream of life,

and that he had this dream on the St. Croix River, when he was quite a young fellow. He fasted ten days for it.

The two human figures at *a*, he told me, represented himself and his guardian spirit, or guide, who spoke to him in his dream, and ordered him to look upwards. When he did so, he saw a large, handsome eagle (a kiniou) sitting in its nest, as is represented at *b*. The double mark under the bird indicates the nest. Above the bird a crown of glistening stars floated, and over them the moon (*d*).

"I often think of this face, this eagle," he said, "and I not only think of it, but I speak to it in a loud voice."

I. "Has it already helped thee?"

He. "Frequently. If it did not help me I should not have taken so much trouble to paint it on my tomahawk."

I. "Canst thou impart to me all the circumstances and course of this dream?"

He. "No; but when I am in great danger, and on the point of dying, then I shall collect all my family around me, and reveal to them the entire history of my dream. And then they will hold a great feast."

The little figures below (*e*) are birds—war birds.

"The rings at *f f f* are marks for the war expeditions which the Ojibbeways have made against the Sioux."

I. "Canst thou not give me closer details of these expeditions, and their meaning?"

He. "No: a very old man made these marks for me. He knew about them; but I do not know."

CHAPTER XIX.

At length the day arrived when we were compelled
to take leave of the Anse and its remarkable inhabitants. It seemed to me as if I left so many fields there
unexamined, so much treasure not raised, and I saw
our little canoe push off from the shore with unfeigned
sorrow.

Once more the little bell in the chapel on the hill
was rung; once more all the guns of the young men
were discharged; and once again the entire population
fell on their knees along the beach to receive the
benediction of their departing shepherd. We had
rowed past the village, and the shots and pealing of
the bell had ceased, when we heard a muttered " Bojo !
bojo !" from behind a bush. It was the old dreamer
Kagagengs, who was sitting on the beach, black, smoke-
dried, and wrinkled, wrapped up in his blankets, and
wishing us farewell.

We paddled along our former route, passed the strangely formed rocks of Anse Bay, up the rivers and lakes of the interior, and arrived, after a pleasant though rather monotonous day, at the lodge of the Canadian Richard, one of the three hermits residing on the Lac du Flambeau.

He was a remarkably merry and humorous fellow, of course descended from an old noble family of Normandy, and the son of a French officer; for the poorest Canadian here will boast of such progenitors. The Canadian half-breeds often swagger with two genealogies—a European, commencing with a "lieutenant du roi," and an Indian, from some celebrated chief. I met one half-breed, a man tolerably well off, who had engraved both his French coat of arms and his Indian totem (an otter) on his seal-ring.

Richard prepared us a famous fish soup, but as he had neither sugar nor salt to give it a flavour, we could not prevent him going to fetch us one of these ingredients, and though the evening was gusty and rainy, he got into his canoe and paddled across the lake to his neighbour, under violent thunder and lightning. I listened to his song the while, for he never once left off singing even in this commotion of the elements, and his really unnecessary trip. His song died away in the obscurity, and at last I heard him coming back and still singing. I thought of Menaboju, who did not leave off singing even in the belly of the great fish-king.* He brought us a lump of maple sugar, and our fish soup was covered with it, after the Indian fashion.

Richard insisted that this was a famous dish, and far

---

* This, with several other legends, I have omitted from the work, because my readers will be familiar with them in the pages of Hiawatha, to which I recommend Mr. Kohl's book as a famous supplement.—L. W.
[See Appendix I.]

better than fish soup with salt and pepper. However,
he was ready to admit that there were other Indian
preparations even better than this.   The most delicate
of all, he said, "a most elegant dish," was a certain
blending of deer meat and young corn, prepared in
the following way : "When the corn (maize) is
still quite young and unripe, they cut it down, husk
it, and boil or bake it in red-hot pits.   These pits are
first filled with burning wood and hot stones, heated,
and then cleaned out.   Then they are lined with the
husks of the young corn, and the corn laid upon them
and covered over with leaves, and upon them earth.
The corn thus baked shrivels up very much, and can
be preserved in this way for a long time; it is eventually boiled with bear or deer meat.   It then swells
up again, having retained all its sweetness and spring-
juices, and imparts a pleasant flavour to the meat."
(This Indian dish enjoys among all European traders
and trappers a certain degree of celebrity.   It is described, or at least alluded to, in Carver's " Voyage
on the Mississippi.)

   " Any person who has grown accustomed to Indian
cookery likes it much, even more than the European,"
Richard said, and I have heard many Frenchmen say
the same.   " Everything remains more natural.   They
refine upon it, too, in their way, by not allowing the
virtue and aroma to escape with the steam.   Thus
they boil or roast turtle usually in the shell, and
thrust a stick into the mouth.   A peculiar Indian
mode of cooking turtle is as follows: They thrust a
piece of "bois blanc" into the mouth.   This wood,
when young, contains a sweet and pleasantly tasting
pith, of which they also make a soup.   After boring
a hole through the pith and lighting it at one end, the

damp steam of the pith passes through the tube into the interior of the turtle, and gives it a flavour. The shorter the stick burns down the further they thrust the turtle into the fire." The largest and most renowned delicacies of the desert are, however, the following four: " the buffalo's hump," " the elk's nose," "the beaver's tail," and the "bear's paws." The two latter I tasted: the beaver's tail, when smoked and then carefully cooked and roasted for a long period, tastes like bacon. The bear's paws are also known among us, but connoisseurs all gave the preference to the elk's nose.

It struck me as curious, too, that the Indians cook their porcupines precisely as our gipsies do hedgehogs. They blow them up, peel off the quills as the gipsies do, and eat them half-cooked.

After enjoying our over-sweet fish meal with such kitchen discourses as these, Richard proposed to give us a Canadian Voyageur song, a " complainte." " Ecoutez !" he began:

> " Je vais vous chanter
> Une complainte, bien composée,
> Une complainte bien triste," &o.

He had not, however, progressed far with this elegiac song, than he grew so affected by it that he began crying.

" Hélas ! je braille," he sighed, " je ne peux pas chanter !"

Between the intervals of smoking and sobbing he began again once or twice, but I could only understand so much that he was singing about a drowned Voyageur and his dog, who discovered its master's body. In a trembling voice he sang:

" On a bien cherché son corps,
Sans avoir pu le trouver.
C'est son chien qui a fait apercevoir
Son maître noyé——

Hélas, c'est si touchant!   Je ne peux plus!"

"C'est qu'il a connu personnellement ce Voyageur," our Voyageur Du Roy remarked.   "Ah, le bon
Richard!   Il a le cœur si tendre!"

Instead of a song we had a perfect scene, and we
found some difficulty in consoling our kind host.   It
seemed to me very curious that these rough, half-
savage bear-hunters had yet retained a "cœur si
tendre" in this icy North.

The following day we marched again through the
wild forests, and, after a few days—or, to use the
Indian phrase, a few "nights"—crossed the lake to
Sault St. Marie, a village on the rapids of St. Mary's
River.

The powerful outpour of water at the eastern end
of the lake, called the St. Mary's River, is a combina-
tion of several very variously formed waters.   The
river divides into several broad arms, which separate,
unite, and then divide again.   Repeatedly these arms
collect in large pools, when they become calm, and
then shoot in narrow passages from one lake to the
other, thus forming the rapids.   In this manner a
labyrinth of large and small islands is formed.

Canoe voyages in this wild water labyrinth are exquisite.   The shores of the islands and continent are
covered with dense forests of leafed wood and firs.
On the Canadian, or eastern side, run the final spires
of the Canadian chain of mountains, which were here
broken through by the water gods, or by Menaboju,

as the Indians say, to give the lake air. These heights are generally covered with forests, though, here and there, masses of naked primeval rock jut out on the shore, and scatter their fragments over river and lakes.

Some of the islands—St. Joseph's, Drummond's, Anebish, and the Sugar Islands—are each as large as a German county, but countless others as small as a salon; and in some places you find yourself surrounded by islands, each of which has scarcely room for a couple of trees.

Through the midst of all this pour the crystalline waters of Lake Superior, here gently circling in large pools, and there foaming through the narrow passages like mountain torrents.

The islands and shores are still in a state of primitive savageness. Their interior is perfectly uninhabited and uncultivated, and so covered with swamps, blocks of stone, logs of wood, and rolling stumps, that the bears could not desire a better thicket. Even the nearest mountain-tops, which you feel inclined to ascend for the sake of the view, can only be reached axe and saw in hand. Most of them are as untrodden as was the Alpine Jungfrau fifty years back.

On one of these rapids there is an Ojibbeway village, an Indian mission, called Rivière au Désert. It is probably a very ancient Indian station, and a Christian plantation may have existed in the old times of the first Canadian Jesuit missions. At any rate, the name Rivière au Désert is ancient, and is mentioned in many of the earlier reports on the country. But its present condition—the Methodist and other Protestant chapels built here by the side of the Catholic church, the Indian families now settled and collected here,

the district marked off as their reserve—all this dates
from modern times.

A person who only consulted a French dictionary
would give a very wrong translation to the name
" Rivière au Désert." He would find under the word
" désert" merely allusions to the Sahara and other uninhabited districts, and would consider his translation,
" Desert River," peculiarly applicable to this Canadian
forest desert. The name, however, is not French, but
Canadian, and the English have correctly rendered it
by " Garden River." How the ideas of " garden" and
"desert" gradually merge into each other, and can
become identical, may appear very strange at the first
blush, but the American traveller easily comprehends
it. Nature is here, at the outset, a pleasing wild forest
garden; but when civilised man breaks into it, his axe
and his fire produce a desert of half-carbonised tree-
stumps and skeletons.

The " improvements," or the patches of oats and
barley sown among the tree-stumps, are so scanty that
they can scarcely be regarded as something agreeable.
Hence, the French Canadians, accusing themselves, as
it were, of being desolators of nature, have named
such a patch of cultivation " un désert."* After a
while the clearing reassumes a garden-like character,
and the English, as I said, translated the desert into a
garden.

The first half of the name, or "rivière," is derived
from a stream that pours down the Canadian mountains, and divides the village into two parts. " On
one bank of the river," I was told beforehand, " are
the huts of the Protestant Indians, with their wooden

* They have also formed a verb of it, "déserter"—i. e. to desolate the
forest, or introduce cultivation.

church, and, on the other, the Catholic huts ranged round their chapel."

I was very curious to visit this settlement, and as my excellent friend, the Catholic missionary, under whose charge it was, was about to go there, and kindly accepted me as a companion, we prepared for our departure at an early hour next morning.

But in these Indian countries, above all, the proverb, " early saddled but late ridden," becomes a bitter truth. Hopes had been held out to us of several ways of travelling, but in the course of the morning these were dissipated through various reasons. At length we found and engaged an Indian who was about returning with his family to Rivière au Désert, and intended starting directly. But the October sun was already setting when we—the Indian, his squaw, their boys and infant, my friend and self—at length embarked in the small, fragile wash-tub of a canoe, and glided down the north-eastern arm of St. Mary's River.

Our Indian and his wife took up the paddles, and kept them going as busily and regularly as a steam-engine. My worthy friend of the Church sat at the stern, and guided our nutshell.

These excellent men, the learned pastors of the Canadian mission, are always obliged to appropriate some of the life and acts of the Canadian Voyageurs. They understand how to steer a canoe, guide a Mackinaw bark, and get ready the dog-sledge. They are good sailors, and wear water-boots and South-westers suited to the swamps and rainy and stormy climate of their widely extending and desolate parishes, so far as this is feasible without entirely abolishing the clerical costume.

Chateaubriand has described in a most attractive and true manner the labours and perils which the old missionaries patiently endured in these wild countries that they might cultivate a garden of the Church; and I may take it on myself to speak on this subject, for I have read all the old journeys of the early messengers of the Church, and followed them with sympathising zeal. In our day, when religious martyrdom no longer flourishes, it is especially refreshing to travel in a country where this epoch has not entirely died out, and to associate with men who endure the greatest privations for loftier purposes, and who would be well inclined even to lay down their lives for their Church.

In fact, everything I heard here daily of the pious courage, patience, and self-devoting zeal of these missionaries on Lake Superior, caused me to feel intense admiration. They are well-educated and learned men, many better educated, indeed, than the majority, and yet they resign not only all enjoyment and comforts, but also all the mental inspiration and excitement of polished society. They live isolated and scattered in little log-huts round the lake, often no better off than the natives. They must draw their inspiration entirely from their own breast and prayer. Only the thought of the great universal Church to which they belong keeps them connected with society and the world. It is true, however, that they find in this an incitement to exertion, which our Protestant missionaries lack. The latter, broken up into sects, labour only for this or that congregation, while the former are animated by the feeling that, as soldiers of the Church, they are taking part in a mighty work, which includes all humanity and encircles the entire globe.

The sheep forming these little flocks are usually scattered over wide deserts, and hence the shepherds are constantly travelling during a great part of the year—in summer in bark canoes, in winter in dog-sleighs—in order to bear to the members of their congregation the consolation of the Church. They must seek them at one time in a secluded bay, at another in the heart of the forest, according as fishing or hunting may be their employment at the moment. Even the daily offices of the Church—a christening, a wedding, consoling the sick, or a burial—are accompanied by unspeakable difficulty and exertions, for here, all these things, which cost our home pastors merely a walk, are connected, so to speak, with an Arctic expedition à la Franklin or Kane.

My companion—a follower of Fathers Allouez and Marquette—told me the following story, as something of ordinary occurrence in this country:

It was not long after the blessed cold Christmas season. Nature lay buried beneath the cerecloth of winter snow and ice. It was evening, and my missionary had just retired, after the labour and fatigue of the day, to his quiet log-hut, where he shut up his breviary and snoozled over the fire. All at once there was a knock at the door, and a breathless stranger, covered with snow and icicles, walked in.

It was an Indian, who had hurried on night and day, in snow-shoes, to inform the missionary that his mother was ill, and requested the presence of the "father," and the consolations of the Church.

The place where she lived was forty miles off, but the necessary preparations for the journey were immediately made, the two dogs fed, the harness and sleigh brought out, the snow-shoes repaired and patched, the sacred vessels packed up, and the next morning, long before sunrise, they had started. The dog-sleigh is naturally only intended to carry the utensils, luggage, the bed, consisting of a blanket, and the provisions, which are reduced to a bag of flour and some bread. The missionary and the Indian walked along side by side in their snow-shoes.

One of the dogs, which belonged to my friend, pulled willingly and well, but the other, hurriedly borrowed from a neighbour, proved to be lazy and obstinate, and would not work without its master. It had scarce been driven a few miles, with considerable trouble, ere it turned savage, snapped at them, tore the harness, and at length laid itself down so sulkily in the snow, that nothing was left but to unharness it, let it run back to the village, and continue the journey with the other dog. In order to help it, missionary and Indian harnessed themselves in turn, and thus they reached at nightfall " the little rapids," the place where they intended to spend the night, because they knew there was a small deserted log-hut there, which would afford some shelter.

The house stood on the other side of the river, which was frozen over. But in the middle of the river the whole party fell through up to their waists. The water froze at once on their bodies, and covered their limbs with a corslet of ice. The sleigh had to be unpacked, and the " butin" was dragged through the river and carried to the ruined hut, in which, after clearing away the snow and icicles, a warming fire was kindled, and a cup of refreshing tea prepared.

For the night missionary, Indian, and faithful dog crept under some moss they collected, and woke the next morning to a repetition of the same difficulties and adventures, which they bravely overcame, and at the end of the third day the missionary was enabled to give the poor dying Indian woman extreme unction, and see her eyes gently close in death.

Would an Oxford gentleman rejoice at being presented to such a living ?

With these, and similar interesting stories my friend told me, night drew on apace, and cold autumn fogs brooded over the quiet water. Our Indian and his squaw ceased paddling at times, and drew the blankets and hides more closely round their children, lest they might take cold. The little ones lay comfortably in the middle of the canoe, between their parents and the seat where I sat cowering.

It is impossible to have a quieter and more polite load than a canoe full of Indian children. The eldest boy played the Jew's-harp incessantly, and the younger children lay listening to him, with their black heads peering out of the woollen rags and pieces of hide in which their parents had wrapped them. I noticed that the latter ever had an eye on the children, and frequently, when they ceased paddling, gazed on them with affectionate sympathy. They would then nudge each other, and exchange some whispered remarks about the children.

It seems to me a settled thing that Indians have an ape-like affection for their children. Even fathers are very kind to their sons, and never treat them with severity. Would that the sons were at a later period equally grateful and patient with their parents ! But love of children is a law of nature, while gratitude or recognition, as the derivation of the word im-

plies, is a higher product of the educated, " sensible "
mind.

Children soon become useful—indeed, indispensable
—to parents, but parents gradually grow a burden on
the children.   It never happens among the Indians
that an infant is exposed, as is the case among our
urban population, who deny the impulses of nature.
On the other hand, you may often hear—at least, of
the very savage tribes—that they expose their old
people in the desert, and leave them to their own resources.

The river was by no means unfrequented.   We repeatedly heard the plashing of paddles, and the almost
noiseless movement of a canoe close to us on the broad
surface of the lake.   As soon as anything of this sort
was noticed in the distance, the paddles were shipped
by both parties, and they remained silent.   In Europe
there would have been a mutual shout and inquiry,
" Who are you—where do you come from?" but our
Indians set to work listening, in order to recognise
some voice in the other canoe, and then muttered to
each other their suppositions as to who it might be.
We were watched with equal silence from the other
canoe, and so the boats glided past each other like
shadows.

These are certainly customs and precautionary
measures originating in the old warlike times, which
were no longer required on this peaceful east end of
the lake.   I was told, also, that the Indians are much
addicted to travelling by night, especially in a canoe,
probably from the sole reason that it is then cooler,
and the mosquito annoyance is less.

We found the bays of the little St. George's Lake,
which we reached in the middle of the night, illumi-

nated by numerous fires. Indians from Rivière au Désert were engaged in spearing fish. The Ojibbeways practise this mode of fishing by night and by torch-light, in the same way as many other nations in Northern Europe. Like the Letts, Finns, and Scandinavians, they suspend a fire-basket in the bows, which makes the water transparent to a great depth. Their spears and poles are much longer, however, and they manage to strike a fish fifteen feet below them. The greater clearness of their waters is more likely to be the cause of this than any increased skill.

There is one peculiarity among these Indians, however, that they also entrap deer by fire, and shoot them from their canoe at night. This curious mode of hunting, which I heard of both among the Ojibbeways and Sioux, is only customary in the mosquito country, for I never heard of it elsewhere; and, besides, mosquitoes are an important factor in rendering it possible. The deer and stags are driven into the lakes and rivers by these little tormenting insects. They will stand at night for hours in the shallow water refreshing themselves, or will walk some distance up the stream. The Indian hunters drift down with the stream towards them; and, in his canoe, an Indian will make less noise than in his soft mocassins on the snow. In the bows burns a light, or torch, which they make very neatly of birch bark. The strips employed for such torches are bound together with a quantity of rings. The flame burns down from one ring to the next, and bursts them one after the other, while the lower ones still keep the torch together. These torches are fixed in a cresset provided with a board behind, like a dark lantern. The light throws its beams forward, while the hunter

cowers in the shadow of the board. The gently-
approaching boat does not, strange to say, startle the
animals in the least : they stand, on the contrary,
quite quiet, and stare at it. When the hunter has so
managed that the animals cannot scent him, he can
come close up to them and kill them at his ease, as the
light shines on them. The animals are so little
startled by the light, that they will, on the contrary,
rush towards it; and cases have been known in which
they wounded the hunter with their antlers. There
is no sort of hunting in which a man can approach
the game with equal security, and nearly all the
Indians of Northern America seem to be acquainted
with this novel mode of hunting.

But if river and lake were lively, our mission, when
we arrived at it, afforded a strange contrast. Not a
light glistened as welcome in a single lodge. Hence
we decided on paddling up to the " Ile au Sucre,"
where a family of hospitable Canadians lived, who, we
were certain, would not feel annoyed at so late a visit.
We certainly disturbed the good people rather cruelly
in their deep sleep, but what can equal the hospitality
of the French Canadians of the old school, especially
if a man arrive in the company of their pastor ?

I spent a number of sunshiny days among these
pleasant and obliging persons. For though the sun
did not shine once during the whole period, I found
sunshine in myself, for I was again enlightened on
many interesting points connected with this curious
race of beings.

Our Canadian hosts had cleared the forest around
to a considerable extent, had made gardens round
their most cleanly and neat dwellings, and thrown
across the forest streams bridges possessing some

architectural pretension. Before all, though, they had made a wooden roof over four trees, and constructed beneath it a pleasant little chapel, in which there was no want of flowers and other gay votive offerings on the altar of the Virgin. In this chapel our whole party was present at mass every morning, and then we took to our canoe, and made excursions to the Ojibbeway village opposite in search of Indian traditions and ethnography.

CHAPTER XX.

My excellent companion pitched his hut at Rivière
au Désert, near his little church, which lies a short
distance from the village. Then he busied himself
with repairing the house of God and arranging the
affairs of his parish. In the tent we had our fire,
where we met to dine and sup. In the mean while I
lounged about th e village, watching Indian life more
closely, and at night we returned to our French Canadian on the opposite shore.

I made the acquaintance of a half-breed in the
village, who kindly invited me into his house. These
men, who have two sorts of blood in their veins, have
also generally two names, Indian and French. My
good friend's French name was La Fleur, his Indian
one Bimashiwin, or, as he translated it, "Une chose,
ou personne, qui marche avec le vent," as we should
say, a sailor. La Fleur was an Indian pipe-cutter,
and his squaw busied herself with embroidering por-

cupine's quills, which work is so much admired by the
Indians. The whole house was an atelier, and reminded me of the lines in Hiawatha :

> At the doorway of his wigwam
> Sate the ancient Arrow-maker,
> In the land of the Dacotahs,
> Making arrow-heads of jasper,
> Arrow-heads of chalcedony.

Red and black pipe-stones, half or quite finished
pipe-bowls, with the little engraving tools, lay in one
corner of the room, and in the other portion, reserved
for the squaw, were clean birch bark and elegantly
carved miniature canoes, and children's pouches
covered with " toutes sortes de plumissages," or that
fantastic and gay embroidery which the Indian women
prepare so cleverly out of porcupine quills. It is an
art that only flourishes in America, and whose mysteries and manipulations were revealed to me here for
the first time.

The body of the American porcupine is covered
with a fine hairy wool, from which quills of various
lengths project, though they never grow so large,
thick, and stiff as those of the eastern porcupine.
They are more elastic and flexible than the quills of
young bird's feathers, and they have a somewhat
harder point at either end. They are naturally white
or grey, but readily take any colour desired. On
these qualities of the porcupine quills the Indian
squaws have based their art.

In the first place; they remove the quills from the
wool, and sort them into large and small. Even the
largest are rarely more than three inches in length.
The longer quills are employed to ornament the pipe-
stems, while the smaller ones, which are not stouter

than a thick thread, are used for embroidery work on
purses, bonbonnières, cigar-cases, &c.

After sorting they are dyed, and for this all sorts of
colouring plants have been found in the forests. A
very brilliant black is produced by the charcoal of a
certain variety of willow, a bright yellow from the
berry of a bush they call "bois de perdrix," and
a pleasant red from the juice of the cranberry. To
produce other colours, when they have no better
expedient, they pluck from old woollen rags dyed in
Europe the threads which possess the colour they
require, and boil them with the porcupine quills, to
which their colour is transferred. Then they prick
the design with a fine needle on the birch bark, of
which the object to be adorned is made. The two
sharp ends of the quills pass through with ease, are
cut off on the inner side of the bark, and form a
coloured mesh on the right side.

By adding mesh to mesh in this way, the "fleuris-
sages" are gradually produced.

I have described on another occasion La Fleur's
own trade. But his wife's mother interested me even
more than the arts he and his wife practised. She
was an old Indian woman, who used to spend the day
with the family, though she had her own wigwam a
short distance off.

Her Indian name, which was told me, but which I
forget, was equivalent in French to "Quand le petit jour
paraît," and is, therefore, almost synonymous with our
Aurora, or dawn. This old Aurora told me that she
originally came from the far west on the Upper Mississippi, but had followed her son-in-law to this part
of the world. When I asked her which place she
liked best, she gave an unhesitating preference to this

eastern Garden River. Here, she said, all was so quiet and secure, while on the Mississippi she had never known a peaceful day through fear of the Sioux. Those wicked men had killed no less than three of her brothers, and ten cousins, uncles, and nephews.

As my good people were quite as curious about me as I was about them, my first day among them was almost entirely lost in questions touching Europe and my country, about which they wished to know all sorts of things. Among other things, they asked me whether Indians ever came " from this island" to Germany. As the war was raging at that time between England and Russia, they addressed several questions to me on that subject, and wished to know whether, in case the English were defeated, the Russians would take all Canada and march on the Kitchi-Gami. As I conscientiously believed I might save them any fears on this head, we separated for the first day in a mutual state of satisfaction. I promised to return the next day, and they, on the other hand, promised that they would keep nothing in their housekeeping concealed from me.

It is surprising how many objects worthy of investigation are presented to a man even in such a wretched little Indian cabin as this of La Fleur.

An ethnographer fancies he will very soon have finished the inventory, but, on looking more carefully round, he finds it as full of interesting matters that have been collected as any magpie's nest. And, lastly, if he take each branch seriatim, the object of his investigation spreads out like a tree, and he finds that the life and requirements of even the savage are far more composite than he at first imagined.

Recently I looked about me a little in the kitchen and cellar at La Fleur's. I confined myself to one special subject, the berries and forest fruits, and saw what stores they had collected of these, and what advantage they derived from them. I began to make out a list of them, but, before I had finished, evening surprised us. Hence, I suspect that my investigation was far from being complete, and that these trifling productions of the woods play a much more important part in Indian housekeeping than I am in a position to describe. However, I will give the result of my notes, such as it is.

When I alluded to the subject, and told the good woman that I should like to see all the berries, nuts, and fruits the Indians have discovered in the forests, and which they are accustomed to eat, she first brought me a handful of " pagessaneg " (des prunes sauvages), for it was now the middle of October, or the time when they are accustomed to collect this ripe fruit. Wild plums are found in large quantities through the whole of Canada. They grow chiefly on the banks of rivers and the smaller lakes, and in rowing past I frequently saw the trees covered with green fruits, and heavy branches pendent to the water. The French Canadians make a very pleasant preserve of the fruit, and though when unsweetened it is of course not to be compared to our garden plum, when boiled with sugar it exhales an extraordinary delicate forest aroma.

The Indians dry it at times, but more usually boil it with maple sugar, and make it into a sort of cake, or dough. They boil and stir the plums in the kettle, until the mass becomes thick; then they spread it out on a piece of skin or birch bark for the thickness of

an inch, and let it dry in the sun. It supplies a tough,
leathery substance, which they roll up and pack in
their "makaks" (birch-bark boxes).   These are then
placed in holes in the ground, like so many other
things of their housekeeping, and covered with earth.
It keeps sweet a long time, and in winter they cut off
pieces, which they boil with dried meat.   " C'est bon
—bon, monsieur—tout à fait."

Whether the art of preserving fruit with sugar is an
old invention of the Indians I am unable to say, but
I believe so, for it has been ascertained that the manufacture of sugar was pre-European among the Indians.
Besides, the use of sugar as the universal and almost
only condiment in Indian cookery is most extended.
Sugar serves them, too, instead of salt, which even
those who live among Europeans use very little or not
at all.   They are fond of mixing their meat with
sweets, and even sprinkle sugar or maple syrup over
fish boiled in water.   They have a perfect aversion
for salt, and I was often told they could not digest
salt meats, and were taken ill if they lived on them
for any time.   A similar dislike for salt is noticeable
among European traders who have lived with the
Indians.   At last they grow quite to give it up, and employ sugar instead of it.   That great cookery symbol,
the salt-box, which is regarded among many salt-con-
suming nations with a species of superstitious reverence,
is hence hardly ever found in an Indian lodge.   But the
large sugar makak may be always seen there, and
when the children are impatient, the mother gives
them some of the contents, and they will sit at the
door and eat sugar by handfuls.

Like the wild plum, the wild cherry is very common in this country.   It is found extensively in the

érablières (sugar-maple plantations) and on the edge
of the smaller prairies in the forest, where hay is
made. The cherries, which are ripe in August, are
called by the English " sand cherry," and by the
Canadians "la cerise à grappe." The women collect
them at the same time as the whortleberry, and prepare them in various ways. One mode is smashing
the cherries between two flat stones, then mixing them
with the fat of roebuck or other animals, and boiling
the whole till it forms a dough. It is then cachéd in
makaks. In winter, when they wish to do a guest
honour, and other fresh things are wanting, they will
produce this. " C'est très bon !"

They also collect and dry the little red apples they
find in their forests, and eat them as dessert.

Another forest fruit which they collect largely is
the Canadian bellois, or English whortleberry. The
berries are generally dried by being laid on frames of
" bois blanc," in which they are suspended over a slow
fire, and " boucaned." When quite dry they are
packed in makaks, and mixed with the bread dough.
They also boil them with fish and flesh, as we do
peppercorns. The sweet berries answer instead of
sugar, which grows rare in winter, and is often entirely
consumed before the fresh spring harvest. They
attach much value to a good whortleberry year. "Oh !
oui, monsieur, c'est une grande ressource pour nous
autres !"

The berries which the Ojibbeways call "mashki
gimin" are, however, of still greater value to them; at
any rate on St. Mary's River. The Canadians here
call them "les ottakas," but this is probably an Indian
word, which the Canadians learned from some other
tribe and introduced here. They have no French

appellation for them. The English call them " cranberries," but they are much larger and finer than our fruit of that name. They grow in swamps, and are ripe in October. I was told that half the Indian families then absent from the village had gone " dans les ottakas," or to the cranberry harvest. All the Canadian, British, and American settlers along this river also preserve large quantities of this pleasant bitter-sweet and refreshing berry. It has recently become a valuable article of export to Lower Canada and America, and one of the settlers boasted that he exported several tons annually. The poor Indians have to do the principal work: they go off with squaw and children into the swamp, often forty miles away, build a temporary shelter there, and pick as many berries as they can. The "great preservers" on the river then buy their harvest of them. Although the berries are ripe in October, it is always better to pluck them later in winter. The fruit has, namely, the peculiarity that it does not fall off of itself; it remains on the branch, and will go on ripening even beneath the snow. The old berries may be seen still on the bush when the new leaves and blossom are already put forth. These ottakas do not require drying or preserving, for they keep through the whole winter in the Indian lodges, and are for a long time as fresh as if just plucked from the tree.

As I had generally heard that the Indians were a marvellously indolent race, who only endured want and hunger through their own laziness and carelessness, I did not expect to find, on closer inquiry, that they employed so many little resources of nature in their housekeeping. They also carefully collect the wild hazel-nuts, rival the squirrels in their search for them, and keep them in bags. They use them, to some extent, instead of butter, for they often eat them with their bread, or the unsalted maize cakes, to which the pounded nuts give a flavour. When they have neither nuts nor fat to take off the insipidity of the maize cakes, they employ a decoction of ashes. "We use very white wood ashes for this," my Indian woman said to me, " and pour warm water on them. The coarse part falls to the bottom. We also filter the ash-water and then pour it on the dough or into the soup." This is, then, a sort of use of salt, and I have read of this decoction of ashes in the oldest writers about the Indians—for instance, in the reports of De Soto's expeditions.

In addition to the bear roots of which I spoke before, I saw among the roots the squaw employed those known by the name of " swan potatoes." They grow in the water, on the banks of rivers and lakes. There is a special season for gathering these, and they are threaded on strings of "bois blanc," and are hung up to "boucaner" in their lodges. When dried, they are very small, and occupy but little space, but in boiling they swell out. "Elles sont beaucoup mieux, monsieur, que les pommes de terre, très sucrées, et molles comme la farine !" When this Indian squaw described her delicacies to me, my mouth always began to water, such exquisite qualities did she give them.

My old lady also showed me another little bag of "delicious and valuable" roots, which she called "wadapinig." These were not tubers like the last described, but long, thin, knotted roots, of a yellowish-brown colour, which I ate with considerable relish, for they had a taste something like watercress. They are principally found in dry localities and in the erablières.

They are boiled before eating, and considered very wholesome. They are also dried, pounded between two stones, and the powder used to make into bread or broth, like wheaten flour. " By making the broth rather thinner, and shredding a little meal into it, we obtain an excellent soup."

They also collect and eat fresh several herbs, plants, and leaves, as, for instance, the leaves of a plant which they call " les feuilles de la truite." These leaves are plucked in early spring, and when quite young and fresh. I know not whether it is called trout herb because that fish is fond of it, or because it is eaten with the trout; but I was assured that the squaws made a very pleasant and nutritious green soup of this herb and fish: the bones and offal are taken out of the latter, then they are pounded between stones, and boiled with the herbs. A Voyageur told me this fish soup was excellent, although he praised their game or venison soup much more: " This is made of the dried venison which is to be found in every Indian lodge; I have seen and tasted it frequently. They have always some in readiness, and if they wish to give a guest something nice, they take a couple of handfuls of shredded meat, throw it in a saucepan with dried plums or whortle-berries, and thus produce a soup which restores the strength of a poor fatigued Voyageur as if by magic."

They prepare several sorts of sugar in their sugar camps at the commencement of spring, when the snow begins to melt. The chief sort is " grain sugar," which is produced by boiling the sap of the maple-tree, and stirring it round and round till it crystallises. Their principal stock of sugar is found in this granulated state.

The second sort is what is termed " cake sugar."

To produce it, they boil the juice, without stirring it, till it becomes thick, and pour it, just prior to crystallisation, into wooden moulds, in which it becomes nearly as hard as stone. They make it into all sorts of shapes, bear's paws, flowers, stars, small animals, and other figures, just like our gingerbread-bakers at fairs. This sort is principally employed in making presents.

A third variety is the "gum," or "wax sugar." This is produced by throwing the thick-boiled sugar into the snow and cooling it rapidly. The sugar in that case does not crystallise, but becomes a soft coagulated mass, which remains tough for a lengthened period, and which can be twisted about between the fingers, or chewed as an amusement.

Generally they prefer their maple sugar to the West Indian cane sugar, and say that it tastes more fragrant —more of the forest.

In truth, when I looked at these various productions of the Indian cooking art, I easily understood why the Eskimos, those train-oil drinkers and whale-fat eaters, are an object of aversion to their Indian neighbours in the south. To my surprise, the Ojibbeways on Lake Superior are all acquainted with the raw flesh eaters, or, as they call them, "Ashkimeg." Before I knew anything of the analysis of this word, I consulted the old Indian woman as to its etymology, and she said: "Ca signifie une chose qui serait casiment sale et pleine de limon. Littéralement ça veut dire une personne qui mange cru. Mais le tout se rime toujours sur le limon de poisson, sur quelque chose dégoûtante qu'on ne peut pas manger." She made such a sour face that it gave me a lively idea of the horror in which these cooking Indians hold the Eskimos. Bishop Baraga says, in his Lexicon, that "Ashki" in composition means "raw," but he does not tell us the meaning of the termination, "meg." Probably this word "Ashkimeg" is very old in the Algic language, and we formed of it our European word, "Esquimaux."

The reader will, no doubt, have learnt from Professor Agassiz's excellent report of the ichthyology of Lake Superior how rich it is in peculiar varieties of fish, most interesting to the naturalist. Here, where my proper study is man, I will restrict myself to describing the sorts of fish I saw and eat, and then proceed to my main object, "the human art and human guile," by which the Indians lure the finny brood "to die in scorching air." (Goethe.)

In all the small rivers running into the lake the delicious trout is found, and we often caught there not only the spotted, delicately marked trout, but also that which Longfellow describes:

> Like the yellow perch, the sahwa
> Like a sunbeam in the water.

There are also large lake trout, which attain a size I never saw elsewhere.

The siskawet is a fish bearing some resemblance to the salmon-trout. As it belongs to the larger fish, and is peculiar to Lake Superior—at least, to the upper lakes of the St. Lawrence—it has attained a certain degree of celebrity, and some persons consider it a delicacy. But it is too fat and soft.

A variety of herring is also found in large shoals in this lake.

The Indians, however, consider the sturgeon "the king of fish," and it plays a very devilish part in their legends. Not only does it swallow the hero, Menaboju, canoe and all, but it is frequently the representative of the evil principle.

"Mais la force c'est le blanc"—the "poisson blanc." This fish may be called the daily bread of the fishermen on this lake; for it is, in the first place, the most abundant, and may be caught the whole year through; and then it is the most wholesome sort of fish, and has a very agreeable taste. The meat is snow-white, and, when carefully boiled, rather flaky, though never dry. You can eat it for breakfast, dinner, and supper, without growing surfeited — especially when cooked by Indian women, for they manage to serve it up deliciously. "The Indians are very particular about their food, and this is specially the case with the atikameg (the Indian name of the blanc); and if it should happen to be watery, or over-boiled, the severe head of the house is sure to give the squaw a hint."

The Ojibbeways have the same methods of fishing as we—with the net, the line, and the hook—and many other varieties in addition.

They have also in their language, first, a general term for "fishing," and then a special word for every description of fishing.

"I fish" generically is, "Nin gigoike" (literally the words ignifies, "I make fish"); "Nin pagidawa" means: "I catch fish with nets;" "Nin pagibadi:" "I catch fish with a line on which there are many hooks." "Nin akwawa" means: "I fish with a spear." We could certainly convey this idea in English with one word, "I spear," still it would not be so comprehensive as the Indian word, in which it is explained that *fish* are speared.

They have also a separate term for spearing fish by torchlight; they call it "wasswewin" (fishing with a spear in the light).

"Nin wewebanabi" signifies: "I fish with a hook;" it

is the only term of the whole category which we can render in one English word, " I angle."

Fish-catching is not the principal means of existence among the Ojibbeways, as among many of the other tribes, for they depend mainly on hunting. If the Eskimos respect the bold whale-spearer or industrious seal-hunter, our Indians regard the active deer-slayer or brave beaver-trapper as a man to be respected, who can support a family, a brave who gains the women's hearts, and whose praises the songs repeat.

They rarely speak of the gagoiked, or fisherman, and the popular poesy seems to devote as little attention to him as does the national religion. Their sacred medicine-bags are made of the skins and furs of all other useful animals, but I never saw one made out of a fish, though such skins might be employed equally well as those of snakes, for instance. Nor among their totem signs or family arms do I remember to have seen a fish, though there was any quantity of birds, and every description of quadruped. Nor do they ever use any part of the fish as an article of clothing. More than this, although they employ feathers of every description, even the quills of the porcupine, as ornaments, they never use the pretty and silvery fish-scales, although they appear so well suited for the purpose. All those parts of the fish they cannot use as food they throw to the dogs. Nor did I ever come across any magic song for catching fish, although I have them for animals of the chase.

If, then, all this goes to prove that the Ojibbeways, in spite of their great lakes, are a hunting nation, they have by no means neglected this source of subsistence, least of all those who dwell near the lake, and the division of the nation into " gens du lac" and "gens de

terre" may be partly founded on the difference of
their occupation.   But, for all that, the lake people
are passionate hunters too, and the "people of the
interior" come at times long distances to profit by the
fisheries.   The migrations of the fish, their regular
arrival and departure, the periods of their spawning,
being out of season and becoming in condition again,
hence have a material influence on the movements of
the population.

Of all the varieties of fishing, the one best suited
to a hunting people appears most extensively used—
namely, spearing.

Most astounding are the many sorts of fish lances
they have invented, and how cleverly they use them.
This is the species of fishing least used among us.
And we might draw the conclusion from this fact,
that the people were at first exclusively hunters, and
then at length applied their hunting operations to
fishing, thus converting Diana's hunting-spear into
Neptune's trident.

They spear fish in winter and summer, by night and
by day.   They spear the huge sturgeon and the little
herring—often, too, even smaller fish.

In winter, spearing is almost the sole mode of catching fish.   Very naturally so, for the firm coat of ice
supplies the secure position so necessary for the fisherman to throw and aim with certainty, and which the
oscillating canoe does not afford him so well.

One of the most remarkable forms of winter spearing of which I was told, is "sturgeon spearing."
They perform it on the ice in this way: they cut
with their ice-chisel a round hole about two feet in
diameter, and over this hole build a hut of bush-work,.
which is again covered with a cloth.   The fisherman

crawls into this hut with the upper part of his body, the legs remaining outside, and places his face over the hole. The light falls through the transparent ice, and illuminates the crystalline waters for a long way round. The artificial darkness over his head keeps off any reflexion from the opening, and he can see clearly to a depth of forty or fifty feet, and watch the movements of every passing fish.

With their long spears and certain thrust, the fishermen strike to an extraordinary depth. Their spears are frequently thirty-five to forty feet in length; but, for all that, they handle them so cleverly that their prey, which they fetch up from such a depth, rarely escapes them. Of course this is only possible in such transparent water as that of Lake Superior.

Were the water beneath quite motionless, the certainty of the blow with the long spear would be increased. But there are currents at many parts of the lake, and in these the largest sturgeon generally lie; as, for instance, in the rapids of St. Mary's River. As the rapid flow of the water would render it quite impossible to reckon on the blow with the long spear, the Ojibbeways, when sturgeon-spearing, usually employ an assistant. He holds a cord fastened to the bottom of the fish-spear, and corrects its movements in the flowing water.

For this purpose, a small channel is cut from the main hole, where the spearer stands, through the ice and against the current. It is from twenty-five to thirty feet in length, and allows the cord to be freely moved. The other end of the line is held by a young fellow, who sits at the extremity of the channel, and moves the cord according to the orders and signals of the fisherman. If the latter see a sturgeon coming

up stream, and, as fish are wont to do, moving along
first quick and then slow, and then stopping altogether,
he tries to get his spear right over the fish's back, and
orders his assistant, by signs, to let go a little, or pull
up slightly, till the moment arrives that the iron is
over the fish's back, when he gives a thrust, and
usually brings up the quivering fish.

Sturgeon generally swim very deep, and, consequently, such an arrangement is required for their
capture. Other fish, however, can be seduced nearer
the surface by a variety of schemes, and are then
speared with no difficulty. The Indians carve for this
purpose small artificial fish of wood or bone, which
they let down into the water as a bait. The Indians
call these little fish " okeau," the English equivalent
being " decoy-fish." I saw several of them, very
cleverly executed, generally in the form of a small
herring. Some were also stained light blue, just like
the real fish. They attach it to a long string, which
is fastened to a piece of wood a foot and a half in
length. It is weighted with a piece of lead, so that it
may sink perpendicularly in the water. The fisherman, lying over the hole as in sturgeon-spearing, lets
his okeau play round the mouth of the fish he is
decoying, draws it up in time, and tantalises the poor
wretch higher and higher, until he can easily spear it.
I could not discover why they did not use our line
and bait, which would be much less troublesome,
I should imagine. Perhaps the fisherman is not so
clever in angling as in spearing, and does not feel so
certain. Perhaps, too, a natural bait is sometimes
rare, and they have nothing edible to spare.

I saw nearly all their varieties of fishing-spears.
They call them generically "anit," but have special

names for the various sorts. They all appeared to be very neatly made, and admirably adapted for the purpose. Some had two prongs, others three. In the trident the centre prong is shorter than the other two, which diverge slightly. At times they use several short central prongs, while they have all barbs on the outer sides.

For catching larger fish they also have a species of spear-head, which, on striking, comes loose from the pole, and is merely attached to it by a cord. The fish darts off, dragging the wooden bob after it, gradually becomes exhausted, and is captured without difficulty.

CHAPTER XXI.

THE dense population of European countries soon
walks and shovels footpaths through the winter snow
from village to village and from house to house.　The
scattered elements of population here are unable to do
this, and hence they require an instrument which will
easily bear them over the loose snow and inequalities
of soil, if they would not be stifled and starved in the
masses of snow.　This is the snow-shoe, which is as
necessary in winter as the canoe in summer.

Through the whole of North America all the warriors, hunters, traders, travellers, church-goers, men,
women, and children, move about at that period in
snow-shoes.　Even the English and French ladies in
Quebec and Montreal have borrowed the custom from
the Indians, and go about the country in snow-shoes.

The Indians possess snow-shoes of very varying

forms and sizes, and for various purposes and occasions, differing according to the nature of the snow
and ice. I am told that the arrangement of the instrument, as the Ojibbeways build it, cannot be improved upon. Their theory was frequently explained
to me. I have attempted to walk in them, and I have
inspected most of the varieties at the places where they
are used.

The ordinary large Canadian snow-shoe, or " agim,"
is made very substantially, carefully, and suitably. It
has, generally, the shape of a boat, or fish with a wide
stomach and head in front, and a long tail behind.
The Ojibbeway name is probably derived from agi-
mak (ash-wood), because the framework is made of
that wood, just as the name of the wigwam is derived,
for similar reasons, from the wigiwass, or birch-tree.

The frame is kept in its fish-like shape by two cross-
bars, one before and one behind. These beams are
called " okanik," and it must be remarked that this
word is not applied to cross-bars generally, but only
to such snow-shoe cross-bars.

The three divisions which the two cross-bars make
with the frame, are filled with close-plaited work of
thin leather cords, whose ends are passed round the
frame and cross-beams, and firmly fastened. In the
front and back compartment the meshes are closer,
in the centre wider.

The most interesting thing in the construction of
the snow-shoe is the little arrangement by which the
foot is fastened in, and brought into connexion with
this huge shoe. The foot rests with the ball of the
great toe on what is termed the " bimikibison," a
word meaning the foot bandage, and also the walking
thong. This is a strong, elastic cross-cord of leather,

which is fastened very securely, not only to the frame,
but also to the front cross-bar, by means of short
cross-bands.

The snow-shoes are generally one and a half feet
broad, five feet long, and even longer, and hence are
a tolerable weight, in spite of their light construction.
On reflection, it will be seen to be impossible to bind
such an enormous sole firmly on the foot in the way
we fasten our skates, for the long snow-shoe would
then have to follow the movement of the foot in
stepping. It would sink into the snow in front with
every step, and be lifted behind by the heel. In this
way the foot would have a very painful and straining
task, which could not be endured for any length of
time.

The great point is that the snow-shoe should never
be pressed into the snow, and the weight be always
equally divided over the loose snow-ground. At the
same time, the snow-shoe must not be lifted from the
ground, but be dragged as gently as possible over it.
It must be allowed to slide along over it in the same
way that many persons shuffle along in their slippers.

In order to effect this, there is a small mesh, or loop,
in the centre of the bimikibison, just large enough to
allow the toes to pass through. The broad ball of the
foot does not pass through with them, but pushes
against it, and in its movement forward drags the
snow-shoe after it. In order to prevent the foot
slipping out behind, another sling passes round the
heel, so that the latter can always freely move up and
down, and at the same time still remain attached to
the whole in the horizontal movement. This heel-
band is called "adiman," and I may remark here

again, that a cord is not generally called adiman, but
only this " snow-shoe heel-cord."

The heel, in going down, rests on the meshwork of
the snow-shoe, but there are no meshes in front before
the toes. There is, on the contrary, a hole, in which
the toes can play in their up and down movement
like the piston of a steam-engine in a boiler. They
call this hole " oshkinjig," or the " eye of the snow-
shoe."

It will be seen from all this that the foot is fastened
to the snow-shoe nearly in the same way as a piston
with two arms—fast in the centre, while the two arms
move freely. The centre (or ball of the foot) is im-
prisoned, while the two arms (heel and toes) have an
upward and downward movement. The toes pass
with each step through the eye of the shoe on to the
snow, which, however, owing to their shortness, they
scarcely touch.

Our mechanicians could not have solved the problem
more carefully or better. Were not the invention a
thousand years old, the Indian inventor ought to receive a premium and a patent.

Like the canoes, the snow-shoes are sometimes
painted all the colours of the rainbow. They also
fasten a number of coloured tassels as an ornament
to the wooden framework. These tassels are called
" nimaigan," a word meaning snow-shoe tassels, and
no others.

The Europeans have imitated the Indian snow-
shoes just as they have done with the canoes, and, I
grant, made them more correctly, with their improved
instruments and mode of manufacture. In the forts of
the Hudson's Bay Company, among the Indian traders,

&c., magnificent specimens of snow-shoes may be seen, just as they have the best and largest canoes. Such snow-shoes, however, intended to satisfy every requirement, need time to make; but sometimes circumstances occur when a man is only too glad to have anything, so long as it is broad, on his feet. It often occurs to the hunter that the camp must be suddenly broken up in the heart of winter, and snow-shoes quickly produced. We will assume that a small band of Indians has tried to stay as long as possible in a neighbourhood, but is compelled to leave it at last. The hunters have returned once more in the evening empty-handed; the kettles and stomachs are equally empty. The snow has fallen deeper during the day. All at once the people are alarmed, and decide on starting the next morning, either for a more productive hunting-ground, or to find some friends better provided than themselves. The old snow-shoes have been broken during the winter, and all the members of the band, even the girls and children, must have snow-shoes in all haste. They work at them all day and all night, and of course cannot turn out such finished and elegant work as that I have just described. In such cases, the makwassagim, or bear's-claw snow-shoes, are made ; they are built after a more simple model, and hence receive a different shape, bearing a fanciful resemblance to that of the bear's claw.

The Canadians call them in the same way "raquettes pattes d'ours," and everybody knows how to cut them out in the forest in case of need.

In many parts they only take a long board, which they cut to the shape of a fish, but, of course, the "eye" of the shoe must be made in this. On such board-shoes a species of trough, or cavity, for the entire foot is chiselled out, so that it may always fall back in its right position. These wooden snow-shoes also have their peculiar advantages under certain circumstances, as, for instance, when the road runs over very soft and watery snow, and over swamps, when they keep out the damp.

The nature of the ground to be traversed regulates to a considerable extent the form and size of the snow-shoe. In forests, where there are many roots and creeping plants, smaller snow-shoes are used ; on plains, larger ones. On any intersected terrain covered with stones, or on lakes and rivers, where the ice has packed, and is not quite covered with snow, they have extremely long snow-shoes, turning up at the front end like the head of a skate or the prow of a ship. These are frequently six feet long, and easily glide over any obstacles on the road. You feel very safe in them on night journeys, when the obstacles are not so easily avoided. In woods and thickets these long snow-shoes with bent points cannot be used at all, for they easily catch in roots and brambles. The prairie tribes, however, are said to have their snow-shoes generally made in this form.

These tribes have not discovered the use of the wheel and vehicles. They do not even appear to use the roller in moving heavy weights, or to have recourse to those round logs and levers found in use among some slightly advanced races in other countries. Here they have not got beyond the sledge, but they have various forms of this. The prairie tribes that have horses form their sledges in the following way : they bind two poles crossways, kept asunder at the top by a cross-bar, and fastened to the harness, so that the ends trail along the ground. At the point of intersection the things to be transported are fastened. At times they fasten boxes on them, in which they lay their old people and invalids, who can hardly find this mode of locomotion pleasant.*

Among these forest tribes—the Ojibbeways—I never saw any of these pole sledges, but the ice sledge is in general use among them. The sledge which is found here on Lake Superior, and among all the tribes of the great Hudson's Bay territory, is made of a long narrow board, bent upwards at the end. It is generally only one foot wide, and nearly eight feet long. They tell me this is necessary, that they may work through the narrow passages of their trails. There may be some slight variations from here to the North Pole in the form of this snow-board, but I describe the details here as I observed them in a sledge on the lake.

The most important thing is, that the board should be as thin as possible, and for this purpose they employ a very elastic wood, which will slide over the surface inequalities like a snake, and not break easily, of which there is considerable risk, owing to the length. In front there is a crooked beak, about one and a half feet long, to which a stout piece of leather is sewn, fastened tightly to the board by two ropes, so as to keep the curvature always rigid. The board is reinforced by two or three cross-pieces fastened on to it. They have no runners, but the sledge glides along with the entire surface of the board.

As draught animals to the sledges only dogs are

* The poles employed are the tent-poles, which the prairie Indians are obliged to carry about with them, owing to the scarcity of wood. On this subject the reader should consult Catlin, who gives several pictures of these primitive sledges.—L. W.

used here, and they are harnessed to two poles jutting out in front of the sledge. The load is divided over the whole of the sledge, and a cord is run along either side of the board and fastened to the cross-pieces. These are used for the purpose of fastening cords over the load and keeping it in its proper place. A cord generally trails along from the back of the sledge, which the drivers seize now and then to act as a check when the sledge is going too fast down hill, or to turn it in another direction. Sometimes, when the descent is too steep and slippery, they will overturn the sledge, load and all, and allow it to slide down on the edge. They told me they had very different sledges for the smooth ice on the lakes, but I had no opportunity of seeing them.

I have often alluded to the "mocassins," but have had no opportunity of describing them. As I am here talking about a matter allied to them, I may be permitted to tag on a word of praise for this Indian foot-covering.

According to the opinion of the Ojibbeways, and other people who live here in the Ojibbeway fashion, the light, thin, soft Indian mocassin is the best foot-covering in the world — incomparably better than clumsy, stiff European boots, which the Indians cannot endure. In their mocassins, which are made of brown tanned deer-hide, they say they can get along much quicker, especially over the swamps, so common in this country, where they would tread deep holes and sink in if wearing heavy boots. The mocassin is very porous, and the perspiration of the foot is not at all impeded, while it protects the foot from slight wounds excellently. From the fact of being so porous, the mocassin dries much quicker, and it may

be allowed to dry on the foot almost without risk.
You do not catch cold in them so easily as in our thick
leather boots.   Owing to the great elasticity of the
mocassin, which follows every expansion or contraction
of the foot like a second skin, the foot always moves
freely in it, and hence remains warmer than in the stiff
European boots, in which it is enclosed as motionless
as in a coffin.   In the severe cold the "nippes" can be
introduced into the mocassins to keep the feet warm
more easily than in our unyielding boots.   If the foot
is injured, and has to be bound round with plaster and
rags, the mocassin offers the pleasantest slipper in the
world.   The Indian mocassin-wearers naturally never
suffer from corns, bunions, pinching of the toes, and
other foot diseases, and they usually have a small and
graceful foot.

There is probably no chapter of Indian ethnography
of which more has been written than about the manners
and customs they observe in war and the negotiations
of peace, and yet I heard here much that was perfectly
new to me, and I will attempt to narrate some portion
of it, while avoiding repetition as far as possible.

Naturally the inducements for their war expeditions
—we may say, more correctly, murder and revenge
expeditions—are extremely various, and the way and
manner in which they are introduced and brought to
an outbreak differ greatly.   Very frequently, however,
the whole undertaking will commence with the wicked
thoughts of revenge, and dreams in the heart and head
of *one* war-desiring chief—just as an avalanche is produced by the fall of a stone.

Good dreams are, before all, necessary for a war, as
they are for hunting and for all other important under-

takings. When a chief is meditating a war expedition, or preparing for it, either a dream he has had was the incitement to it, or in case the determination preceded the dream, he now seats himself for the express purpose, concentrates his every thought on the subject, and seeks to gain good dreams for it before he proceeds to carry it into execution.

He keeps apart from his family, and, like a hermit, retires to a solitary lodge, built expressly for the purpose. There he sits whole evenings on a mat, beating the drum and muttering gloomy magic songs, which he will break off to sigh and lament. He has all sorts of apparitions while lying in his bed: the spirits of his relatives murdered by the enemy visit him, and incite him to revenge. Other spirits come and show him the way into the enemy's camp, promise him victory, tell him at times accurately where and how he will meet the foe, and how many of them he will kill.

If his drum and song are heard frequently in the evenings, a friend will come to him, and, sitting down on the mat by his side, will say: "What is the matter with thee, Black Cloud? Why dreamest thou? What grief is oppressing thee?" The Black Cloud then opens his heart, tells him how his father's brother was scalped three years back by their hereditary enemies, the Sioux, his cousin last year, and so on, and how thoughts of his forefathers had now come to him. They had often appeared to him in his dreams, and allowed him no rest with their entreaties for vengeance. He will tell him, too, a portion of the auguries and signs he has received in his dream about a brilliant victory he is destined to gain, and of the ways and means that will conduct him to it. Still, only "a portion," for he generally keeps the main

point to himself. It is his secret, just as among us
the plan of the campaign is the commander-in-chief's
secret.

The friend, after listening to all this, if the affair
seems promising, will take to the drum in his turn,
and "aid his friend with his dreams." The latter, if
placing full confidence in him, appoints him his associate or adjutant, and both place themselves at the
head of the undertaking, or become "chefs de guerre,"
as the Canadians express themselves. They always
consider it better that there should be two leaders, in
order that, if "the dreams of one have not strength
enough," the other may help him out.

These two "chefs de guerre" now sit together the
whole winter through, smoke countless pipes, beat the
drum in turn, mutter magic songs the whole night,
consult over the plan of operations, and send tobacco
to their friends, as an invitation to them to take part
in the campaign. The winter is the season of consultation, for war is rarely carried on then, partly
because the canoe could not be employed on the
frozen lakes, and partly because the snow would
betray their trail and the direction of their march
too easily.

If the two are agreed on all points, if they have
assembled a sufficient number of recruits and allies,
and have also settled the time of the foray—for instance, arranged that the affair shall begin when the
leaves are of such a size, or when such a tree is in
blossom, and this time has at length arrived—they
first arrange a universal war-dance at the cemetery
with their relatives and friends, at which the women
are present, painted black like the men. The squaws
appear at it with dishevelled hair, and with the down

of the wild duck strewn over their heads. A similar war-dance is also performed in the lodges of all the warriors who intend to take part in the expedition.

If the undertaking and the band of braves be at all important, it is usually accompanied by a maiden, whom they call "the squaw of sacrifice." She is ordinarily dressed in white; among the Sioux, for instance, in a white tanned deer or buffalo robe, and a red cloth is wrapped round her head. Among several prairie tribes, as the Blackfeet, this festally adorned "sacrifice squaw" leads a horse by the bridle, which carries a large medicine-bag and a gaily-decorated pipe. A reverend missionary, who described her to me, called her "la conductrice du calumet." Among the Ojibbeways, who have no horses, and usually make their expeditions on water, this maiden is seated in a separate canoe.

When all have taken their places in full war-paint, they begin their melancholy death-song, and push off.

If the expedition is really important—if the leader of the band is very influential—he will have sent tobacco to other chiefs among his friends; and if they accepted it, and divided it among many of their partisans, other war bands will have started simultaneously from the villages, and come together at the place of assembly already arranged.

They naturally take with them as little as possible, and are mostly half naked, in order to march light. They do not even burden themselves with much food, for they starve and fast along the road, not through any pressure of circumstances, but because this fasting is more or less a religious war custom.

They also observe all sorts of things along the road, which are in part most useful precautionary measures,

in part superstitious customs. Thus, they will never
sit down in the shade of a tree, or scratch their
heads, at least not with their fingers. The warriors,
however, are permitted to scratch themselves with a
piece of wood, or a comb.

The young men who go on the war trail for the first
time, have, like the women, a cloth or species of cap
on the head, and usually walk with drooping head,
speak little, or not at all, and are not allowed to join
in the dead or war songs. Lastly, they are not permitted to suck the marrow from the bone of any
game that is caught and eaten during the march.
There are also any quantity of matters to be observed
in stepping in and out of the canoes on the war
trail. Thus, the foot must not, on any condition, be
wetted.

The only things they carry with them besides their
arms and pipes, are their medicine-bags. These they
inspect before starting, as carefully as our soldiers do
their cartridge-boxes, and place in them all their best
and most powerful medicines, and all their relics,
magic spells, pieces of paper, &c., in order that the aid
of all the guardian spirits may be ensured them.

On approaching the enemy's country they build a
large branch lodge, and repeat in it all the ceremonies
they performed during the course of the winter. At
this performance there is something for the young men
to do who have not before been to war. A bar is
laid on two forked sticks, and they jump over it in a
state of nudity.

On the march through the enemy's country the
mysterious tobacco-smoking becomes more frequent,
for they have now all sorts of information to acquire,
to divine, to guess, and beg from the spirits. At one

moment a doubtful trail of the foe is discovered, and
it is necessary to know where he is hidden. At
another moment they desire a little rain, or fog, to
secure themselves from detection; and this must be
produced by incantation. The leaders of the band
then take up the decorated war-pipe, which is always
carried before them, and one offers it to the other,
that he may try his strength; but through modesty,
or want of confidence, no one is particularly desirous
of taking it. At times the pipe will go the round
twice or thrice before any one will accept it. At
length a great clairvoyant or "jongleur" will step
forward—generally the commander-in-chief—seize the
pipe, and prophesy that by the time he has smoked it
so deep, or when he has smoked it out twice or thrice,
the hoped-for fog or rain will arrive, and with it the
time for attacking.

If they are lucky in their prophecies, and at the
same time victorious in action, they hang up after the
engagement some deer-skins, or other matters, in the
trees on the battle-field, as a species of expiatory sacrifice; for they appear, to a certain extent, to regard
their murderous attacks as something godless, and
hope by such sacrifices to prevent the manes of their
murdered foemen, and the spirits in heaven, being too
angry at their barbarous cruelty. Many of them will
bring locks of hair, cut from their deceased relatives,
on to the battle-field, and have a habit of thrusting
them into the wounds they have dealt on the enemy.

I have been assured that they will frequently cut
fingers, arms, and other limbs from their enemies,
which they carry home to show to their families.
These limbs, which finally grow quite dried up, they
carry about with them for a long period. Like the

scalps, they are produced at the war-dances, and the braves will grow so excited over them as to break off and swallow a finger. " Oui, monsieur, j'ai vu tout ceci souvent, et c'est plus vrai que leurs histoires de Menaboju."

The stories told of the Indians' daring deeds seem almost incredible, as well as of the undaunted courage they evidence on the field of battle. " As a general rule, however, perfect belief may be placed even in the most extraordinary stories," so said an esteemed friend of mine, who had travelled much in the far west, and who told me the following story of the behaviour of an Indian on the battle-field:

He was a Sioux warrior, and had received such a terrible wound in fighting with the " Blackfeet"—the arch-foes of his tribe—that he at last sank on his knees and let his weapons fall. Several Blackfeet rushed upon him, brandishing their knives, for the purpose of killing him. " Stay!" the menaced man shouted; " wait an instant! Before you kill me I have something to say to you. You do not know yet who I am. Listen! Ye have made a good capture! for I have spent my whole life in fighting against you." Then he told them that he was the celebrated So-and-so, reminded them of many well-known forays made by the Sioux into the Blackfeet country, and described the occasions on which he had scalped or killed their people.

The Blackfeet, like all Indians, very curious in such matters, "lent him their ears" eagerly, and formed a listening group around him. Some, in their amazement, came quite close to him, leaning on their knives and hatchets with outstretched head, and quite forgetting the fight.

The Sioux, who had been watching his opportunity, ended his narrative with the words, " And see ! now you have me! now I must sing my death-song, and go along the wearying dark path to the west; but I will take some of you with me as company and attendants." Yelling these words, he collected all his strength, cut frantically around him, killed one of the enemy, and wounded several, before they could recover from their surprise and cut him in pieces. After doing this, even the Blackfeet were obliged to admire his craft and courage, and called him a brave whenever they told the story.

Even more astounding than their bravery are the stories told of their incredible self-command and patience in enduring bodily suffering. In a skirmish between the half-breeds of Pembina, on the Red River, and the Sioux, one of the latter was shot through both arms, and rendered perfectly defenceless. The Indian fell, and, knowing his hopeless position, determined on feigning death as the only chance of saving his life. He sank on the ground, stretched out his full length, as if dead; and the half-breeds, really believing he was so, came up and scalped him. Without moving a feature, or evidencing life by a single convulsive spasm, the Sioux endured this operation, and then fled to the forest when the battle-field was free. The next day several prisoners were brought into the half-breeds' camp, among them, to their amazement, the man they had scalped for dead. He told the story how he had deceived them, and in what way he saved his life. He was cured, and lived a long time after.

In their horse-thefts — and the majority of their thefts are of this nature—the Indians of the west

prove themselves frequently as clever as they are
bold.   Once a Sioux, whose piebald horse had been
shot in a skirmish, desired to have another piebald.
He crept by night into the camp of the enemy, the
Blackfeet, in order to steal one.   On entering the
camp he came across a splendid horse, so conve-
niently tethered that he could have carried it off
without difficulty.   But it was not of the colour he
desired; it was black, and he wanted, as I said, a piebald.   Indian thieves are very peculiar in their fancies:
they do not take the first thing they come across, but
try to obtain some remarkable thing of which they
have dreamed, or on which they have set their fancy.
The thief, or, as the Indians would call him, the hero,
crept along on all fours very noiselessly—more noiselessly than a serpent—through the village, and discovered another horse; but, on examining it in the
obscurity, it proved to be brown.   Crawling still
further on, he came to a piebald exactly as he wanted;
but it was tethered very close to a tent, and the bridle
was carried inside.   He gave it a tug to see in what
way it was fastened, and suddenly heard a stir in the
tent.   A sleeping Blackfoot, the owner of the horse,
had bound the bridle round his arm, as they so frequently do for the sake of security, and jumped up as
quick as he could to see what had been tugging at
the rein.   The Sioux had fallen on his stomach long
before, and crawled like a snake through the grass.
The sleepy Blackfoot looked round, but on seeing
nothing, went back into the tent with the bridle, and
was soon snoring again lustily.   In a quarter of an
hour the Sioux crept up again, and reached the bridle
so gently that not even a blade of grass crackled.   He
would have found it easier to take off the bridle, but
he wished to have that too; hence he seized it with

both hands, and, reckless whether the bridle or the arm were broken first, gave such a violent tug that the horse came loose at once. In a second he leaped on its back, and trotted away. A general commotion was aroused in the camp, shots were fired after the thief, and a suddenly mounted band of half-naked sleepers galloped out after him into the prairie. Bullets and arrows soon flew around him, and as at starting he had missed the direct route to his home, and was compelled to make a circuit, he was caught and surrounded by several of the enemy. He was obliged to have recourse to his own weapons, but he had soon expended all his arrows, and, to add to his trouble, his bow-string snapped. The foremost of the Blackfeet barred his way, and seeing him taking aim, the Sioux couched his last remaining arrow, galloped on his foe, and pierced him through the chest in the ardour of the encounter. After thus clearing the path he discovered that he had stolen the right horse, for the piebald steed carried him off with the speed of the wind far away, and before day broke he was once more among his friends, and laughingly telling them his predatory exploits.

War goes on almost uninterruptedly between the Sioux and the Blackfeet, the Ojibbeways and the Sioux. Now and then, growing tired of the contest, they will make a truce; but the story of their peace contracts is nearly as sorrowful and bloody as that of their quarrels. Sometimes the peace negotiations themselves give occasion for a renewal of the bloodshed, and the messengers of peace are cut down on the homeward path by the men to whom the peace was an annoyance.

The story of the events that happen on such an occasion is often most interesting, especially when heard from persons thoroughly acquainted with all the circumstances.

In the spring of 1838 an educated half-breed was engaged on the Upper Mississippi as land-surveyor in the service of the American government. He had pitched his tent on an isolated lake about fifty miles to the north of Fort Snelling, which had just been built as an American fortress in that immense flow of water.

One evening, while eating his supper, "Hole-in-the-day," the celebrated Ojibbeway chief, walked in. He appeared on that occasion quite unexpected, although on friendly terms, and indeed related, with his host.

But more than by the visit was the latter surprised by the fact that the chief had blackened his face. There had been for several years a very welcome peace between the Sioux and the Ojibbeways, and some of the hostile bands had come to live on such friendly terms that they would spend months on each others' hunting-grounds and hunt together. Hence the astounded half-breed asked his friend what reason he had for making his appearance in such solemn and martial fashion. The latter replied, that something fearful had happened, and worse things were at hand. When requested to explain, he said that the whole affair was at present a secret, and he did not know whether some tribes of his own race were not implicated in it. But as he had a man now before him in whom he placed entire confidence, and who was his relative, he would tell him the whole affair. It was, indeed, his duty to bring the whole matter before the government of the white men.

"Thou knowest, my uncle," he then continued,

"that I, Hole-in-the-day, and my cousin, Strong-ground (nearly as powerful a chief as myself), entered into a treaty a year ago with Wapeassina, one of the greatest Sioux chiefs. Our great father in Washington desired this. We also wished it, in order to put a stop to the constant bloodshed. The Sioux also said to us, 'Such a peace between you and us will be of advantage to both. You have in your forest many things we need; and we have on our prairies much game which you do not possess.'

"We made a peace, and invited the Sioux during the next winter to hunt with us in our forests. They came, and we agreed for the whole winter, while hunting bears, elks, foxes, and deer.

"When spring arrived, only a few weeks back, the Sioux invited us to join them and kill buffalo with them during the summer. ' Still,' Wapeassina, the Sioux chief, said, 'before you accept this invitation, we wish to have a secret conference with you. Will you come to our camp at midnight ?'

"We both accepted the invitation without hesitating, and went at the appointed time. We found a large new wigwam built for the purpose of our conference. All the Sioux chiefs and warriors sat in the centre of the hut, on both sides, and round a gloomily burning fire, as is generally the case at nocturnal conferences which must be kept secret, at warlike undertakings, or in conspiracies.

"We began to feel awkward, for all the warriors sat there so solemnly and quietly, offering no salutation, and saying not a word; and it almost seemed as if there were cause for apprehension. As, however, we had come, and were not disposed to offend the Indians, we walked quietly and firmly through the two

ranks of warriors, and took the place of honour indicated to us in the rear of the hut.

"When we were seated, Wapeassina's skabewis
(servant) came in with a very handsomely ornamented pipe, in which the tobacco was already
lighted. I was about to take it and smoke, when
Wapeassina rose, and, turning to me, said, 'Stop,
Hole-in-the-day! smoke not yet! Listen to me first.
When ye have heard me ye can smoke or not, as ye
please. Know, then, that this pipe which we offer
you has a distinct meaning—we have a secret to impart to you. If ye will promise not to tell it to any
one, not to the American agents, white traders, or
half-breeds, that live among you—if ye two chiefs
will keep it deeply hidden in your breasts, under
every circumstance—then smoke!'

"I answered to this: 'Ye have lived the whole
winter with us peacefully and hunted: you meditate
no harm to us; and we, for our part, will not break
our young friendship by any treason. Hence, I will
take the pipe and smoke.'

"Strong-ground also said that he was of the same
opinion; and we then both took the offered pipe, and
smoked. After this, Wapeassina told us in full detail
how their land belonged to the Sioux and Ojibbeways,
and how the white men had torn it from them by
force: how these pale faces were always extending
further and growing more dangerous, and were collecting daily more troops in their newly-built and
troublesome Fort Snelling, on the Upper Mississippi.
He said that the danger was pressing: either the giant
must be strangled in the cradle, or he would trample
on all the Indians far and near. His chief bulwark
was Fort Snelling, and all the Sioux tribes, from the

Mississippi to the Missouri and the Rocky Mountains, had joined together to destroy it. Warriors would soon arrive from all parts of the prairies to attack and destroy that bulwark of the pale faces. He was determined on inviting their brothers, the Ojibbeways, who also lived in this neighbourhood, and would be so useful in a war, to join them. ' Help us, brothers,' he said; ' let our quarrel be at last utterly forgotten, and ally yourselves with us. Send us warriors, and come yourselves, at the appointed time, and let us secure the freedom of our country by our united strength!' When the speaker ended, we were rather surprised at the magnitude and difficulty of the enter-prise. We were thoroughly opposed to the whole plan, and did not believe that it could be carried into effect, for we lived nearer to the white men, and knew their strength better. Hence, circumstances would demand caution and cleverness.

"I then explained to the assembled Sioux, in an equally long speech, in what a difficult position we Ojibbeways stood. We had many half-breeds and white men among us, and were related to them. Even if we chiefs, Strong-ground and myself, declared our-selves for the attempt, it was doubtful whether this plan would prove acceptable to our people, whose interests were so greatly interwoven with those of the white men. Hence, we could give no decided answer, but promised once again to keep the affair secret.

" The Sioux declared themselves, apparently, satis-fied with this, but we received no shout of applause from the war meeting, though that is usual with agreeable speeches.

" Wapeassina, however, invited us repeatedly, no matter how other affairs stood, to come with them on to their prairies, and hunt with them the beavers, musk-rats, and buffalo.

"The next day we started, and though I and Strong-ground objected, a party of our people went off with the Sioux, to reside as their guests on the prairies. On the third day another party of our people started, in their desire to hunt the buffalo. But the latter returned soon after at full speed, and with signs of the greatest consternation, and told us they had hardly gone far on the prairie, than they saw the corpses of all their friends and countrymen who had started with the Sioux lying uncovered on the road, and their limbs scattered about. The Sioux probably lost confidence in them through their dubious answer, and even if Wapeassina and the other chiefs did not play a traitor's part, there were many young and unbridled men in their bands who performed this bloody stroke under the influence of the old quarrels. This, my uncle, is the latest news I bring thee, and this is the event which caused me to travel quickly home in the state thou now seest me, and think thou what measures we must now take."

The measures the half-breed surveyor took, after hearing this story from Hole-in-the-day, were dictated by the duties of his position. He denounced the whole affair as soon as possible to his government, and, in consequence, several squadrons were sent to Fort Snelling, and this important post was saved. The measures taken by Hole-in-the-day and his friends, however, consisted in immediately beating the war-drum. During the same year several large bands of Sioux were surprised and cut down by the Ojibbeways in the most barbarous manner, and for the next six or seven years the "two races were always red with the blood of their enemy."

CHAPTER XXII.

CANNIBALS—PRIVATIONS IN CANADA—LIVING ON ROAST LEATHER—FRANK-
LIN'S EXPEDITIONS—FORCED ANTHROPOPHAGY—THE WINDIGOS—DREAMS
AND THEIR CONSEQUENCES—MURDERS AND LYNCH LAW—MISSABIKONGS
—HIS STRANGE VOYAGE—OUTLAWS AND THEIR FATE—FEMALE WINDIGOS
—VOYAGEUR STORIES—A WINDIGO TURNS CHRISTIAN—TRIPE DE ROCHE—
GIANTS AND DWARFS—AN INDIAN HOP-O'-MY-THUMB—FAIRY SPORTSMEN
AND SAILORS.

IT is pretty generally accepted and allowed that the
Indian North American tribes are not anthropopha-
gists, and have never been so. Still, as I have just
mentioned, owing to their barbarous war habits and
wild thirst for revenge, they will sometimes sin by
swallowing human flesh. It frequently happens, too,
in these barren and poor countries, that men are so
reduced by hunger and want, that in their despair
they shoot down their fellow-men like game, and eat
them in the same way.

"In my utter misery," a Canadian Voyageur assured me, "I have more than once roasted and eaten
my mocassins."

Many educated traders also assured me that if they
had to reckon up all the leather articles they have
devoured in their life, they could easily make up a
couple of dozen skins.

In a country where such scenes and events as
Franklin described in such heartrending fashion in his
first Arctic voyage are among the things which every
man endures once or twice through life, we can
easily imagine that men like that cannibal half-breed
whom Franklin's companion shot, should not be a
rarity. In fact, my ears still tingle with the tragic
stories I heard of an Indian who killed his two squaws
and then his children, in succession; of another who
murdered his friend; of a third who wandered about
the forests like a hungry wolf, and hunted his fellow-
men; stories, one of which happened in 1854 on Isle
Royale, another on the north bank of the lake, the
third occurred somewhere else in the neighbourhood,
and were told me in their fullest details.

But even these cases of unnatural attacks on one's own
brethren, produced by unspeakable want, are only ex-
ceptions to a rule. The Indians here, on the contrary,
have always returned to a state of natural repugnance
against cannibalism, and they have, indeed, a decided
aversion from those who have committed the crime,
even when in extreme want, and almost in a state of
rabid frenzy. They give them the opprobrious name
of " Windigo," which is nearly synonymous with our
cannibal. And it is quite certain that if a man has
ever had recourse to this last and most horrible method
of saving his life, even when the circumstances are
pressing and almost excusable, he is always regarded
with terror and horror by the Indians. They avoid
him, and he lives among the savages like a timid head
of game.

Any one that has once broken through the bounds
does so easily again, or, at least, the supposition is rife
that he can do so. Hence he becomes an object of ap-

prehension, and must live retired from the rest of his fellow-men. He does not enjoy their fraternal assistance, and thus his hostile position towards society soon drives him back into the same difficulty and temptation. In this manner, or nearly so, a class of windigos is called into existence.

I was told of a man who wandered about in the forests on the northern bank of the lake. He was known perfectly well, and his name was even mentioned to me. I learnt that during a hard winter he had killed and eaten his squaw: after that he had attacked, killed, and also devoured a girl. This man always went about hunting by himself, and whenever his canoe was seen, the sight produced terror and alarm, and all the world fled from him. He was equally a burden to himself as to the others, and, in consequence of all the agony he endured, he had fallen into a state of brooding melancholy and a fearful affection of the brain. The murder of his wife was the result of a state of delirium, produced by his sufferings; and now, report added, his brain was quite softened, and the sutures of his temple had begun to give way. He was regularly hunted down, so people said, and he would before long receive a vengeful bullet from society.

It is very natural that in a country which really produces isolated instances of such horrors, and with a nation so devoted to fancies and dreams, superstition should be mixed up in the matter, and that at last, through this superstition, wonderful stories of windigos should be produced, as among us, in the middle ages, the belief in witches produced witches. Just as among us some people really did unusual things through electro-magnetism and spiritualism, and per-

formed incantations, and as superstition endowed these
magicians and witches with greater and more dangerous
powers than they really possessed, and people grew
at last into giving themselves out as witches and magicians—here, too, some men have become windigos
by necessity; in the same way fear has caused some
gloomy-minded people to be regarded as windigos; and,
worst of all, this fear and the general opinion have so
worked upon some minds, that they believe themselves
to be really windigos, and must act in that way.   In
all physical and mental diseases incidental to humanity,
there is a certain epidemic tendency, and a spontaneous
self-production and propagation.   It is just like the
" Sorrows of Werther."   First, there is a Werther in
real life, whom the poets render celebrated, and at last
the nation is inoculated with Werthers.

It is a universal tradition among the Indians that in
the primitive ages there were anthropophagous giants,
called Windigos.   The people's fancy is so busy with
them, as well as with the isolated cases of real cannibalism, that they begin to dream of them, and these
dreams, here and there, degenerate to such a point
that a man is gained over to the idea that he is fated
to be a windigo.

Such dreams vary greatly.   At times a man will
merely dream that he must kill so many persons
during his life; another dream adds that he must also
devour them; and as these strange beings believe
in their dreams as they do in the stars, they act in
accordance with their gloomy suggestions.

Some few years back a man lived here who dreamed
that he must kill seven men during his life, and would
not be suffered to stop till he had completed that
number.   He was naturally not at all bloodthirsty or

of murderous propensities; merely the dark destiny in which he believed drove him to such deeds of horror. He had dreamed of it, perhaps, several times: the dream made him melancholy and brooding, but he must obey it, and so soon as an opportunity offered, he killed a fellow-being. Thrice had he already thrust his knife into the heart of his innocent brethren, when punishment or destiny overtook him. He had not been caught committing one of his murders, not one of his crimes could be proved by testimony, and yet suspicious signs repeatedly pointed to him as the source of all the misfortunes preying on the community. He had also friends cognisant of his dreams, for such poor tortured dreamers can rarely keep their secret entirely to themselves. A gloomy cloud hung over him, rumour had long before branded him, and so, as he was sitting one day with his back to a tree, brooding and solitary, an axe cleft the wicked dreamer's head asunder. A few of his victims' friends had joined together to put him out of the way. They did so, and the whole community applauded them for freeing them from such a monster.

In our countries very possibly these incidents I narrate will be regarded with suspicion, and I shall be asked for my authority. In that case, I can only answer that I am speaking of matters current among the people here.

The story of the man I have told who struck down others in consequence of a dream, is not actually cannibalism. But a case of the sort is frequently connected with cannibalism, and, at any rate, depends from the entire chain of superstition I describe here, and of which the windigo forms the termination. The windigo mania rarely breaks out spontaneously; it must have its predecessors and degrees. If a man live much apart and out of the world, if he appear to be melancholy and is tortured by evil dreams, then people begin to fear he may end by becoming a windigo, and he is himself attacked by the fatalistic apprehension, and is driven towards a gloomy fate. At times, when a man is quarrelling with his wife, he will say, "Squaw, take care. Thou wilt drive me so far that I shall turn windigo" (que je me mettrai windigo).

I was told the following story of a young man, with whose conduct and mode of life people were not satisfied, and of whom it was feared "that he might yet end as a windigo:"

Missabikongs was a young Indian, who from his youth up had offered signs of a very strange and adventurous character and manner. When quite a lad, he once ran away from his father, while on a journey, without bow or arrow, provisions, or any means of kindling a fire. His terrified parents sought him everywhere, and he was found a month later on the banks of a small lake called Lac de Patates. On what he had lived for so lengthened a period, or why he had run away, no one ever really found out. His parents took him back, and he remained quietly for the rest of the winter with his father, who watched him closely.

The next spring, however, when his father went with other savages to a great council, his little son disappeared again, and all seeking was in vain. At length, at the beginning of autumn, he came down the river in a canoe, and joined his family. He told them piecemeal the adventurous history of his six months' wanderings. He had a dream, so he said, that he must go eastward, where the sun rose. He had made his way at first along the southern shore of Lake Superior, at times living on roots and wild berries, at others shooting squirrels. At Anse Bay the Indians received him kindly, and gave him food; and he had gone from them to Sault Ste. Marie, the eastern outlet of the lake. There the Indians had adopted him as a son, and he spent some time with them. But he had run away from them again in two months, and had gone on eastward to Penangouishine, on Lake Huron. At last he got tired of travelling, as there seemed no end of journeying eastward, and determined on returning to his parents. At the end of several months' journeying westward, he at length reached a river which people told him led to his father's village. The Indians there also gave him the canoe in which he descended.

The parents and all the hearers wondered at his story, and the extraordinary lad thenceforth received the name of Missabikongs, which means " the little man of iron," because he had endured so much fatigue like child's play. To us the life of ordinary Indian hunters appears sufficiently wild and exposed, but to many Indian characters it is still far too tame and regular. They grow tired of respectability, and desire a perfectly savage life. I have already alluded frequently enough to children who ran away from their parents, and to young men who undertook great peregrinations through an adventurous or romantic temperament.

Missabikongs, or The Little Man of Iron, when grown up and independent, undertook many similar wanderings, whose details no one knows but himself, and he has sunk deeper and deeper into a state of savageness.

He still lives. " Il déteste la multitude. Il ne fume
pas avec les autres. Il n'aime que la sauvagerie. Il
ne mange ni souvent ni beaucoup. Il marche avec
rien du tout. Et quand on lui offre, il n'accepte pas."
In these words a Voyageur who knew him well described him. " He is unmarried, and for months he will
wander about alone in the forest, and build his own
lodge. He rarely visits his relatives, but he is known
far and wide, and people are afraid of him. He, on
the other hand, believes that he is persecuted by his
fellow-men. For some time past he has supposed
that the Americans are hunting him, and wish to kill
him. One evening he appeared at our fire in a very
savage condition, thin and pale, ' et la vue tout-à-fait
égarée et la bouche ouverte.' He looked at our
women preparing the supper. We offered him some
food. ' No,' he said, ' the Americans want to kill
me.' And then he opened his mouth again all so
stupidly, and looked so wild. ' If thou wilt not eat,
Missabikongs, then retire from here. No one wants to
kill thee, but thou mayst be thinking of killing a
fellow-man. Go away !' Very quietly he rose, and
went out into the forest, where he disappeared. Since
that time I never saw him again."

" Do you believe that the man is a windigo ?"
" No; not yet— perhaps not yet ! But if such an
outlaw were to be in great need—if winter and
hunger were to fall on him with all their terrors—
if he were to be driven almost to madness by his
sufferings—then you can understand how he might
step over all bounds and become a savage. Then he
will shoot his best friend and bury him in the snow,
to feed on him like a wolf."

They believe that the windigos have an understanding with the evil spirits, who help them. Hence,
a windigo can go on for a long time before a punishment fall on him and the avenger appear. They
imagine that a real windigo is very difficult to kill,
and that, in order to destroy him thoroughly, he must
be torn in pieces. Otherwise, he may easily come to
life again.

There are also windigo women — " des femmes
windigo"—in Indian, Windigokwé.

A Canadian Voyageur, of the name of Le Riche,
was once busy fishing near his hut. He had set one
net, and was making another on the beach. All at
once, when he looked up, he saw, to his terror, a
strange woman, an old witch, une femme windigo,
standing in the water near his net. She was taking
out the fish he had just caught, and eating them raw.
Le Riche, in his horror, took up his gun and killed
her on the spot. Then his squaws ran out of the
adjoining wigwam and shouted " Nish !"—(this was
the name Le Riche had received, as the Indians cannot pronounce the letter " r")—" Nish ! cut her up at
once, or else she'll come to life again, and we shall all
fare ill."

I do not know where Le Riche obtained his " firm
conviction" that the old woman he shot was really a
" femme windigo." But it seems as if people's eyes
and minds were practised here in the matter, for another half-breed told me how he met a windigo and
fired on him at once, like a rattlesnake:

" I was once shooting ducks in that swamp," he
said, as he pointed to a bed of reeds. " I fancied I was
alone : but suddenly, while aiming at a brace of ducks,
I saw a windigo crouching in the reeds. I recognised

him at once, and knew that he had come down from
the interior to the lake. He had been going about for
some time in our neighbourhood, and he was said to
have killed two men already. He had his gun to his
shoulder, and was aiming at me, just as I was doing to
the ducks. On seeing this, I did not make any sign
that I had recognised him, but walked quietly on towards my ducks. He hesitated about firing, probably
in the hope that I should soon stand still. I took advantage of the interval, squinted round from my gun,
made sure of his position, and, suddenly turning, I shot
him down. His charge went off harmlessly in the air.
But he soon picked himself up and disappeared in the
reeds, for I had merely wounded him. I had not the
courage to follow him, but he soon left these parts
over the ice, for it was winter. We followed his
blood-trail for some distance, and afterwards a report
spread that he had fallen through the ice on his flight,
and had perished."

Here is another windigo story I wrote down at
Sault Ste. Marie: An Indian had sought shelter at
that place, where he lived two years, no one knew
exactly how, and his origin was also unknown. At
length some persons sent a message from Grand
Portage, at the other end of the lake, that the fellow
was a windigo who had devoured his mother-in-law,
his wife, and children, and he had fled from there
because people tried to shoot him. He was obliged
to be very cautious at Sault Ste. Marie for some time;
but then he was converted to Christianity, confessed
his sins, and died as a Christian.

There seems not a doubt that these poor people,
persecuted and shot as windigos, are, like our witches,
very often wretched persons driven to extremities by

starvation. This will be seen from the fact that the Indians, during the celebrated expeditions of Franklin, gave the name of Windigo wakon (Windigo cabbage) to what is termed " tripe de roche" by the Canadians. This is well known to be a very bitter rocky growth, which, however, contains some nutriment. Only those who are driven to madness by fasting and want pick it from the rocks and use it as food. The Indians, who, as I said, call it " Windigo cabbage," seem to indicate by this that these poor starving wretches have recourse to honest food as long as it is possible, and only descend into the lowest depths of brutalisation when that herb gives out.

We may generally express our admiration, and indeed gratitude, that this degeneration only occurs in isolated cases, and that the nation, though so sorely ill-treated, has not given way to it *en masse*, like several other nations who inhabit, however, other more gifted countries. To this I may add, that you hear more frequently of windigos than you find or see them; and I may further remark that the word is much more frequently used with reference to the giant race of cannibals known by the name, than to the monsters now having their being among us. Stories are told of these old fabulous windigos which are quite as amusing to listen to as our " Hop-o'-my-Thumb." It is curious enough, too, that the Indian fancy, like that of the Scandinavians and other nations, invented and created a dwarf-like race by the side of the cannibal giants. They believe that these pigmies, though not visible to all, still really exist, and they populate all the forests with them. It seems, too, as if these Indian pigmies had even guns, for many a time I was told that a hunter, in walking through

the forest, had heard a little snapping shot, only ex-
plicable by the fact that a hunting pigmy had just
passed close by him.   These dwarfs, too, have delicate little canoes like the Indians, and glide over the
lakes and rivers.   Some Indians have so sharp a sight
that they can distinctly see them moving along in the
reeds and narrow channels between the broad leaves
of the water-plants.

I wish I could have learned more about these interesting little people, or spirits; but I thought I had
better at least mention them at the end of a chapter
which will not produce very agreeable sensations
among my readers.

CHAPTER XXIII.

" AH!" old Aurora, La Rose's mother, said to me,
with a sigh, this morning, when I called once again
to listen to her stories—" ah!" she said, " my head
has grown quite weak lately. I have lost my memory.
The Ojibbeways have all lost their memory. The
Americans have made them weak. Our people do
not talk so much about their own affairs now as they
used to do. They no longer feel the same pleasure
in telling the old stories, and they are being forgotten,
and the traditions and fables rooted out. You often
ask after them, but you seldom find any one who can
give you the right answer. Our nation is fallen; and
this came quite suddenly, since the Kitchimokomans,
or ' Long-knives,' entered our country."

Lake Superior and the Ojibbeway tribes around it
have already been under three European masters:

first, under the French; then under the Britons; and, lastly, under the Long-knives, which is the Indian name for the Americans of the United States. I frequently heard it asserted here that the people and country were tolerably free and independent under the French and British, but suddenly fell, and are rapidly proceeding to ruin, since the Americans have taken them, and they already call the recently expired period of British dominion "the good old times." The time of the French, or Wemitigoshis, as the Ojibbeways call them, was naturally still older and better. It was what we may call a silver age; and, of course, the time when there were no pale faces—the primitive times, when the Indians lived entirely alone—was the golden era.

My old lady talked to me about these old times in broken Canadian-French, after her fashion. I was much inclined to give her characteristic speech just as she held it, and in her broken Indian-French. But I fear lest the reader may hardly understand it, and so many explanatory remarks would be requisite. Hence I will translate it as carefully as I can, now and then quoting her own words:

"Beng! à cette heure!"* she began, when I asked her about the old times; " à cette heure c'est longtemps. C'était du vieux temps dont je te parle, beng beng vieux" (at this moment it is very long since. It is from the old times of which I am speaking to thee, very, very old), "when there were no white men at all in the country. Then the Indians were much

---

* The Canadians always say, instead of " à present," " à cette heure," and pronounce it exactly "asteur." Their "bien" sounds like "beng," and when they wish to strengthen it, they repeat it several times, after the fashion of Indians and children, thus: " Beng beng vieux," or "très vieux."

better than at this hour. They were healthier and
stronger, et beng plus forts pour la médecine. (This
Indian idea may be translated into European as
"stronger in their faith, more pious and religious.")

"They lived long and became very old. Beng
rarement que se meurt un sauvage. They could all
fast much longer.* They ate nothing at all for ten
days and longer. Hence they had better dreams.†
They dreamed of none but good and excellent things,
of hero deeds and the chase, of bears, and stags, and
cariboos, and other great and grand hunting animals,
and when he had dreamed, the Indian knew exactly
where these animals could be found. He made no
mistake. Il alla tout droit. Il tua, quoiqu'il avait ni
poudre ni fusil. Now their dreams are weak. They
often make a mistake, and even if they have dreamed
well, they do not know how to find the animals at
the right place.

"It is true all the beasts were more numerous then.
All the forests were filled with them. Çà et là et partout. Bears and deer, stags and foxes, cariboos and
beavers. All the rivers were full, full of fishes. And
the Indians had great power over them. C'est vrai
ils n'avaient pas le bon pouvoir. Ils n'étaient pas
Créquins (Christians), mais, au reste, ils vivaient
comme des rois. All they wanted they could make for
themselves. They made axes and arrows of sharp
stones; knives and lances of bones, et ils tuèrent pour
leur nourriture et vêtement les animaux tout roide.

---

* The reader will have had several opportunities through the course of
this work to see that the power of abstaining long from food is the sign of
a good and brave man.

† "Dreams" is always employed for thoughts, determination, and plans
of life.

C'est vrai ils n'avaient pas le butin* comme à cette heure. But they had a many hides and skins, and birds' skins, which were very good; and their squaws made of them the most useful and prettiest things.

"I allow that they did not know much about God at that time. They said, it is true, that there was a God, but they did not know Him so accurately as the Christians have now taught them. However, those who dreamed of heaven, said, at that time even, that it was the Good Spirit who evidenced to the savages mercy and sympathy. Still, the black priests taught us that afterwards better, and have brought it about that so many persons do not now dream of the Evil Spirit who lives at the bottom of the water.

" Beng, aussitôt que le blanc a débarqué icit. It was the Frenchman who landed first, and took land at Quebec, I believe, and came up the great Montreal river. There he found the whole country full of savages. Everywhere nations lived. Les sauvages ont dit, 'Qui est cet homme blanc-là? on ne l'a jamais vu dans notre pays.' They held a council together, and decided that they would make war on him, and send him back to his own country.

"The first year the white man did go back. But the second year he came again, and sailed up the whole river and the lakes,† and brought many fine things with him. Then the savage saw all sorts of things

---

* "Le butin " is a Canadian Voyageur expression, probably derived from the field. They mean by it not only their hunting effects and trading articles, but their household utensils and gear, clothing, &c.

† I thought it possible that in this story of my old woman, of two French landings, there was a reference to the first undertaking of the French under Cartier (in 1534), and the second series of conquests which recommenced in the beginning of the seventeenth century under Champlain.

which he had never seen before, and wished to possess them.

" Good, that ! the Frenchman began to give them presents, but not such presents as at the present time. The French presents were good and solid presents, wholesome food, fresh pork, stout knives, lasting guns, and good clothes. Ce n'était comme ce qu'on nous donne à présent. The savage loved the Frenchman, and accepted the French religion and the French trade; and the French ' black coats' took good care of the Indian, and lived with him in his wigwam. And the savage went hunting for the Frenchman, and so he hunted the game for him a long, long time, and both lived together in peace and friendship.

" At length, however, the Yaganash* came. Il est entré avec la force, et il est venu partout avec la force. He took away the whole lower land from the French. The Indians, because they loved the French, all dug up the tomahawk for them, and many braves set out too from Lake Superior to help the Frenchman. But the Englishman at last conquered everything.

" At first the Indians did not love the Yaganash. He also brought much ishkotewabo (fire-water) with him. The Frenchman had also fire-water with him, but not so much as the Englishman. Hence things have now grown much worse in the country. When the Indian had many furs, he drank much fire-water. And my grandfather, who was old, very old, old, often told me this sorrowful story. He often told me that more than one-half of the Indians died of this ' whisky water.'

* The Englishman. The word is probably an Ojibbeway corruption of the French " Anglais."

"And would to God we had taken an example from it ! Like the men the animals die out; and in the English time already there were many hunting districts where no game was to be found.

"But the Long-knives brought us even more whisky-water than the Englishman, and these killed more men and animals for us, and the times always became worse, worse. The presents and the salt pork grew ever worse, and the hunting-grounds have failed: besides, more and more land was taken from us.

"When the English were at war with the Americans (1812-1814), the savages were almost as kindly disposed to the former, their old friends, as before to the French, and they helped the English, and stood up for them, and sent their braves to help them against the Long-knives. When the English made a peace with them, and gave up to them the whole southern half of Lake Superior, the savages would not hear of it, and still lived for a long time in good friendship with the English, and were, from ten to twenty years, as independent on the lake almost as they had been before.

"Now, however, since the copper mines have been discovered, and the great steamers have appeared on the lake, and since the canal has been dug, which brings their ships easily from Huron Lake into our waters, and that all the men have come to seek copper, and look at our lake, it has all been over with the Ojibbeways. Their strength is broken, and they have lost their memory. Their tribes have melted away, their chiefs have no voice in the council. Their wise men and priests have no longer good dreams, and the old squaws forget their good stories and fables."

My path frequently led me here at our little Rivière au Désert, past the grave of the former chief of the tribe, and as I learned to regard this rough monument from a picturesque side, I made a sketch of it.

Like all Indian graves, it was made of clumsy axe-hewn tree-stumps, formed in a long quadrangle, and wedged into each other at the corners. It formed, in this way, a species of small house, and, like a lodge, had a roof of birch-bark strips. At the front end a lofty pole was raised, and from it fluttered a broad long cloth, like a flag, and rather larger than the usual grave flags, as a sign that a chief was interred here. This block mausoleum was situated near the river bank, and was mirrored in the water. The large flag, which formed a contrast to the dark rear of the forests, could be seen fluttering for a long distance.

As this looked to me at times very poetical, I inquired as to the history of the man who rested here. The people were astounded that I did not know Shinguakongse (The Little Pine), and they told me he had been a great warrior, and celebrated far and wide. He was the last brave their tribe and village had produced, and they told me so much about him that I began to feel an interest in the man, and obtained a tolerably perfect description of his life and deeds. But in attempting to repeat it here to my readers, I do so less for the sake of Shinguakongse himself than for that of the Indians, whose characteristics I chiefly keep before me. It is very possible that Shanguakongse has already been described as a brave in English and American histories I am unacquainted with, and that his biography, with all the necessary dates, figures, and facts, may be found elsewhere. I make no pretensions to writing a history here, and dates are a matter of indifference to me; I only care for the way in which Indians draw such life-histories of their heroes, and what they say to each other about them.

Shinguakongse, so the Indians told me at the place, was the son of an Indian woman and a British officer of Scotch birth. This mixture of blood produced, as usual, a famous half-breed race. After being separated from her officer, who was removed to the lower districts of Canada, the mother kept the boy, and educated him among the Indians and in the Indian way. " The child had, from youth up, powerful and good dreams," or, in other words, he was a talented and gifted lad. At an early age he distinguished himself by his abstinence, and in his tenth year fasted twice ten days in succession, without taking a particle of food. When grown up he showed himself strong in fasting, and for the last twenty years of his life always fasted, that is, lived temperately, and only took so much food as was required to keep his body strong. It is very natural that the Indians should make a great faster into a brave, for they are so often obliged to fast involuntarily, that the energetic defeat of hunger and thirst must become a national virtue among them. They make a virtue of a necessity.

Shinguakongse, however, nearly resembled an ancient stoic. He said he fasted not to obtain a great name and respect among his people, but because he always wished to have fine dreams—that is, wished to keep his head and thoughts clear. He wished to know everything that a savage can know on earth and in heaven. Hence, in his later years, he always fasted regularly—once most severely—principally in the spring, when all animals, and men, and spirits

receive renewed activity, and the whole of nature is
in a state of fermentation.

The very first dream Shinguakongse had in his life
was connected with great matters, and showed him
that a grand destiny was prepared for him. This
took place on a cold night, as he lay in his mother's
hut, freezing and half naked on his hard bed.

I ought to have remarked before, that his mother,
after parting from her European lover, had married
an Indian, who treated the son of love harshly, and
even the mother, who was immoderately fond of her
new husband, neglected her first child, and often left
him to starve and freeze in a wretched state.

Shinguakongse, however, endured this very patiently, and as, after his step-father's death, his mother
grew more attached to him, he entirely forgot her
former heartless conduct, took care of her like a good
son, and was wont to say that the torments of his
youth had prepared him famously for his future
career, and that with all the hunger, cold, and thirst,
he had always enjoyed splendid dreams.

This was more especially the case, as I said, on
the evening when he lay, half-naked and sleepless,
trembling with cold and hunger, on his hard bed.
He whimpered for a long time, but at length fell into
a state of half dreaming and half waking, Then he
fancied that a gentle voice said, sympathisingly, to
him, " Thou, poor Shinguakongse, thou art wretched;
come to me!" He looked around him, but he could
see nothing. But he perceived a path hovering in the
air, which gleamed in the darkness, and which, commencing at his bed, ran upwards through the doorway of his cabin. He comprehended that it was a
way on which he must walk. He went upon it, and

kept on rising higher and higher into heaven. There he found a house, from which a man came out to meet him, wrapped from head to foot in white garments, like a priest. " I called thee, O Shinguakongse, to me, to show thee something glorious. Look thither, towards the rising sun." When he looked, Shingua-kongse perceived the entire field full of tents and troops, among them being the great tents of the kings and chiefs, and a multitude of braves, warriors, and leaders, sitting together at the war-council. His eyes were, as it were, blinded by the dazzling brilliancy, and he felt a longing to be among them. " See, Shinguakongse," the white-robed man proceeded, " I give thee this picture; thou art still young, and thou art at the same time poor, wretched, and persecuted. But hereafter thou wilt be as grand as those thou seest there in the field, and will become, thyself, a mighty hero. I will always think of thee, if thou dost the same by me, and give thee this symbol in remembrance of this moment."

With these words he handed little Shinguakongse a gay fluttering pennant, and, with this in his hand, he again descended his hovering path. This path, too, was decorated on either side with fluttering pennants, through which he marched in triumph. The flags in the glistening path extended down to his hut, and the last of them stood by his bed. When the rough winter's wind again blew right coldly through the hut, he started and woke up, and, lo! all had suddenly disappeared.

But the glorious reminiscence remained to him, and the lad believed firmly from that moment that he would once become a great chieftain of his people. And the dream was really fulfilled. He became the greatest "general" of his race, and was known and celebrated everywhere among the Ojibbeways on the entire lake of Mitchigaming (Michigan Lake) and Kitchi-Gami.

After that dream he also changed his name of Shinguakongse, which, as I said, had the very trivial meaning of "The Little Pine." He called himself from that time forth Sagadjive-Osse, which means almost identically "When the sun rises." "It was amusing," my narrator added, "how highly he adored the sun from that time forth; and when he dreamed of it, he ever saw it before him, like a person walking before him and conversing."

When his step-father was dead, and his mother lived on closer terms of familiarity with her growing son, she took him once to the town of Detroit, where his real father, the English officer, was stationed. The latter gazed with pleasure on his grown-up "savage" son. He felt proud of him, "et il voulait le mettre blanc" (and he wished to educate and establish him as a white man), as his father was brought up. He proposed to him to enter the English service, and become an officer. "Mais Shinguakongse ne voulait pas se faire mettre blanc." He had a settled desire to remain with his mother and his Indian relatives. The father, however, dismissed mother and son with handsome presents, and from that time kept an eye upon them, and often sent them up messages to Lake Superior.

He had also soon an opportunity to send his son, who, a few years later, distinguished himself in a war on behalf of England, a silver medal, as reward, in the name of the British government. Shinguakongse also distinguished himself greatly in the war between Eng-

land and America. Once he fought so bravely for two
months against the Yankees, that a number of young
Ojibbeways collected around him, and the English
general, who was just setting out to besiege Mackinaw,
took him and all his comrades with him. When the
time came to attack this American fort in the most
effectual manner, the general even asked Shinguakongse for his advice. "I will dream about it to-
night, general," Shinguakongse said in the evening,
when the question was proposed to him, and the following morning he said: "I have dreamed, general."
"I have dreamed too," the general replied; "let us
compare our dreams." "I," Shinguakongse said,
"dreamed that a thick fog came two hours before
sunrise on the next day, so that nothing could be
seen on the lake round Fort Mackinaw or on the
island. Further, I dreamed that thou, general, pre-
paredst, with drum-beating and great noise, to attack
the fortress in front, while I and my Indians, concealed
by the fog, paddled out in our canoes, went round the
island, climbed the heights, unnoticed and unopposed,
and then made an unexpected and fresh attack on the
rear of the Americans. Thou hadst drawn them all
to the front, so I dreamed I climbed the undefended
walls in their rear, fired on them, and they surrendered, filled with terror. I saw their great star-
spangled banner fall down."

"Thou didst dream well, Shinguakongse," the general said, "and I have dreamed also like thee. Let
us set to work quickly." The dream was fulfilled
literally. Shinguakongse appeared at the decisive
moment in the rear of the Americans. They surrendered; and the young Indian was knighted, as we
should say, but, as it is called here in Canada, he re-

ceived as reward a chèferie. The British general appointed him official chief of a tribe, and procured him more silver medals, which from this time were repeatedly bestowed on the young brave. He, however, never wore them himself, but he always gave them to his young men, warriors, and friends.

In all wars he was on the side of the British, and remained faithful to them till his dying day. When peace was proclaimed, and the shore of the lake on which he lived was surrendered to the Americans, he left his residence, and followed the British to the English or Canadian bank. He would never accept a "chèferie" from the Americans, nor would he allow his sons to enter their service.

At the same time he was continually engaged in the wars going on among his own race. He fought all round Lake Superior, at every point of the compass, and led more than one expedition into the Sioux country from Lake Superior to the Mississippi.

He was, of course, equally skilled in hunting as in war, and extraordinary deeds are told as performed by him in both branches of Indian activity. He had educated and trained a pack of sporting dogs. One of his sons told me that these dogs had been his father's friends and playthings. He would lie on the grass for hours, watching the sport of his dogs. He had one which could catch beavers alive and bring them to his hut from the water. This dog would even tear down and destroy the beaver dams, if they were not too strongly built, and fetch the beaver out by the scurf of the neck, though there was generally a good hard tussle between them. Still the dog was sure to be the victor if he could only get the beaver on dry land, where this aquatic animal is helpless. Shingua-

kongse would lie on the grass the while, and feel a
delight in the bravery and skill of his dog.

Of course Shinguakongse, who, as I said before, had
dreams so distinct in his tenth year, and loved the sun
so passionately, was a great medicine-man, and was up
to his neck in the superstitions and incantations of his
people, as is the case with every great Indian hunter
and brave. The jossakids and warriors always go
hand in hand like the patricians and augurs in ancient
Rome. Shinguakongse knew and employed a number
of magic spells. As he was tall and strong, and at
times rich in productions of the chase, he was in a
position to obtain many such recipes, and he had
more than one medicine-bag full. He also had a
number of birch-bark written songs and traditions.

"Once, on my journey through the interior of the
country to Lake Superior," an American told me,
whose mother also belonged to the Ojibbeways, "I
came to a district where Shinguakongse was hunting
at the time, and where he had erected his hunting-
lodge. Another chief, of the name of Kiguash, was
hunting at the same time, for some months, in the
neighbourhood of Shinguakongse. When I entered
the lodges I only found the two hunters' wives at
home. They told me their husbands had left them
for some days past, and were busied in a special lodge
together over medicine matters. The women pointed
out to me the little forest meadow on which their
husbands' lodge stood: they had built it, expressly for
the purpose, of fresh branches. As a general rule,
it is not advisable or allowed to disturb the chiefs
when they have retired together for the purpose of
discussing high political and mysterious matters. But
I was very intimate with both; and as they also

regarded me as belonging to the tribe, through my
mother, I proceeded to join them. The entrance to
the wigwam was covered by a blanket, and I heard
for some distance the murmur of the song and the
drum-beating of the two men. As I addressed them
when a pause ensued, and they recognised my voice,
they received me very kindly, and allowed me to
enter. I found a very pleasant, new, and cleanly hut,
hung with fresh, gaily dyed mats. The chiefs themselves were in their grandest holiday state, adorned
with all their eagle feathers, medals, bears'-claw
necklaces, and other insignia derived from European
and native; with their faces painted bright red and
other glaring colours, and wrapped in their long white
blankets, on which the signs of their totems were
sewn with blue thread. In the middle of the wigwam a white cloth was spread out, at the ends of
which they sat opposite each other. By their side
lay their open medicine-bags, with their contents displayed on the white cloth. They consisted of small
pieces of copper and other metal, bones, shells of various sizes and colours, small packets of roots, papers
or bags of red, or green, or yellow coloured powders,
and other substances unknown to me, many wrapped
in swan's-down. Painted or written birch-bark
books also lay among them. Behind Shinguakongse
packets of peltry were piled up—beaver and bear-
skins—as well as coloured calicoes, silks, and many
yards of blue and scarlet cloth. I soon perceived
that they had been imparting to each other, explaining, and exchanging their various family and tribe
secrets. The principal buyer was Shinguakongse,
who was always eager for such things. He gave old
Kiguash, who was deeply engaged in these mysteries,

whole bales of beaver skins for a couple of powders
and the necessary instructions. Still, it could not be
said that Kiguash was taking him in, for he had himself, probably, paid very dearly for these matters.

" As the display of these mysterious articles, the
explanation of their virtues, the settlement of the
price, and the inspection of the goods, proceed very
slowly and cautiously, and as magic songs have to
be sung, the drum beaten, and many calumets of
peace smoked in the intervals, days are often spent
before the Indians have completed such negotiations.
One really takes lessons of the other, and, in order to
be able to receive them without disturbance, they
order their squaws to build them separate wigwams
for the purpose.

" The news I had to tell Shinguakongse was soon
told, and I then took my leave again, very well satisfied at having had a glance at a scene which even a
person like myself, so intimate with the Indians, does
not often have an opportunity of seeing. When Shinguakongse eventually turned Christian, and the heroic,
adventurous, and superstitious employments of his
youth no longer appeared to him in the same rosy
light, he often confessed to me that he had spent a
large fortune in superstition. He calculated, he said,
that he had paid at least forty packets of beaver skins
for medicine. Each packet contained one hundred
pounds of beaver skins, and though now it is not calculated at more than one dollar a pound, in those days,
when Shinguakongse was both young and superstitious, beaver was worth eight to ten dollars a pound.
Forty packets hence represented at least a minimum
value of thirty thousand dollars, and Shinguakongse
could carry off in one medicine-sack all the recipes

he obtained for them." It will be seen, from this instance, how valuable their religious traditions appear to the Ojibbeway braves, and what squanderers superstition renders them. It is like when a gentleman among us expends half his fortune on a church.

As long as Shinguakongse was a pagan, he was continually fighting. " Il aimait la guerre, et il guerroyait partout." For thirty years he lived in this way, something like the mediæval knights-errant. " Enfin, il s'est mis de la religion." It was the Englishman who ever said to him, " Shinguakongse, wander about no longer ! Settle quietly down and become a Christian !"

It is often the case that Indian chiefs can be converted, towards the end of their life, to Christianity, and a quiet, settled mode of life. But as long as they are young, superstition and patriotic views are too powerful in them. Generally, they can only be converted when children or old men. Frequently, too, only on the death-bed.

Shinguakongse, then, lived for a long time as Christian in the village of Rivière au Désert, highly esteemed by his family and the English. Before his house a lofty pine-tree was raised, from which the British flag fluttered as symbol of his dignity. When he lay on his dying-bed, the people of his tribe were sorely grieved. They wished to do something to save him, and they hit on the idea of putting up a new and second flag-staff before his house. Hence, they prepared, at their own expense, another one like the first, and put up a second flag in the name of his Indian community. They hoped that the freshly fluttering flag would give fresh play to his drooping spirits; but, for all that, he died. Still, at the time of

my visit, the two flags might be seen flying before his
house, and the question, which of his two sons should
be his successor and hoist the flag in front of his
house, was not yet decided.

I heard that Shinguakongse possessed a large
pagan Indian library—I mean, a collection of written
and painted birch-bark books—and as I hoped to
obtain some valuable addenda on this interesting subject, I was taken to his eldest son's house. I found in
him a powerful and handsome man in the prime of
manhood. He told me, however, that his father destroyed all his papers and birch-barks, and painted
dreams, dances, and songs, shortly before his death.
I inquired whether none of his family remembered
them, and the son said his father had often shown
and explained the things to him, and he knew the
most of them by heart. He could certainly draw
most of them for me, but it would require at least
six months' time.

CHAPTER XXIV.

AN INDIAN SCRIBE—MENABOJU AND THE DELUGE—THE TERRORS OF WAR—
CREATION OF KINNI-KANNIK—MENABOJU BECOMES YOUNG AGAIN—LOVE
SONGS AND INCANTATIONS—A SPRING SONG—WHEN THE SWALLOWS HOME-
WARD FLY!—THE DREAM OF THE MORNING STAR—A HUNTER'S DREAM—
THE FRENCH TRAITEUR—EUROPEANS AND THEIR HATS—THE WAR EAGLE
—A GREAT FAST—THE DREAM OF A BRAVE—THE TEMPLE WIGWAM—THE
FOUR VICTIMS.

As I was continually asking at our little mission
about pictorial writing, the Indians at length told me
they had a man among them of the name of Ojibiwas, who was very clever in drawing and writing.
He could make me as many books as I might wish to
have. He could write down anything told him, and
had already written much for other persons.

I at once made the acquaintance of this Indian "scrittore," and begged him to call on me with birch barks
and the other requisite writing materials. The next
morning he made his appearance in my little arbour.
It seemed as if he had peeled an entire birch-tree, for
he had at least half a quire of this Indian paper under
his arm, as well as a large knife and a bone pencil in
his hand.

I first asked him to write down or paint something

after the manner of his people. He asked me what? and I told him it was all one, he could follow his own imagination; it might be a story about Menaboju, or any other pleasant narrative which he could describe in picture and writing.

"Good!" he said. He would do so.

I gave him a good English pencil, but he said his sharp bone was much better for drawing. Nor would he take a seat in the shady arbour, where I had arranged a convenient table for him. He assured me that he must sit in the sunshine outside. And so he went out into the weeds and scrub, and worked away busily in his hiding-place for several hours, during which I did not hear a sound from him.

I do not know how many chapters of Morgan's excellent work on the Iroquois I had read through, when my little scrittore crawled in again, and told me he had drawn me some anecdotes of Menaboju, the great demi-god of the Ojibbeways. He then showed me a birch bark, on which the figures opposite were drawn.

As the product of two hours' labour, they did not appear to me very important; but Ojibiwas said it was very hot, and the work had caused him no slight trouble.

Then began a long lesson, and detailed interpretation of the figures, which cost teacher and scholar a considerable amount of perspiration ere they arrived at a mutual clear understanding.

It was, I soon saw, very nearly the story of Menaboju's deluge. I had heard it several times before, but now there were some variations. My painter had also episodically introduced other anecdotes about Menaboju. It will be seen that he arranged his pic-

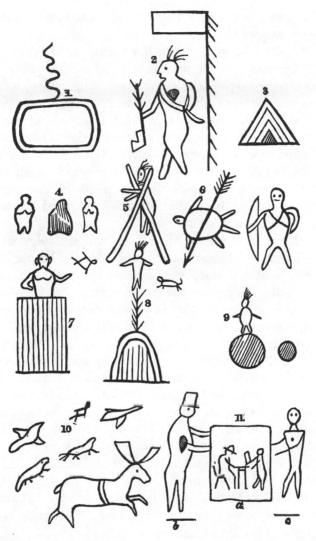

torial stories much like Töpfer has done his about
Monsieur Jaunisse," " M. Sabot," &c.

I have numbered the separate pictures, and will

now give my Indian "Töpfer's" explanations as accurately as possible.

"No. 1," he said, "was the earth, called 'Aki' by the Ojibbeways. It was painted there in order to have a proper foundation for our entire story, for it was the scene of all the events. The perpendicular undulating line over it is a great river. It is really not necessary there," my artist remarked, "for it is not alluded to in my story till later. But I have drawn it on the Aki figure, because the rivers flow on the earth. When we come to the point in the story where the river is needed, thou wilt be good enough to remember this stroke.

"No. 2 is Menaboju, in all his military splendour. He was a great brave and chief. Hence he has the flag-staff at his side, the feathers on his head, his sword, and the pipe of peace. (I suspect that Ojibiwas placed him here in the same way as we give in our biographies the portrait of the hero, adorned with all his orders.)

"No. 3 is Menaboju's wigwam, in which he lived, sometimes with one squaw, sometimes with two. In this lodge many events occurred to him, such as the following: Once Menaboju's two squaws quarrelled. This quarrel between the squaws, which I have represented at No. 4, is very celebrated among us. They wished to get to blows, but Menaboju said, 'Stop!' and commanded peace. I have shown this order of Menaboju's by a mountain or rock between the two squaws. Dost thou see it? This rock is a word signifying so much as 'stop!'

"No 5 relates to another little anecdote about Menaboju. It represents him as he was once caught between two trees. It often happens in our forests that two trees, with their great thick branches, are driven so close against each other that they continually rub, as the wind shakes them. Hence a jarring sound is produced through the entire forest. At times, too, such rubbing of two trees produces heat and a fire. Menaboju, either because he wished to put an end to the noise, or feared a fire in the forest, climbed up the tree to break the branches asunder. But they flew back again and squeezed him, as the figure shows. He remained between the trees for three whole days, without eating or drinking, and in vain begged all the animals that passed to liberate him. First came the wolves, but they said, ' Oh, Menaboju! thou art well taken care of there !' and even ate up his breakfast, which he had left in a cloth under the tree. Next came the squirrels. Although these began, on Menaboju's entreaties, to gnaw the trees a little, they said at last that they would get toothache by it; they were not used to such hard woodcutter's work, but only to crack sweet nuts. Similar excuses were made by other animals to whom Menaboju applied. At length the bear came, and he helped the poor man out of his fix. When Menaboju reached home he scolded and beat his wives, because, as he said, they were entirely to blame for the whole unlucky event. His squaws said truly that they knew nothing about it. But what injustice will not a man commit when he is in a bad temper !

" Menaboju had a little grandson, who one day, in hunting, came to a river. (That is the river," Ojibiwas said, " which I drew at No. 1.) The king of the turtles (No. 6.) sat on the bank of this river, and Menaboju's grandson begged him to help him over. But, instead of doing so, the king of the turtles was so malicious as to make the river broader, so that the little one, when he at last ventured to leap across, fell in and was drowned. The king devoured him, but was caught in the act by Menaboju, and killed. Thou seest in my picture that he already has Menaboju's arrow in his back.

"When the turtles on this declared war against Menaboju, and produced the great deluge, Menaboju first carried his grandmother on to a lofty mountain (No. 7). He, himself, mounted to the top of the tallest pine, on the tallest mountain in the world, and waited there till the deluge was over. Thou probably knowest how the loon and the musk-rat came to him there? I have drawn them on either side of Menaboju.

"At No. 9, two islands are represented which Menaboju made: a little one, which did not bear his weight; and then a large one, which supported him, and afterwards became the new world.

"After Menaboju had thus restored the world, he called all the birds, animals, and men together, displayed himself to them in his full war-paint, with the lance in his hand and the horns of his strength on his head, and made a speech: 'Our children the savages will be constantly warring, and at times they will sign a peace. Hence, the laws of peace and war must be settled.'"

On this Ojibiwas produced a long series of small pictures, representing the calumet-dance, the war-dance, the medicine-dance, and the other Indian dances and ceremonies, which he stated Menaboju ordered. But I have omitted these, as rather too long-winded.

At the end of the series of pictures (No. 10) I

found a group of animals, and, on asking Ojibiwas
what they meant, he said, " Those are the animals
which Menaboju sent forth to look for his grandmother, to inform her of the new creation of the
world, and lead her back from her mountain."

At the end of the row I noticed the sketch at
No. 11. "What is this, Ojibiwas?" I asked. "That
is a thing," he said, very modestly and seriously,
" which I have painted in remembrance of our meeting. That in the centre (at *a*) represents our arbour,
and thou and I in it, as we are speaking. Those are
our portraits. The figure outside (at *b*) is thyself,
and at *c* myself, as I hand thee the portrait as a
remembrance."

"My good Ojibiwas," I said to him, "but thou
hast flattered me greatly by giving me so great a
heart. Would to God I had such a one. And thou,
too, art so modest, I can scarcely perceive the dot for
thy heart."

In truth, this is the only way in which Indian por-
trait-painters can flatter their customers and patrons.
I own it appears, too, very original, that Ojibiwas
found it necessary to paint us first in the actual portrait, and then represent the presentation of it in the
bargain.

We were satisfied with each other, and I requested
my artist to return the next day. He came, seated
himself again in the weeds, and engraved with his
migoss, or pencil, most busily for several hours.
After some days' labour, he brought me a little library
of birch-bark books, and told me the stories relating
to the pictures. I will not copy the whole of his
library here, as it would be tedious to my reader.
Many of the sketches were so piquant and improper,

and the Indian wag Menaboju proved himself in them
such a coarse and loose fellow, that, for that reason, it
would be impossible to reproduce them. Still I will
give, as further specimens, two or three of the Menaboju fables I heard on this occasion, while leaving out
my painter's designs.

Menaboju was once travelling quite incognito, and
found some other braves, who were also on their
travels. He asked them where they were going, and
for what object; and they told him that they had set
out to fight against Menaboju and slay him.

Menaboju bit his lips, and said to the men, "That
is all right!" But, then, he ran back to his lodge as
quickly as possible, and raised a war-cry, and began
beating the drums to collect his own warriors.

The noise excited the curiosity of one of his small,
impudent boys, and he crept to the door of his father's
lodge and peered in. Menaboju, who noticed him,
and thought this interruption of a solemn war council
highly improper, struck him so violently on the head
with the drum-stick, that he fell back dead on the spot.

This sent Menaboju's squaw, who saw the deed,
almost out of her mind. "What! monster!" she
yelled; "thou killest thy own children! and that,
too, was our best son!"

"Peace!" Menaboju replied, calmly. "Console
thyself, wife. These are times of war. For the following centuries the same will constantly happen in
wars and revolutions. Husband and wife will quarrel.
Brother will kill his brother, a father his son. And
even worse things than this will happen. Such is the
harsh destiny of war!"

On one of his wanderings, Menaboju was once lying by his camp fire, but, to his annoyance, his tobacco-pouch was empty. When a savage cannot smoke he goes to sleep, and so did Menaboju. But he lay so awkwardly, that, in his dream, he rolled too near the fire, and burnt all his back and loins. He woke up, yelled, and rushed, tortured by pain, through the bushes. Some of these bushes, which he grazed, received the singed odour of the demi-god's scorched skin, and thus became perfumed, and henceforth suited for smoking. These now supply the Indians with kinni-kannik. And thus poor Menaboju had to suffer like a martyr, in order that his children, the Indians, might never henceforth fall into the dilemma in which he found himself. They now find tobacco everywhere in the forests and shrubs.

Menaboju once lived with two squaws, for he gave the Indians the notion of polygamy. The squaws were young, but he had already aged a little, and noticed that he did not please his squaws so much as before, for they neglected him slightly now and then. This annoyed him greatly, and he determined on making a change.

One evening he did not return to his lodge at the usual time, and the squaws began to feel uneasy about him. All at once a voice was heard sounding through the forest, " Your Menaboju is dead in the bushes; go and fetch him!" The squaws were frightened, but obeyed the voice; and as they found his apparently stiffened corpse, they bore it home.

" Now comb and dress his hair," the voice was again heard pealing through the wigwam. The squaws be-

lieved that it was a voice from the spirits, and combed
their Menaboju.

Then the voice commanded again: "Paint his whole
face pleasantly of a red colour, put on him a new robe,
and lay him so adorned in the branches of a tree."
The squaws, in their terror, did all rapidly that the
spirit-voice commanded them, and laid Menaboju in
the branches of a tree. "To-morrow," the voice
shouted once more, "a young, handsome, red-painted
Indian will knock at your door. Let him in, and take
him as your husband, and treat him kindly; and if
you do not so, I will visit you again, and plague and
torment you. The man, who will come to-morrow
can alone protect you from me."

The next day a neatly-combed, red-faced, freshly-
clothed Indian appeared before the wigwam of the
squaws. It was Menaboju himself thus metamorphosed.

He had only feigned death, and the spirit-voice
which had caused his squaws so wholesome a terror
was nothing but the produce of his ventriloquism, in
which he, like many an Indian of the present day, was
very clever.

His squaws found him rejuvenated in the pretty
toilet with which they had themselves decorated him.
They had learned how much the attention a squaw
pays to her husband, aids in making him young, and
in future they were more patient with him.

In my inquiries after poetry and pictured writing
among the Indians, I at length grew weary of the
eternal dream-stories and magic spells that crossed my
path. I would so gladly have met with purely poetic
outbursts of a free and disinterested enthusiasm, in

which poesy might appear for itself, and without the
secondary intention of catching fish or deer.

But such songs are a *rara avis* among the Indians.
It seems as if they only possess "poetry with a purpose." As in revolutionary times all the poetry as-
sumes a political tone, though it may be published
under the name of spring or autumn songs, or love
strains or elegies (in the same way as among the old
English Puritans every poem, even the war-songs,
was a species of hymn), so among these superstitious
Indians, whose entire poetry moves amid dreams,
visions, fear of spirits, and magic, every song is at
once a magic spell, specially designed to ensnare
beavers and bears. Every sorrowful or joyful emotion that opens their mouth is at once wrapped up in
the garb of a "wabano-nagamowin" (chanson magicale). If you ask one of them to sing you a simple,
innocent hymn in praise of Nature, a spring or jovial
sporting stave, he never gives you anything but a
form of incantation with which, he says, you will be
enabled to call to you all the birds from the sky, and
all the foxes and wolves from their caves and burrows.
If, again, you ask him for a love-song, he will give
you a philter, or a powder with the proper form of
incantation, and assure you that this is a most effec-
tive love-song.

I experienced an instance of this on one occasion.

I was once sitting with a young unmarried Indian
in his lodge, with whom I was talking on various
matters. At length I asked him if he had not yet
fallen in love with any fair one of his tribe.

"Oh yes, I have," he said.

"Hadst thou then no pretty songs and poetry for
thy beloved?"

" Of course I had them, and have them still."

And when I begged him to let me see them (of
course laying a packet of tobacco on his knee at the
same time), he went and fetched his medicine-sack,
and produced a small paper parcel. At the same time
he looked round timidly to see if we were quite alone,
and no one observing us. Then he produced all sorts
of things from the paper: first, a small figure carved
out of wood, which, as he said, represented his beloved; and then another figure, intended for himself.

In the bosom of the female figure the heart was
indicated by a hole, and thence a line (the line of
speech) ran, as usual, to the mouth. The heart holes
were painted red, and there were several small dots
round them.

After this he produced from his packet five small
bags. Each was made of a single piece of leather and
carefully fastened up, and in each was a different
coloured powder—red, blue, yellow, grey, &c. He
told me that sometimes when he was alone in the
forest he put some of the powder in the heart holes of
the small figure, and then he sang and beat the
magic drum. All the powders produced a different
effect: one aroused gentle feelings and longing for
him, while another caused his sweetheart pain, and
terrified her so much that nothing was left her but
to yield to him.

" Look at this needle in his packet," my interpreter
said, drawing my attention to it; " with that he
pierces the heart and breast of his sweetheart every
now and then, after dipping its point into one of the
powders. He fancies that every stab goes through
her soul. This causes the numerous dots on the

hole, or heart, which looks like a worn-out rifle target. These barbarous lovers often have spells, by which they believe that they can torture girls, who spurn their offers, to death. When very violently inflamed with love, they often busy themselves for hours in the forest with such recipes and the songs that accompany them, which are partly elegiac, partly malicious, and almost criminal forms of incantation. They call these love-songs ' masaminik,' while the Voyageur term is ' gatins.' "

While our young barbarian was repacking his traps, I noticed that the bags and figures were fastened with a lock of black hair. On my inquiry, he told me that it came from his sweetheart's head, and a friend had procured it for him, as it was indispensable for the whole process.

At length I found an Indian who wrote me down something that really approaches to a simple spring song. The man's name was Bebamisse, which may be translated " L'Oiseau Voltigeur."

The pictured writing which was given me as " a song of praise on the arrival of the birds in spring," contained the figures to be found on the next page.

The writing, or song, I was told, must be sung from right to left, and the birds were arranged in the same order as they arrived in spring. The bird at No. 1, I was further told, was an " oiseau de passage," the " pluvier," and came first of all.

No. 2 represented the little duck which the Indians call " kangkangouè," " which always keeps timidly a great distance from land."

No. 3 is another variety of duck, called by the Ojibbeways " jishib," and by the Voyageurs canard de France.

No. 4. "Voilà l'aigle, ou le migissi, qui s'élève pour prendre son air."

No. 5. "That is the great kiniou, which the Voyageurs call 'le quiliou'" (the celebrated war-eagle, from which the Indians derive their handsomest war-ornament). "Descending from the heavens, he brings with him the fine weather.

"And next to the kiniou will be seen, at the top of the fir-tree, the piskiniou, which the Voyageurs call the quiliou bâtard. These are the two birds which fly the highest in our land, and are nearly always in the uppermost clouds.

"No. 7 is the hopping crane, the 'adjijag,' which arrives the last, and brings the summer with it."

No. 8. " C'est le chèfre du beau temps. He bran-
dishes a knife, and is adorned with numerous wampum necklaces and a belt, and summons the birds
and the spring."

I say that in this song something may be recognised
bearing a resemblance to a song of spring, or a poem
on the arrival of the birds. In the soaring eagle and
the descending kiniou some pastoral allusions may
also be traced. A Voyageur, before whom I laid
this drawing, told me it is true that the birds really
arrived, or, as he said, " d'après leur naturalité," in a
very different succession; but it is too much to expect
fidelity to natural history in a song.

As I was once walking out of my village, an Indian
stalked along before me, wrapped in his wide blanket.
In the centre of the back was the following figure
drawn with coarse purple strokes.

I joined him, and he told me that his name was
" Makwa" (the Bear), (here every fourth man is called
the Bear, as, among us, Smith or Thompson), and we
walked some distance together. I asked my friend
Makwa the meaning of the grand star on his back.
He replied that it was his dream. " It is the fine
star," he said, " which thou seest glistening when
thou risest early, over there" (here he pointed to the
east). " I met it once in a dream. It glistened and
shone continually on my path, now rising, now sinking. At length it spoke to me, and said: 'Makwa, I
will be thy guide. Thou shalt glisten and shine as I

do. Like me thou wilt once set. But so long as
thou livest, I will float over thee and protect thee.'
Since that period, I have always painted it on the
back of my blanket, and carry about its picture in remembrance."

The readers of Longfellow's "Hiawatha" will be
here reminded of the poetic canto, "The son of the
evening star," and I was very pleased to find at this
place a confirmation, to some extent, of the poet.

From an Indian of the name of Amongs (The Little
Wasp), I received the following picture, representing
his greatest dream:

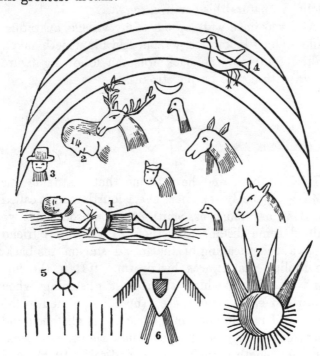

I will accompany it with some explanatory remarks:

No. 1 is the dreamer, lying on his bed of moss and grass.

No. 2 is his guardian spirit, or the person who spoke to him in his dream, and explained the occurrences that took place in it.

In the present case, these events seemed to be limited to the fact of the dreamer seeing the sky expanded above him, and full of birds and animals. It is a real hunter's sky, and the whole a simple hunter's dream.

Only the heads and long necks of the animals appear. Several varieties may be recognised—the stag, the elk, a roebuck, and two large birds.

Amongs also dreamed on this occasion of a Frenchman, represented at No. 3 as a figure wearing a hat. The Indians picture themselves without a hat, because they usually have no other head-gear than their matted hair, or at most an animal's skin, worn turban-wise round the head. The hat, however, appears to them such a material part of the European, as much fastened to their heads as is the horse to the Centaurs, that a hat in a picture-writing always indicates a European.

It was not at all stupid of Amongs to dream of a Frenchman. For of what use would a sky full of animals prove to him unless he had a good honest French " traiteur," to whom he could sell the skins, and receive in exchange fine European wares?

The vault of the sky is represented by several semi-circular lines, in the same way as it is usually drawn on their gravestones. On some occasions I saw the strata or lines variously coloured—blue, red, and yellow, like the hues of the rainbow. Perhaps, too, they may wish to represent that phenomenon as well. But that the whole is intended for the sky, is proved

by the fact that the ordinary colour is a plain blue or
grey. The bird soaring in the heavens (4) was meant
for the kiniou, which so often appears in the dreams
of these warlike hunters.

When I asked the dreamer what he meant by the
strokes and figures at the foot of the drawing, he said:
" It is a notice that I fasted nine days on account of
this dream. The nine strokes indicate the number
nine, while the small figure of the sun (No. 5) over
them means days."

His own " me " he indicated by the human figure
(6). It has no head, but an enormous heart in the
centre of the breast.

Though the head is frequently missing, the heart is
never omitted in Indian figures, because they have, as
a general rule, more heart than brains, more courage
than sense. " I purposely made the heart rather
large," the author of the picture remarked, " in order
to show that I had so much courage as to endure a
nine days' fast. He omitted the head, probably because he felt that sense was but little mixed up with
such nonsensical fasting.

I. " But why hast thou painted the sun once more,
and with so much care over it ?"

He. " Because the very next morning after my fast
was at an end the sun rose with extraordinary
splendour, which I shall never forget, for a fine sunrise after a dream is the best sign that it will come to
pass."

On a journey I once took on the St. Peter's River,
in the Sioux country, accident brought me together
with an Indian known as " Le Rond Vent." He was
bedizened with many eagle feathers and other trophies,
and had a painting on his pipe, which he told me

represented a glorious dream. He had dreamed it twenty years previously, and always connected it with the greatest exploit in his life—the slaughter of four Ojibbeway Indians.

As he noticed that I evinced an interest in his life-history, he offered to draw the whole dream distinctly in my book, and he eventually supplied me with the following picture :

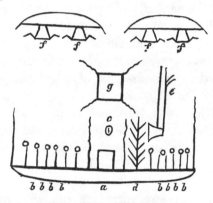

After having fasted, sung, and beaten the drum for a long time, he said it seemed to him as if he were entering a temple or great medicine wigwam (the door of this temple is indicated at *a*). Round it sat many old wise men, the warriors and chiefs of the nation since olden times. They are indicated on the drawing by the perpendicular lines *b b b b*. They bade him welcome, allowed him to enter the sanctuary, and permitted him to beat the drum and sing in honour of the Great Spirit near the great stone in the centre (*c*). The large pipe of peace, adorned with feathers (*e*), hung suspended from a lofty tree (*d*) above his head. While sitting to pray and sing in the midst of these men, he heard something coming towards him through the air.   He could not at first detect what it was, but gradually saw that there were two canoes floating in the air, in each of them two men of the Ojibbeway tribe being seated (ff).   The faces of these, his enemies, were blackened, and they had sung their death-song.   The men and the canoes came floating up quite close to the door of the temple, when suddenly a large hole (g) opened in the ground.   The men with the canoes paddled into the hole, and they were swallowed up close before his eyes and feet.

Directly after the whole dream melted away.   Still he knew that he was destined to kill four Ojibbeways, and he had therefore set out after certain preparations (which, by the way, often last for months), had crept into the Ojibbeway land, found the four men in their canoes at the right spot—and this was also indicated to him in his dream, though I know not how—killed them one after the other, and brought home their four scalps.

He had, therefore, carried about with him through life a memorial of this deed and his dream.   I had no reason to believe that he was deceiving me, for the two canoes were represented in his drawing inverted with the men.

CHAPTER XXV.

THE bears, it appears, perform certain wanderings,
regulated by the season, from north to south, or from
the forest-clad districts to the more open parts.   In
spring and summer, so I was told, they migrate to the
south, where a richer harvest of fruit and grain awaits
them.   In autumn, however, they return to the great
forests, in order to stow themselves away for the
winter, in what the English call the pineries, the
French, "les bois forts."   In winter they would positively starve on the prairies and more open plains.

In these excursions, the bears, although rarely or
never found in large bodies, have certain places on the
rivers, where they are in the habit of crossing.   A
very celebrated ford of this description is said to be
the "passe à l'ours" on the St. Croix, a confluent of

the Upper Mississippi. It is at no great distance from
the mouth of the little Yellow River on the Mississippi,
and is well known to the traders and hunters in these
parts. One of them gave me the following description of the hunting and locality there:

" The northern shore is thickly clothed with wood,
for a spur of the great northern forests runs down to
that point. The south shore, on the contrary, is a
fine open prairie. On this bears arrive almost daily
in the month of October, to swim through the water,
and then creep into the forest thickets. In order not
to disturb them in this, all the travellers and traders
quit the south shore of the St. Croix during this
period, and give similar directions to their people,
although the trail along the south shore is far more
convenient than that on the other bushy and swampy
side. The bears would immediately notice the footsteps of men and become shy. The hunters who
await the bears here, and give them chase, naturally
also keep on the northern shore, where they lie in the
little forest bayous in their canoes. The bears usually
arrive in the night. The night is fine and calm, the
moon shines brightly, the water is as clear as a mirror.
Suddenly the hunters hear a trampling in the reeds,
on the shore, and the dry grass. Here's Bruin ! Away
the animal splashes into the water, and paddles
along, snorting violently; only its black head is
visible on the moon-illumined waters. The hunters
aim at this, and usually give the bear a mortal wound.
They hurry up in their canoes and pull the beast
alongside with iron hooks. If it is dead, these prevent it sinking, while, if still living, they drag the bear
to the north shore, lest the body might float down and
the scent of the blood cause an alarm among the fol-

lowing bears. This bear migration at Passe à l'Ours is said to last three to four weeks."

As I said, there may be other bear passages besides the one I have mentioned, and which I merely chose as an instance. Several years have become remarkable for enormous bear migrations. Thus, I heard much at Rivière au Désert of the year 1811, as a perfectly extraordinary bear year. It is natural enough that, if the bears are wandering, they must appear in large numbers on this river at the eastern point of Lake Superior, where two large peninsulas join to form an isthmus. In the said year, however, they migrated the whole summer through from the northward across the river to what is called the "upper peninsula of Michigan." Above six thousand bears are said to have been killed on the island and banks of this moderately long river. Many traders bought five hundred or six hundred skins in the course of a year, and several even more. A hundred bears were sometimes killed in a night, and many a clever hunter brought down as many to his own gun during the season. Young bears were even taken out of the water by the hand. At least, this happened to an Indian squaw, while crossing the river in a canoe, and who ran against a young footsore animal, which was unable to follow the others in their hasty course southwards, and was wearily floating in the water. The squaw took the struggling beast out, and as she could not pacify it otherwise, she thrust it under a sack, on which she sat down, and it scratched and yelled away till she reached the shore and killed it.

In the same year, 1811, the " twenty dogs of Maguesh" each received a bearskin cover, as skins were nearly as cheap as calico. This Maguesh was

an Indian, who lived without family and children,
and, instead of them, kept a quantity of dogs, which
he nursed like children, shared his breakfast with
them every morning, often held a dialogue with them,
and warned them like children to behave properly
and not quarrel. Although, since 1811, many other
hunters have been richer in skins than the ordinary
average, such an instance as this never occurred again.
Nothing certain was offered me in explanation of this
extraordinary phenomenon, although every one here
was thoroughly conversant with the fact.

Some of the Western Indian tribes have what they
call a "couteau d'ours." This is a knife drawn
through the mouth and grinders of a dead bear—
doubtlessly with certain forms and ceremonies—and
thus receives magical qualities. Such a knife as this,
which is certain to kill, and at the same time make
the owner brave, can only be purchased at a high
price. There is also only one way of transferring it
to another owner, so as not to destroy its power. The
buyer must permit the seller to throw it at his breast
like a javelin, and catch it in the air. If he has not
the courage for this, or misses it, the knife loses its
qualities, and the clumsy purchaser his life in the
bargain.

Of all the animals that exist in their forests, the
Indians respect the bear most. They regard it almost
in the light of a human being. Indeed, they will
often say that the bear is an "Anijinabe" (Indian).
They will converse with it, thinking all the while the
animal must understand them. The little bear-pups
are so droll, and so full of life and comical liveliness,
and the old bears are so remarkably clever and crafty,

that it may be easily understood how the Indians can imagine that they see enchanted beings in them.

The things told me here about the tricks and cheating of the bears are almost incredible. But everybody repeats them to me, and believes them. Thus, a hunter told me recently of the tricks and schemes a bear will perform, when it knows itself pursued, and wishes to deceive its follower as to the direction it has taken.

This is most difficult to perform in winter, when the ground is covered with snow and the rivers with ice. In summer the bear will often take to streams and brooks, and run up or down their bed. The hunter in pursuit is then unable to say in what direction it has gone. In the winter, when the snow betrays the bear everywhere, it has to think of other devices. Then it leaves the treacherous ground as frequently as possible, and springs along on the tree-stumps, which lie about all these forests, piled up on each other. At times, when a violent storm has raged, whole districts in the forests for miles round will be covered with overblown trees. Thus is formed what the French Canadians call a " renversi." Fortunate for the flying bear if it can reach such a spot. It then balances itself along on the stumps, and takes long flying leaps. Less snow usually lies on these trees, and, besides, wind and sun melt it away more easily than on the ground. If, however, the bear sees the mark of its footprints left upon them, it will steer a zig-zag course, turn back on the same trail, or leap aside. I was even told that at times Bruin will purposely return on his trail, and thus produce a perfect labyrinth of foot-marks, in which the hunter can find no Ariadne's thread. " Il embrouille sa piste," the Canadians say.

At times, too, the animal will climb up trees stern foremost, so as to make the pursuers, when they notice the marks on the tree, fancy that it has come down again.

I was also told that a bear will wait and watch about for perhaps three days before it will enter the hollow tree in which it intends to pass the winter. My half-breed friend, La Fleur, told me the following instance:

Not far from Grande Isle, on the southern shore of Lake Superior, there were large and fine beech woods, said to be a perfect paradise for bears and hunters. The bears like the sweet mast-nuts, and hence are always collected in large numbers in this wood. La Fleur was once hunting them with a friend. They discovered the trail of a bear in the snow, and followed it. The animal very soon found out the game, retired, and fled many miles to the south, with the hunters after it. They followed its trail for eight days, losing it at times, and then taking it up again.

At length they came to a woody district, where the nature of the ground and of the trees altered. The snow ceased there, and it was impossible to follow the bear's trail over the rocky ground. My hunters, therefore, considered the animal lost, and gave up the chase. As, however, they knew there was a beaver dam in the vicinity, they started on the back trail for that place, so that they might take their revenge on the beavers. But they had hardly inspected the locality after arrival, ere they found the trail of their bear again. They followed it afresh, and soon stood before a hollow tree, in which they killed the animal. It was plain to them that the bear had only described a semicircle on the unsnowed rocky ground, which did not suit it. It was well aware (so La Fleur declared) that the hunters would lose its trail at the edge of the snow-land, and then it could return comfortably to its beloved beech forest, where it crawled into a hollow tree, to rest from its eight days' exertions. The hunters' wish to pay the beavers a visit unfortunately foiled the success of Master Bruin's plan.

The Canadians and Indians believe that the bear always crawls into the tightest-fitting tree it can find. It thrusts itself forward with its long paws and sharp muzzle like a wedge, and thus forces its way into holes which it finds at times too narrow when desirous to emerge from them. When the bear chooses a suitable tree for the winter's sleep, it prefers one with a smaller orifice, because it is warmer. For the sake of warmth, the bear will also stop up the hole with moss and branches. (Il bouche son arbre.) In spring, then, it sometimes happens that Master Bear cannot get out again, and they have frequently perished in their confined holes. Even when they are killed with bullets in the cavity, the greatest difficulty is experienced at times, and the hole has to be cut open to get the body out. The hunters fancy that the hole in the tree grows tighter, and closes up after the entrance of the bear. But the fact may be, probably, very simply explained in this way: the bear has more strength and force to push through anywhere in autumn, while in the spring it is weakened and exhausted by the long winter's sleep.

The bear is said to have a piece of meat grow under its great tongue. The Indians call it " the little tongue (la languette). The hunters cut this off when they kill a bear, dry it, and pocket it, because they consider it very influential for their future success.

It happens at times that an Indian will kill three
bears in one day. He cannot drag them home by himself, but he trails his gun after him through the snow,
so that he may find his way back. When the successful hunter returns home in the evening, and sits with
the other hunters round the fire, he is at first as quiet
and sparing of words as he would be had he killed
nothing. He places his gun quietly in a corner, and
lets the others talk. When asked at last, "And what
hast thou killed?" he will produce his three languettes,
lay them on his hand in a row, and show them to the
others, who laud him. The next day he sends his
squaws out to follow the trail of his gun-stock, and
drag home the shaggy carcases.

I heard at this Rivière au Désert for the first time in
my life of a most extraordinary trade the Ojibbeways
carry on. I was told, namely, of their birch-bark
biting, and of pretty figures of every description which
they contrive to bite on the bark with their teeth.

This is an art which the squaws chiefly practise in
spring in their sugar plantations. Still they do not all
understand it, and only a few are really talented. I
was told that a New York gentleman was so pleased
with the productions of this remarkable trade, that he
gave numerous orders for the Eastern City. I learned
that a very celebrated birch-bark biter resided at the
other side of St. Mary's River, in Canada, and that
another of the name of Angélique Marte lived in our
cataract village. Naturally, I set out at once to visit
the latter.

Extraordinary geniuses must usually be sought here,
as in Paris, on the fifth floor, or in some remote fau-
bourg. Our road to Angélique Marte led us past the
little cluster of houses representing our village far out

into the desert. We came to morasses, and had to leap from stone to stone. Between large masses of scattered granite blocks, the remains of the missiles which the Indians say Menaboju and his father hurled at each other in the battle they fought here, we at length found the half-decayed birch-bark hut of our pagan artiste, and also herself living in it like a hermit.

The surrounding landscape seemed better adapted for a renversi than for an atelier. When we preferred our request for some specimen of her tooth-carving, she told us that all her hopes as regarded her art were now concentrated on one tooth. At least, she had only one in her upper jaw properly useful for this operation. She began, however, immediately selecting proper pieces of bark, peeling off the thin skin, and doubling up the piece, which she thrust between her teeth.

As she took up one piece after the other, and went through the operation very rapidly, one artistic production after the other fell from her lips. We unfolded the bark, and found on one the figure of a young girl, on another a bouquet of flowers, on a third a tomahawk, with all its accessories, very correctly designed, as well as several other objects.

The bark is not bitten into holes, but only pressed with the teeth, so that, when the designs are held up, they resemble to some extent those pretty porcelain transparencies made as light-screens.

Our Indian woman told us that this operation was called, in Ojibbeway, " ojibagonsigen." I cannot find this word in any lexicon, but I conjecture that it is correct, and derivable from the verb "nin ojibian," which Bishop Baraga thus interprets in his dictionary, " I make marks on it." It will be seen once again, from this instance, that the Indians have not only their trades absolutely necessary for their livelihood, but their " beaux arts " as well.

I have been told of many ways in which the Indians manage to let their absent friends know at what time any event happened.   One of the simplest modes will be found in the following method, which fishing or hunting-parties frequently employ when compelled to leave their camp at a certain time, and they wish to indicate the exact period to any friends away hunting. For this purpose they make a circle on the ground, in winter on the snow or ice, in summer on the sand. In the middle of the circle they place a stick, and draw on the snow or sand the line on which the sun threw the shadow of the stick at the time of their departure. When the friends come up afterwards, they find the shadow of the stick diverging from that line, and can tell by the difference the lapse of time since their friends started.

This is surely the most natural commencement of the invention of the sun-dial.

Of course, this method can only be employed on the supposition that the friends are expected on the same day, or the weather keeps bright.

An Ojibbeway, of whom I inquired why a white colour was so specially esteemed by the Indians, told me that the cause was as follows:

" When the first man on earth fell sick, and saw death before his eyes, he began to lament and complain to the Great Spirit about the shortness and sufferings of this life. The Great Spirit listened to him, and summoned " all those that are created in heaven" to a grand council. The angels whom the Great Spirit questioned, replied, ' Thou hast created us, and thence wilt best be able to judge how this can be most easily helped.' They consulted for six days, and during all this time there was peace throughout nature: no wind, no rain, no war or bloodshed among the animals. At length, the council came to an end, and God sent messengers down, bearing to the suffering man his Midé-wiwin (Indian magic teaching or revelation). These messengers brought down at the same time a white hare-skin, the feathers of a white-headed eagle, and a medicine-sack of white otter-skin. These contained all the Indian medicines and benefactions of the Great Spirit to mankind. And from this time forth white became a sacred colour among the Indians."

As far as I have myself noticed, or learned from others, the mighty Menaboju, the Indians' favourite demi-god, is never named in their religious ceremonies. This is strange, and almost inexplicable to me, for they ascribe to him the restoration of the world, the arrangement of paradise, and so much else. Nor did I hear that they ever prayed to Menaboju, or sacrificed to him. And yet, all along Lake Superior, you cannot come to any strangely formed rock, or other remarkable production of nature, without immediately hearing some story of Menaboju connected with it. He is also the legislator of the Indians, and the great model or ideal for all their ceremonies, customs, and habits of life. Nearly all their social institutions are referred to him. It was Menaboju who discovered that the maple-tree could produce sugar. He went one day into the forest, made an incision in a maple-tree, found the exuding sap to be sweet, made sugar of it, and since that period the Indians have imitated him. Menaboju taught the

Indians hunting, fishing, and canoe building, and, as we have seen, discovered kinni-kannik, at considerable expense to himself.

The same god seems also to have invented the art of painting the face. I asked an Indian why he and his countrymen painted their faces so strangely, and he replied: "Menaboju did it so. When he was once going to war he took red earth, burnt it to make it still redder, and smeared his face with it that he might terrify the foe. Afterwards, on returning from the wars, he also took some of the yellow foam that covers the water in spring (probably the yellow pollen that falls from the pine), and made pleasant yellow stripes on his face." And that was the reason why the Indians have since painted their faces.

Stories about Indians, male and female, curing diseases, which white doctors could not cure, are very common. Thus, we were told a similar case here. A white boy lay ill of a very severe scurf and hair disease. All the white doctors in vain tried their skill on him. An Indian woman, who accidentally saw the boy, said she would prepare something that would infallibly cure him. She proceeded to the forest, and in a few days returned with a salve, which she rubbed into the boy's head, as well as a powder, afterwards strewn on his hair. Very soon after it was found possible to comb his head, and within three weeks the lad was all right again.

The Indians, as far as I know, are universally accused of being very serious and morose people; and there is also, perhaps, some truth in the charge. But that it is only true under certain circumstances, is proved by the fact that an Indian when travelling, exposed to danger or hard paddling in canoes, grows

much better tempered, which is not the case with
Europeans. I have had occasions to notice this myself several times. And the Canadians have confirmed
my views—"ils ont presque toujours la misère, et
pourtant ils sont presque toujours gais. Ils sont
patients dans tout ce qu'ils font." At dangerous
rapids, where the Europeans quarrel and curse, the
Indians jest. When a canoe is upset in the cataracts,
and the Canadians sigh " Ah, misère!" the Indians
will shout, " Tiwé! Tiwé!" which is about so much
as our " Hurrah, hurrah!"

The Indians practise many Christian virtues naturally, and hence they are quite easy to them when
they are converted. Among these more especially,
the doctrine " Take no thought of the morrow," &c.

A Protestant missionary told me how he noticed
this very closely in a good old Indian woman. She
was a squaw he had himself baptised, and visited occasionally in her lodge on the shore of Lake Superior.
On one visit he found the old woman eating her last
maize porridge. She had just one handful of meal
left for the evening, but seemed quite free from apprehension when she threw it into the pot for him.

"Art thou not alarmed, then, at thy solitude and
empty larder?" the missionary asked, in surprise.

" No," the old woman said. " I always pray well
and easily."

" But art thou not alarmed as to thy morrow's
meal?" he asked further.

"By no means," she replied, simply. "I know
from experience that God always sends me something
at the right moment, even if I do not know precisely
whence it will come."

As the missionary happened to have plenty of provisions, he left her a good allowance, and thus confirmed her in her belief.

An influential and well-informed American gentleman gave me a very lively idea of the peculiar Indian
laziness and sloth, by describing a meeting he once
had with Pawaushek, a chief of the Sauks and Foxes.

He was with the Indian at the entrance of his
village. My narrator was standing upright, but the
Indian sitting on the prairie grass, half-naked, and
with a stick in his hand, which he idly thrust into the
ground.

"Well, Pawaushek, I am now returning to Washington," my friend said, who always liked to give the
Indians some good advice prior to his departure;
"what shall I say there to our Great Father at the
White House, if he asks after thee? Thou dost not
know him personally, but he knows thee; he has thy
name on his list, and has heard of thee as a respected
man among the Indians. What good shall I tell him
of thee when he asks how thou art—how thou livest
—if thou hast much cattle—if thou cultivatest the
ground steadily with thy people—if thou providest
thyself properly with clothing—how thy lodge is
arranged, and how thy fields look? Further, what
sort of grain thou cultivatest—what use thou makest
of the axes, hammers, ploughs, and other things sent
to thee? And what, further, shall I tell him of thy
family—how thou bringest up thy children, and what
they learn? Speak, Pawaushek; what shall I say to
our Great Father in Washington about all this?"

Pawaushek still kept his eyes fixed on the ground,
and dug his stick repeatedly into the grass.

"Come, Pawaushek," my friend continued, " I will

look thy Father so in the face as I now do to thee. I will speak to him with just a straight, unforked tongue, as I am now speaking to thee, and will tell him how I found thee. I will describe thy house to him, and tell him that thou hast no house, but only a wretched, smoky, damp, ragged lodge; that thy clothing is not worth mentioning, and that thou hast scarcely a whole shirt to thy back; that a quantity of weeds, but no corn, grows on thy fields; that thou possessest many useless dogs, but no oxen at all; and that thou makest no use for thy children of the school we established for thee and thine."

Pawaushek went on thrusting his stick in the ground, played the elder Tarquin by decapitating the flowers, but made no reply.

"In Heaven's name, Pawaushek, bestir thyself! Speak, man, and tell me what you fellows mean to do. How will you defend yourselves, when the white settler comes here? At present your prairies are still free from squatters, but these are close at hand. When they come and find that you do nothing, and have not taken possession of any territory, they will take it all as good prey. You can avoid this, and prepare for their reception, by behaving as much like them as possible beforehand. But when they find you all so wretched and half naked, as thou now sittest before me, they will despise you, and you will fare badly. Tell me, Pawaushek, what thou thinkest of all this?"

Pawaushek at length opened his lazy mouth, and rolling himself out to his full length, put an end to the conversation by the simple remark:

"Well! I hope that when the white people, with whom thou threatenest me, come, and find me thus

stretched out on my prairie, they will go round me
and not tread upon me !"

My friend, completely defeated by the imperturba-
bility of the man, left him lying quietly on the prairie.

At times, some of the natives who live scattered
through the forests and mountains of Lake Superior
will come down to the lake, where they cause no
slight excitement, and are gazed at by the Ojibbeways
as something quite out of the common.

Thus, a short time back, one of the so-termed Montagnais, or " gens des hauteurs," came down to the
lake and paid visits to several Ojibbeway villages.
These Montagnais derive their name from the fact that
they wander about in the savage, rocky ranges sepa-
rating the Hudson's Bay waters from the St. Lawrence
system.   A lake Indian, who lodged this visitor from
the north for some time, gave me such a lively description of his savage state, that I clearly saw how incomparably higher he estimated the state of civilisation
existing among his people, the Ojibbeways.

" These Montagnais," he said, " are astoundingly
barbarous. They sleep in the middle of winter on the
naked snow, at the most with un petit brin de sapin as
shelter over it.   They live not much better than the
beasts, and are as timid and shy as they. Il paraît
qu'ils ont peur de tout le monde et de toutes choses:
ça ne parle pas, ça n'aime pas à causer comme les
Sauteurs (Ojibbeways). When you speak to them,
they turn their heads away; and when they speak to
you, you can only understand a couple of words out
of what they say. The rest is lost. C'est terrible
comme ça mange. If one of these hunters brings home
twenty hares, his squaw throws ten of them into the
kettle, and puts the rest on the spit, and they eat

them all up. When they have enough, they will eat
the whole night and day through. On the other hand,
they will march five days and nights without eating a
morsel. They dress in hare-skins, which they fasten
tightly round their bodies, and wear them till they
drop off. When they are utterly worn out and starving,
and do not know how to help themselves, they come
wandering down to us people on the lake, pour mendier
un peu de butin."

My good friend, who gave me this picture of an
Indian, drawn by an Indian, spoke nearly as a European would do of a remote savage people, and seemed
quite to forget that one might say of his own remarks,
" Et de te fabula narratur."

The beaver dams—so persons conversant with the
subject assured me—all have owners among the Indians,
and are handed down from father to son. The sugar
camps, or " sucreries," as the Canadians call them, have
all an owner, and no Indian family would think of
making sugar at a place where it had no right. Even
the cranberry patches, or places in the swamp and
bush where that berry is plucked, are family property ;
and the same with many other things. If this be so,
and has been so, as seems very probable, since time im-
memorial, we can easily imagine how the irruption of
the white men into their country must have been a
tremendous insult and infringement of law in the eyes
of the Indians.

The Ojibbeways have their devil-incantations, and,
judging from what I heard, the ceremonies performed
bear some affinity to those of Caspar and Max in the
wolf's ravine.

The earliest Christian visitors here regarded the
whole Indian system of necromancy, or, if I may so

term it, the religious medicinal system, as bedevilment. But the Indians make a very sharp distinction between the magic formulæ obtained from the good spirits through the Midé rite, and in an honest and traditional manner, and those derived from the evil spirits, or, as they express themselves, through " dreams that are not good."

The evil spirit, Matchi-Manitou, according to their idea, resides at the bottom of the water; and hence their invocations of the devil usually take place on the water. " Dost thou know any instance of this?" I asked an Indian with whom I was recently conversing on this subject. He replied in the affirmative, that a man had once been here who had very bad dreams. But he was long dead, and had plunged himself and his family into misery and the grave by his evil dreams. When I inquired more closely how this all happened, my bonhomme told me the following story:

The man of whom he was speaking had once dreamed ten nights in succession that a voice spoke to him, saying that if he wished to have something very fine, which would make him happy, he must one night strike the water with a stick and sing a certain verse to it.

He told this dream to his friends, who, however, dissuaded him, and said, " Do not go, my friend—do not accept it."

On the eleventh night, when he dreamt the same thing again, he awoke his squaw, and said to her: " Dost thou not hear in the distance the drums clashing on the water? I must go there." The squaw assured him, on the contrary, that she heard nothing;

all was as quiet as mice. But he insisted that the drum could be heard quite plainly from the water, and he felt an irresistible call.

With these words he sprang up and hurried out. His wife went after him, because she was afraid that her husband might be somewhat distraught. She saw him cower down by the edge of the water, and prepare for an incantation. He drew his magic staff and struck the water, just as the Midés employ the drumstick in their ceremonies. At the same time he sang magic songs, first in a muttering voice, and then aloud.

The water began gradually moving beneath the influence of his drumming, and at last a small whirlpool was formed. He struck more rapidly, and his song grew quicker. The whirlpool became larger and more violent. The fish were at length drawn into it, and soon after them the other water animals. Frogs, toads, lizards, fish of every description, swamp and aquatic birds, with enormous swarms of swimming and flying insects, were drawn into the whirlpool, and passed snapping and quivering before the eyes of the enchanter, so that he nearly lost his senses.

At the same time the water rose till it wetted his feet and knees. At length he stood in the middle of the commotion he had created, like Goethe's apprentice to the magician. He felt a degree of horror creeping over him, but he held his ground manfully. He went on striking the angry waves, and sang his gloomy incantations, till the water rose to his chin and seemed ready to swallow him up.

But, as he would not give way yet, and more and more insisted that the king of the fishes should appear, the latter found himself at length compelled to yield. The waters calmed down, the whirlpool and animals disappeared, the enchanter stood once more on the beach, and the water-king emerged from the placid lake, in the form of a mighty serpent. "What wilt thou of me?" he said. "Give me the recipe," he replied, "which will make me healthy, rich, and prosperous." "Dost thou see," the snake said, "what I wear on my head, between my horns? Take it: it will serve thee. But one of thy children must be mine in return for it."

The Indian saw between the horns of the water-king something red, like a fiery flower. He stretched out his trembling hand and seized it. It melted away in his finger into a powder, like the vermilion with which the Indians paint their faces. He collected it in a piece of birch bark, and the serpent then gave him further instructions.

In accordance with these, he was to prepare a row of small flat pieces of wood, twenty or more, and lay them in a semicircle around him on the beach. On each board he must shake a pinch of the red powder, and then the water-king counted all the diseases and ills to which Indian humanity is exposed, and also all the wishes, desires, and passions, by which it is usually animated, and each time that the enchanter shook some powder on one of the boards, the wicked water-spirit consecrated the powder, and named the illness which it would avert, or the good fortune it would bring.

"Every time that thou mayst need me," he then added, "come hither again. I shall always be here. Thou wilt have, so long as thou art in union with me, so much power as I have myself. But forget not

that, each time thou comest, one of thy children becomes mine!"

With these words the water-king disappeared in
the depths. His adept, however, made up each powder in a separate parcel and went home, where he
found his squaw, who had watched all his doings
with horror, already dead. Like her, the children
were killed one after the other by the water-spirit.
The wicked husband and father, who gave way to
such bad dreams, was, for a long time, rich, powerful,
and respected, a successful hunter, a much-feared
warrior, and a terrible magician and prophet, until
at length a melancholy fate befel him, and he ended
his days in a very wretched manner.

I had already heard on the Mississippi that the
Indians have as great affection for their home and
scenery as we have, and was told that many Indians,
exiled from that river, would return to its banks, and
take another longing, lingering glance at it.

At Rivière au Désert I was also assured that the
Indians living round Lake Superior are as attached
to their Kitchi-Gami as the French Swiss to their
Lake of Geneva. Mr Schoolcraft, in his large work
on the Indians, tells an affecting story in confirmation
of this. Some time back a young girl had carried her
dying father from the interior for many miles through
the forest, because the old man wished to see the lake
once more ere he died.

When the report was spread some years back
among the Indians that the United States government
had decided on removing all the subjugated Indians
from the lake, and settling them in the interior, a
great excitement arose among the people, and they

determined on emigrating to the Canadian shore, on the northern side of the lake, and becoming British subjects. They packed up their traps, and prepared their families, in all seriousness, for this emigration, so that they might not be deprived of their lake. The report was fortunately unfounded, and they remained where they were.

ABOARD THE STEAMER "NORTH STAR."

We were unfortunately compelled to make up our minds to leave our little Garden River, although my good missionary had not yet completed his church, nor I my Indian studies. But there are through life all sorts of pressure and untoward circumstances which check the very best designs in the midst of their course. Many important affairs were awaiting my friend at "Sault," and the steamer *North Star* myself, which was to carry me away from this Indian dream and fairy land, and the lake which had become so interesting to me. Hence we got into our canoe, took leave of our kind Canadians, Indians, and half-breeds, and paddled up the river.

It is extraordinary how much one sees and discovers when gliding in a canoe, like a duck, through the forests. The same country which appears to a man who hurries through like an eagle on board a steamer, desolate or possessing no interest, shows itself to the canoe traveller full of all sorts of remarkable phenomena, and rich in pleasant and interesting revelations and experiences in natural and human life. I could write a chapter about all the little things characteristic of land and people, which occurred to us as we paddled along this misty day over the broad waters of St. Mary's River, landed here and there, and visited the scattered forest settlers, who had built their solitary cabins on the river bank.

It was to me, in some measure, a recapitulation of all I had seen on Lake Superior. Once we put in to "allumer" at a Frenchman's,* and amused ourselves for a quarter of an hour with his cleanly household and his sonorous French conversation. Another time we came to a jolly Irishman, who had cleared a small potato patch in the forest, and lived there alone with his spade and his axe, without family, friends, or neighbours, defying fate and the blue devils, and had nothing living to console him save a cat, which followed him everywhere. On a third occasion we "took a handful of fire" at the hut of a half-breed, the bonhomme La Battu. This gentleman was an industrious bark-canoe builder. He had a number of them always on the stocks, and carried on a lively trade with the foresters, who nearly always prefer a canoe to using their feet, for in this watery, swampy, inaccessible land the latter can scarce be used to pay a neighbour a visit, much less to travel. He was married to an Indian woman of the "Crees" tribe, a most respectable-looking housewife, who told us many curious things about her northern home and people. Unfortunately, though, we could stay nowhere long enough to examine the peculiar circumstances under which men live here. For, after a short stay, the shout would be heard, "Au large! au large!" and we were forced to hurry on to reach our night's resting-place betimes. This occurred when darkness already brooded over the face of the waters, and the roar of the cataracts convinced us that we had really arrived

* The word "allumer" in the Canadian language means, "to call at a person's house while travelling."

at the "Villa ad Cataractas Sanctæ Mariæ,"—or, as
this village at the efflux of Lake Superior is usually
called, at Sault.

It was only, however, an arrival to depart again;
for the steamer which was to bear me away, and on
board which I date my last salutation to Lake Superior, started the next morning. I bade adieu to many
worthy men—perhaps for ever—and my departure
rent the thread of many studies I had arranged, as it
did of my newly-formed friendships. I left behind me
fairy tales for a New Arabian Nights' Entertainment,
and I had hardly succeeded in securing two or three
of them. Rapidly disappearing nations remained behind me, whom I shall never see again, and who yet
appeared to me so deserving of a thorough study,
when I had myself scarce laid my fingers' ends on
them. Hundreds of questions crossed my brain,
which—had not the last grain of sand fallen in my
hour-glass—I should have wished to propose to the
willing echo of the lake, and reap copious replies. I
felt like the poet when he described Hiawatha's departure :

> And I said : Farewell for ever !
> Said : Farewell, O Hiawatha !
> And the forests dark and lonely,
> Moved through all their depths of darkness,
> Sighed : Farewell, O Hiawatha !

THE END.

APPENDIXES

APPENDIX I

TALES FROM THE OJIBWAY

Menaboju and the Deluge[1]

"Poetry is gold; a litle bit of pleasing
Metal, shaped with skill, will stretch
to gild our worlds."

RÜCKERT

As in other parts of the world, there is probably no people
in North America that does not have stories to explain the various upheavals in the history of creation. They tell of repeated
destructions of the world through fire and water and describe
a rebirth of the earth out of the wet element.

Although the Ojibways tell the history of these upheavals

The stories in this appendix were translated by Ralf Neufang and
Ulrike Böcker. The text has thus endured several translations: Kohl's
informants spoke in Ojibway, his translator related the stories to
Kohl in French, Kohl wrote them in German, and they are here
presented in English. These translations follow Kohl's words as
closely as possible, although the translators have modernized some
spellings and usages chosen by Lascelles Wraxall, the translator of
the 1860 edition. Unless otherwise noted, the footnotes printed here
are Kohl's. For discussions of the structure of the German edition
and the alterations in the English edition, see pages xxxvi–xxxvii and
xl–xlii.

1. This story and the three that follow appear in the second book of the

and rebirths with many variations, their Menaboju[2] always plays the main part. And although Menaboju is not the original creator of the universe, in most stories he is the creator of the earth as it is now – of the river beds, of the shapes of the lakes, and of rugged mountains as we find them today.

Occasionally during my stay at L'Anse I visited the mother of the half-breed La Fleur in the evening in her tent. She narrated for me the history of the deluge and of Menaboju's second creation of the world. I will try to repeat her stories exactly, in details and in manner.

"All animals," the old woman began, "were relatives and kinsmen of Menaboju. He could speak with them and he lived together with them in great friendship. Once Menaboju had his hunting camp in the middle of the forest, far away from the whole world. Times were bad for him. The hunt was unprofitable. He had to fast, and he was starving.

"In bare distress he went forth to the wolves and talked with them. 'My dear little brothers, would you give me something to eat?' The wolves said 'Yes!' and they fed him.

"Since he liked their food he continued, 'Would you allow me to go hunting with you?' They gave him their permission, and thus Menaboju went hunting with the wolves, and he shared their camp and their meals.

"In this manner they managed well for ten days. Then, one day, they came to a crossroads. The wolves wanted to go on a side road, but Menaboju wished to follow the wide path. They argued about their different opinions and, since both parties stubbornly persisted in their views, they finally de-

German edition of *Kitchi-Gami* as letters six through nine, dated "At L'Anse, September 1855." Had Wraxall chosen to include them in his translation, they would appear between chapters 15 and 16 of this volume. – *Trans.*

2. This mythical person is also mentioned among other Indian tribes. He has different names, but usually the same stories and deeds are ascribed to him. Among the Iroquois and their kin he is called Hiawatha.

cided to go separate ways. Menaboju asked, however, that at least the youngest wolf go with him. He loved this young wolf very much and even used to call him his little brother. The little wolf, too, did not want to part with Menaboju. Hence the two continued on their way together while the other wolves followed the side road.

"Menaboju and his beloved pet built their camp in the middle of the forest, and they hunted together. Once in a while the little wolf went hunting all by himself.

"Menaboju cared very much for this wolf and he said to him, 'My dear little brother, did you see the lake just west of our camp? Do not ever go there! And never go on the ice. Do you hear me?' Menaboju said this very forcefully, since he knew that in that lake lived the Snake King, his worst enemy, who would do anything to irritate and distress him.

"The little wolf promised indeed to do as Menaboju had told him and not to do what Menaboju had forbidden, but he thought to himself, 'Why does Menaboju forbid me to go on the ice? Perhaps he believes that I would meet my brothers the wolves there. But I truly love my brothers.'

"And he said that to himself the first evening, and he said that to himself the following evening. And on the third morning he still thought the same. He finally went to the lake and ran about on the ice looking for his brothers. But when he came to the middle of the lake the ice broke. He sank into the water and drowned.

"Menaboju waited the whole evening for his little brother. He did not come. He also waited the following day, but in vain, for the wolf did not come. And so he waited for five days and five nights. Then he started moaning and mourning, and he cried for his little brother so loud one could hear it at the other end of the forest.

"For the rest of the sad winter Menaboju lived in loneliness and sorrow. But he knew well who had killed his brother. It was the Snake King. During the winter Menaboju could not get at him. But then spring finally arrived. On a beautiful warm day Menaboju went out to the lake where his little brother had been killed. All winter he had not been able to make up his mind to visit this site of horror and grief. At one place in the sand that had not been covered by the snow, he could still find his little brother's footprints. And when he saw them he burst into mourning so loud one could hear it far and near.

"Even the Snake King could hear it, and since he was curious to find out where the noise came from, he rose to the surface and stuck his horned head out of the water. 'Ah, there you are,' Menaboju said to himself, drying his tears with his sleeve. 'Now you will suffer for your misdeed.' Quickly he changed himself into a tree trunk, and in this disguise he planted himself at the shore of the lake.

"The Snake King and all the other snakes who appeared behind him were curious to find out who had started the lament. But they could not find anything wrong with the tree trunk, although they had not seen it at their lake before. 'Stop,' one of the snakes said, 'be on your guard. There is more to it than meets the eye. Perhaps it is even our enemy, the cunning Menaboju.' The Snake King immediately ordered one of his snake followers to go to the tree trunk and examine it. And this gigantic snake wound his body, twenty ells[3] long, around the trunk, pressing and squeezing it in order to see whether it was just wood or perhaps a living being.

"The bones in Menaboju's body cracked, but he stood still and did not utter a sound. So the snakes calmed down and said, 'No, it is not him! We can go to sleep without fear. This is nothing but wood.' And since it was a hot day they lay down on the sand of the beach and fell asleep.

3. The length of the German *ell* varied regionally between 55 and 80 centimeters. – *Trans.*

"No sooner had the last snake closed his eyes than Mena-boju slipped out of his tree trunk. He grabbed his bow and arrow and shot down the Snake King. He also riddled three of the King's sons with his arrows. Then the other snakes woke up and, slithering into the water, they screamed, 'Alas! Alas! Menaboju is among us, Menaboju will kill us!'

"They made a dreadful noise about the whole lake and whipped the water with their long tails. Those among them who were the most apt shamans got out their medicine bags, untied them, and sprinkled the whole contents, all their charms, over the beach and all over the forest and into the air.

"Thereupon the water began to rise and to circle in muddy swirls. The sky was covered with clouds that dropped torren-tial rains. The entire neighborhood was flooded, then half of the earth, and in the end the whole wide world was covered with water. Poor Menaboju, frightened to death, had long since escaped. He jumped from one hill to the next, not know-ing where to turn because the rising waters followed him everywhere. Finally he discovered a very high mountain where he could rescue himself. But even this mountain was soon flooded. So Menaboju climbed on a fir tree that stood one hundred ells tall on the highest peak of this mountain. He climbed to the very top of that tree while the water was still rising beneath him. And then the water reached up to his belt, and then over his shoulders, and then to his mouth. Suddenly it stopped rising, either because the snakes had exhausted their charms, or because they thought they had used enough of them, believing that Menaboju could not possibly have escaped.

"Menaboju, notwithstanding his uncomfortable position, held out in his tree for five days and nights, vainly racking his brain for a way to help himself. Finally, on the sixth day, he saw a solitary bird — it was a loon — swimming in the water. He called him to come over and said to him, 'Brother Loon, you are a skilled diver! Please do me a favor and dive down to the bottom and see whether you can still find the earth, without which I cannot live, or whether it is completely drowned.' The loon did as he was told and dived down several times, but he could not get down deep enough. Time and again he came up without having accomplished anything, reporting the dismal message that the earth could not be found.

"Menaboju almost gave up hope. But on the following day he saw the stiff corpse of a small muskrat floating toward him in the waves. He caught him, took him in his hands, and put life back into him by blowing his warm breath on him. Then he said to him, 'Little brother Rat, neither of us can live without the earth. Dive down into the water and bring me some soil if thou canst. Even if it is only a little bit, even if you only bring three grains of sand, I will be able to make something out of it for you and me.'

"The obliging little animal dived down immediately and came back to the surface after a long time. But he was dead and floated on the water. Menaboju caught the little body and examined its paws. In one of the little front paws he discovered a few grains of sand or dust particles. He took them out of the paw, put them on his palm, and dried them in the sun. Then he blew them away across the water, and wherever they fell they floated on the surface. They grew and expanded, either due to the earth's own natural power, or because it had received this power through Menaboju's magic breath.

"First of all small islands were formed, then they expanded quickly and grew together to form larger ones. Finally Menaboju was able to jump down from his uncomfortable seat in the tree onto one of these islands. He navigated it like a raft, helping the other islands to get closer and to grow together, so that in the end they became big islands and continents.

"Diligently and actively he marched back and forth, arranging everything and setting up nature in its former beauty.

Now and then he found small root systems and little plants that had been washed up onto the beach. He put them into the ground, and thus grassland, shrubbery, and forests appeared again. Also many stiff animal corpses were washed onto the beach. Menaboju carefully picked up all of them and blew life into them. Then he said to them, 'Leave for your places at once.'

"And so each animal went to its place. The birds built nests in the trees. The fishes and beavers chose for themselves small lakes in the forests and rivers, and the bears and the other four-footed animals roamed about the land.

"Menaboju had his long measuring string in his hand, and he walked all over the earth measuring everything. He decided on the length of the rivers, on the depth of the lakes, on the height of the mountains, and on the shape of the lands so that everything would be in good proportion."[4]

At this point the old woman suddenly ended her story, but she added, "This earth that had been created by Menaboju in this manner was the first land in this world inhabited by Indians. The earlier one that was drowned in the waters had only been occupied by Menaboju and the wolves, and by the Snake King and his monsters."

I asked her, "Does this mean that your story of Menaboju's creation of the world comes to an end at this point? And what happened to the snakes? Did they later give up their war against Menaboju?"

Here La Fleur interrupted, "Did the story come to an end?! For heaven's sake, no! The sagas of our storytellers do not end

4. "Il a roulé sur la terre, et il a fait la mesure des fleuves, des lacs, des mers et des montaignes." These were literally the words of the old woman as translated by La Fleur. I thought it rather peculiar that the savages give the creator of the universe a measuring tape, which means that they have observed the wonderfully harmonic proportions of the sizes and dimensions of all creatures and natural objects.

that quickly. Even if you stayed with us for the whole winter my mother could continue telling stories every night for three months."

I answered that in any case I would be in the neighborhood for another few days and would like to come back the following evening. And if La Fleur's mother was inclined to go on we could take up again the thread of the story. We agreed to do that, and I said good-bye and left.

Menaboju and His Friend the Marmot

"Talk and pictures just continue
Where they yesterday had stopped."

The story about Menaboju that I recounted in the previous letter is to a certain degree complete in itself. When the old woman picked up again the thread of the tale during my later visits, she told only fragments—in a way they were fairy-tale arabesques, without beginning or end. But they were nevertheless unusual enough to be worth hearing and retelling.

The Indian Menaboju is not only the father or re-creator of our earth. Unlike the creators in other myths, who retreat to heaven after they have finished their work, Menaboju stays on the earth, living as an Indian among Indians and having all sorts of adventures. The Ojibways weave into their stories of Menaboju all the incidents, conditions, and phases of their own lives, although in a very fantastic and grotesque way. One can recognize the suffering, the miseries, and the troubles that an Indian hunter had to endure year after year on his path through life in the suffering, the miseries, and the troubles Menaboju has to overcome. Menaboju's courage, as displayed in the cunning and tricks that helped him win, is a true copy of the courage and the cunning of which Indians are capable.

The charms successfully used by Menaboju are the charms the Indians believe in, and the monsters and bad spirits who threaten and oppress the mythical hero are the same that the superstitious Indians believe to be their enemies in the forest, in the water, and in mountain hiding-places.

The person who undertook to collect all Menaboju stories and attempted to bring them together in a book could easily give it the title "Les Indiens peints par eux mêmes." To avoid repetition, however, he would have to choose the stories very carefully, because the same sagas and incidents reappear with various ornaments and in different disguises. Indians are familiar with this method and do not easily tire of the same old meal served repeatedly with only a different dressing. But Europeans might be satiated much earlier.

For a while, however, I want to walk along on the chosen path, less because of the value of the stories themselves than because of the way in which they are recited. If the reader sees how the Indians continue their stories and how they use a theme introduced earlier and elaborate on it, then he can imagine how these stories can be continued endlessly.

"You told me yesterday how Menaboju made this new world for himself after the wicked snakes had destroyed and drowned his old creation. But tell me, where were the snakes in the meantime? Did they stop bothering Menaboju in his new world? Were they dead or had they disappeared?" This was how I began asking questions the next day when, cheerfully smoking my pipe, I had resumed my seat on the mat beside La Fleur's mother.

When I arrived she was engaged in an occupation that harmonizes very well with storytelling. She was twisting ropes from the fiber of the so-called bois blanc. She had a great many thin twigs of this tree lying in a water container in front of her. One by one she pulled them out of the water, carefully split them lengthwise, and cautiously cut out the tough fiber. Then she wound such ropes as the Indians use – as we use our hempen ropes – for various tasks in their households. They use them for their nets, for their boats, for their sacks and baskets, for tying up their bundles of merchandise, and in their construction of houses. This is a noiseless task that can be combined with storytelling almost better than work on our spinning wheel.

"The snakes were by no means dead nor had they disappeared," the old woman began. "They still lay in ambush in their hiding places at the bottom of the lake. Evil does not disappear totally from this world. But fortunately they deceived themselves in their expectation that Menaboju had drowned or that he was dead or had vanished; for good also exists forever and is created new out of every destruction.

"When the snakes, however, noticed the newly created islands, the beautiful forests, rivers and prairies, and rocks and mountains, they began to doubt their assumed success in destroying Menaboju. And so they talked among themselves: 'Could this insufferable creature still live, after all? Could these pretty continents possibly be his work again? Perhaps he is wandering around on them, hunting as he did in the old days. Much to our chagrin, Menaboju may be enjoying life while many of our own people are still laid up with the wounds that his wicked arrows inflicted on them. These people still wait in vain to be healed and they do not have the consolation of knowing they have been avenged.'

The old woman explained at this point, "The arrows that Menaboju used to wound and kill the snakes were by no means common arrows. They were magic arrows, and wounds inflicted by them do not heal very quickly." And here I would like to remark that with Indians we get closest to the truth when we understand that all elements of nature are magic products or are endowed with marvelous properties. Copper and iron are not prosaic copper and iron, but are something quite mystical. A yellow buttercup is not a yellow buttercup, but, if not a bewitched princess, at least an otherwise spiritual being. One cannot catch fish or kill enemies with a simple hempen net or with iron arrows. Even the best iron and the best hempen net give almost no help unless they are assisted by a strong belief and some charm.

"You must keep this in mind always," the old woman continued, "or you will not understand anything of our tales. At first the snakes did not know how to find out whether their sworn enemy was still alive.

"They held a big council to discuss the question, and even the chiefs and kings of the turtles were asked to participate. That is because the turtles are in league with the snakes, and they are considered extremely cunning. After a long discussion the turtles finally advised the snakes to make ropes out of 'bois blanc,' as I am doing here, and to spread them crosswise like a net over the whole earth. One of the turtles would then tie the ends of the ropes of this net to one of his legs. Since the fidgety Menaboju, if he really were still alive, was unable to rest, he was bound to bump into one of the ropes when he went hunting. The turtle on guard would immediately feel this tug with his leg and would promptly run to the snakes and deliver the news.

"The snakes liked this advice very much. Therefore, they and the turtles set out to twist as many pieces of bast from 'bois blanc' as were necessary to cover the whole world with a net. They gave a feast for the turtles with songs and magic, and during the festivities the ropes were spun as thin as spiderwebs, so that Menaboju would not become suspicious."

At this point of her story the old woman elaborated on the subject of making rope from "bois blanc" and on how the turtles and snakes went about it. She explained how they chose the wood, how they soaked it in water, how they cut it, and how diligently they twisted the ropes. She also recited the

magic songs that they sang while working. But for the benefit
of my readers I will pass over these details, and only say that
when the net was almost finished, it was spread over the whole
world.[5] In order to complete it, however, they needed a little
more "bois blanc." So one of the snakes, in the guise of an old
woman, went out to search for it in the forest.

"Menaboju happened to be out hunting when he met the old
woman, who was moaning and crying noisily as she looked for
the 'bois blanc.' He approached her and asked: 'Why do you
cry?' When Menaboju asked her sympathetically for the reason of her wailing the old woman answered: 'Oh, my sons are
laid up with severe wounds. They are dying. Do you perhaps
know a remedy? Maybe you would take the trouble to go to
my cottage and try to cure them!'

"Menaboju: 'Who was it then that put them into this pitiful
condition?'

"The old woman: 'Oh, it is their archenemy Menaboju who
is tormenting them! My sons mistakenly killed a little wolf
who was very dear to Menaboju. And he started such an uproar and dispute over this that the world almost perished.'

"Menaboju: 'Aha? Ahem? Menaboju? Really Menaboju? It
was he? Just fancy that! – Now then. That Menaboju, he certainly is the greatest archrogue in the whole wide world.'

"Old woman: 'Yes, my good friend, there you might be
right! But that wicked person! This time he shall not escape
us. We have taken excellent precautions and surrounded the
whole earth with a magic net. Perhaps he will get caught in
it. Or, if that does not happen, we will at least know where
he is whenever he is snared in it with one foot. The turtles
who tie the ends of the net to their legs will feel precisely
where he is every time. We need only a few more loads of
"bois blanc" to finish our net, and I came out to search for it.'

5. One is almost led to believe that when creating this tale the Indians had
knowledge of the telegraph network that we have now spread across the globe.

"Menaboju: 'Why, bravo! Splendid! – And when you finally catch him, what will you do with him?'

"The old woman: 'Well, you see, Menaboju, who does not know what is good, does not like water, which is best of all the elements. We have an abundance of it and we tried before to destroy him with it. But we were careless, and he survived. This time, when we catch him again, we are going to let the waters rise up to the sun. We will set him under water in such a way that no loon and no rat will be able to help him out of the predicament.'

"Menaboju: 'That is befitting. Give it to him soundly. But let us come back to your poor sons; where are they wounded?'

"Old woman: 'Oh God, it is a miserable sight. The oldest of them, here in the neck. The second oldest, here in the side. And the third and youngest has an arrow stuck in his knee joint.'

"Menaboju: 'Well, well. But then, how do you treat the wounds?'

"Old woman: 'I beat the drum and in addition I sing a magic song.'

"Menaboju: 'That is quite appropriate! But what is the name of the song? Let us once sing it together.'

"Until this moment the snake still had not recognized Menaboju, since his medicine was stronger than hers.[6] He blinded her so that she could not see him. She took him for a common human being. But when she began her magic song, and Menaboju was at once able to join in aptly and skillfully, a misgiving befell her and she became suspicious. And struck by that sudden fear she exclaimed: 'Alas! Are you Menaboju, by chance?'

" 'Yes, that is exactly right!' he answered, 'I am Menaboju!'

6. "His medicine is stronger (Sa medicine est plus fort)." That is what the Indians say of a shaman and also of a hero whose charms, strength, and talents are more significant than those of others, and who is able to dupe others.

He took his knife, killed the old woman, and skinned her immediately. He dried her skin over a fire, put it on, and applied her old wrinkles to his forehead and cheeks. He also clapped her unkempt scalp or her wig on his head, bent his back as she had, started to cough and gasp like her, cried and moaned as she had over her wounded sons, and scolded violently about that 'bewitched Menaboju.' And in this disguise he went to the house of the snakes.

"When the three injured sons heard the old woman approach, coughing slightly and moaning, they started shouting from a distance: 'Alas, there comes our old, good, crying mother!'

"Menaboju: 'Yes, here I am, my little darlings. Well, how are you? Do you feel a little better?'

"The sons: 'No, certainly not, we still feel rather sick. But hast thou found the missing "bois blanc" so we can finally catch that scoundrel, Menaboju?'

"Menaboju: 'Calm down, my darlings! I brought it and I have already delivered it to the turtles who now are busily completing their work. But now come close to me, my children, I have brought more fresh herbs to treat your wounds.'

"The children: 'You are certainly quite hungry, good mother. Do you not want to eat something first? There is still a paw of that detestable little wolf of Menaboju. We did not eat it all up and we left you something good.'

"Upon this offer and at the sight of the tender paw of his darling, Menaboju became quite furious and could hardly hold himself in. He ground his teeth and murmured: 'No, my children, first I have to attend to your wounds.'

"Children: 'As you will, mother.'

"These were the last words the snake princes said, because Menaboju could not restrain himself any longer. He attacked them. And since he knew from the former conversation with the old woman where the arrows stuck, he quickly grabbed them and, instead of pulling them out, drove them completely into their bodies and into their hearts and killed them.

"Then there was a sudden uproar throughout the snakes' camp, and everybody knew now who had come to them as mother of the snakes. While taking his leave, Menaboju tore off the skin of the old woman, threw it at his enemies, and exclaimed: 'So will I treat all of you.' Having said this he made off.[7]

"In the camp of the turtles and snakes, however, began a general mourning and howling. 'Alas! Alas!' they cried, 'Menaboju, that arrant knave, has killed the mother and also the three royal princes of the snakes!' And in their mourning they were joined by all the water animals, by the frogs and the bullfrogs, by the toads, by the otters and peccans (fishers),[8] and by whoever else lives in the water, and who can make more noise than the fish.

" 'Menaboju,' said the people who heard what had happened and who met him on his retreat, 'this will bring you dreadful consequences! Hurry to safety and provide for the coming winter, because dire need will fall upon you.'

"Everyone who saw Menaboju repeated this advice, and since they all fled, and nobody stayed to help him, he finally started worrying himself. He retreated to a small hill close to his wigwam and started practicing his magic arts. He beat his drum, shook his calabash, and for hours on end he mumbled his charms to himself. But still he could not regain his inner peace. And nobody came by to ask him against whom he was preparing to fight and to offer him assistance, as is usually done when an Indian warrior sings his songs of war and vengeance and thinks of aiming a blow at someone.

7. Disguises, sneaking up on enemy camps, and similar undercover surprise attacks to subdue enemies are often part of Indian war stories.

8. The English call this animal, which is very similar to the otter, "the fisher."

"Frightened by the vengeful grief of the water animals, all his friends seemed to avoid Menaboju, and he remained alone for a long time. At last, however, and only very late one night, a little friend joined him. It was 'Siffleur,' the Canadian marmot. This little animal, although usually daring, like Menaboju does not enjoy water, and he always builds his den where it is dry, on high ground; and, by laying the entrance downhill and the living area uphill, he arranges it to be dry no matter how much it might rain.

" 'Do you fear water, Menaboju?' the little marmot began. 'Would you like me to build you a dry den?'

" 'Yes, please, my best friend, do that rather quickly! The very thought of how I froze and suffered in the water when the snakes drove me up to the highest top of the tallest tree of the whole world with their blasted flood, and I was nevertheless drenched, still gives me goose flesh. Get to work, my friend, scratch, and scrape, and dig, and hurry. I will go hunting quickly and get food for the two of us.'

"Hereupon the little marmot started working on the den, and Menaboju went hunting. He shot ten bears, twenty caribou, thirty deer, fifty roe deer,[9] and many other animals. He dried all the meat in the sun and over a fire, thus preparing it for fall and winter reserve.

"Once in a while, when he came home from his hunt, loaded with game, and saw the little marmot diligently digging away, he jumped into the hole and tried it to see whether it was big enough. 'Quick! my friend, quick!' he shouted to him, 'the hole has to get wider yet.'

And then some big raindrops started to fall, and Menaboju shook them off, remembering the first deluge when water had plagued him so. But fortunately the marmot had just finished his work. Menaboju tried the entrance and all rooms of the

9. A small Asiatic and European deer that does not exist in North America. — *Trans.*

underground lodgings one last time, and he found everything large enough for both of them and comfortable. Quickly they stored their provisions and then hid behind their boxes and cases. There they enjoyed their meal and slept through the whole night on the furs with which they had covered their chambers. It was very cozy, despite the rain that poured out of the sky.

"All the rain ran down the slopes of the mountain where they had built their den, and it did not do any damage. No drop of water reached them through the downhill passage. Menaboju defied the impotent floods, and both of them passed the time as well as they could. The marmot turned funny somersaults and danced and Menaboju sang and made music to accompany him.

"This irritated the angry water animals, and since they feared that the rain would help them this time as little as it had the first time, they stopped it rather soon. But then they brought on a hard winter and made so much hail and so many blizzards that soon all the trails and passages were covered with snow. The snow lay on top of the mountain and on the slopes and in front of the hole, and so they finally thought they could totally cover Menaboju, suffocate him, starve and bury him, and even save themselves the cost of burial.

"This was a winter as had never been seen before. The snow in the forests and on the prairies lay as high as a house, and rivers and streams froze up so much that it was difficult to find drinking water.

"But every time fresh snow fell, the little marmot reopened the entrance and all the breathing holes, so they had fresh air all the time, and sometimes they could even go outside. Often poor people came to them with empty stomachs and limbs chilled through, complaining bitterly of the outrageously hard winter, of the want of game, of the paths that were covered with snow, and of the countless animals and human beings who perished from want. Menaboju and the marmot received everyone hospitably and shared with them what they had. They rubbed the frozen limbs of these people with snow and cured them. They kept a fire burning in their den so that they would always have something warm for themselves and others to eat.

"So far so good! Late one evening in the depth of the winter, when the two occupants of the den had just finished enjoying a good deer soup, someone knocked at their door.

" 'Stop,' said Menaboju to the marmot, 'what is this? That is no good visitor, my friend. We will have to be on our guard. I know this is Peccan. And undoubtedly he is on the side of the water animals. Quickly, put the bones and the rest of our evening meal away. And do not show that we just ate well.'

"And so it was. The water animals had been curious and wanted to know how Menaboju was coping with the hard winter and the snow. Therefore, they had sent out their friend 'Peccan,' the fisher, to find out what condition Menaboju was in, and whether he was close to his end.

"Menaboju let the fisher in, cordially shook his hand, and then, with a sorrowful expression, started a heartbreaking complaint of the hard times, of the famine, of the harshness of the winter, and of all the suffering caused by it. 'This,' he said and produced a gnawed bone, 'this is our last bone, and we have been gnawing at it for three weeks already.'

" 'Yes,' the little marmot confirmed, 'it may even have been four weeks by now.' 'Oh,' Menaboju said, 'you should see us in daylight, dear Peccan, and you would know how thin we are. Nothing but skin and bones! Whenever I try to walk both my knees tremble!' 'Yes,' the little marmot agreed, 'and for me it is even worse – my four knees tremble.' They went on to say, 'Dear Peccan, surely you brought something for us to eat? For we cannot offer you anything but a cold bed on harsh ice and snow, of which our home is full.'

"The fisher apologized and said that unfortunately he, too, had no food with him. And, laughing up his sleeve, he made off as quickly as possible to deliver the good news to the camp of the turtles and snakes. 'Let it freeze and snow heavily for a few more months, and he will certainly die.'

"Thereupon thunderstorms began, and it started hailing and snowing again, so heavily that soon even the tops of the highest fir trees did not reach out of the snow.

" 'Quick, my friend, quick!' Menaboju shouted to his little marmot, and the marmot scraped, scratched, and shovelled so quickly with his paws that it was pure fun to watch him. As fast as the snow fell, he cleared it away, and he kept all the breathing holes open. And thus they stayed lively and healthy and nourished themselves. It was, however, somewhat uncomfortable for them to walk for almost a mile through snow tunnels whenever they wanted to go outside.

"Finally, shortly before spring came, and at a time when need among Indians is usually greatest, the snakes and turtles sent their fisher again to find out whether Menaboju was dead. The latter and his marmot noticed him from afar, and so they lay down on their beds pretending they were sick and almost dead, and they put their moccasins close to the fire.

" 'Hey, Menaboju! Do you still fast or are you already dead?' the fisher shouted into the den. 'Oh yes, good Peccan,' Menaboju answered with a most pitiful and weak voice, 'yes, I am almost dead and I am still fasting.' 'Yes, we are still fasting,' the little marmot whispered with an even thinner voice.

" 'Come in, good Peccan!' Menaboju continued, 'and see for yourself. I have already put my two moccasins close to the fire. We will have to fry them now to keep us alive.' 'Yes,' the little marmot added, 'my four little moccasins are also lying in the ashes like sweet chestnuts, representing my last hope.'

" 'You poor people,' the fisher said, with a shrug. 'How unfortunate that I am unable to help you.' And he hurried

back to give the turtles and snakes the good news that Menaboju and the marmot were on their last legs and that they
would starve to death after they had eaten their moccasins. 'It
is all over with them,' he said. 'The snow did good service.
There is no more need for snow, and spring can come in fourteen days. Spring will make the flowers bloom on Menaboju's
grave.'

"At that the turtles and snakes started a general joyful dance
in celebration, and when spring came all the frogs and bullfrogs, the toads, and the otters and fishers shouted and
whistled louder and more joyfully than ever before.

"But how surprised they were, and how shocked, when on
a lovely spring evening they suddenly heard Menaboju's drum
join in their songs, and they saw him sitting with his little
marmot on the flowery top of their hill, both rather round and
fat and lively after the long winter that fortunately was now
behind them! – 'That Menaboju!' they cried. 'He is invincible!
He is immortal!' And they gave up their war against him. At
least for that year."[10]

The Story of the Loon

"I am the sovereign of the sea,
A king in the kindgom of the waves."

The loon, or the so-called northern diver,[11] is the king of the
waterfowl on the Canadian lakes. This bird is common in
northern America as well as in Scandinavia. It lives on all the
lakes and rivers of the Hudson Bay country and on the great

---

10. Obviously this interesting story symbolizes the hard struggle of the
people here against the forces of nature.

11. In German it is called the "Seeflunder"; in Icelandic, "Lunde." English
and American natural scientists usually call it "the northern diver." In Canada,

waterways of the St. Lawrence system. Sometimes the bird moves toward the Mississippi and even farther south.

The loon is as big as a goose but has a different body structure. Its legs are short and stand out far to the rear of the almost tailless body. Because of that it has difficulty moving about on land. Since the loon does not fly very adroitly, it is not often seen in the air. It lies deep on the water, its proper element, like a heavily laden vessel. The size of its body is not immediately apparent, especially because its long neck is usually bent and drawn in and is only occasionally visible at full length. At the end of the neck is a large head. The whole body seems designed mainly for diving. The heavy head presumably sinks like a plummet and the feet are at the other end, right where they can best aid in pushing downwards. Diving is therefore the bird's main maneuver. It dives with the greatest dexterity and endurance, and this gave the loon its name "the northern diver."

It is covered with a thick and heavy feather coat. While the bird's colors are only white and black, these colors are spread over the entire body in a most elegant and regular design. Sometimes the Indians use the whole feathered skin to cover their bags and pouches, and when they make proper use of the bird's design, the objects look very pleasing, almost splendid.

Loons seldom live in large groups or communities. Often one can be seen alone in the midst of the watery waste of the lakes, enjoying its life and freedom. Even if a few of them are together, you will not find them in coveys or bands like the ducks or wild geese, but separated over great distances as if each needed a large space for itself.

---

it is called "Maug," by the Ojibways, "Huard" by the French, and "the loon" by the English. The last word certainly must originally have meant "a clumsy lad," and the name might have been given to the bird because of its awkwardness.

The Indians as well as the French Canadians are preoc-
cupied with this animal and often speak of it, even though it
is not good to eat. I mentioned earlier that the Ojibway have
a totem, or clan, of the loon.

Now I will tell the story the Indians have created to explain,
historically or mythically, the peculiar anatomy of the loon: its
taillessness and the strange placement of its feet, off the usual
center of the body. I have certainly heard the story told elsewhere, but it is, like all such tales, narrated differently in each
place. And I will retell the story now just the way it has been
told to me here at L'Anse.

Everyone knows that Menaboju, the Indian Hercules or
Prometheus, the creator or reviver of the world, is responsible
for the formation or deformation of the loon. Once, Menaboju
sat in his canoe on the shore of Lake Superior, fishing and
singing a beautiful magic song to lure the fish he wished to
catch. He had hardly cast the fishing line when an enchanted
little fish wagged to the hook and snapped at the bait.

Menaboju pulled the line in and saw that it was a lively, little, silvery-shining trout. "You lively, little, silvery-shining
trout," he said to her, taking her off the hook and throwing
her back into the water, "you are not the fish I want." The cat-
fish heard this and since he thought himself big, he now swam
to the hook. But he too was rejected and set free again. "I
angle for a much bigger and nobler fish," Menaboju said and,
continuing his song, he cast his fishing line again.

Soon something again thrashed on the end of the line. This
time it was a brightly speckled, fat siskawet[12] that was
trapped, attracted by the magic songs. "Brightly speckled, fat
siskawet," Menaboju said a little impatiently, letting the fish
back into the water, "you are not the animal I fish for, either.
It is, in one word," he shouted out so loud that it could be

12. The siskawet is a rather large and very fat fish found in the Canadian
lakes.

heard across the whole water, "it is the great Fish King himself that I am fishing for."

"What do I hear? What does the insolent Menaboju say?" said the mighty Fish King when he heard this. Is he fishing for me, the lord of Lake Superior? Well! Well, Menaboju! Ho, I am already on my way to try your bait!"

With a few swishes of his tail, the gigantic Fish King shot like an arrow through the waves and reached Menaboju's bait. With one gulp, he swallowed the bait and the hook and the fishing line and also the fisherman, Menaboju, together with his canoe. Everything tumbled in an instant down into the enormous mouth, gullet, and stomach of the angry Fish King. He sailed triumphantly out into the vast waters of Lake Superior, and boasting to all the world that he had finally put an end to the intolerable Menaboju by swallowing him. "If it only agrees with him," the other people said, shaking their heads.

To Menaboju, all this happened rather unexpectedly, and at first he found the surrounding darkness disconcerting. But, like a good Indian, he quickly adapted to the new situation, and, since he discovered that his prison in the Fish King's stomach was spacious enough, he began to sing and dance to pass the time away. To defy the Fish King, he performed the war dance and sang boldly of all the noble deeds and cunning tricks he had performed in his life.

The Fish King, who thus discovered that Menaboju was much harder to digest than he had imagined, was very angry. He thought that the fellow would settle down after a while, but Menaboju's hero's song in the Fish King's stomach lasted all night. It just did not want to end. And at last Menaboju screamed and raged and made such noise, stamping his feet and throwing his fists in such a way, that the Fish King became quite ill, and he decided to part with the uncontrollable fellow. He tried to bring him up again.

But one is not so easily rid of everything that one gulps down in passion. For Menaboju, it was not at all enough to be spit out into the water again. Tenax propositi vir, he still adhered to the plan he had in mind when he first began fishing: to catch and kill the mighty Fish King himself.

As soon as he noticed that his whole prison, the stomach, began to swing like a shovel to throw him out, he quickly seized his canoe and shoved it into the gullet of the monstrous creature, where it stuck firmly. In spite of all his efforts, the Fish King could not move it forward or backward and thus died a miserable death. His body drifted calmly on the water like a shipwreck; to be sure, Menaboju himself was still a prisoner in this wreck. Since his canoe blocked the passage through the throat, he vainly racked his brains for three days for a way to get out.

Finally, on the third day, he heard a scratching, scraping, and picking above his head. It was the seagulls, who had flown hither to feast on the corpse of the Fish King. Menaboju's hiding place finally grew a little lighter and at last a small hole was picked into the stomach. So Menaboju himself began conversing with the gulls. He told them that he was trapped inside and asked them to make the hole still a little bigger. This the good animals did, so he could slip out into the daylight. His canoe, too, was set afloat again. He tied the fish he had caught to the stern and triumphantly paddled home, inviting the gulls to a great feast to show his gratitude. All the other waterfowl were also invited to this festivity and also all the animals from the forests and plains. And they made very merry, since the gigantic body of the dead fish offered meat and fat for many a hundred.

The bear profited most. He drank fish oil in tankards and grew so fat that afterwards he had to sleep for six months, all winter, just to grow a little thinner. To this day, from this heavy meal, fat is layered over his body.

But not all the animals knew how to help themselves like the bear with his big paws. The skinny little American hare was only able to lick up a few crumbs that had fallen under the table. And now, when a hunter shoots a hare, he finds only a little fat in the back of its neck.

The prairie pheasant did not fare much better at fattening himself. Like the hare, he only picked up some scraps, and he now shows at the most a little fat under the wings.

After he had in this way fed all the creatures as well as possible, Menaboju let the music and the dancing begin. His mouth watered when he saw all these well-fed, sleek animals dancing past him. And since he had not enjoyed any food so far this day – partly because as a well-behaved host he had to fulfill so many duties, partly also because fish oil was not quite to his taste – this sight now aroused in him an irrestible appetite. He therefore told the animals, one and all, to close their eyes and dance past him as in blind-man's bluff. This, he said, would be fine fun.

The animals, who foresaw no harm, did exactly that: they closed their eyes and danced merrily past Menaboju. But when a couple of animals that appealed to him came close, he grabbed them by the neck and threw them behind him, into the kitchen. There his wife immediately began to slaughter and cook them.

He had put aside a good many roasts and still the foolish animals waltzed toward him with closed eyes. The loon waltzed with his small cousin and good friend, the bird whom the Indians call Skabewis and the English call the little diver. Both of them moved a little slowly and cautiously and were among the last couples.

"Skabewis," said the loon, "dost thou not notice that it is growing quieter and quieter in the hall? How peculiar!" And in saying this, driven by curiosity, he blinked with one eye and saw Menaboju just then strangling a couple of rather fat geese.

"Oh, you animals!" the loon suddenly cried out, "Menaboju is strangling the geese! Menaboju will kill all of us!" All the animals opened their eyes and, seized with terror, fled and fluttered, crawled and leaped, hopped and swam all and sundry away in a hundred different directions.

Menaboju was beside himself with anger that the loon had in this way utterly ruined his fun. He pursued him, and, had he caught him, he would without a doubt have slain him, too. But the loon was already at the water's edge and was jumping into the waves just as Menaboju caught up with him. His pursuer had only enough time to kick him violently in his wrath. This kick displaced the entire body structure of the bird, robbed it of its tail, and moved its legs as far back as one sees them to this day, as I have described earlier. Since that time, it has also been a very shy bird, and when it notices one of Menaboju's relatives, an Indian, even far off in the distance, it dives into the deep. It is very difficult to shoot.

Legend of the Origin of the Bears

"But you were my dear amusement,
Golden Fantasy!"

Not only Menaboju himself, but also his whole family seems to have performed heroic deeds of all kinds. At least the people around me frequently mention a "son" or a "grandson of Menaboju," whose deeds are only slightly less fantastic than those of his great ancestor.

One of these "grandsons of Menaboju" went out hunting one day. He roamed freely through forests and plains far to the west and finally came to the foot of a great and desolate mountain range, where to his astonishment he saw bones of humans as well as animals scattered over the entire region.

White as snow, these infinite masses of bones covered the mountain tops, the slopes, and the plains far and wide. In all the bushes and trees high up onto the mountains hung skeletons, horns, and antlers.

This filled the hero's heart with terror, for he concluded very rightly that a merciless monster must dwell here. And he fled back eastward to hold council with a prophet and magician he knew. Even the most valiant Indian heroes do not think it beneath their dignity to use caution and to make use of the advice and the charms of prophets, just as the Greek heroes consulted the oracles.

The prophet listened to him and then said: "From thy very vague account, I cannot yet judge what it may mean. Take courage. Go there one more time and bring me full particulars. I will give thee a magic remedy which may help thee escape in case of need."

So the next day, after staying the night with the prophet, the hunter again set out westward. Once more he came to the chalky mountains covered with bones. And he overcame his repugnance when he had to push away entire heaps of decayed bones to clear a path or when bones hanging from the trees struck him in the face as he slipped through a grove.

Reaching the top of the mountain, he saw a kettle-shaped hollow, filled with a lake, and on the opposite shore of this lake lay a sleeping, snoring, shaggy, black monster. It was as big as a house and its teeth were like rows of knives. The young man's hair stood on end. But when he discovered that this beast had a most valuable necklace of shells slung around its neck, he was seized with an irresistible craving to possess it.

He immediately returned to the prophet again, to confer with him anew. He gave a description of the mountains explored, the animal, and the necklace of shells and asked the prophet to help him acquire it.

The prophet then said to him: "From your description I gather that the animal you have seen is the Bear King. But I cannot help you get his string of pearls. I do not have enough power. Farther east, however, lives another prophet; perhaps he has some advice for you."

At once Menaboju's grandson started eastward to visit the second prophet and report his adventure to him, too. The prophet listened to him patiently. But at the end he, too, explained that he would not be powerful enough to help the grandson get the necklace. But he said that farther east there lived still a third prophet who might have advice and a method to offer.

So the hunter went even farther east to the third prophet, and this one finally decided to become his advocate and to supply him with what he needed. The Ojibways seem to believe generally that the farther east a prophet lives, the more powerful he is.

The most eastern prophet brewed, boiled, sang, and beat the drums all night. Finally, in the morning, he gave his heroic visitor a small potion wrapped in paper, which he was to keep in his pocket, and some strategic rules for attacking the enemy.

Thus equipped, the hero set out on his journey anew. When he passed by the two western prophets and told them that he was now on his way to rob the Bear King of his jewelry, they were struck with terror. They immediately abandoned their homes, fled eastward to the third prophet, and placed themselves under his protection.

The young man had taken his canoe along and dragged it up the mountain. He found the bear asleep, as before, on the other side of the lake, and he let his canoe down into the water. The magician had advised him to use the canoe, for the bear would move much more slowly in the water than the swiftly gliding Indian canoe. If the bear should wake up, he would know this and choose the overland route around the lake. Since the bear would have to circle the lake entirely, the young hero would at least have a head start and could cut diagonally across the water on his retreat.

It happened as the prophet had foreseen it. The Indian approached the snoring bear as quietly as possible, fearlessly unfastened the beautiful necklace of shells, and carefully pulled it away from his neck. But he had hardly got back into his canoe with his valuable prize when the bear awoke and leapt around the lake, howling and growling so that the whole mountain trembled. This was a very long journey, however, and the young thief reached the other side much sooner than the bear in spite of the bear's great efforts. And hurrying across the bone-covered plains, he soon reached the homes of the first and second prophets. Finding their houses abandoned, he sped on to the third prophet, where he found all three together, badly frightened.

When they saw him coming with the necklace, they rejoiced. They summoned the courage to unite and face the approaching Bear King.

All three of them beat their drums, shook their schischiguas,[13] and sang their magic songs. The Bear King, who at first roared toward them like a storm, checked his speed a little when he heard the magic songs of the prophets' triumvirate. At last the drums and songs broke his spirit, and he sank down onto the grass unconscious. Thereupon Menaboju's grandson stepped forward and put an end to him with knife and tomahawk.

Then the immense corpse was cut up into pieces, all the neighbors were invited, a big feast was held, and all the people ate with great pleasure. On this occasion, the bear's head was set in the middle of the board and decorated with its string of

---

13. These gourds, filled with beans or small stones, are shaken during all magical performances.

pearls, as if in ridicule. But the gnawed-off bones that they carelessly threw out became alive again right away: each put forth a head, a tail, and four legs, and ran off as young bears. And from them originated the present, slightly less gigantic, family of the bears. Since that time it has been customary with the Ojibways to hold such a feast when they have killed a bear and to decorate the bear's head with a string of shells or wampum, just the way Menaboju's grandson and his three prophets did after the killing of the ancestor of the bears in ancient times.

The Legend of Beaverhead Rock and of the Origin of the St. Marys River[14]

"Look near the rocky prominence
Back the swollen waters whirl.
Roll and dawdle, flee and hasten
Back into the magic circle."

SCHIMPER

A few miles from the mouth of the St. Marys River, with its many whirlpools and rapids, on whose banks also our small village Rivière au Désert is built, lie a large number of broken, dark, granite rocks. Among some which are scattered along the banks the British from Upper Canada found copper-bearing rocks and established a small mining town called Bruce Mines. One of these huge black boulders has fallen into the water, and its high, rounded-off top towers above the crystal-clear river. The Indians and Canadians call it the Beaverhead. And the former, as is their custom, tell a legend of its origin, which I shall relate here, because it was the first one I was told

14. This story, dated "Rivière au Désert, October 1855," appeared as the second letter in Book III of the German original. Had it been included in the 1860 English translation, it would fall between Chapters 19 and 20. — *Trans.*

in Rivière au Désert and because in it the Indians also express their view on the formation of the labyrinth of streams, described above, that connect Lake Superior and Lake Huron.

Like the rock pillars and the waterway at the mouth of the Mediterranean Sea that date from Hercules, according to Greek mythology, and like the mountain gaps and rocky cliffs in the Pyrenees that are regarded as a work of the great Roland by the people of those mountains, the St. Marys River outlet, according to the Indian legend, results of course from Menaboju.

There was a time when all of broad Lake Superior was nothing but a big beaver pond. The Beaver King reigned there with his family while Menaboju lived the life of an Indian hunter in his hut on the upper, most western tip of the lake. He hunted and killed the animals of the woods, ate their meat, and dressed in their coats.

But one winter the fox hunt was extremely unproductive and so Menaboju said to himself: "Now the Beaver King and his family have to assist me." He decided to catch them all. And to bring this about, he hit upon the same techniques the Indians now use during the winter when the whole lake is frozen up and they want to set the beaver high and dry and pull him out from underneath the ice. They cut the beaver's dike, which has dammed up the water, and drain the lake. In the opening of the dam they place a latticework made of poles that allows the water to pass through, but not the beavers that follow. No longer held up by the water, the hollow sheet of ice sinks partly in, and the frightened beavers hurry to the outlet. To be sure, sometimes the ice does not fall in or does not sink far enough, and then the beavers stay underneath in some pool of water. In that event, trained dogs may well be sent under the ice to fetch the beavers. But usually, as I said before, the beavers follow the water that drains off, reach the fence, and fall prey to their pursuers. For greater security, some guards may also be positioned around the lake in case it should occur to the beavers, against the rule, to slip away in an unexpected direction. The Indians have also trained their dogs to stand sentry. They stay right where their master puts them, carefully watch every movement in the water and among the floating ice, and report if a beaver dares to slip away somewhere.

As I said before, Menaboju observed all these precautionary measures in the war he declared against the Beaver King. At first he cut the big eastern dam that separated Lake Superior and Lake Huron. The water from Lake Superior began to drain off and thus formed the wide and clear river of the present day, which the French have dedicated to the Virgin Mary. There, where the big cataracts and rocks are today in this river, the so-called Sault de Ste. Marie, Menaboju drove in his pegs and his latticework, with which he hoped to confine the Beaver King and his family.

When he had thus started to drain off the water, he positioned his faithful dog to guard the northern shore of the lake. And he placed his aged mother on the neck of land that is today called Cape Iroquois.[15] He ordered his old mother to guard the outlet and the latticework at the cataracts carefully and, if she saw the beaver come near, to whistle twice loudly at once.

But he himself then proceeded back to the western side of the lake to watch the gradual dropping of the water level and, at the same time, to prepare his bow and arrows and other hunting equipment. He presumably also wanted to keep the Beaver King from escaping across the narrow isthmus to the waters of the Mississippi or the Hudson Bay region.

He was now certain that with such careful preparations his prey could not escape from him. A fierce cold spell set in, and

15. This is a point made very famous by a battle with the Iroquois at the entrance to the easternmost bay of Lake Superior.

when the Beaver King, following the draining water, came to
Cape Iroquois and the latticework, the old mother was unfortunately either wrapped up too deep in her furs or she could
not purse up her frozen lips to whistle twice, as she had been
told. In short, she whistled a little too late, and even though
Menaboju was there in two strides from the west side of the
lake as soon he heard the whistle, the Beaver King, with
irresistible force, had already broken through the latticework
and swum into the St. Marys River. Many stumps from the
posts and pegs he broke are stuck there in the ground to this
day, causing the spraying and roaring of the cataracts.

When Menaboju came near and saw that the Beaver King
had slipped away, he was so angry that he not only scolded his
old mother rudely for her negligence, but he even forgot himself so far as to slap her face. This slap in the face was so hard
that – our European sentiment resists believing and retelling
it, but the barbarous Indians relate it without hesitation – the
slap in the face was so hard that blood ran from the old
woman's parched lips; this blood was flung far out to the west
against the rugged sandstone cliffs that the Americans call
"the pictured rocks." To this day the rocks carry the red
stripes that came from that violent and vicious slap in the face.
It is hardly possible to discover a more unromantic and barbarous origin of a natural scene so beautiful and romantic.

Then Menaboju immediately set out again to pursue the
Beaver King. He jumped into a canoe and navigated the wild
St. Marys River, brandishing his deadly spear in his right
hand. When the Beaver King saw his archenemy behind him,
he dived under. And with this plunge developed an immense
whirlpool, which swirls up to this time and is familiar to the
boatmen of the river.

Menaboju knew well that the Beaver King could not stay
underwater for long and that he soon would have to come up
for air. Therefore he quickly canoed to the place where the

aforesaid town of Bruce Mines now lies, near where the St. Marys River runs into Lake Huron. And there he sat down on the tall granite rock, which at that time was still unbroken and served as a rather comfortable seat for such a giant as Menaboju.

The Beaver King kept swimming underwater for some time. Finally he had to surface; unfortunately, he chose exactly the place where his deadly foe sat on the rock. From sheer weariness and fatigue, Menaboju had just fallen into a slumber, but the breathing, wheezing, splashing, and spitting of the Beaver King woke him up quickly enough. Thus alarmed, he sprang up so briskly from his rocky seat and gave it such a push that it broke into a thousand pieces under him. The tremendous heaps of rocky debris near Bruce Mines still bear witness to this event today. Some colossal pieces of rock tumbled down into the water and towered high above the waves. And on one of these blocks, after he had finally killed, skinned, and butchered his foe, Menaboju stuck the head of the Beaver King. Fur and meat he took home, but the head he left standing on the top of the rock. In the course of time it grew together with the stone and became stone itself. And it still has today, as I said before, the physiognomy of a beaver and the name "Beaverhead."

APPENDIX II

SOME OBSERVATIONS ON THE OJIBWAY LANGUAGE[1]

"These thighs
Flew more nimbly through the snow
Than the stag of twenty points
Than the mountain deer."

SCHILLER

I said above that the most important invention the Indians have devised is the birch-bark canoe, but this must be understood with one qualification. The invention and development of their language, as far as it can be attributed to their own mental power, is immeasurably more remarkable and admirable. I deeply regret that I can enter so little into this subject, which is by far the most interesting aspect of research on the ethnography of the Indians. But of course, I cannot avoid it; indeed, I encountered it everywhere. All the thinking and experience of a people are reflected in their language. Lan-

---

1. These paragraphs were translated by Ralf Neufang. They appeared at the beginning of the sixth letter in Book III of the German edition of *Kitchi-Gami*, dated "Rivière au Désert, October 1855." Had they been included in the 1860 English translation, they would precede the text that begins on p. 332. – *Trans.*

465

guage accompanies the entire life and conduct of the Indian; it is like a great collection of commemorative medals, in which he has gathered all the expressions he has coined for sense perceptions or spiritual life, for observations in nature, and for his artistic creations. One can only understand the Indian condition, and one can only pursue it into all nooks and crannies, when using the bright light that the language shines on the path of the ethnographer.

However! – for my limited subject, I elaborate too much. For here I do not want to speak of the great grammatical mysteries or historical riddles and questions that are in language, or of the psychological revelations that can result from its study. I have nothing more in front of me than an Indian snowshoe, and I admire its sensible construction as much as the rich terminology of the language. I have brought this tool forward mainly to show both how far into detail the language of the Indians goes with its word-coinage, and how fixed and definite the expressions for such objects of perception are. This will also prove how fixed, definite, and well-thought-out are the parts of the artwork itself, for in the area of the arts, language only forms permanent and generally accepted expressions for those things that play a role in the mechanism.

On the occasion of the building of the canoe, I have already indicated that every string and peg is necessary for the whole, and the Indians have given them all definite names. They use detail just as minute to describe their arts and crafts as they use for nature. In their woods, swamps, lakes, and prairies nothing crawls, flies, swims, or grows that they do not observe and that they do not give a name, no matter how very small it might be. If this were the case only with the useful plants and animals, I would certainly not have found it so amazing. But what I admired so much was that when I sat down in the grass with an Indian and asked about the most useless things flitting about, he always knew a name for them. Naturally I could conclude from this that he had observed them all, held them in his hand, and investigated them curiously, and had differentiated them according to their essential characteristics. We educated people are motivated by scholarly curiosity, the admiration for God in all his works, the endeavor to have our systems complete and to discern all the links of a chain, in order to develop a rich terminology without any gap. But I admit that I was at times hard pressed to explain the reason for such a rich terminology with the Indian. Superstition may sometimes cause him to notice a peculiar being or a curious plant and name it. Sometimes he may name things to differentiate them from other products of nature expedient and useful to him. But sometimes, I have to believe, curiosity or a touch of scholarly inquisitiveness into nature alone leads him to take pains over the aforesaid.

INDEX.

Note: Kohl never gave the name of the priest who accompanied him from La Pointe, Wis., to L'Anse, Mich., and at Sault Ste. Marie. From the evidence the priest can be identified as Father Frederic Baraga; he is thus indexed by name.

VON HUMBOLDT, Alexander, ethnologist, xxi, xxii
Voyaguers, characterized, 72; method of carrying goods, 168–69; songs, 253–65, 301–2; identify with Indians, 260–61. *See also* French Canadians

WABASHA, Sioux chief, 250–51
Walking, method described, 4–5, 8
Wampum, described, 49, 135–36
Wapeassina, Sioux chief, 351, 352, 353, 354
War of *1812*, impact, 372; battles, 377–78
Warfare, expense, 67; revenge as motive, 67, 127–28, 253, 340, 341, 445; exploits memorialized, 159; expeditions planned, 340–42; customs, 343–45; trophies, 345. *See also* Ojibway-Sioux warfare
Wattab, Ojibway warrior, 22–24
Weapons, bow and arrow, 8; magic knife, 408. *See also* Firearms
Weasels, pelts used, 47
Whiskey, use by Indians, 115; introduced, 371–72
Whitefish (*poisson blanc*), caught, xv; prepared, 326
Whites, relations with Indians, 54, 55, 350, 418–20; initial encounter with Indians, 243–47; undermine chiefs, 270–71; object of warfare, 352–53; impact on Indian culture, 367–68, 421; in hieroglyphics, 401; medicine inferior, 416; characterized, 417
Whortleberries, preserved, 320
Wigwams, construction, 3–5, 9–10;

repair, 11, 12; name, 12; for summer, 12; hieroglyphics on, 144; described, 231
Wild rice, name, 117
Williams, ——, informant, 161
Willow, used, 89, 316; in tobacco mix, 284
Windigos, discussed, 356, 357–60, 362–65
Winter, time of storytelling, 86; games, 90; travel, 120, 177–80, 307–9, 332, 338–39; hunting, 123, 461–62; ice fishing, 328–29; season for planning war, 342
Wolves, pelts used, 47; in legend, 432–33, 437
Women, 67, 272, 273, 276–77, 412; build wigwams, 3–5, 9–10; Ojibway described, 4; weave mats, 10–11; face painting, 18; make canoes, 29, 31, 32; participate in Mide rite, 46, 47, 127; games played, 81, 83, 90; storytellers, 88, 91–104, 367–68; receive annuities, 112, 114, 115; war exploits, 125–26, 127–28; indicated in sign language, 140; names, 274; embroider, 315–16; role in warfare, 342, 343; as windigos, 363; decorate birch bark, 412–14; cure diseases, 416
World, creation story, 150–51, 194–202; re-created, 431–32, 436 37
Wraxall, Lascelles, translator, xxv, xxxvii, xl–xli, 431n

YEAR, names of months, 120. *See also* Seasons